RELIGION, LANDSCAPE AND SETTLEMENT IN IRELAND

Matthew Stout, *The Irish ringfort* (1997)

P.J. Duffy, David Edwards and Elizabeth FitzPatrick (eds), *Gaelic Ireland c.1250–c.1650: land, lordship and settlement* (2001)

James Lyttleton and Tadhg O'Keeffe (eds), *The manor in medieval and early modern Ireland* (2005)

Elizabeth FitzPatrick and Raymond Gillespie (eds), *The parish in medieval and early modern Ireland: community, territory and building* (2006)

Linda Doran and James Lyttleton (eds), *Lordship in medieval Ireland: image and reality* (2007)

James Lyttleton and Colin Rynne (eds), *Plantation Ireland: settlement and material culture, c.1550–c.1700* (2009)

Margaret Murphy and Matthew Stout (eds), *Agriculture and settlement in Ireland* (2015)

Bernadette Cunningham and Harman Murtagh (eds), *Lough Ree: historic lakeland settlement* (2015)

James Lyttleton and Matthew Stout (eds), *Church and settlement in Ireland* (2018)

Religion, Landscape and Settlement in Ireland

From Patrick to Present

Kevin Whelan

FOUR COURTS PRESS

In association with the Group for the Study of Irish Historic Settlement

Set in 10.5 on 12.5 point Ehrhardt for
FOUR COURTS PRESS LTD
7 Malpas Street, Dublin 8, Ireland
www.fourcourtspress.ie
and in North America for
FOUR COURTS PRESS
c/o IPG, 814 Franklin Street, Chicago, IL, 60622.

A catalogue record for this title
is available from the British Library.

ISBN 978-1-84682-756-3

Printed in England
by TJ International, Padstow, Cornwall

Published in association with the
Group for the Study of Irish Historic Settlement

'One eye sees, the other feels'.

Paul Klee (1879–1940)

For our family, Anne, Bébhinn, Fionn, Ruaidhrí and Eamonn.

Contents

Illustrations

FIGURES

TABLES

Abbreviations

AAI, i	R. Moss (ed.), *Art and architecture of Ireland, volume I: medieval, 400–1600* (Dublin, 2015).
AAI, iv	R. Loeber et al. (eds), *Art and architecture of Ireland, volume 4: architecture, 1600–2000* (Dublin, 2014).
AFM	*Annala rioghachta Eireann; Annals of the kingdom of Ireland by the Four Masters*, ed. J. O'Donovan, 7 vols (Dublin, 1851).
Anal. Hib.	*Analecta Hibernica* (Dublin, 1930–).
Archiv. Hib.	*Archivium Hibernicum: or Irish historical records* (Maynooth, 1912–).
Atlas of Irish rural landscape	F. Aalen, K. Whelan & M. Stout (eds), *Atlas of the Irish rural landscape*, second edition (Cork, 2011).
BL	British Library.
Cal.	Calendar [in the short titles of calendared series].
CELT	Corpus of Electronic Texts, University College Cork.
CSO RP	Chief Secretary's Office, Registered Papers, National Archives of Ireland.
CSPD	*Calendar of State Papers, domestic series, 1547–1580* [etc.]
CSPI	*Calendar of State Papers of Ireland.*
DIB	*Dictionary of Irish biography*, ed. J. McGuire & J. Quinn, 9 vols (Cambridge, 2009).
FDJ	*Faulkner's Dublin Journal* (Dublin, 1725–1825).
FJ	*Freeman's Journal* (Dublin, 1763–1924).
FLJ	*Finn's Leinster Journal* (Kilkenny, 1767–1801).
HMC	Historical Manuscripts Commission.
IFC	Irish Folklore Commission.
IHS	*Irish Historical Studies* (Dublin, 1938–).
JCHAS	*Journal of the Cork Historical and Archaeological Society* (Cork, 1892–).
JGAHS	*Journal of the Galway Archaeological and Historical Society* (Galway, 1900–).
JRSAI	*Journal of the Royal Society of Antiquaries of Ireland* (Dublin, 1892–).
NAF	National Archives of France, Paris.
NAI	National Archives of Ireland.
NGI	National Gallery of Ireland.
NHI	*A new history of Ireland*, 9 vols (Oxford, 1976–2005).

NLI   National Library of Ireland.
NMAJ   *North Munster Antiquarian Society Journal* (Limerick, 1936–).
NMI   National Museum of Ireland.
OS   Ordnance Survey.
OS letters   M. Herity (ed.), *Ordnance Survey letters*, 18 vols (Dublin, 2000–16).
PRIA   *Proceedings of the Royal Irish Academy* (Dublin, 1836–).
PRONI   Public Record Office of Northern Ireland, Belfast.
QUB   Queen's University Belfast.
RCB   Representative Church Body, Dublin.
SOC   State of the Country Papers, National Archives of Ireland.
Studia Hib.   *Studia Hibernica* (Dublin, 1961–).
TCD   Trinity College Dublin.

Preface

THERE ARE MANY PASTS within the past. Irish history is often past and furious: its fields are also mine fields. This book offers an exercise in one-handed history: it refuses fence-sitting 'on the one hand/on the other hand' approaches, avoids extended discussion of historiography, and makes firm judgments. I focus on the comparative, the recent, the little-known or the neglected in terms of bibliographic material.

My approach blends the insights of historical geography (with its field-based emphasis on environment, context and continuities), archaeology (with its site- and artefact-based focus), and history (with its emphasis on archival evidence). The book unapologetically ranges across many fields: I endorse the approach of Max Weber (1864–1920): 'I am not a donkey and I do not have a field'.

To use the terms of the novelist Thomas Hardy (1840–1928), this book explores texture rather than veneer, seeking to establish the continuous grain that runs through and across periods. The focus is on the lived experience of real people in real places rather than the abstractions of nationality, class and race. Life as it is lived – incorrigibly untidy, incomplete, messy and contradictory – always finds ways to seep in and through and around these scholarly abstractions.

John O'Donovan (1806–61), the greatest of Irish topographers, described his motivating passion as being 'to connect history with topography and thus give it a particular or local instead of a general interest'. A distinguished scholarly line (Vidal de La Blache, Meinig, Glassie) has read the cultural landscape, while in Ireland the historical geographers (Evans, Jones Hughes, Smyth) have been busy, bringing the real landscape and the paper landscape into an animated dialogue. The greatest attraction of the Irish landscape is that so many sites are so well preserved and I have spent many happy decades absorbing Ireland through the soles of my feet in wise and congenial company. While I have certainly 'coughed in ink' (Yeats) in the libraries and archives that I love, I have also explored in detail all thirty-two counties.

This book considers the complex relationship between memory and history. Joyce in *Finnegans wake* called 'm'm'ry' 'the hole truth' [460.20] and he ranged through other puns that illustrate the complexity of this apparently simple concept: 'maimeries' [348.7], 'mummery' [310.23], 'murmury' [254.18] and 'murmoirs' [294.7]. I seek to honour that complexity, while also keeping the discussion accessible – 'as simple as possible but no simpler' in Einstein's unbeatable formula. To help locate sites, modern counties are used

xv

anachronistically. I draw on a wide array of sources and external commentators, ranging through writers in Arabic, Latin, Greek, Irish, English, French, Dutch, German, Italian, Spanish and Icelandic. Translations from Irish, Latin and French are mine unless otherwise stated. Because religion played such a pivotal role in Irish life, a book like this presents an oblique history of Ireland. It seeks to convey a fuller and more rounded sense of who we are, showing us how we got to be where we are, even as we leave it behind.

I thank colleagues for assistance generously proffered: Maggie Arriola, John Banville, Gloria Binions, Hilary Bishop, Robert Black, Diogo Bolster, Jack Burtchaell, Michael Byrne, Róisín Byrne, Aedín Clements, Clare Carroll, Billy Colfer (1940–2013) RIP, Jane Conroy, Sarah Covington, George Cunningham, Seamus Deane, Paul Ferguson, Mick Gibbons, Seamus Heaney (1939–2013) RIP, Ken Hemmingway, Michael Herity (1929–2016) RIP, Arnold Horner, Eoghan Kavanagh, Rolf Loeber (1942–2017) RIP, Magda Loeber, Gerry Long, Gerry Lyne, Finbar McCormick, Micheál Mac Craith OFM, Niall McCullough, Con Manning, John Mannion, Paul Muldoon, Tomás Ó Carragáin, Conchubhar Ó Crualaoich, Caoimhín Ó Danachair (1913–2002) RIP, Diarmuid Ó GIolláin, Tim O'Neill, William Roulston, Michael Ryan, Geraldine Stout, Matthew Stout and Christopher J. Woods. Many improvements are theirs: many remaining imperfections are mine.

A warm thanks to the Group for the Study of Irish Historic Settlement, especially James Lyttleton and Matthew Stout, for adding this volume to their series. Grateful thanks to Four Courts Press for their characteristic friendliness and professionalism and to Martin Fanning for his flexibility. Lisa Scholey compiled the index and Eoghan Kavanagh generously gifted me the cover image. My greatest debt is to my accomplished friend Matthew Stout who did all the heavy lifting on the technical side of this book.

Introduction

RELIGION MAKES PEOPLE, religion breaks people. The ties that bind become the ties that blind. There remains a compelling argument for inserting both landscape and religion into the heart of history.[1] As early as 1642, the philosopher Thomas Browne (1605–82) claimed that the landscape provides 'that universal and publick manuscript that lies expansed unto the eyes of all',[2] while the American geographer Wilbur Zelinsky (1921–2013) stressed that religion is crucial to understanding 'the dynamic fabric of lived-in space'.[3] Landscape transcends its merely economic or environmental aspects to encompass its experiential, customary and symbolic forms. For example, the medieval Irish imagination, nurtured on a rain-stained, wind-whipped island, regarded hell as wet, cold and miserable, rather than as burning hot.[4] The Irish conceived of the otherworld as a lively Tír na nÓg (the land of youth), or Tír na mBeo (the land of the living), rather than the desolate classical underworld, peopled by greyer shades of pale.[5]

The geographic approach can homogenize unduly – the personal experience of religion varied by class, gender and language group (post-Christian Ireland was always multi-lingual), and heterogeneity was never lacking within regions. There are conceptual difficulties with deficit models (where Ireland is regarded as lacking some element present elsewhere considered to be normative), linear models, like tradition/modernization (where Ireland is held to lag behind 'progress' elsewhere), or the Devotional Revolution models, which imply a straight-line progression from one stage to another. Instead, renewed attention on continuities and transitions – for example, from late antique to early medieval, and from early to late medieval – is fruitful. Historians are addicts of rupture narratives, compelled 'to segment time into trim periods' but 'the massive fact of continuity' remains inescapable in human culture.[6] Forces of continuity need to be considered and breaks should be defined precisely, pinpointing diagnostic changes that are carefully differentiated from what went before.[7]

---

1 J. Guldi, 'Landscape and place' in S. Gunn & L. Faire (eds), *Research methods for history* (Edinburgh, 2012), pp 66–80. 2 T. Browne, *Religio-medici* (London, 1645), p. 30. 3 W. Zelinsky, 'The uniqueness of the American religious landscape', *Geographical Review*, 91:3 (2001), pp 565–85. 4 S. Ó Súilleabháin, *Miraculous plenty: Irish religious folktales and legends*, trans. W. Caulfield (Dublin, 2012), p. 124. 5 P. Mac Cána, *Celtic mythology* (Feltham, 1983), p. 52. 6 H. Glassie, 'Tradition', *Journal of American Folklore*, 108:430 (1995), pp 395–412. 7 M. Ó Siochrú, 'Rebuilding the past: the transformation of early modern Irish history', *The Seventeenth Century* (2018) online.

All living landscapes and buildings are fundamentally palimpsests. They are invariably layered, ferrying multiple meanings across accumulating time frames. The architectural insistence on the 'original', with its presumed pristine integrity, can be widened and enriched by tracing the multiple afterlives of buildings, their complex self-renewing braiding of past and present. Such an approach sharpens the focus on memory, routinely disparaged in once-dominant revisionist Irish historiography with its archival fetish. Ireland is home to globally significant memory troves, material that admirably augments landscape studies. A landscape emphasis brings us face to face with the palpable presence of the sites and the objects themselves, opening a dialogue with archaeological and museological approaches.[8]

Edward Said (1935–2003) commented on that dynamic balance between inside and outside, home and away, vernacular and cosmopolitan, that establishes an appropriate distance from which to hazard judgments:

> The more one is able to leave one's cultural home, the more easily is one able to judge it, and the whole world as well, with the spiritual detachment and generosity necessary for true vision. The more easily too does one assess oneself and alien cultures with the same combination of intimacy and distance.[9]

This is too easily treated as a call for detachment from, and harsh judgment of, one's own culture, but Said is arguing for the equal need for empathetic understanding of one's own cultural world. Maeve Brennan (1917-93) noted that an exile (and this applies equally to scholars and artists) 'knew of a country that made all other countries seem strange'.[10] Ireland is that country.

---

8 K. Robertson, 'Medieval things: materiality, historicism and the pre-modern object', *Literature Compass*, 5 (2008), pp 1–21. The Irish material remains ripe for a sustained treatment of this kind.   9 E. Said, *Orientalism* (New York, 1978), p. 10.   10 Cited in J. O'Leary, 'What makes a waif?', *London Review of Books*, 40 (17), 13 September 2018, p. 36.

CHAPTER ONE

The Early Medieval and Medieval Church in Ireland

I RELAND, SHROUDED IN MURK, was perched on the sill of the known antique world, at a time when the Atlantic was regarded as the world's watery boundary. For the Romans, Hibernia, the wintry island, was 'in ultimo orbis' (Horace) and constituted 'another world' (Solinus).[1] Giraldus Cambrensis (1146–1223) in his *Topographica Hibernica* of 1188 believed that on the west coast of the island 'beyond the whole horizon, only the ocean flows, carried on into boundless space through its unsearchable and hidden ways'.[2] The Irish were self-aware about these perceptions. The earliest poem on Ireland (in Latin) talks about 'the island of Ireland' on 'the edge of the ocean'[3] while Cummian's letter of 631–2 acknowledged that the Irish were regarded by Rome as 'almost at the end of the earth and, if I may say so, a pimple on the face of the earth'.[4]

Adaptations of Christianity flourished around the ragged and culturally porous edges of the Roman Empire. It is chimera-hunting to expect strict uniformity throughout the West in Late Antiquity and Merovingian times: Christianity proved promiscuously permeable to local cultural influences, and there was always diversity within ecclesiastical practice. This tolerance accelerated rather than slowed the flow of Christianity. The remote Irish location in north-western Europe mirrored other equally remote (judged from an eastern Mediterranean perspective) expansions of Christianity, for example,

---

1 K. Lavezzo, *Angels on the edge of the world; geography, literature and English community, 1000–1534* (Ithaca, 2006); T. O'Loughlin, *Adomnán and the holy places* (London, 2007).   2 [Giraldus Cambrensis], *The history and topography of Ireland*, ed. & trans. J. O'Meara (London, 1982), p. 31.   3 A. O'Hara, 'Carmen de hibernia insula: the earliest poem about Ireland' in S. Ryan (ed.), *Treasures of Irish Christianity, volume 3. To the ends of the earth* (Dublin, 2015), pp 20–4; *Jonas of Bobbio; life of Columbanus, life of John of Réome, and life of Vedast*, ed. & trans. A. O'Hara & I. Wood (Liverpool, 2017).   4 *Cummian's letter* De controversia Paschali *together with a related computistical text* De rationae computanti, ed & trans. M. Walsh & D. Ó Cróinín, (Toronto, 1988), pp 74–5. For the wider context, see J. O'Reilly, 'Islands and idols at the ends of the earth: exegesis and conversion in Bede's *Historia Ecclesiastica*' in S. Lebecq, M. Perrin & O. Szerwiniak (eds), *Bède le vénérable* (Villeneuve d'Ascq, 2005), pp 119–45; K. Lilly (ed.), *Mapping medieval geographies: geographical encounters in the Latin West and beyond, 300–1600* (Cambridge, 2013); M. Egeler, *Islands in the West: classical myth and the medieval Norse and Irish geographical imagination* (Turnhout, 2017).

the syncretic[5] Coptic and Ethiopian churches that formed out of the encounter with existing cultures and religious forms.

Patrick regarded himself as fulfilling a central Christian prophecy by ministering on the edge of the known world, with an uninhabitable void beyond it, 'that you may bring salvation unto the end of the earth'. The explicit instruction of Jesus was to preach his message 'even to the uttermost part of the earth' (Matthew 28:19–20). There is a palpable pride in Columbanus: 'We Irish, inhabitants of the world's edge, are disciples of Saints Peter and Paul'. He exulted that the name of Rome 'has been published far and wide through the whole world, even as far as the Western regions of earth's farther strand, miraculously unhindered by ocean's surging floods, though they leaped and rose beyond measure on every side'.[6]

The Irish church was buoyed up by its sense of occupying a privileged place in a providential and eschatological[7] geography, allowing it the honour of fulfilling the Gospel message and perhaps triggering the end times.[8] This awareness conferred such extraordinary self-confidence that the Irish felt sufficiently emboldened to engage in prolonged theological and intellectual disputes with Rome. The Irish 'on the extremities of the earth' (Honorius 1, Pope 625–38) relished taking on the ancient centres of wisdom: they challenged with alacrity Hebrew, Egyptian, Greek and Roman learning, and even the Papacy itself. Cummian, an exasperated Romanist, expostulated that only the Irish asserted that they, and they alone, know what is right: 'Rome errs, Jerusalem errs, Alexandria errs, Antioch errs, the whole world errs'.[9]

After gaining its foothold in early medieval Ireland in the fifth century, Christianity developed a high density of churches there.[10] The 5,529 known churches[11] suggest arguably 'one of the most comprehensive pastoral organizations in Europe'.[12] Bishoprics and kingdoms were coterminous, and eighth-century

---

5 **Syncretism** in religion combines different beliefs through the blending of originally distinct traditions, thus asserting an underlying unity and allowing for an inclusive approach to other faiths.   6 *Roma orbis terrarum caput est ecclesiarum* in *Sancti Columbani opera*, G. Walker, ed. & trans. (Dublin, 1956).   7 **Eschatology** (from Greek ἔσχατος eschatos meaning last) is the theological concept that addresses the final events in human history, sometimes referred to as the 'end of the world' or 'end times'. In the Christian tradition, it meditates on death, judgment, the afterlife and the ultimate destiny of the entire created order.   8 St John D. Seymour, 'The eschatology of the early Irish church', *Zeitschrift für Celtische Philologie*, 14 (1923), pp 179–211.   9 Walsh & Ó Cróinín, *Cummian's letter*, pp 80–1.   10 A clear and well-illustrated survey is 'Early Christianity AD *c.*300–500' in M. Stout, *Early medieval Ireland* (Bray, 2017), pp 19–34.   11 M. Stout, 'The distribution of early medieval ecclesiastical sites in Ireland' in P.J. Duffy & W. Nolan (eds), *At the anvil: essays in honour of William J. Smyth* (Dublin, 2012), pp 53–80. Ailbhe Mac Shamhráin curated the superb Monasticon Hibernicum, a database of Early Christian ecclesiastical settlement in Ireland from the fifth to the twelfth centuries. It lists 5,529 sites, of which 4,396 are located: monasticon.celt.dias. ie/about.php   12 R. Sharpe, 'Some problems concerning the organization of the church in early medieval Ireland', *Peritia*, 3 (1984), pp 23–70; R. Sharpe, 'Churches and communities

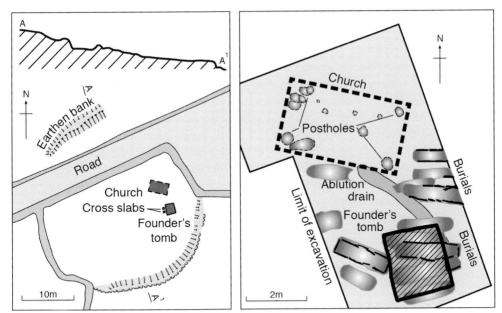

Fig. 1 The earliest securely dated Irish church was excavated at Caherlehillan (Co. Kerry) by John Sheehan. It dates from the early sixth century. It was a tiny building, with external measurements of 3.8m x 2m. The construction technique was post-and-wattle, infilled with sods. The principal components of an early medieval ecclesiastical site are already in place: the enclosure, the church, the founder's shrine and the burials.

Irish law mandated that each of the 180 túatha[13] should have at least one communal church.[14] Every túath formed a little diocese of its own, containing its episcopal mother church (possibly distinguished by the special name domhnach). Domhnach churches can be regarded as early pastoral churches of particular local kingdoms in contrast to sites that originated within monasteries.[15]

A diffuse power structure fostered a surprising density of minor ecclesiastical sites, establishing a consistent density of churches.[16] There were small churches

in early medieval Ireland: towards a pastoral model' in J. Blair & R. Sharpe (eds), *Pastoral care before the parish* (Leicester, 1992), pp 81–109. **13** During the eleventh century, the 180 túatha were being transformed into the trícha cét administrative unit (P. MacCotter, *Medieval Ireland: territorial, political and economic divisions* (Dublin, 2008), pp 40–4, 91–3). **14** The twelfth-century text *Críchad in Chaílli* listed the túath church of every district within the kingdom of Fir Maige (Co. Cork): P. MacCotter, 'Túath, manor and parish: kingdom of Fir Maige, cantred of Fermoy', *Peritia*, 22 (2012), pp 211–48. **15** L. Breatnach, 'Canon law and secular law in early Ireland: the significance of *Bretha nemed*', *Peritia*, 3 (1984), pp 439–59; D. Flanagan, 'Ecclesiastical nomenclature in Irish texts and placenames: a comparison', *Proceedings of the tenth International Congress of Onomastic Science* (1969), pp 355–88; C. Downham, *Medieval Ireland* (Cambridge, 2017), p. 121. **16** T. Ó Carragáin, 'Christianizing the landscape of Mag Réta: home territory of the kings of Laígis' in J. Lyttleton & M. Stout (eds), *Church and settlement in Ireland* (Dublin, 2018), p. 61.

within each túath, many of them proprietary family churches, served by a single priest. Despite political fragmentation, the galvanizing power of the church made Irish culture more cohesive in the early medieval period, as centripetal ecclesiastical forces counteracted centrifugal political ones. Monks, priests and poets enjoyed immunity when travelling between the various túatha, ensuring a high degree of cultural cohesion, and a consciousness of Ireland as a whole. The island, bound together by its possession of a highly prized language, was the only European country where Latin never became a vernacular: vernacular literacy emerged early in Ireland, the Irish retained their language and regarded it as at worst the equal of Latin, Greek and Hebrew.[17]

Early Christianity disdained entanglement in earthly living circumstances.[18] Emergent Christianity was marked by an urgent desire to detach itself from antique sacrality, as expressed in either temples or pantheist paganism. The earliest Christian architecture was composed of three functionally separate sites, sometimes linked (in palaeo-Christian clusters) but not unified within a single architectural structure. The first was the church, defined by its altar, the second was the martyr's chapel, founded on relics, and the third was the baptistry, centred on the baptismal pool or font. The principal transformation of ecclesiastical buildings in the early Middle Ages combined these diverse sites into a single building, a church serving the three functions of the Eucharist, baptism, and the veneration of saints.

This protracted development was completed by the eighth century, when the rule that every church site should possess relics was formalized. The burial site of a founder saint, marked by his tomb or relics, was regarded as a place possessed of a powerful intercessory energy where heaven and earth met.[19] The saint's remains sacralized the church, conceived of as a vast stone reliquary.[20] The church was then regarded as the essential sacramental site of Christians gathered in community: baptism, Eucharist, penance (and reintegration of penitents), death. The physical church functioned as the animating nucleus of a community-based spatial dynamic: a collection of concentric ecclesial zones radiated from the altar and church –

17 The Monk of Saint Gall (usually identified with Notker Balbulus, *ob.*912) recounted an astonishing story in *De Carolo Magno* (Life of Charlemagne): 'When the pursuit of learning had been almost forgotten throughout all his realm, two Irishmen came from Ireland to the coast of Gaul along with some British traders. These Irishmen were unrivalled for their skill in sacred and secular learning and when the crowd pressed around them every day for business, they exhibited no wares, but shouted "Hey, anyone that desires wisdom, draw near and get it from us; we have wisdom for sale" … Charlemagne asked them what price they asked for it; and they answered, "We ask no price, O king, only a fit place for teaching, quick minds to teach, food to eat and clothes to wear" ' (pp 60–1).   18 P. Browne, *Through the eye of a needle: wealth, the fall of Rome and the making of Christianity in the West, 350–550 AD* (Princeton, 2012).   19 K. Ritara, *Pilgrimage to heaven: eschatology and monastic spirituality in early medieval Ireland* (Turnhout, 2016), pp 28–9.   20 D. Iogna-Prat, 'Churches in the landscape' in T. Noble & J. Smith (eds), *The Cambridge history of Christianity: early medieval Christianities* c.600–c.1100 (Cambridge, 2008), pp 363–79.

cemeteries, churchyards, sanctuaries, parishes – each contributing significantly to where settlements were sited and how their inhabitants were controlled.

Monastic churches had become the largest landowning institution in Ireland by the seventh century.[21] Their estates were worked by para-monastic *manaigh* (lay tenants of a religious establishment) down to the late twelfth century.[22] Foreign travel by clerics and pilgrims alerted the Irish to technological advances that might otherwise have reached them much later. An example is the early presence of tillage within monastic estates, and the precocious adoption of the horizontal water mill.[23] By the Carolingian period, manuals on the management of royal properties (for example, Charlemagne's *Capitulare de Villis c.*771–800) were circulating and great monasteries presumably had equivalent manuals. The Saint Gallen plan from *c.*820 supplied a template for an ideal early medieval monastic community.[24]

Irish church leaders became a self-perpetuating elite, defined by birth, tradition, profession and outlook. Their superiors tended to be hereditary, drawn from aristocratic lineages, like the Uí Sínaigh abbots of Armagh, the Uí Cinnachta of Lusk (Co. Dublin) and the Mac Colmáins of Trim (Co. Meath).[25] Monasteries established by the same founder saint or his successors could form a federation of churches – his *paruchia* – under the jurisdiction of the church where the saint was buried, eclipsing the older, free-standing episcopal churches in power and wealth.[26] Belonging to a prestigious *paruchia* – an affiliation of churches – offered the inside track to ecclesiastical advancement, wealth, patronage and influence.[27] The church elite of the eighth and ninth century was already 'rich, comfortable and powerful'.[28] Celebrated churches like

21 T. Ó Carragáin, 'Churches and social power in early medieval Ireland: a case study of Fir Maige' in J. Sánches Pardo & M. Shapland (eds), *Churches and social power in early medieval Europe* (Turnhout, 2015), pp 99–156.   **22** On the manaigh, see D. Ó Corráin, *The Irish church, its reform and the English invasion* (Dublin, 2017), pp 11–14, 36–7. For the wider picture, see F. McCormick, 'Agriculture, settlement and society in early medieval Ireland', *Quaternary International*, 346 (2014), pp 119–30; A. O'Sullivan & F. MacCormick, 'Early medieval Ireland: investigating social, economic and settlement change, AD 400–1100' in M. Shanley, R. Swan & A. O'Sullivan (eds), *Stories of Ireland's past* (Bray, 2017), pp 10–32.   **23** N. Brady, 'Mills in medieval Ireland: looking beyond design' in S. Walton (ed.), *Wind and water in the Middle Ages: fluid technologies from antiquity to the Renaissance* (Tempe, AR, 2006), pp 39–68.   **24** Since 2012, Saint Gallen has inspired a proposed full scale reconstruction project, using only hand-based Carolingian-style tools and materials at Campus Galli (near Meßkirch in Baden-Württemberg, 30km north of Lake Constance).   **25** D. Ó Corráin, 'Ireland *c.*800: aspects of society' in D. Ó Cróinín (ed.), *A new history of Ireland, i: prehistoric and early Ireland* (Oxford, 2005), p. 586.   **26** C. Stancliffe, 'Religion and society in Ireland' in P. Fouracre (ed.), *The new Cambridge medieval history, c.500–c.700* (Cambridge, 2005), pp 397–425.   **27** D. Ó Corráin, 'Island of saints and scholars: myth or reality?' in O. Rafferty (ed.), *Irish Catholic identities* (Manchester, 2012), p. 35; D. Ó Corrain, 'From sanctity to depravity: church and society in medieval Ireland' in N. Ó Ciosáin (ed.), *Explaining change in cultural history* (Dublin, 2005), pp 140–62.   **28** Ó Corráin, 'Ireland *c.*800', p. 584.

Armagh or Clonmacnoise were able to attract the most widespread paruchiae. Succession disputes triggered conflicts. While these sites undoubtedly attracted multiple activities,[29] the 'monastic town' concept has weakened in more recent scholarship, and the eccelesiastical context of 'civitatis' has been re-established.[30]

THE ARCHITECTURE OF EARLY MEDIEVAL CHURCHES

Unwavering conservatism and uniformity distinguished early medieval Irish churches. The astonishing consistency of Irish sites within their circular enclosures implied a deeply held set of shared ideas, while attachment to the sacred microcosm of the quadrangular church itself was sanctified by enduring links to venerated founders. Sites, initially chosen on the basis of mundane criteria such as land grants, were retrofitted with a predestined, intrinsic sanctity. While building within monastic precincts exhibited an organic quality, the architectural pattern still operated within a highly disciplined choreography.[31] A governing template was laid out at the beginning and then incrementally infilled. By the late sixth century, all churches were single cell rectangles with one lintelled western door.[32] Inherited architectural forms emphasized unbroken continuity, especially when augmented by shrine tombs. Authenticity and aura were much more highly prized than innovation. Even when striking round towers were inserted in the tenth century, the interventions respected the integrity of the initial quadrangular church, modelled on the Roman basilica.

How can we best interpret this seven centuries of conformity in Irish church architecture?[33] Although plain in plan, these churches expressed sophisticated theological understanding, steeped in scriptural and patristic moulds. The transmission of the ancient form was more vital than actual ancient materials. A useful comparison is with Japanese and Korean wooden temples, where the materials were perishable but the style was stable, allowing the building

29 J. Soderberg, 'Feeding communities: monasteries and urban development in early medieval Ireland' in S. McNally (ed.), *Shaping communities: the archaeology and architecture of monasticism* (Oxford, 2001), pp 67–77; J. Soderberg, 'Anthropological *civitas* and the possibility of monastic towns', *JRSAI*, 144–5 (2014–15), pp 45–59; T. Ó Carragáin, 'Is there an archaeology of lay people at early Irish monasteries?', *Bulletin du centre d'études médiévales d'Auxerre* (2015), pp 1–29. **30** M. Maddox, 'Re-conceptualizing the Irish monastic town', *JRSAI*, 146 (2016), pp 21–32. Armagh, Derry, Downpatrick, Kells, Kildare, Kilkenny, Trim and Tuam are covered in H. Clarke, 'Quo vadis? Mapping the Irish "monastic town"' in S. Duffy (ed.), *Princes, prelates and poets in medieval Ireland: essays in honour of Katharine Simms* (Dublin, 2013), pp 261–78. **31** T. Ó Carragáin, *Churches in early medieval Ireland: architecture, ritual and memory* (London, 2010). **32** Downham, *Medieval Ireland*, p. 175. The Roman arch had not entered the Irish architectural repertoire presumably because of the dominance of wooden construction techniques. **33** A. O'Sullivan, F. McCormick, T. Kerr & L. Harney, *Early medieval Ireland AD 400–1100: the evidence from archaeological excavations* (Dublin, 2013).

to be incrementally renewed, piece by slow piece.[34] While the church might experience multiple iterations, the sense of permanency was achieved through replicating its ideal shape rather than through preserving venerable fabric.

The skills of masons and carpenters, based on arcane knowledge, were handed down in construction practices, zealously guarded within families. These practices were transmitted informally, through observation, followed by participation, then active and repeated imitation. Local styles evolved in Ireland (for example, the distinctive north-west Clare/south-west Galway masonry style of the eleventh and twelfth century), perpetuating inherited solutions habitualized through repetition.[35] The concept of the original is itself misleading within an iterative and incrementalist architectural culture that expressed a fluid and recursive rather than a linear and fixed sense of time. The Irish deliberately 'distressed'[36] monuments, as, for example, in the archaicizing Irish-language inscription on the 1402 tomb of the chieftain Maoilsheachlainn Ó Ceallaigh at Abbeyknockmoy (Co. Galway), or the reimagining of earlier doors at Ardfert (Co. Kerry), Inishmurray (Co. Sligo), Clonfert (Co. Galway) and Clonmacnoise (Co. Offaly).[37] There is absolute clarity of continuity at Inishmurray, an unchanging site that remained in active use until the seventeenth century, but that is unusual.[38] Ideal forms were constantly deflected or defeated by the resistance of real situations.[39] The repairs of various ages tended towards patchwork building 'like a geocach's breeches' [geocach: a strolling mummer, vagrant, cadger].[40]

Earth and timber construction imprinted a lighter archaeological record than stone.[41] Differential survival can distort our interpretation of these early churches. When Bede referenced building 'in the manner of the Irish', he had in mind wooden churches of hewn oak.[42] 'Dairthech', the word for

34 J. Cannon, *The secret language of sacred spaces* (London, 2013).　**35** T. Ó Carragáin, 'Habitual masonry styles and the local organization of church building in early medieval Ireland', *PRIA*, 105, C (2005), pp 99–149.　**36** A term in the antiques trade for objects that are deliberately treated to make them appear older than they actually are.　**37** C. Manning, 'The adaptation of early masonry churches in Ireland for use in later medieval times' in M. Meek (ed.), *The modern traveller to our past: festschrift in honour of Ann Hamlin* (Southport, 2006), pp 243–8; T. Ó Carragáin, 'Skeuomorphs and spolia: the presence of the past in Irish pre-Romanesque architecture' in R. Moss (ed.), *Making and meaning in insular art* (Dublin, 2007), pp 95–109.　**38** J. O'Sullivan & T. Ó Carragáin, *Inishmurray: monks and pilgrims in an Atlantic landscape: archaeological survey and excavations* (Cork, 2008).　**39** N. McCullough, *Palimpsest: change in the Irish building tradition*, second edition (Dublin, 2014), p. 12.　**40** *OS letters, Mayo*, p. 147.　**41** M. Bridge, 'Locating the origins of wood resources: a review of dendroprovenancing', *Journal of Archaeological Science*, 39:8 (2012), pp 28–34.　**42** R. Moss (ed.), *Art and architecture of Ireland, volume I. Medieval, 400–1600* (Dublin, 2015), p. 20 [henceforth AAI, i]. Axes for chopping and adzes for planing were tried, trusted and well-known tools – hence the well-judged gibe 'adze-head' on new styles of clerical tonsure. Sawn timber appeared in Ireland in the first half of the seventeenth century, when saw technology was first imported from Yorkshire to the Shillelagh estate (Co. Wicklow) to work oak trees there.

a church, meant oak house.[43] Early medieval Ireland became a repository for Roman woodworking technology that had been abandoned elsewhere in Europe.[44] In the seventh century, surviving fabric from bridges[45] and mills[46] both show a sharp break with the indigenous past, and churches presumably also embraced precision Roman carpentry – tight-fitting rectangular mortises supporting tenoned uprights as wall posts, carefully inserted into sole-plates. The 'saer muilinn' [millwright] and bridge builders enjoyed elevated status, as presumably did the masons who constructed impressive timber churches like the well-known example at Kildare. Even Bernard (1090–1153) of Clairvaux, so rudely dismissive of the Irish, grudgingly praised the church at Bangor (Co. Down) 'made of planed logs but closely and strongly fastened together, an Irish work not devoid of beauty'.[47]

These wooden buildings, anchored by wall posts and roof sockets, supported shingled or overhanging thatched roofs to carry off rain. The infill of walls was composed of sods and organic materials, retained within woven wattle (and occasionally plank) shuttering. Wooden churches displayed similar carpentry techniques to those evident in the contemporaneous horizontal water mills.[48] In the early Irish sources, artisans in wood were assigned to two grades: the most skilled could build churches, bridges, ships and mills,[49] while a secondary grade fashioned houses, chariots and shields. Wood was so prevalent in Irish use that its presence impeded pottery production. The replacement of wooden structures (churches, high crosses) with skeumorphic[50] stone equivalents

---

43 C. Manning, 'References to church buildings in the Annals' in A. Smyth (ed.), *Seanchas: studies in early medieval Irish archaeology, history and literature* (Dublin, 2000), pp 37–52.   **44** M. Geaney, 'Timber bridges in medieval Ireland', *Journal of Irish Archaeology*, 25 (2016), pp 89–104.   **45** The early medieval wooden bridge discovered in 1994 at Clonmacnoise crossed the Shannon just downstream of the monastic site and dendrochronology indicated that it was built in 804. A. O'Sullivan & D. Boland, *The Clonmacnoise bridge: an early medieval river crossing in County Offaly* (Bray, 2000).   **46** N. Jackman, C. Moore & C. Rynne (eds), *The mill at Kilbegly* [Co. Roscommon] (Dublin, 2013).   **47** H.J. Lawlor, *St Bernard of Clairvaux's Life of St Malachy of Armagh* (London, 1920), p. 32.   **48** C. Manning, 'A note on dairthech' in E. Purcell, P. McCotter, J. Nyhan & J. Sheehan (eds), *Clerics, kings and Vikings: essays on medieval Ireland in honour of Donnchadh Ó Corráin* (Dublin, 2015), pp 323–5. John O'Donovan noted that (with the exception of damliac) every word in Irish to express church was derived from Latin. Báisleac: basilica; Kill: cill, ceall, cella; Teampull: templum; Eclais: ecclesia; Regles: reg-ecclesia [an abbey church or one belonging to the regular clergy]: Domhnach: Dominica aedes (*OS letters, Roscommon*, p. 108).   **49** As late as 1634, Pheenesse Hardinge of Ilanemore [barony of Kilmaine (Co. Mayo)], a 'mill carpenter', contracted with Myles second Viscount Mayo, to build, repair and lease two corn mills and a tucking mill at Belcarra (NLI, MS 40,892/2 (7–9)).   **50** A **skeuomorph** is a physical ornament or design on an object that deliberately resembles another material or technique. The word can be applied to elements that serve the same function as they did in a previous design. Skeuomorphs render a new look more familiar and comfortable by recognizing cultural constraints. Interactions with new forms are filtered through and learned from culture and users more readily interpret and accept a new object if it is based on a known appearance.

('damliac') is replicated at so many Irish sites after AD 900 that it can be considered as a guiding principle, representing the Irish affinity for trusted structures even while embracing new technology.[51]

This wooden world proved surprisingly durable. In 1512, a wooden church was constructed at the Franciscan friary of Creevelea (Co. Leitrim):[52] it was petrified as late as 1536 after a fire.[53] Shingles remained a common post-medieval roofing material, especially in Ulster.[54] Assaroe (Co. Donegal) in 1589 and Abbeyknockmoy (Co. Galway) in 1620 were still roofed by shingles,[55] while Lough Derg (Co. Donegal) retained its shingle roof until 1632.[56] Timber fortifications were still being constructed in Ulster in the sixteenth century.[57] Fires in predominantly wooden towns remained a disturbing fact of urban life until well into the eighteenth century.[58] The presence of abundant timber resources until the seventeenth century skewed the archaeological record: north Wexford, for example, has few identified church sites, although the

---

51 O'Sullivan & Ó Carragáin, *Inishmurray*, p. 236.   **52** Margaret O'Brien, wife of Eoghan Ó Ruairc (*ob.*1512), sponsored Creevelea (C. Ó Clabaigh, 'The church 1050–1460', p. 510); C. Ó Clabaigh, *The friars in Ireland, 1124–1540* (Dublin, 2012), p. 21.   **53** AAI, i, p. 206.   **54** In 1684, the shingles for re-roofing the friary at Kilnalehin (Co. Galway) were ready (Dudley Pearce (dean of Kilmacduagh) to Francis Marsh, archbishop of Dublin, 22 Dec. 1684 in HMC, *The manuscripts of the marquis of Ormonde preserved at the castle, Kilkenny*, 14th rep., app. vii (London, 1895–1909), p. 312). Shingles for re-roofing the church in Ballyshannon (Co. Donegal) were carried there from Enniskillen in 1692, presumably via Lough Erne. The oak shingles on Enniskillen church were renewed in 1698, but were replaced by slate in 1737, because sufficient shingles could no longer be found (H. Dixon, *List of historic buildings in Enniskillen* (Belfast, 1973), p. 16). The famous 1707 fire at Lisburn (Co. Antrim) started on a shingled roof (P. Barry, 'The journals of Samuel Molyneux in Ireland 1708–9', *Anal. Hib.*, 46 (2015), pp 1–84 [quotation at p. 22]). The shingles at Killucan (Co. Westmeath) church were renewed in 1730 (Register and Vestry minutes of Killucan parish 1696–1786, RCB). The roof of Kildress church (Co. Tyrone) was shingled in 1739 by James Rodgers (cited in W. Roulston, 'The role of the parish in building and maintaining Anglican churches in the North of Ireland 1660–1740' in E. FitzPatrick & R. Gillespie (eds), *The parish in early medieval and early modern Ireland* (Dublin, 2006), pp 325–44).   **55** R. Stalley, *The Cistercian monasteries of Ireland* (New Haven, 1987), p. 48.   **56** James Spottiswoode, bishop of Clogher, destroyed Lough Derg in 1632: 'I undermined the chapel, which was well covered with shingles and brought all down together' (S. Leslie, *Saint Patrick's Purgatory: a record from history and literature* (London, 1932), p. 80).   **57** C. Donnelly, P. Logue & J. O'Neill, 'Timber castles and towers in sixteenth-century Ireland: some evidence from Ulster', *Archaeology Ireland*, 21:2 (2007), pp 22–5.   **58** Limerick experienced devastating fires in 1618 and 1620. Galway had a major fire in 1619 (J. Hardiman, *History of the town and county of the town of Galway* (Dublin, 1820), p. 101). A fire in Cork in 1622 claimed 1,500 houses (R. Caulfield, *The council book of the corporation of Cork from 1609 to 1643 and from 1690 to 1800* (Surrey, 1876), pp 101–2). In 1635, a fire destroyed 164 houses in New Ross; the Civil Survey listed 383 dwellings in the town so this represented a significant proportion of its urban fabric (B. McGrath, 'A fragment of the Minute Book of the Corporation of New Ross 1635', *JRSAI*, 144–5 (2014–15), pp 100–12). In Enniskillen in 1705, 114 families were reduced to penury by a fire that swept through the town (*Henry's Upper Lough Erne in 1739*, ed. C. King (Dublin, 1892), pp 75–8).

Fig. 2 The exposed roof timbers of the nave of Saint Mary's Church in Youghal (Co. Cork) demonstrate high-quality carpentry. Some of its oak scissor trusses have been carbon-dated to the late twelfth century. Nine surviving medieval roof structures have recently been identified in Ireland. Thomas Dineley [Dingley] described the rood screen in 1681 as 'very rich and well carved and doubly gilt over which are painted the arms of the twelve tribes of Israel'. It was subsequently removed and the absence of their timber furnishings deprives modern visitors of a real sense of what medieval churches in Ireland originally looked and felt like (photo: Kevin Whelan).

1657 map of Scarawalsh barony[59] shows dense settlement within the wooded Dufair (Duffry).[60] Ferns church was described as 'adorned with wonderful carvings and striking ornament':[61] hardly a single scrap of that carving in wood survives.[62] Contrast stone and metalwork.

---

59 This faded map showed intense settlement within the woodlands. It is reproduced (poorly) in A. Smyth, *Celtic Leinster: towards an historical geography of early Irish civilization, AD 500–1600* (Blackrock, 1982), between pp 67–8.   60 The anglicized Duffry derives from *dufair*, which may be derived from an early compound of *dubh* + *tír*.   61 C. Plummer (ed.), *Beatha naem nÉrenn*, 2 vols (Oxford, 1922), ii, p. 118.   62 In 1816, when the ruins of the old cathedral were removed, the date 632 (the year of Aidan's death) was found inscribed on several pieces of timber, and also on a huge beam of oak (Lewis, *Topographical dictionary*).

THE VIKINGS

The sense of the Irish as a distinct people strengthened in the aftermath of the Viking onslaught after 795.[63] Even when the coastal Hiberno-Norse towns nudged settlement towards the east coast, a self-contained geography persisted, notably uninfluenced by external factors, with its centre of gravity firmly focused on the centre of the island. Within the early medieval Irish world, the dominant action was in the midlands, and there was a striking lack of interest in navigable river systems like the Three Sisters. Few regional patterns were exhibited, ogam script being an obvious exception, with seventy per cent of ogam stones located in Waterford, Cork and Kerry.[64] This geographical predilection for the monastic midlands received a robust challenge with the arrival of the Vikings.

What motivated the Vikings? The Vikings 'spilled rivers of blood, seized women and children and property, raided and everywhere destroyed and burned. The people who lived on these shores [of the Caspian sea] were in turmoil'.[65] The Vikings exalted death in battle, making them fearless in pursuit of glory. Valhalla, the halls of the slain, fostered a warrior cult marked by extreme aggression. There is overwhelming archaeological evidence of extreme violence in the Viking homelands with many exacavated piles of slaughtered dead. The Vikings, a proud pagan culture, never doubted that Thór was greater than Jesus, and they were determined to resist aggressive Christian intrusion: Sweden was Christianized as late as the twelfth century, Lithuania in the late fourteenth century and animistic religion remained strong in the countryside there until the eighteenth century.[66]

The Vikings were supremely confident pagans who despised meek-and-mild turn-the-other-cheek Christians. The casual starving to death of Etgal, abbot of Skellig, in 823 and the butchering of Blathmac of Iona in 825 for his refusal to reveal the hiding place of the shrine of Columba showed extreme contempt for devout Christians.[67] That is why the Vikings so relished attacking the monasteries. Cinaed mac Conaing, who sided with the Vikings, was accused by Mael Sechnaill in 851: 'Why did you burn the oratories of the saints and why did you along with the Norse destroy their holy places and the books of the saints?' (§234). A contemporary ironic comment on the efficacy of prayers occurs in the notice of a raid on Armagh in 895: 'Alas, holy Patrick! Your prayers are useless – the Viking axes are hacking your oratories'.[68]

63 D. Griffiths, *Vikings of the Irish Sea: conflict and assimilation, AD 790–1050* (London, 2010).   **64** F. Aalen, K. Whelan & M. Stout (eds), *Atlas of the Irish rural landscape*, second edition (Cork, 2011), p. 44 (henceforth *Atlas of Irish rural landscape*).   **65** Mas'údi, *The meadows of gold: the Abbasids*, ed. & trans. P. Lunde & C. Stone (London, 1989), p. 19.   **66** C. Milosz, *The Issa valley*, trans. L. Iribarne (New York, 1981).   **67** B. Smith (ed.), *The Cambridge history of Ireland, volume I, 1000–1550* (Cambridge, 2017), p. 19.   **68** Translation by D. Ó Corráin, 'Viking Ireland: afterthoughts' in H. Clarke, M. Ní Mhaonaigh & R. Ó Floinn (eds), *Ireland and Scandinavia in the early Viking Age* (Dublin, 1998), pp 485–98.

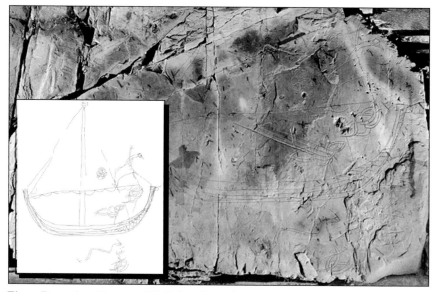

Fig. 3 Deep ploughing near Kilclief on Strangford Lough (Co. Down) revealed a buried stone with a graffito displaying a Viking-type ship with a furled sail. Finbar McCormick dates it to the eleventh century. The ship displays close similarities to ship graffiti in Viking Dublin and in the Scandinavian homelands and it may represent an Irish ship copying a Viking template (Northern Ireland, Department for Communities: Historic Environment Division).

This warrior cult was soon undermined by the absence of women. Only fourteen per cent of Viking graves in Ireland were of women, and the inference has to be that Viking beds were occupied by Irish Christian women, who imparted their religious traditions to their mixed-race children. Intermarriage promoted co-existence of the two traditions, and a distinctive Hiberno–Norse world emerged with Dublin at its epicentre. The 'Viking towns' of Ireland were actually Hiberno–Norse creations: the Vikings entirely lacked an urban culture when they first landed in Ireland.[69]

EARLY MEDIEVAL GRAVEYARDS: HIDDEN 'DEBTHS'[70]

No known culture has ever proved indifferent to dead bodies.[71] Human communities have all consistently felt the obligation to stage the transition

---

69 H. Clarke, R. Johnston & S. Dooley, *Dublin and the Viking world* (Dublin, 2018), pp 103–12.   70 Joyce's pun in *Finnegans wake* [deaths, depths, debts].   71 The three finest recent cultural histories of death are J. Derrida, *The work of mourning* (Chicago, 2001), R. Pogue Harrison, *The dominion of the dead* (Chicago, 2003) and T. Laqueur, *The work of the dead: a cultural history of mortal remains* (Princeton, 2015).

of their dead out of this life. Within the Christian tradition, consecration of graveyards created a bounded sanctified space for the dead.[72] Burial connected the living and the dead in a continuum, a time horizon that linked past, present and future – the *communio sanctorum*.[73] Graveyards marked deep time in a local space, representing a single parish over multiple generations, an embedded shared memory.

Between antiquity and the Middle Ages, the relationship between the living and the dead underwent a revolution that profoundly impacted topography. After centuries of separating the living and the dead through extra-mural necropolises, the middle ages integrated the dead into the world of the living. Medieval people felt and expressed a desire to connect the living and the dead in a single imagined community enduring across the generations.[74]

Settlement archaeology has revealed that this was a protracted process with at least three distinct phases: first, necropolises in the open, then interment within the settlement itself, and finally the clustering of graves in consecrated zones around churches. The practice of communal interment of Christians separate from non-Christians first appeared in the sixth century. It was much later, however, that this interment zone was reserved exclusively for Christians by its consecration as a ritual site. The earliest consecration rituals for a cemetery appear in tenth-century pontificals (no documented example exists before the mid-eleventh century), and canon lawyers did not furnish a definition of the Christian cemetery as land consecrated to the faithful departed before the twelfth century. From the 960s, pontificals record an *ordo* (an order or regulation) for the consecration of cemeteries, supplementing the church dedication rite itself. This late definition of the space as exclusive to the Christian dead occurred within the contemporary context of the expulsion of heretics, Jews and Muslims – the three emblematic figures of the 'persecuting society'.[75] In both Islam and Judaism, mosques and synagogues remained sharply divided from cemeteries; only Christianity integrated the burial and the ritual site.

The transition from cremation to inhumation in Ireland came in the late fourth to the fifth century. No inferences about Christianization can be derived from it, as the burial style was not just Christian but universal in the Roman and Western European world. Inhumation was marked by east–west orientation, with an extended (not flexed) corpse in a supine position, wearing a shroud (wooden coffins appeared only in the late twelfth century), and burial in lintel

---

72 L. Stutz, 'Building bridges between burial archaeology and the archaeology of death: where is the archaeological study of the dead going?', *Current Swedish Archaeology*, 24 (2016), pp 13–35.   73 AAI, i, p. 124.   74 N. Mandeville Caciola, *Afterlives: the return of the dead in the Middle Ages* (Ithaca, NY, 2016).   75 R. Moore, *The formation of a persecuting society: authority and deviance in Western Europe, 950–1250* (London, 2007).

graves rather than the earlier slab- or stone-lined versions.[76] Graves had not been specifically marked at the beginning of early medieval Ireland. In Ireland, earlier cemeteries from the fifth to the seventh century were characterized by the absence of a church, enclosures (notably smaller than their ecclesiastical successors) and a mixture of burial and settlement evidence. The number of burials was small (often less than twenty) at these more intimate sites, suggesting kin group utilization.

In the earlier period, there were very few burials, implying kin group or exclusively clerical usage – three Kerry examples yielded eighteen at Caherlehillan,[77] thirty-three at Church Island (Valentia harbour)[78] and forty-two at Reask.[79] At Ard Oileán (High Island, Co. Galway), an undisturbed monastic cemetery, the graves have cross slabs, every burial was male, and they were all late in date.[80] In the seventh and eighth century, Tíreachán, Muirchú and Adomnán (624–704) all condemned the tradition of burial within circular ditched enclosures known as ferta (ancient burial mounds and enclosures). By the eighth century, burial in ferta had all but ceased.[81] After that, burial in non-ecclesiastical settings faded to vanishing point.[82] There are forty recorded ferta sites: ancestral burial places prominently located on boundaries and often reused.[83]

A long period of co-existence, reflected in diverse burial practices, only finally clarified in favour of Christianity in the seventh century, marking the conclusion of a complex and piecemeal process. The slow adoption of Christian churchyard burial in Ireland should not be regarded as indicating a recalcitrant conversion process, but as simply one among other evolutions in what being a Christian entailed over the many centuries of the early medieval period.

---

76 E. O'Brien, 'Burial practices in Ireland: first to seventh centuries AD' in J. Downes & A. Ritchie (eds), *Sea change: Orkney and Northern Europe in the later Iron Age, AD 300–800* (Angus, 2003), pp 63–72.   **77** J. Sheehan, 'A peacock's tale: excavations at Caherlehillan, Iveragh, Ireland' in N. Edwards (ed.), *The archaeology of the early medieval Celtic churches* (Leeds, 2009), pp 191–206.   **78** M.J. O'Kelly, 'Church Island near Valencia, Co. Kerry', *PRIA*, 59, C (1958), pp 57–136. A reinterpretation can be found in A. Hayden, 'Early medieval shrines in north-west Iveragh: new perspectives from Church Island, near Valentia, Co. Kerry', *PRIA*, 113, C (2013), pp 67–138.   **79** T. Fanning, 'Excavation of an early Christian cemetery and settlement at Reask, Co. Kerry', *PRIA*, 81, C (1981), pp 67–172.   **80** J. White Marshall & G. Rourke, *High Island: an Irish monastery in the Atlantic* (Dublin, 2001): G. Scally, *High Island (Ard Oileán), Co. Galway: excavation of an early medieval monastery* (Dublin, 2014).   **81** E. O'Brien, 'Burial among the ancestors to burial among the saints: an assessment of some burials in Ireland from the fifth to the eight centuries AD' in N. Edwards, M. Ní Mhaonaigh & R. Flechner (eds), *Transforming landscapes of belief in the early medieval insular world and beyond* (Turnhout, 2017), pp 259–86.   **82** E. O'Brien, 'Pagan and Christian burial in Ireland during the first millennium AD: continuity and change' in N. Edwards & A. Lane (eds), *The early church in Wales and the West: recent work in early Christian archaeology, history and placenames* (Oxford, 1992), pp 130–7.   **83** Out of 183 sites listed on the 'Mapping death' burial database.

The establishment of ecclesiastical consecrated burial grounds began in the seventh century, an innovation marked by emergence of the word *reliquiae* (relics, remains of a saint) to denote a 'reilig' (cemetery), as specified by Tíreachán.[84] The transition from ferta to reilig represented the formal claim of the church over burial. It was presumably accompanied by the translation or enshrinement of the relics of the founder saint at the ecclesiastical graveyards. This practice marked the church taking exclusive ownership of burial.

From the eight to the tenth centuries, cross slabs became a status symbol, especially at prestige sites like Clonmacnoise (Co. Offaly), Inis Cealtra (Co. Clare), Glendalough (Co. Wicklow) and Inishmurray (Co. Sligo).[85] An intimate link was established at cemeteries through the use of relics: hence the cross slabs at, for example, Iona and Clonmacnoise, where three-quarters of almost 700 cross-inscribed sandstone slabs bear Irish-language inscriptions from the eighth to the tenth centuries. Are these pilgrim memorials or grave slabs?[86] The Clonmacnoise specimens are so homogeneous that they suggest the products of a single workshop. Specimens can be found in adjacent graveyards within a 25km radius at Clonfert (Co. Galway), Fuerty (Co. Roscommon), Tisaran, Leamonaghan and Gallen (Co. Offaly) and Inishboffin and Hare Island (Co. Westmeath). The consolidation of burial at fewer sites indicated the emergence of a more concentrated power structure that further strengthened the sense of a parish community.

The defining characteristic of an ecclesiastical site was a distinct enclosure, practically and symbolically marking the boundary between the secular and the ecclesiastical realms. The graveyard enclosed within its own boundary was easily absorbed into the existing Irish ecclesiastical complexes, because the monastic tearmon supplied a ready-made demarcation that required no further building work. There could be a series of internal boundaries, with the graveyard located at the centre alongside the church. Synchronicity between the church and the graveyard signalled that the living (in terms of worship) and the dead were now bound together.[87] This followed developments in Late Antique Rome where Christian burials migrated from the catacombs to being located in and around churches.

These new concepts fitted fluently into the Irish veneration of the shrine tomb of the founder, as followers sought burial as close as possible to the saint's

84 T. Ó Carragáin, 'The architectural setting of the cult of relics in early medieval Ireland', *JRSAI*, 133 (2003), pp 130–76.   **85** P. Lionard, 'Early Irish grave-slabs', *PRIA*, 61, C (1961), pp 95–170; 'Clonmacnoise cross-slabs', AAI, i, pp 465–6.   **86** P. Harbison, *Pilgrimage in Ireland: the monuments and the people* (London, 1991), p. 301 suggested that these were pilgrim memorials rather than grave slabs.   **87** An exception is Iona where a vallum separated the church from the burials: F. McCormick, 'Iona: the archaeology of the early monastery' in C. Bourke (ed.), *Studies in the cult of Saint Columba* (Dublin, 1997), pp 45–68.

protective ambit, awaiting favourable judgment at the resurrection.[88] Saints were regarded as patrons of a kin group so burial at his or her site was a mark of loyalty to one's kin. Irish hagiographers chose the saint's *locus resurrectionis* as the defining characteristic, and ultimate focus, of their principal ecclesiastical centres. The saint's body, his or her *praesentia*, marked the spot where heaven and earth met, a punctum of the profane and the sacred, where real presence and real power conjoined.[89] In the earliest Latin *Life* of Ciarán, the saint arrived at Cluain Mac Nóis (Clonmacnoise, Co. Offaly) and said: 'Here I will live: for many souls will leave this place for the kingdom of God, and my resurrection will take place here in this place' and it was believed that the muster of the Irish dead would occur here on the day of judgment.[90] So much clay was taken from the grave of Ciarán that the walls of Temple Ciarán became unstable and began to lean. Belief made the site, as much as the site made the belief.

Across Western Europe, the evolution of the parish system and burial at the parish church went hand in hand in the tenth-to-twelfth-century period. The realignment was powered by a fresh emphasis on communal burial, as opposed to the familial 'private' tomb, which may also mark a transfer in allegiance from the kin group to the church community. That transition was smoothed in Ireland, where ecclesiastical sites were already regarded as closely aligned to dominant kin groups.

The consecrated graveyard came into existence in tandem with the parish system and it was established relatively late.[91] Exclusive burial in sanctified churchyards accelerated in Europe in the eleventh century.[92] This development showed the progressive coming together of the living and the dead, marking a break with classical antiquity, when graves were sequestered at a safe distance from the settlements. The migration from isolated burial grounds to the churchyard was protracted, still evolving in the eleventh century, expressing a profound change in the attitudes of the living towards the dead. The building of the parish church fostered the gathering of graves around it in the churchyard. Parish churches accrued burial rights from the ninth century in Italy, and the tenth to the twelfth century in France and England.[93]

---

88 R. Bartlett, *Why can the dead do such great things?: saints and worshippers from the martyrs to the Reformation* (Princeton, 2013).   89 W. Christian, *The stranger, the tears, the photograph, the touch: divine presence in Spain and Europe since 1500*, second edition (Budapest, 2017).   90 P. Ó Riain, *A dictionary of Irish saints* (Dublin, 2011), p. 175. This tremendous book navigates with ease through the amazing proliferation of Irish saints.   91 J. Graham-Campbell (ed.), *The archaeology of medieval Europe, i, eighth to twelfth centuries AD* (Aarhus, 2009), i, p. 103; A. Cherryson, Z. Crossland & S. Tarlow, *A fine and private space: the archaeology of death and burial in post-medieval Britain and Ireland* (Leicester, 2012).   92 M. Carver & J. Klapste (eds), *The archaeology of medieval Europe, ii, twelfth to sixteenth centuries* (Aarhus, 2011), ii, p. 516.   93 Carver & Klapste (eds), *Archaeology of medieval Europe*, ii, p. 516; E. Zadoro-Rio, 'The making of churchyards and parish territories in the early medieval landscape of France and England in the 7th-12th

This transformation instigated a more tightly defined relationship between burials and the church, marking the evolution from a diffuse funerary area to the concentrated churchyard, and it corresponded to a pivotal phase in the reconceptualization of the parochial community. The right of burial was reserved for the parish church solely. The parish churchyard within its own walls solidified as a distinct element in the landscape, as opposed to the preceding early medieval pattern of scattered burials spread loosely over ruined buildings. The burial ground around the church embodied the physical expression of the parish.

The transition from family cemetery to burial at community churches in Ireland began in the eighth century, accelerated in the tenth and was still in progress in the eleventh century.[94] Recent excavations have revealed many examples of hitherto-disregarded early medieval enclosed burial sites that lacked a church.[95] Examples include Knowth (Co. Meath), Ballymacward (Co. Donegal), Eelweir Hill (Lehinch, Co. Offaly), Farta (Co. Galway) and Holdenstown (Co. Kilkenny).[96] At Ballykilmore (Co. Westmeath), a fifth-to-sixth-century cemetery within an enclosure preceded a later ninth-/tenth-century church: over 1,000 years of continuous burial occurred at the site, and there was a later cillín phase.[97]

Ballyhanna (Co. Donegal), another lost graveyard, lacked upstanding remains or burial markers, but it contained 1,296 burials, dating from 1200 to 1650. Burials, representing a broad based late medieval Gaelic population, occurred for over 900 years, before the site was abandoned (and perhaps deliberately levelled?) shortly after the Ulster Plantation.[98] These were typical Christian shrouded east-facing burials in simple shallow earth-lined graves. Children were also buried here with white quartz pebbles stones in their hands: an early medieval reliquary shrine contained eighty quartz fragments.[99]

---

centuries: a reconsideration', *Medieval Archaeology*, 47 (2003), pp 1–19; E. Zadora-Rio, 'Territoires paroissiaux et construction de l'espace vernaculaire', *Medievales*, 49 (2005), pp 105–20. **94** T. Ó Carragáin, 'From family cemeteries to community cemeteries in Viking Age Ireland?' in C. Corlett & M. Potterton (eds), *Death and burial in early medieval Ireland in the light of recent excavations* (Bray, 2010), pp 217–26. **95** The Stouts were among the earliest to identify the distinctiveness of these sites: G. Stout & M. Stout, *Excavation of an early medieval secular cemetery at Knowth Site M, Co. Meath* (Dublin, 2008). **96** O'Brien, 'Burial among the ancestors to burial among the saints', pp 259–86. **97** J. Channing, 'Ballykilmore, Co. Westmeath: continuity of an early medieval graveyard' in Corlett & Potterton (eds), *Church in early medieval Ireland*, pp 23–38. **98** E. Murphy et al., 'The "lost" medieval Gaelic church and graveyard at Ballyhanna, Co. Donegal' in Corlett & Potterton (eds), *Church in early medieval Ireland*, pp 125–42; C. MacKenzie, E. Murphy & C. Donnelly (eds), *The science of a lost medieval Gaelic graveyard: Ballyhanna* (Dublin, 2015); C. MacKenzie & E. Murphy, *Life and death in medieval Gaelic Ireland: the skeletons from Ballyhanna, Co. Donegal* (Dublin, 2018). **99** E. Murphy & M. Le Roy (eds), *Children, death and burial: archaeological discourses* (Oxford, 2017).

THE MEDIEVAL CHURCH

THE MEDIEVAL PARISH

A reactive energy was injected into European Christianity by the rise of Islam to the east and by the Great Schism of 1054. The jolt to Christianity triggered innovations such as the parish, the advent of the European monastic orders,[100] and the determination to cover Christendom in a 'white mantle of churches'.[101] The delimitation of parishes was a medieval innovation, a novel way of marking off space; still in its infancy in the ninth and tenth centuries, it did not mature until the eleventh and twelfth centuries. The word 'parish' only acquired a distinct territorial meaning in the twelfth century. Spaces delimited by beating the bounds (of churchyard, cemetery and parish) achieved a territorial actuality.[102] Feudalism involved *encellulement*, the widespread organization of people by firmly attaching the populace around the castle, the church, the cemetery and the parish. Cells served as gravitational poles for grouping, controlling and ruling people. Local communities formed distinct cells, but religious, cultural, social, economic and political currents continuously linked them through capillary networks that ensured a common underlying framework.[103]

Centred on the church, concentric zones were defined by the *circuitus*, evoking both the ancient Roman juridical practice of delimiting property by perambulation, and the consecration of cemeteries by a ritualized circuit around the site carrying relics.[104] The outer concentric zone was defined by the parochial boundary. These tightly controlled and overlapping feudal networks generated obedience, submission, solidarity and salvation, guaranteed not through individual efforts or attainments but through involvement in the community.

Two principal factors combined in the genesis of the medieval parish. The first stemmed from tithing, which was obligatory from the Carolingian era

100 C. Corlett & M. Potterton (eds), *Settlement in early medieval Ireland in the light of recent archaeological survey* (Bray, 2011).   101 Rodulfus Glaber (*ob.*1047), *Historiarum libri quinque*, III, iv, 13, 162–5. 'Throughout the whole world, but most especially in Italy and Gaul, men began to reconstruct churches, although for the most part the existing ones were properly built and not in the least unworthy. But it seemed as though each Christian community vied to surpass all others in the splendour of construction. It was as if the whole world were shaking itself free, shrugging off the burden of the past, and cladding itself everywhere in a white mantle of churches. Almost all the episcopal churches and those of monasteries dedicated to various saints, and little village chapels, were rebuilt better than before by the faithful'. These new churches proclaimed *Romanitas* (Romanness) by their construction in stone, Rome's premier building material. They were inspired by specific ancient churches, notably Constantine's Saint Peter's basilica in Rome and his Anastasis rotunda above the Holy Sepulchre in Jerusalem.   102 'Riding the franchises' was a secular equivalent.   103 C. Wickham, *Medieval Europe* (New Haven, 2016).   104 For the role of relics in consecration rituals, see A. Wycherley, *The cult of relics in early medieval Ireland* (Turnhout, 2015).

onwards. The parish then became primarily a fiscal unit, the precinct within which the faithful contributed to the upkeep of both the incumbents and the church fabric itself. The second historical factor was the cemetery. The faithful could now expect to be buried in the place where they were tithing. A parishioner was defined by paying tithes and enjoying reciprocal rights/rites of burial in that same parish. In this way, the reciprocity of church and community was expressed through the provision of material support in return for spiritual services.

As opposed to the administrative units of antiquity and of the early Middle Ages, the radical novelty of the medieval parish lay in its size. The new network was the first administrative pattern adjusted to the scale of farming communities, integrating the religious and social practices of local populations. The process of sub-infeudation calibrated the secular and agricultural world of the manor to the framework of the parish system. If the will to marshal communities into a coherent and precisely delimited ecclesiastical territory was clearly documented by the twelfth and thirteenth century, its enactment was fraught with obstacles and it was often thwarted and delayed, assuming a significant timelag between conceptual decisions and their practical application. By the end of the thirteenth century, parochial boundaries were hardening across Europe and they remained consistent thereafter. A key nexus was that manor and church tended to coincide.[105]

The countryside was so much larger when travel was so much slower. If the parish was to function properly as a gathered community, its church should be accessible on foot. A two-mile radius was considered as within reasonable walking distance, so four miles was the ideal distance between churches in densely settled land. Medieval Irish churches, to judge by County Meath, were centrally located within their parish.[106] The parish enclosed a familiar walkable world, under the aegis of its dedicated protective saint, within the sound of its church bells (which resonated more in a working agricultural world lived outdoors).[107] Many earlier hand bells were struck (as in Hare Krishna rites). A Christianized landscape was always a soundscape.[108] The faiche [green] in front of a ringfort was regarded as extending 'as far as the sound of a bell or the crowing of a cock' could be heard.[109] The distance across which church bells

---

105 Carver & Klapste (eds), *Archaeology of medieval Europe*, ii, p. 471. **106** See the map in M. O'Neill, 'The medieval parish churches of Co. Meath', *JRSAI*, 132 (2002), p. 4. **107** The classic study is A. Corbin, *Village bells: sound and meaning in the nineteenth-century French countryside* (New York, 1998). An earlier study is F. Peacock, 'Church bells: when and why they were rung' in W. Andrews (ed.), *Curious church customs* (Hull, 1895), pp 33–48. **108** On soundscapes, see J. Obert, *Postcolonial overtures: the politics of sound in contemporary Northern Irish poetry* (Syracuse, 2015). **109** Smith (ed.), *Cambridge history of Ireland, 1000–1550*, p. 24. The phrase occurs in the bechtbretha – Old Irish legal judgments on bees. The **honeybee** (Old Irish bec) was highly valued in the early medieval world. Honey (Old Irish mil, hence the later phrase Mil na h-Éigse for an anthology in Irish) remained the essential sweetener prior to the advent of slave-sugar in the seventeenth century. Scriptoria

were audible, especially when tolling the dead, generated community identity and a shared social field – the Italian *campanilismo*. The bell on Inis Cloithrín (Inchcleraun or Quaker Island) in Lough Ree could allegedly be heard on the Roscommon shore seven miles away.[110] A fifteenth-century Irish reference defined the essential function of church bells: '*Deum colo verum, plebem voco, colligi clerum, defunctus pluro, pestem repellem, cunctorum terro sum demiorum*'.[111]

Parochial boundaries were stitched into communal memory through a public process of collective assent – a perambulation of the perimeter, in the presence of old and locally respected tradition bearers.[112] As late as 1654, the outsider William Petty (1623–87) emphasized 'the memory of the ancient bounds'.[113] If we accept the later civil parish as a reliable proxy, there were 2,428 parishes in medieval Ireland, each containing a church within its boundaries. The size and distribution of civil parishes presumably reflected medieval population patterns.[114]

The Romanesque style arrived in Ireland towards the beginning of the twelfth century, inspired by the Gregorian reforms (Gregory VII, Pope 1073–85). Churches should visibly reflect current papal teaching, notably on the real presence, and the consequent need was to separate the officiating cleric from the congregation. Belief in the actual transformation of the species (the term transubstantiation appeared around 1140) magnified the time of the sacrifice (the Mass), but equally sanctified its site (the church), now given a specific name as though it were a person.[115] Consecration symbols appeared in Irish churches, with surviving examples at Churchtown (Co. Wexford), Castlemartyr (Co. Cork) and Old Leighlin (Co. Carlow). The Fourth Lateran Council in 1215 decreed that the bread and wine was 'transubstantiated' into the body and blood of Christ, which charged the altar space with gravitas.[116] A clear early Irish example is the apse on St Peter's church in Waterford.[117] This concept encouraged the careful elongation of earlier buildings – often by adding a

required considerable beeswax (Old Irish céir) for candles, seals, waxed tablets (to practise scribal techniques), and adhesives. Swarms, their tracking and their ownership, were enormously important and occasioned many judgments. T. Charles-Edwards & F. Kelly (eds), *Bechbretha: an old Irish law-tract on bee-keeping* (Dublin, 1983). **110** *OS letters, Roscommon*, p. 140. **111** 'Worship the true God, call the people, gather the clergy, lament the dead, repel the plague, terrorize all demons'. Commonplace book, TCD, MS 667 cited in Ó Clabaigh, *Friars in Ireland*, p. 240. **112** A. Wood, *The memory of the people: custom and popular senses of the past in early modern England* (Cambridge, 2013). **113** A. Horner, 'Through the fractured lens of the Civil Survey: an appraisal of buildings across the mid-seventeenth-century Dublin region' in Duffy & Nolan (eds), *At the anvil*, p. 246. **114** S. Ní Ghabhláin, 'The origin of medieval parishes in Gaelic Ireland: the evidence from Kilfenora', *JRSAI*, 126 (1996), pp 37–61. **115** **Transubstantiation** is the Catholic doctrine that the bread and wine offered in the sacrament of the Eucharist during the Mass are changed into the body and blood of Jesus Christ. **116** There are no known surviving Irish altars from the early medieval period, presumably because they remained wooden until the turn of the twelfth century. **117** See the photograph in Stout, *Early medieval Ireland*, p. 222.

chancel, as at St Mullins (Co. Carlow). As opposed to the venerable single west door, more variable door piercing appeared. The enhanced status of the stone altar (Irish altars remained wooden until the late twelfth century)[118] affected the hitherto sacrosanct quadrangle by promoting the nave and chancel shape.[119] Eighty per cent of mortared stone churches (teampall) became parish centres as the parish system consolidated in the late twelfth and early thirteenth century.

Irish medieval churches get short shrift from art and architectural historians who regard them as gaunt grey boxes, plain and architecturally unelaborated: the English poet Ted Hughes (1930–98) described them as 'grey crumble'.[120] Bare walls were once plastered and painted: wooden interiors have now vanished as well as rood screens, pulpits, lecterns and images of the saints. A reminder of what was once there are the twenty-three fifteenth-century oak choir stalls with carved misericords[121] in the choir of Limerick cathedral. The dismissive attitude is more concerned with what they were not – embellished English and continental churches – rather than what they were – churches well suited to their Irish context and conditions, utilizing easily worked and fine-textured limestone to achieve their own robust clarity of line.[122]

Before 1169, the Irish church and clergy were already adapting this new parish model, and Irish ecclesiastical practices were aligning more closely with the pyramidal structure of the Continent.[123] Rather than being externally imposed, this impulse was generated by charismatic but fanatically driven internal figures like Máel Máedóc Ó Morgair (Malachy) (1094–1148), and it signalled a destabilizing reform agenda that emerged from within the Irish church.[124] Around 1100, Dyflinaskiri, the area stretching south of Dublin dominated by the Hiberno-Norse, incubated an early parish network: innovative stone churches with coeval nave and chancel appeared. Early examples include Killiney and Palmerstown, and the new style spread quickly in the twelfth century.[125] The word 'teampall' (stone church), rare before the mid-eleventh

---

118 AAI, i, p. 254. 119 AAI, i, p. 254. 120 Cited in H. Murtagh, *Lough Ree: a short historical tour* (Athlone, 2017), p. 22. 121 A **misericord** (from the Latin for mercy or relief) was a bracket (often grotesquely or humorously carved) beneath a hinged seat in the choir stalls of a medieval church: when tipped up, the seat supported a standing cleric during a lengthy service. In 1828, the connoisseur Puckler-Muskau was taken by them: 'I admired five hundred year old seats, beautifully carved out of bogwood, which time has turned black as ebony. The lavish ornamentation consists of exquisite arabesques and peculiar masks, different on each seat' (*Letters of a dead man*, p. 501). These seats were not made of bog oak but of the genuine article, likely derived from Cratloe woods. 122 R. Stalley, 'Masons and their materials in medieval Ireland' in V. Olson (ed.), *Use of limestone in medieval buildings* (Farnham, 2011), pp 209–26. 123 M.-T. Flanagan, *The transformation of the Irish church in the twelfth century* (Woodbridge, 2013). 124 'The English invasion brought chronic warfare, renewed conflict in the church and the wider society, legal inequity and severe social disruption' (O Corráin, *Irish church*, p. 116). 125 AAI, i, p. 173; R. Moss, 'Continuity and change: the material setting of public worship in the sixteenth-century' in T. Herron & M. Potterton (eds), *Dublin and the Pale in the Renaissance, 1494–1660* (Dublin, 2011), pp 182–206.

century, suddenly spiked.[126] Mellifont was called 'an mhainistir mhór' – an indication that its large size was regarded by the local population as marking a definitive break with the preceding huddles of small buildings. The adoption of ashlar[127] rather than rubble masonry required the location and exploitation of quarries[128] and the importation of stonemasons skilled in these techniques.

Manipulating space into regular proportions constituted the arcana of medieval masons, with their ability to lay out coherent and integrated ground plans. The plans of medieval churches indicate that two proportional systems generated the dimensions of chancel and nave.[129] The first was based on the root-two extension of a square (the length of the diagonal of a unit square acts like a square root of two), while the second relied on the golden section.[130] Geometric ratios were manipulated using pegs and rope. Interior widths and lengths could then be pegged out, foundations dug outside these lines, and wall thicknesses remained consistent at 0.9m. The width of the nave or chancel governed all other dimensions. These proportions hold good for Meath, south Dublin,[131] Offaly,[132] Louth[133] and Kildare.[134] Over one-quarter display a nave width of five metres, equivalent to sixteen feet and six inches, the length of the medieval perch/rod/pole.

This system also explains the plan consistency of medieval parish churches in Ireland. According to John O'Donovan, who visited most of them, those constructed after 1180 averaged 18m x 6m (108 square metres).[135] The average of medieval churches in the diocese of Elphin was 16.2m x 5.7m (92 square metres).[136] Assuming that three standing people occupied one square metre, and that one-third of the space was required for liturgical purposes, congregations of around 200 could be accommodated. If sufficient parishioners lived over two miles distant from the central church, they were entitled to erect their

---

126 Ó Carragáin, *Churches in early medieval Ireland*, p. 111.   127 **Ashlar** masonry is cut or worked stone, usually quadrilateral, which facilitates very thin joints between blocks. The visible stone face may be dressed in a variety of ways (tooling, polishing, rendering with another material) to create a smooth unified effect. Less expensive rubble masonry employs irregularly shaped stones, sometimes selected for similar size, but minimally worked.   128 See map of quarries around Kilkenny city by John Bradley in *Atlas of rural Ireland*, p. 308.   129 This paragraph relies on pioneering research by Michael O'Neill.   130 In mathematics, two quantities are said to be in the **golden section** (Greek letter phi (φ or ϕ), 1.618) if their ratio is the same as the ratio of their sum to the larger of the two quantities. The golden section was used to generate harmonious relationships between the width and height of a building, the proportions of the portico and the position of columns supporting the structure.   131 M. Ní Mharcaigh, 'The medieval parish churches of south-west Co. Dublin', *PRIA*, 96, C (1997), pp 245–96.   132 E. FitzPatrick & C. O'Brien, *The medieval churches of Co. Offaly* (Dublin, 1998).   133 V. Buckley & D. Sweetman, *Archaeological survey of Co. Louth* (Dublin, 1991).   134 M. O'Neill, 'The medieval parish churches of Co. Kildare' in W. Nolan & T. McGrath (eds), *Kildare: history and society* (Dublin, 2006), pp 153–93.   135 *OS letters, Galway*, p. xxi.   136 T. Finan, 'The medieval bishops of Roscommon and the lost church of Kilteasheen' in Duffy (ed.), *Princes, prelates, poets*, p. 360.

own chapel.[137] In the Irish context, a more decentralized system based on the centrifugal impact of the townland favoured dispersion and encouraged church construction.

Bede in 731 had offered a generous appreciation of Irish spirituality, commending Aidan of Lindisfarne, for example, for travelling on foot rather than on horseback when he arrived there in 635. By contrast, a fat and corrupt ecclesiastic insisted on travelling by chariot, as recounted in the life of the ascetic Cainnech.[138] For the historian and ecclesiastical leader Bede (672–735), remoteness was congenial to austerity, and austerity was congenial to spirituality. But with the Anglo-Normans – unsentimental, hard-nosed, men of the world – geographical morality was reconfigured. After the Crusades, the pestilential was regarded as emanating from the Islamic world. Giraldus Cambrensis (1146–1223), historian of the conquest of Ireland, relocated the noxious to the European margins: he was writing shortly after the Fall of Jerusalem (1187) and the launch of the Third Crusade (1189–92). He emphasized a Latin West increasingly centred on Rome rather than Jerusalem, and his map cast Ireland off onto the very edge of the wild Atlantic, at a debilitating distance from Rome.[139]

This geopolitical reconfiguration downgraded Ireland's distinctive monastic culture. Distance from the centre was now regarded as a blemish rather than a blessing. Monastic enclosure and withdrawal into remote places was regarded as a sulky repudiation of the secular world. Urbanity conferred civility, a shared and supportive human context, lacking in the merely rural.

---

137 N. Whyte, *Inhabiting the landscape: place, custom and memory, 1500–1800* (Oxford, 2009), p. 2. In 1657, the Cromwellian government sought to reorganize the parish system so that every parishioner would be within three miles of a church. In 1670, Oliver Plunkett noted that 'The people are so devout that they will go three miles to hear Mass – very often in the rain' (*The letters of Saint Oliver Plunkett, 1625–1681*, ed. J. Hanly (Dublin, 1979), p. 74). In 1719, 'An act for the better maintenance of curates within the Church of Ireland' permitted chapels of ease to be built where a group of parishioners lived more than six miles from the parish church (6 George I, c. 13). In 1763, the same permission was granted if inhabitants resided more than three miles from the parish church, and more than two from another parish church (3 George II, c. 22). In 1824, the Catholic archbishop of Tuam Oliver Kelly reported to the Commission on Education: 'I have known them to resort to a place of worship from 4, 5 and 6 miles' and in 1853, Paul Cullen allowed priests to hold stations in private houses 'if the church is more than two miles away' (quoted in E. Larkin, 'The Devotional Revolution in Ireland 1850–75', *American Historical Review*, 87 (1970), p. 647. In 1954, the approved distance for expecting attendance at Mass in Limerick was 1.5 miles on foot and five miles on a bike (*Our Catholic Life*, 1 (1954), p. 30). **138** T. Charles-Edwards, *Early Christian Ireland* (Cambridge, 2000), pp 261–4. **139** Lavezzo, *Angels on the edge of the world*.

In the medieval period, Paradise was reimagined as a holy city rather than as a pastoral Eden. Earlier versions of monasticism were criticized as anti-social, an inbred spiritual solipsism that generated seclusion and insularity, impeding proper pastoral provision. Giraldus added a novel twist: the filthy and paganized Irish contaminated a pristine island, because they lacked the necessary skills to profit from its God-given abundant resources. A colonial and ecclesiastical agenda conveniently dovetailed: like the Holy Land infected by the heathens, Ireland was in urgent need of Christian cleansing.

THE REGULAR ORDERS

It is useful to revisit the difference between a monk and a friar. The monk came first: the word is derived from the Greek *monakhus*, meaning solitary or apart. Monks lived in spiritual communities that had withdrawn from the secular world to concentrate on meditation, prayer and personal piety. To ensure their autonomy, their foundations should be financially self-sufficient, sustained by their own endowment of landed property. The monastic reform movement regarded this model as self-indulgent aloofness. Friars (Latin *fratres*, brothers) sought solidarity with the world and to assert a difference in it. They practised mendicancy to express their trust in providence and to ensure that they remained in constant contact with ordinary life, remaining barefoot – discalced – to signal this point. Reliance on the kindness of others put friars in intimate touch with people's lived experience, their joys and their solace, more so their sorrows and their burdens, especially in the effervescent early decades before their orders also subsided into institutional orthodoxy.

Rather than contemplative withdrawal into serene monasteries beyond the boundaries of the everyday, exclaustrated friars sought engagement with the messy noisy world. That drew them to the towns, themselves undergoing an explosive burst across Europe at this time. The friars emerged to serve the new pastoral demands of these rapidly growing towns, disrupting the incumbent secular clergy. A second reforming impulse was towards community-oriented liturgy and preaching rather than private prayer. To ensure that preaching friars gained a sophisticated knowledge of the world, professional training was needed, hence their attraction to university towns. The charismatic friars Dominic (1170–1221) and Francis (1182–1226) exuded spiritual energy, dedicated to a social engagement that married passion to purpose.

Friars engaged the materialistic world in its increasingly significant urban settings. Mendicant spirituality was expressed topographically in the urban fabric, with friars favouring sites on well-trafficked main roads into the towns.[140]

---

140 Ó Clabaigh, *Friars in Ireland,* p. 204.

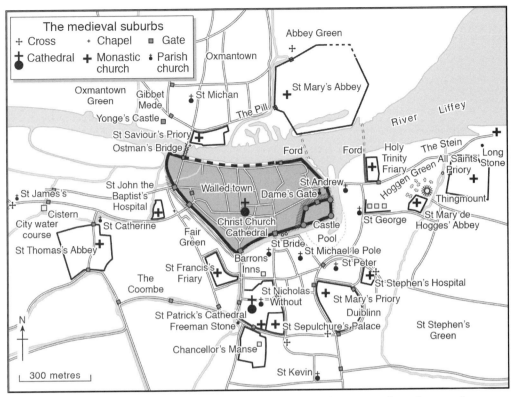

Fig. 4 Churches in medieval Dublin. The extra-mural concentration of monastic foundations is noticeable.

Irish locations in towns broadly resembled European friary locations: peripheral but adjacent to town walls and gates.[141] Friary churches were characteristically conceived as long, large preaching halls, providing significant congregational space, punctuated at two-thirds of their length by rectangular belfries. In 1125, Benedict cautioned against ostentatious churches, where 'the eyes of the rich are fed at the expense of the impoverished': 'Omitto oratoriorum immensas altitudines, immoderatas longitudines, supervacuas latitudines, sumptuosas depolitiones, curiosas depicdones, quae dum in se orandum retorquent aspectu, impediunt et affectum'.[142] Benedict recommended simplicity instead, a frugality that warded off the corrosive personal effects of power, avarice and luxury.

141 A. J. Lafaye, 'The Dominicans in Ireland: a comparative study of the east Munster and Leinster settlements', *Journal of Medieval Monastic Studies*, 4 (2015), pp 79–108.   142 Churches of 'soaring heights, extravagant lengths and excessive widths, their expensive decorations and their novel images, which beguile the attention of those who should be praying, and impede their devotion': Benedict, *Apologia ad Guillelmum abbatem*; trans. M. Casey (Kalamazoo, MI, 1970), p. 12.

Over 400 abbeys, priories, friaries and nunneries were established in medieval Ireland. Two hundred religious houses for men and forty for women had been established by 1230, mostly under Gaelic patronage. In the 1220s, the mendicants (Dominicans, Franciscans, Carmelites, Augustinians) first arrived. As preachers, they sought out urban locations to exercise their very public ministry: they shunned property owning and avoided landed endowments, so their foundations were significantly cheaper to establish and accordingly they could spread more quickly. Mendicant foundations tended to exhibit piecemeal extrapolation from a humble and constrained start, but becoming incrementally claustral. They favoured plain narrow churches, as at Ennis (Co. Clare) and Nenagh (Co. Tipperary).

The Dominicans appeared in 1224 in Dublin and Drogheda, followed quickly in the same decade by Cork, Limerick, Waterford and Kilkenny. By 1291, there were twenty-three Dominican foundations. The Franciscans arrived in 1230 (they had thirty-two foundations by 1336, most established by 1270), the Cistercians followed in 1142, the Augustinians in 1281, the Friars of the Sack (with only one enigmatic foundation) in 1268 and the Carmelites in 1271. In Ireland, 114 nunneries were established, sixty-five between 1100 and 1540, of which thirty-one were founded during the twelfth century. Forty of these, the vast majority, were Augustinian of Arrouasian[143] observance,[144] eight were Augustinian, six were Cistercian, four were Franciscan, one Benedictine and six were of unknown affiliation. This contrasted with the British preference for the Benedictine or Cistercian orders.[145]

All these orders developed their own binding rules on observance, spirituality and liturgy. Their reimagined version of the monastic life was expressed architecturally through a unified layout of domestic spaces arrayed

---

143 Arrouasian meant belonging to the order of canons regular of Saint Augustine or the associated order of nuns, founded at Arrouaise Abbey (northern France) in 1090, who followed the modification of the Augustinian rule by Nicholas of Arrouasia. The Order of Arrouaise was basically Augustinian with some more austere Cistercian elements added. The zealot Malachy promoted the rule of Arrouaise as a means of reform and found widespread adherents in Ireland. The Irish proved unwilling to attend the annual chapters, fomenting tensions between Arrouaise and the Irish houses. As time passed, the distinction between the Arrouaisians and other Augustinians softened sufficiently that Arrouaisian houses in their later history were often referred to as simply Augustinian. **144** P.J. Dunning, 'The Arrouasian Order in medieval Ireland', *IHS*, 4 (1944–5), pp 297–315. **145** T. Collins, 'An archaeological perspective on female monasticism in the Middle Ages in Ireland' in J. Burton & K. Stöber (eds), *Women in the medieval monastic world* (Turnhout, 2015), pp 229–51; T. Collins, 'Isolated in the wilderness?: an archaeological exploration of nunneries in the medieval landscape of Ireland' in Lyttleton & Stout (eds), *Church and settlement*, pp 142–56; T. Collins, 'Timolin: a case study of a nunnery estate in later medieval Ireland', *Anuario de Estudios Medievales*, 44:1 (2014), pp 51–80. For the post-Reformation period, see B. MacShane, 'Negotiating religious change and conflict: female religious communities in early Modern Ireland, *c.*1530–*c.*1641', *British Catholic History*, 33:3 (2017), pp 357–82.

around a courtyard, anchored by large cruciform churches with integrated conventual buildings. These were modelled on the cloister template developed by the Benedictines at Cluny when it was rebuilt after 1088, and by the purity and simplicity of Cistercian cloisters after 1125.[146] Architecture structured the monastic space just as the liturgy structured monastic time. The cloister concept, originally designed to keep out scorching sun, proved equally useful in keeping out the Irish rain.[147] The filiation system offered an effective mechanism for rapid diffusion of architectural innovations within highly organized orders like the Cistercians.[148] The new styles carried Irish ecclesiastical architecture into the European mainstream, but with a notable drop in distinctiveness.

By the late thirteenth century, the elaboration of monastic infrastructure had everywhere attained its mature phase: the surge of foundations was largely complete and the diffusion of the various orders of mendicant friars was petering out. The church-building phase in England had peaked by 1280. By 1290, Britain and Ireland contained almost 1,500 monastic foundations. England accounted for seventy per cent: two out of three houses of mendicant friars were in England, as were three out of four monasteries, the more expensive foundation.[149] Ireland boasted the next greatest number of religious houses – one-fifth of the total, with an estimated one regular cleric for every 280 people. The parish evidence mirrored broadly the picture conveyed by religious houses: of 12,190 parishes in Britain and Ireland, England had sixty-six per cent, Ireland had twenty per cent, while Scotland and Wales together accounted for just fourteen per cent (despite comprising one-third of the land area). Although well endowed with parishes, religious houses and regular clergy, the Irish church was comparatively poor in ecclesiastical income.

A clear geography characterized the Irish church at the end of the thirteenth century. Dublin, Ferns and Ossory were the three richest dioceses as measured by ecclesiastical taxation and all three were located in the east.[150] A second tier

146   R. Stalley, *The Cistercian monasteries of Ireland: an account of the history, art and architecture of the White Monks in Ireland from 1142–1540* (New Haven, 1987).   **147**   T. Coomans, *Life inside the cloister: understanding monastic architecture: tradition, reformation, adaptive reuse* (Leuven, 2018).   **148**   E. Jamroziak, *The Cistercian Order in medieval Europe, 1090–1500* (Abingdon, 2013).   **149**   B. Campbell, 'Benchmarking medieval economic development: England, Wales, Scotland, and Ireland *c.*1290', *Economic History Review*, 61:4 (2008), pp 896–945.   **150**   Valuations of Irish dioceses for ecclesiastical taxation from 1303–6 survive for most dioceses; G. Hand, 'The dating of the early fourteenth-century ecclesiastical valuations of Ireland', *Irish Theological Quarterly*, 24:3 (1957), pp 271–4: T. Barry, 'The Pope Nicholas IV taxation of the early fourteenth century and Irish medieval rural settlement archaeology: a case study', *L'urbanisme: mélanges d'archéologie médiévale* (2006), pp 8–15. Only data for Ferns is missing. Meath, Waterford, Cashel, Emly and Cork have additional taxation returns for 1319–22. This Irish material is erratically calendared (understandably because the medieval placenames are garbled) in H. Sweetman & G. Handcock (eds), *Calendar of documents relating to Ireland*, 5 vols (London, 1875–86), v, pp 202–323. In sharp contrast, the English and Welsh materials are now brilliantly edited and

Table 1: Ecclesiastical wealth per diocese in Ireland, 1303–6: total tax value in pounds

Tier one		Tier two		Tier three	
Dublin	2,814	Cloyne	583	Killala	96
Ferns	1,250	Limerick	392	Derry	76
Ossory	1,049	Tuam	360	Annaghdown	73
		Killaloe	318	Kilmacduagh	63
		Emly	313	Clogher	60
		Cork	284	Elphin	69
		Clonfert	206	Kilfenora	60
		Ardfert	179	Raphoe	59
		Waterford	126	Ross	45
				Dromore	42
				Ardagh	39
				Achonry	35
				Clonmacnoise	25
				Kilmore	23
				Armagh	11

straddled Munster and inner Connacht, followed by a noticeably impoverished third tier along the Atlantic West and especially in Ulster.[151] The 1324 proposal (but never implemented) for the abolition of dioceses worth less than sixty pounds annually was seen as explicitly anti-Gaelic.

accessible on line. The Irish materials can be sifted to infer valuable settlement evidence as in S. Ní Ghabhláin, 'Church and community in medieval Ireland: the diocese of Kilfenora', *JRSAI*, 125 (1995), pp 61–84.   **151** Values per parish for 1538 can be found in the *Valor beneficiorum ecclesiasticorum in Hibernia: or the first-fruits of all the ecclesiastical benefices in the kingdom of Ireland, as taxed in the King's books* (Dublin, 1741) (available on Internet Archive). Figures for Catholic parish income in 1800 are listed in C. Vane (ed.), *Memoirs and correspondence of Viscount Castlereagh*, 4 vols (London, 1849), iv, pp 97–172. Detailed figures are supplied for Achonry, Ardagh, Ardfert, Armagh, Cashel & Emly, Clonfert, Down & Connor, Dromore, Dublin, Elphin, Ferns, Galway, Kilmacduagh, Kildare & Leighlin, Kilfenora, Killala, Meath, Ossory, Tuam, Waterford and Lismore. Only aggregated data is extant for Clogher, Cloyne & Ross, Derry, Killaloe, Kilmore, Limerick and Raphoe.

CHAPTER TWO

The Gaelic Church

F EW ADDITIONAL RELIGIOUS HOUSES were founded after 1300, with the exception of the Franciscan Third-Order Regular[1] friaries in Ireland. The Black Death first appeared in the ports (notably Drogheda, Dublin, New Ross, Waterford, Youghal and Cork) and ravaged the Pale area between 1348 and 1350, leaving the Gaelic areas relatively unscathed. Religious communities were especially susceptible, and perhaps close to half their members died: twenty-five Franciscan friars died in Drogheda, twenty-three in Dublin, and eight Dominican friars died in Kilkenny in a single day in March 1348. Geoffrey Le Baker, a contemporary English chronicler, concluded that the plague in Ireland 'killed the English inhabitants there in great numbers, but the native Irish, living in the mountains and uplands, were scarcely touched'.[2]

Several existing houses were either merged or dissolved in the fourteenth and fifteenth centuries. The observant reform movement of the late fourteenth and fifteenth centuries had its epicentre in the west, a reversal of the expected direction of innovation flow in Irish settlement geography. There was a pronounced late fourteenth-century shift into Gaelic areas: forty new houses and forty-nine lay tertiaries of the observant movement were established between 1426 and 1539. The Tertiaries, laymen who took simple monastic vows, suited the erenach families. The Augustinians favoured local autonomy and that proved equally congenial to the Gaelic world. The first Augustinian Observant friary was established in 1423 at Banada (Co. Sligo) and by 1517 they had eight houses. In total, 190 new Dominican, Augustinian and Franciscan houses appeared between 1400 and 1508, of which sixty-eight were in Tuam and Armagh.[3]

Connacht was the seedbed for a remarkable second flowering of the reform movement that established almost 100 new mendicant houses. After 1371, the Observants went west, adding twenty-one new foundations before 1510 and peaking at sixty-one houses. In the fifteenth and sixteenth century, forty-six

---

1 Initially an internal reform movement, the Third Order Regular was formalized in 1447. Tertiary communities were small groups of both clerical and lay brothers.   2 M. Kelly, '"Unheard-of mortality": the Black Death in Ireland', *History Ireland*, 9:4 (2001), pp 12–17. 3 Smith (ed.), *Cambridge history of Ireland, 1000–1550*, p. 505.

more houses of the Third Order of Saint Francis were founded – a surge that was not replicated in England. Between 1426 and 1539, forty-nine houses of regular tertiaries (about whom little is known) appeared. The Dominicans added thirty-five houses from 1224 to 1507, while the Augustinians established eight new friaries in their secondary expansion between 1380 and 1500, of which only one (Callan, Co. Kilkenny) was in the east. The more Gaelic areas were benefitting from a booming fishery at this time.[4] In 1578, the well-informed Sir Owen O'Sullivan noted that the O'Sullivans in west Munster 'liveth only by the sea, and the commodity thereof, as of his fishing, his wrecks and such like', 'the country being all valleys, cragged rocks and hills'.[5]

There was an architectural caesura in the mid-fourteenth century, driven by the Black Death, followed by the Irish Revival flourish of late Gothic in the west of Ireland.[6] These late medieval buildings like Quin Abbey (1433, Co. Clare) were marked by slender square belfries, curvilinear tracery windows, stepped battlements and a preference for local grey limestone (rather than sandstone and imported Dundry stone),[7] which took and held sharply chiselled detailing. These new buildings expressed a new theological perspective.[8] There was also a renewed emphasis on Christ as the 'Man of Sorrows', who had a particular empathy for the poor: 'Íosa Críosd cara na mbocht' (Jesus the friend of the poor), as he was termed by the poet Pilib Bocht Ó hUiginn (*ob.*1487) (the 'bocht' (poor) nickname signaled that he was an observant Franciscan following vows of poverty).[9]

In 1606, Donncha Ó Maonaigh (Donatus Mooney (1577–1629)) described Moyne Friary on Killala Bay (Co. Mayo) (founded for Observant Franciscans in 1460): 'Round the convent were gardens, meadows and orchards enclosed within a strong stone wall'. A spring supplied clean water, there were two mills while adjacent Bertragh island 'abounded in rabbits'. Burned shells 'make a wonderfully binding cement'. Fish were plentiful there, as well as fresh vegetables and shellfish; 'Who can lack these when they can be gathered on the shore with minimal labour?'[10]

4 T. O'Neill, *Merchants and mariners in medieval Ireland* (Dublin, 1987), p. 36.   5 'A note describing the ancient customs of the divisions of land time beyond the memory of man among the O'Sullivans of Beare and Bantry' in *CSPI, 1586–8*, pp 365–8.   6 R. Stalley, 'Gothic survival in sixteenth-century Connacht' in M. Meek (ed.), *The modern traveller to our past: festschrift in honour of Ann Hamlin* (Dublin, 2006), pp 302–14.   7 **Dundry stone** came from Dundry Hill in the Mendip Hills in the English county of Somerset near Bristol, the principal trading port of medieval Ireland. The yellow oolitic limestone is easily carved. The stone was much used in medieval Bristol. A large cube (1.5m each edge), still standing in the churchyard of St Mary Redcliffe in central Bristol, is widely considered to be an early advertisement for Dundry stone.   8 M. Krasnodebska-D'Aughton, 'Prayer, penance and the passion of Christ: the iconographic program of the Franciscan friary at Ennis, Ireland', *Studies in Iconography*, 37 (2016), pp 75–108.   9 C. Mac Mhurchaidh (ed.), *Lón anama: a collection of religious poems in Irish with translations in English* (Dublin, 2005), p. 163.   10 Ó Clabaigh, *Friars in Ireland*, pp 125, 256–7. This detailed material is presented in Latin in B. Jennings, 'Donatus Moneyus, de Provincia Hiberniae S. Francisci', *Anal. Hib.*, 6 (1934),

Gaelic learned families embraced these friaries whence emanated effective preachers, simple and direct in style, but above all equipped with knowledge of the vernacular. This underpinned their pastoral and educational mission in Connacht and Ulster, which later proved crucial in preventing Gaelic Ireland from embracing the Reformation as readily as Gaelic Scotland proved willing to do.

This friar-based system also assigned prominence to the laity and especially to devout women, operating within domestic spaces rather than churches, and perforce diminished the priest's role.[11] Mairgréag Ní Chearbhaill (*ob.*1451) of the leading Gaelic family of Co. Offaly was praised for repairing roads, erecting bridges and churches, making a pilgrimage to Santiago de Compostella, and sponsoring Mass books.[12] Infusion of the spiritual into the secular life was demonstrated in the spiritually themed sculptures at Ardamullivan Castle (Co. Galway).[13] In a sample of 2,000 Bardic poems, one in five was explicitly spiritual in theme.[14] The Mac Aodhagáin's legal school at Ballymacegan (Co. Tipperary) possessed an impressive collection of vernacular religious material.[15]

Land, lineage and kinship characterized the culture of late medieval Gaelic Ireland. Surnames had stabilized by the eleventh century, conferring clarity and public visibility on kin relationships in a lineage-based society. A confident Gaelic society resisted tightening ecclesiastical prohibitions on kin marriage until the seventeenth century. The parish was utilized as a staging post for family interests. In Clare, notable lineages included Kelly of Killard, Tulla and Inis Cathaigh, O'Hogan of Inis Cealtra, Considine of Killone and Mac Craith of Clare Abbey.[16] An abiding sense of tradition infused the western church because the erenagh [airchinneach]/coarb families as chief tenants and managers clung like limpets to the termon lands of ancient sites – for example, O'Dea at Dysert O'Dea, Quinn at Killinaboy and O'Grady at Tuamgraney. This continuity was exhibited in a clear preference for local over universal saints, a preference that dictated the distinctive geography of Christian names.[17]

pp 12–138. *The Franciscan Tertiary* (1894–9) published an English translation 'A history of the Franciscan Order in Ireland by Donagh Mooney' in sixty-seven monthly installments from volume 4:10 (Feb. 1894) to its last issue volume 10:4 (Aug. 1899). **11** L. Lux-Sterritt & C. Mangion, 'Gender, Catholicism and women's spirituality over the longue durée' in L. Lux-Sterritt & C. Mangion (eds), *Gender, Catholicism and spirituality: women and the Roman Catholic church in Britain and Europe, 1200–1900* (Basingstoke, 2011), pp 1–18. **12** Ó Clabaigh, *Friars in Ireland*, p. 99; AFM, iv, pp 972–3; D. Hall, *Women and the church in medieval Ireland c.1140–1540* (Dublin, 2003). **13** K. Morton, 'A spectacular revelation: medieval wall painting at Ardamullivan', *Irish Arts Review*, 18 (2002), pp 104–13. **14** K. Simms, 'Bardic poetry as a historical source' in T. Dunne (ed.), *The writer as witness: literature as historical evidence* (Cork, 1987), p. 71. **15** W. Follett, 'Religious texts in the Mac Aodhagáin Library of Lower Ormond', *Peritia*, 24–5 (2013–14), pp 213–29. **16** L. McInerney, *Clerical and learned lineages of medieval County Clare* (Dublin, 2014). **17** W.J. Smyth, 'Excavating, mapping and interrogating ancestral terrains: towards a cultural geography of first names and second names in Ireland' in H. Clarke, J. Prunty & M. Hennessy (eds), *Surveying Ireland's past: multidisciplinary essays in honour of Anngret Simms* (Dublin, 2004), pp 243–80.

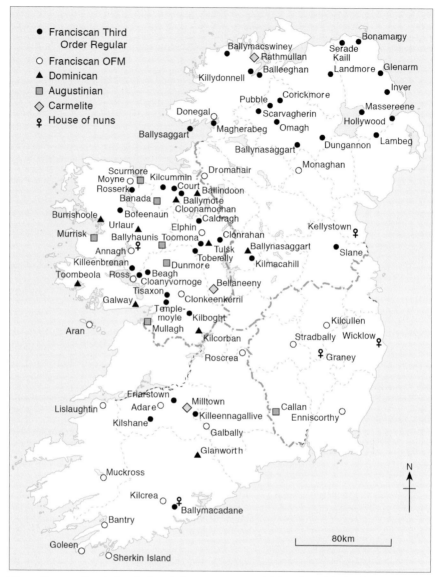

Fig. 5 Late medieval church foundations, 1420–1530 (*Atlas of rural Ireland*, p. 58).

In Irish society, the hereditary principle was so ubiquitous that it was natural for it to be applied within the church as well. Retaining a family member on ecclesiastical land granted through Irish law conveniently met the requirement that such land could not be alienated in perpetuity from the family. Lineages controlled benefices within the sphere of influence of the hereditary lands of their kindreds. Ecclesiastical fashions fluctuated but the key families occupied their accustomed sites. At Clonkeenkerrill (Co. Galway),

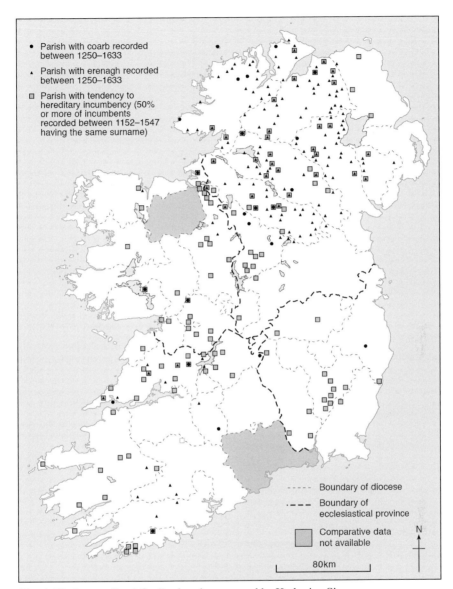

- ● Parish with coarb recorded between 1250–1633
- ▲ Parish with erenagh recorded between 1250–1633
- ☐ Parish with tendency to hereditary incumbency (50% or more of incumbents recorded between 1152–1547 having the same surname)

----- Boundary of diocese

.—.— Boundary of ecclesiastical province

Comparative data not available

N

80km

Fig. 6 The late medieval Gaelic church as mapped by Katharine Simms.

for example, the Franciscan Tertiaries (OSF) took over an existing church site but its O'Mulkeerill clerical family came along too. Later the site reverted to the Franciscan Minors (OFM), but the O'Mulkeerills were still there.[18] In late medieval Clare, these firmly established families ensured that there was little

18 Ó Clabaigh, *Friars in Ireland*, pp 205, 311–12.

overlap between clerical and learned lineages – each stuck to their expertise – and to their separate ecclesiastical and lay patrons.

The process of hereditary lineages infiltrating benefices was accelerating in the mid-fifteenth century. The pluralist MacNamaras and O'Briens in east Clare were able to penetrate Augustinian houses (the Franciscans resisted) as a means of advancing career and income. A quasi-hereditary clerical succession remained a feature of the Irish church.[19] All three sons of an abbess of Killone in Clare (including one whose father was the local bishop) were dispensed to become clergy.[20]

The shielding effect of dominant local families underpinned the robust continuity of Gaelic culture that remained cohesive over many centuries in its ancestral power bases. In the Gaelic world in general, there was a sophisticated hierarchy of autonomies: 'Sinsir la fine, febta la flaith, ocus ecna la eclas' (seniority in family, dignity in the lord, wisdom in the church).[21] Clients and cattle counted as much as acres, and status had to be earned as well as inherited. The stability mechanisms within the Gaelic polity were sustained by the cultural discipline embedded in its institutions: the dearbhfhine (creating a pool of senior policy makers), the tánaiste (effective in managing the disruptive interregnum), cinn comhfhogais (the consensual collective decision making of hillside assemblies),[22] cóisireacht (regular visiting of clansmen as a way of cementing loyalties and keeping leaders close to and familiar with those that they led), a predilection for cousin marriages that softened kin asperities after bitter succession disputes, and the advisory role of an intellectual class of lawyers, priests, poets and doctors.[23]

These strategies generated an agile and capable leadership cadre, as the 'Discourse on the mere Irish of Ireland' of 1608 lamented:

---

19 K. Simms, 'Frontiers in the Irish church: regional and cultural in colony and frontier' in T. Barry, R. Frame & K. Simms (eds), *Medieval Ireland: essays presented to J.F. Lydon* (London, 1995), pp 177–200; M. Haren, 'Social structures of the Irish church: a new source in papal penitentiary dispensations for illegitimacy' in L. Schmugge (ed.), *Illegitimitat im spatmittelalter* (Munich, 1994), pp 207–26.   20 Ó Clabaigh, *Friars in Ireland*, p. 301. Daniel O'Donnell, dean of Raphoe, was accused in 1463 of melting down a silver paten and a chalice to make ornaments for a concubine (AAI, i, p. 260).   21 Cited in C. Mac Aonghusa, 'Thomond in a European context: the Ui Bhriain dynasty 1450–1581' (MA, University College Cork, 2005), p. 14.   22 Map of inauguration sites by Elizabeth FitzPatrick in *Atlas of Irish rural landscape*, p. 61; C. Ó Crualaoich, 'The identification of Leac Mhic Eochaidh in north Wexford 1592' in *The Past*, 32 (2016), pp 52–72. A proverb stated 'Dána gach fear go tulaig' ('Every man is bold until he is on the hill' at a public assembly). The Irish held public assemblies on traditionally designated hills; hence the secondary meaning of tulach, a hill (as in this proverb) to mean a place of assembly. Aonach, 'an assembly', means a fair in modern Irish but 'a hill' in Scots Gaelic.   23 An edited collection of relevant documents from the Mac Ghiolla Phádraig family can be found in D. Edwards, 'Lordship and custom in Gaelic Leinster: select documents from Upper Ossory 1559–1612', *Ossory, Laois & Leinster*, 4 (2010), pp 1–47.

He that must be the chief lord must be the valiauntest and stoutest of that family or house. And besides this, this valiauncy must be determined amongst all the family, so as every chieftianship of every family is by this means made elective, now consider what manner of preparation this is for rebellion. For the custom being thus every one of that family being as likely to be the best, as another will strive to advance their own fortunes above the rest, and by this emulation they become wonderful active in exercise of arms, and thus the chiefest of all must of necessity prove exquisite, so as they will be sure never to want a leader or governor in all their attempts.[24]

Surnames utilized in Sligo placenames were derived disproportionately from clerical and learned families, occurring primarily on church lands. Examples on the ancient church lands of Drumcliff in the Rosses include Ó Beolláin, Ó Coinéil, Mac an Fhirléinn, Ó Gealáin, Ó Dálaigh and Mac Aogáin.[25] Paradoxically, Gaelic surnames in townland names occurred more frequently in areas that experienced substantial Anglo-Norman settlement. In south Wexford, Anglo-Norman surnames abound in townland names, to the extent that they overwhelm indigenous Irish surnames even in placenames derived from the Irish language.[26] The striking contrast with Irish-dominated areas stemmed from divergent legal systems – freehold under English law prevailed in areas of Anglo-Norman settlement, while land was held 'at will' from the dominant family in areas under Irish law. Land rarely became the exclusive property (freehold) of occupants under Irish law, even where long-term occupancy was the reality (professional families were the exception), generating a much weaker impetus to attach surnames to townland names. That long-term occupancy is clearly attested on the church lands.

The quasi-hereditary clergy tightly bound into this Gaelic matrix provided a significant force for continuity. They held their ground until the pressure ratcheted up in the turbulent sixteenth century when their room for manoeuvre inexorably narrowed. The reinforcing impact of the Reformation and Elizabethan campaigns to obliterate the autonomy of the Gaelic lordships marked a watershed, as corrosive external forces, initially by stealth, then by law and finally by military aggression, intruded English and Protestant power. The learned lineages had initially controlled four areas of specialist knowledge – seanchas (history), filíocht (poetry), féineachas (law) and leigheas (medicine)

24 'Discourse on the mere Irish of Ireland', 1608 [CELT]. **25** C. Ó Crualaoich, 'Townland and defunct placenames in Sligo: evidence for surnames' (forthcoming). **26** C. Ó Crualaoich & A. Mac Giolla Chomhghaill, *Logainmneacha na hÉireann IV; Townland names in County Wexford* (Dublin, 2016), pp 83–107. This discussion makes Tom Jones Hughes's earlier map of baile/bally placenames all the more revealing: T. Jones Hughes, 'Town and baile in Irish placenames' in N. Stephens & R. Glasscock (eds), *Irish geographical studies* (Belfast, 1970), pp 244–58 [map at p. 254].

– and did not pursue clerical careers. With the Catholic Reformation, these learned classes actively entered the church, supplying the intellectual heft required to resist the intrusive twin threats of Protestantism and anglicization in a joint resistance to a relentless common adversary.

A similar existential threat loomed over the admirably resilient airchinneach/erenagh institution. These resident para-clerics, drawn from hereditary families, managed church lands, maintained church fabric, supplied hospitality, backboned the diocesan clergy and dominated the cathedral chapter well into the modern period.[27] The system of hereditary erenach families was tied to the church's termon lands, following the transfer of church lands from the monasteries to the erenachs on the back of the twelfth-century reform. The subsequent dominance of the erenach septs within the diocesan hierarchy conferred stability on the ecclesiastical structure. In 1622, the Protestant bishop of Derry was aghast that there was a 'priest placed in every parish', responsible for 'carrying the natives after them generally'.[28] These families disproportionately supplied the diocesan clergy in the Gaelic areas. In 1703, the majority (nineteen of twenty-seven) of the Derry clergy was drawn from erenagh families like Crilly in Tamlaght O'Crilly and Scullion in Ballyscullion (Co. Derry), Colgan in Carndonagh (Co. Donegal) and Mac Cathmhaoil in Omagh (Co. Tyrone), a pattern that fostered intimate local bonds.[29] The Irish term dúthasach (anglicized 'doughasa') signified a native holder of hereditary erenach land.[30]

No wonder that in the early seventeenth century the Protestant bishop of Derry first identified the erenaghs, then attacked them and finally eliminated them.[31] Erenagh families active in Fermanagh included Ó Conghaile, Ó Taichligh, Ó Corcrain, Mac Arachain, Ó Donnacháin, Ó Gabhann, Ó Corragáin, Ó Caiside, Ó Sleibhine, Ó Breasláin, Ó Cianáin, Ó Luinín, Ó hOgáin, Ó Banáin, Ó Breasláin, Ó Fiaich, Ó Treasaigh, Mac Gilla Coisgle (Cosgrove) and Mac Maghnusa.[32] In 1609, twenty per cent of County Fermanagh was

27 H. Jefferies, 'Erenaghs in pre-Plantation Ulster: an early seventeenth-century account', *Archiv. Hib.*, 53 (1999), pp 16–19; H. Jefferies, 'Erenaghs and termonlands: another early seventeenth-century account', *Seanchas Ard Mhacha*, 19:1 (2002), pp 55–8. 28 Ecclesiastical visitation to diocese of Derry by Bishop George Downham, TCD, MS 550. 29 H. Jefferies, 'Derry diocese on the eve of the plantations' in G. O'Brien (ed.), *Derry: history and society* (Dublin, 1999), p. 192. 30 This term, which designated a member of a long-established local family, appeared in an early seventeenth-century Fermanagh inquisition: *Inquisitionum in officio rotulorum cancellariae Hiberniae repertorium*, 2 vols (Dublin, 1826–9), ii, p. 57. **Dúchas** is a core word in Irish, representing the dynamic unity of place and people, a cumulative effect achieved over multiple generations. 31 H. Jefferies, 'Bishop George Montgomery's survey of the parishes of Derry diocese: a complete text from *c.*1609', *Seanchas Ard Mhacha*, 17:1 (1996–7), pp 44–76. 32 C. Ó Scea, 'Erenachs, erenachships and church landholding in Gaelic Fermanagh, 1270–1609', *PRIA*, 112, C (2012), pp 271–300. His detailed map of Fermanagh erenachships and coarbships was constructed from many sources, most notably

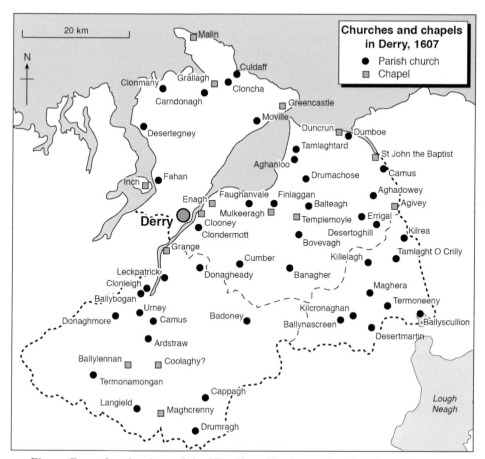

Fig. 7 Even after the chaos of the Nine Years War (1593–1603) in Ulster, there were forty-five parishes in the diocese of Derry in 1607, served by twenty-seven priests and a tight network of churches and chapels. This is apparent on this map by Henry A. Jeffries, capturing the intact and functioning Gaelic church before the Plantation shattered this venerable system.

church land: the comparable figure for Tyrone and Dublin was twenty-five per cent.[33] In both Tyrone and Roscommon,[34] a feature of the medieval church lands was their predominant location in areas of low townland density and depressed land value.[35] John O'Donovan recorded the latest glimpse of an erenach in

the annals, the 1603 Survey and the 1609 Inquisition. The erenach lands comprised 17,282 acres (164 out of 679 townlands). Of these families, Ó Casaide, Ó Cianáin, Ó Luinín and Mac Maghnusa were also distinguished for their scribal activities. **33** P. Robinson, *The plantation of Ulster: British settlement in an Irish landscape, 1600–1670* (Dublin, 1984), p. 195: Downham, *Medieval Ireland*, p. 298. **34** P.J. Carty, 'The historical geography of County Roscommon' (MA, University College Dublin, 1970). **35** Ó Scea, 'Erenachs, erenachships and church landholding'.

action at Uarán Uí Chlabaigh (Co. Roscommon). Until recently 'the senior of the O'Clabys used to appear at the pattern and show the people the extent of his termon lands and how his ancestors were deprived of them' and 'they then made a collection for his support'. O'Donovan described the contemporary family as 'still in the neighbourhood' 'but very poor, all paupers'.[36]

THE FRIARS

After 1610, the mendicant friars, fugitive and peripatetic, haunted their ruined friaries, without habits, observance or statutes, awaiting a thaw in the penal cold.[37] The pastoral emphasis dominated. In pop-up novitiates, local religious leaders addressed their financial problems by ordaining after a mere year of clerical formation – an improvised solution unique to Ireland.[38] In 1662, the archbishop of Armagh objected to the Franciscans and Carmelites accepting novices 'in cabins, huts, woods and caves'.[39] The more socially elevated Jesuits and Capuchins (recruited from the Old English of the Pale) refused to countenance makeshift novitiates but mainstream mendicant orders reacted in this way to the exacting conditions of Ireland, rather than allowing their novices to go soft in more pampered continental conditions.[40] The Old English supplied 217 of 287 known early Jesuits in Ireland.[41] Irish novices who could endure rough living conditions and meagre diets would adapt more readily to the hardship of the mission.[42] Oliver Plunkett (1625–81) concluded in 1674 that '*la tempesta gioverá piu che la bonaccia*'.[43]

The social centre of gravity of recruiting dropped to meet the harsh new reality. In 1732, a Galway priest identified 'the sons of shepherds and peasants' as the social base of vocations.[44] The more fastidious were appalled by plummeting standards: from Co. Monaghan, the *Comhairle Mhic Clamha ó Achadh na Muileann*, a pungent late seventeenth-century satire on badly trained clerics from families who could not afford to send their children abroad for a proper education, excoriated the 'sagart bhocht na droch-Laidne/an uair do mhilleas an soisgéal' (the poor priest with bad Latin, who butchered the gospel message).[45] Archbishop Oliver Plunkett literally held the nose on his Pale face when saying Mass in Gaelic south Armagh in 1677:

---

36 *OS letters, Roscommon*, p. 36. 37 H. Fenning, *The undoing of the friars of Ireland: a study of the novitiate question in the eighteenth century* (Louvain, 1972), p. 55. 38 Fenning, *Undoing of the friars*, p. 56. 39 Fenning, *Undoing of the friars*, p. 58. 40 Fenning, *Undoing of the friars*, p. 70. 41 V. Moynes (ed.), *The Jesuits Irish Mission: a calendar 1566-1752* (Rome, 2017). 42 Fenning, *Undoing of the friars*, p. 224. 43 'The storm will prove of more benefit than the good weather': Plunkett to Falconieri, 12 Feb. 1674 in Hanly (ed.), *Letters of Oliver Plunkett*, p. 401. 44 Fenning, *Undoing of the friars*, p. 39. 45 *Comhairle Mhic Clamha ó Áchadh na Muileann: the advice of Mac Clave from Aughnamullen*, ed. & trans. S. Ó Dufaigh & B. Rainey (Lille, 1981), p. 85.

'if the bishop has a nose at all, he won't fail to notice a trace of the odour of the stable at the altar'.[46]

The innovation of questing for oats, wheat, barley, turf and hay began in Connacht in 1620 and escalated into claims to exclusive right by regulars.[47] Questing within their impoverished host communities proved an inexhaustible spewer of clerical squabbles. In Galway town in 1775, there were seven Franciscans, six Dominicans and five Augustinians, totalling eighteen friars to be maintained by 15,000 Catholics. This ratio of one friar per 850 people guaranteed only a spartan diet of potatoes and milk, low incomes and constant spats over burials and funeral offerings.[48]

The regular clergy were treated best in Connacht, where they were most numerous, and where there was the strongest survival of Catholic gentry, especially in Galway and Mayo.[49] The archbishoprics of Dublin and Armagh later allowed regulars to quest 'si alia stit in Connacia suae stent consuetudini' (as was always the custom in Connacht).[50] The friar's right to binate,[51] (exercised by saying a second mass in the homes of Catholic gentry), was regarded by the diocesan priests as mere moneygrabbing.[52] The 'ruagairí reatha' (vagabonds) – 'rambling friars' exempt from episcopal control – sought to exempt their faithful too.[53] This worried both Catholic bishops (concerned about clandestine marriages) and the Protestant state that abhorred their mobility and lack of accountability (as opposed to the sedentary parish clergy). In 1711, a Galway magistrate encountered 'extraordinary opposition' from 'those moles', 'the friars that work underground'.[54] Because they owed allegiance to foreign

---

46 Hanly (ed.), *Letters of Oliver Plunkett*, p. 498. Plunkett never really reconciled himself to being back in Ireland: of 229 surviving letters, only 19 are in English and the vast bulk are in Italian. **47** H. Fenning, *Irish Dominican province, 1698–1797* (Dublin, 1990), p. 416; Fenning, *Undoing of the friars*, p. 47. **48** Fenning, *Irish Dominican province*, p. 508. **49** Mary Beaufort, wife of Daniel Augustus Beaufort (1739–1831), recounted an amusing anecdote about **Christopher St George** (1754–1826) of Kilcolgan Castle (Oranmore, Co. Galway). She encountered 'a well-looking house built in the castle stile by Mr St George's father who lives there, keeps a *chere amie* and to please her is turned Roman Catholic. A story is told of this dissolute old gentleman, which one can scarcely credit. The first day he went to chapel, it happened that the host was then elevating, at which every one kneels. He supposed this obeisance was performed in honour of him and bowed all around. When service was over, he came forward & made a fine harangue returning the congregation thanks for their great civility to him. It must be an unpleasant circumstance to his son who is a moral domestic county gentleman to have his father living so near him (not two miles from his gate [Tyrone House]) so despicable'. Mary Beaufort, A journal of our tour to the westward to inspect the Charter Schools 1808, TCD, MS 4035, ff 102–3. Christopher St George lived with Rebecca Clyne: M. Keegan, 'Index to persons in household account book kept by Christopher St George of Kilcolgan Castle 1810–1819', *Irish Genealogist*, 7:1 (1986), pp 101–12. **50** Fenning, *Irish Dominican province*, p. 417. **51** **Bination** in the Catholic tradition means celebrating Mass twice on the same day. **52** Fenning, *Irish Dominican province*, p. 128. **53** Fenning, *Irish Dominican province*, p. 168; Fenning, *Undoing of the friars*, p. 52. **54** R. Strong, Headford (Co. Galway) to Archbishop J. Ryder, Tuam (Co. Galway), 23 July 1711, MS in Damer House, Roscrea (Co. Tipperary).

superiors, the Pope and a Jacobite king, the friars bore the brunt of state violence. Of 162 Catholics killed for their religious beliefs between 1529 and 1629, forty-eight were Franciscans, who remained the dominant influence in the Gaelic church.[55] The Observant friars withdrew over almost a century to the Gaelic west and north, where they remained active in and around their ancient former friaries. Their survival strategies were fortified by membership of an international order.[56]

The Post-Reformation period generated ghost friaries, not actually functioning but claimed to assert ancient rights.[57] The Dominican bishop Thomas Burke (1709–76) offered a neat summation when describing the situation in 1726:

> Ruri etiam conventus omnes, paucis duntaxat exceptis, unum alterumve conduxerunt agrum, ubi domum quidem lapideam, stramineo tamen sub tecto, & sacellum excitarunt, ibique vicinam plebem catechismis, & concionibus instruunt. Huc haud raro convenient omnes istius respective caenobii sodales, majori nihilominus anni parte tres quatuorve domi manent, caeteris vel parochos adjuvantibus, vel apud ditiores laicos munus obeuntibus capellanorum, vel inter rusticos vitam satis austeram ducentibus, hordeum nempe & avenam, pro domus sustentatione, pro solutione pensionis annuae aedium, proque amictu mediocri, colligentibus.[58]

At Kilconnell (Co. Galway) in 1709, 'two of ye [Franciscan] Fryers are yet alive, and live, tho' blind with age, on ye charity of the neighbouring papists, in a poor cabin, in a very small island, which they shew'd me, not half a mile from Killconell, in a bog: they employ one to begg [quest] for them, and by that means subsist near their old habitation'.[59] The Canons Regular opened a novitiate at Cong (Co. Mayo) in 1740 in a house adjoining their old abbey.[60] They built an oratory in the ruins, with a choir, pulpit and sacristy for daily Mass. Their accoutrements included cheap pewter chalices and vestments.[61] They were able

55 A. Ford, 'Martyrdom, history and memory in early modern Ireland' in I. McBride (ed.), *History and memory in modern Ireland* (Cambridge, 2001), pp 50–4.   **56** J. McCafferty, 'A mundo valde alieni: Irish Franciscan responses to the Dissolution of the Monasteries, 1540–1640', *Reformation & Renaissance Review*, 19:1 (2017), pp 50–63.   **57** Fenning, *Irish Dominican province*, p. 448.   **58** 'In the country, all the convents with few exceptions rented one or two fields where they built stone houses roofed with thatch and a chapel, and there the friars instructed the local people through the catechism and sermons. The members often return to their respective convents but only three or four remain at home for the greater part of the year. The others are absent helping the parish priests, acting as chaplains to the wealthier laity or leading a fairly hard life among the country people collecting barley and oats to support the house, to pay the annual rent of the building and to provide the rough clothing of the community': T. Burke, *Hibernia Dominicana: sive historia Provinciæ Hiberniæ Ordinis Prædicatorum, ex antiquis manuscriptis, probatis auctoribus, literis originalibus* (Cologne [Kilkenny], 1762), p. 716.   **59** 'Molyneux tour', p. 40.   **60** Fenning, *Undoing of the friars*, pp 83–4.   **61** Fenning, *Undoing of the friars*, p. 70.

to operate openly because of support from George MacNamara, the 'Prince of Cong', a Catholic who lived adjacent to the abbey, with his private chapel, his nine children, his garden and his pleasure boats.[62] In 1761, the density of Catholic burials at Cong struck a traveller, as it is 'reckoned by the Papists very holy ground and many covet to be buried there'.[63]

The bishops of Connacht employed the regulars as chaplains to gentlemen, as curates and as substitutes for sick or suspended priests.[64] By 1761, they were mostly private chaplains, parish priests and curates[65] – 'roving about without any function but to say Mass, to marry young couples, and to empty barrels'.[66] The 1750 decrees recommended that regulars should follow a fixed communal life in convents, rather than a rambling individual life. Otherwise they were to be absolutely subject to the bishops who would be authorized to transfer them as they saw fit. In 1751, draconian decrees barred new novices except for those going abroad.[67]

62 B. Clesham, 'A voyage to the kingdom of the Joyces in 1756', *Journal of the South Mayo Family Research Society*, 7 (1994), pp 2–5. **George MacNamara** (*ob.*1760) held the abbey lands in Cong from the Tasburgh family from 1722 and lived in a house in the grounds called 'the Palace'. 63 J. Kelly (ed.), *The letters of Lord Chief Baron Edward Willes to the earl of Warwick, 1757–1762* (Aberystwyth, 1990), p. 88. 64 Fenning, *Irish Dominican province*, p. 457. 65 Fenning, *Irish Dominican province*, p. 296. 66 Fenning, *Undoing of the friars*, p. 115. 67 Fenning, *Irish Dominican province*, p. 314.

CHAPTER THREE

The Reformations Protestant and Catholic

THE DISCOVERY OF THE ATLANTIC in 1492 propelled the great extraversion of Europe away from its Mediterranean inland lake – Plato had accused the Greeks of plopping like frogs around a pond. A fresh tide of energy swept along the Atlantic façade, from Cadiz to Nantes, from Amsterdam to Bristol and from Dublin to Galway.[1] By the time of Elizabeth I, the tightly woven fabric of European Christianity had suffered an internal gash, creating a new internal religious frontier to rival its old external one with the Islamic world. In crude brush strokes, the European south remained Catholic, the north-west turned Protestant, and eastern Europe embraced the Orthodox church, and these choices were underpinned and reinforced by the pre-existing linguistic divisions of Roman, Germanic and Slavic. For cultural reasons, Ireland found itself marooned on the wrong side of that sectarian frontier. Inishowen (Co. Donegal) became the most northerly settlement of Catholics in the entire world.[2]

Across Europe, Catholics and Protestants jostled and bristled each other in the aftermath of the Reformation, precipitating protracted wars of religion. This confrontation also unsettled the narrow ground of Ireland, on which the English kept a gimlet eye for fear of meddling by Catholic Spain. European states, pursuing a systematic policy of religious homogeneity, detonated a cascade of expulsions across the Continent, rendering the religious refugee a mass phenomenon. Between 1609 and 1614, 300,000 Muslims were forced out of Iberia, 200,000 Huguenots escaped out of France after 1685, 20,000 Protestants fled Salzburg in 1731–2 (the last large-scale religious pogrom in pre-modern Europe), while the British forcibly relocated at least 11,000 French Catholic settlers from Acadie after

---

1 D. Dickson, 'Seven sisters?: the seaport cities of mid-eighteenth century Ireland' in T. Truxes (ed.), *Ireland, France and the Atlantic in a time of war* (Abington, 2017), pp 93–107. 2 **Donegal** was considered 'the Connaught of the North' (J. Glassford, *Notes of three tours in Ireland in 1824 and 1826* (Bristol, 1832), p. 112). In 1835, John O'Donovan observed of Kilcar in Donegal that the people there 'live in what may be called the extreme brink of the world, far from the civilization of cities and the lectures of the philosopher' (*OS letters, Donegal*, p. 105).

1755.[3] The Irish Catholic diaspora formed part of this brutal resorting along confessional lines.[4]

Europe eventually fought itself to an exhausted stalemate.[5] Weary acceptance of the Erastian[6] solution staunched the bloody wars of religion that had gouged the Continent for a century. Minority religions were henceforth allowed to live separately within parallel societies, as states no longer sought to flense all internal religious difference. That solution forced non-state religions to withdraw into the domestic sphere.[7] In turn, clandestine churches were permitted, as long as they remained supinely discreet almost to the point of invisibility.[8] English Protestantism developed an invincible conviction that civil and religious liberties required the demise of Catholicism, so that English democratic institutions were founded on the most naked of sectarian principles and with an in-built resentment towards the principal Catholic European powers.[9]

In the early modern period, the medieval Christian concept of individual identity as indivisible from communal identity was replaced by a version that conceived of the self as singular and autonomous. The logic of individualization that animated the enclosure movement invaded the domestic as well as landscape space: what happened in the fields also happened in the domestic house.[10] The early modern period witnessed a remodelling of the house. The older medieval house had a high central hall with a central open hearth, a hole in the roof and a stone staircase. The hearth was now replaced by a lateral fireplace, with a chimney and a ceiling: that created space for a room or rooms upstairs, accessible by an internal wooden staircase. A tripartite house evolved with the hall in the middle, the kitchen/dairy on one side and the parlour on the other. Thatch and shingles gave way to tiles and slates and glazed windows were added. The new spaces allowed for greater specialization in room uses and the physical separation of master and servants, parents and children.[11]

---

3 N. Terpstra, *Religious refugees in the early modern world: an alternative history of the Reformation* (Cambridge, 2015). 4 C. Carroll, *Exiles in a global city: the Irish and early modern Rome, 1609–1783* (Leiden, 2018): K. Whelan, 'Paris: capital of Irish culture' in P. Joannon & K. Whelan (eds), *Paris capital of Irish culture: France, Ireland and the Republic, 1798–1916* (Dublin, 2017), pp 33–76. 5 M. Greengrass, *Christendom destroyed: Europe, 1517–1648* (London, 2014). 6 An **Erastian** state is one in which the church is entirely under the jurisdiction of the state and which enforces state supremacy in ecclesiastical affairs. 7 Recent scholarship includes A. Ryrie, *Being Protestant in Reformation England* (Oxford, 2013); P. Marshall (ed.), *The Oxford illustrated history of the Reformation* (Oxford, 2014); P. Marshall, *Heretics and believers: a history of the English Reformation* (New Haven, 2017); E. Duffy, *Reformation divided: Catholics, Protestants and the conversion of England* (London, 2017). 8 B. Kaplan, *Religious conflict and the practice of toleration in early modern Europe* (Cambridge, MA, 2007). 9 C. Fatovic, 'The anti-Catholic roots of liberal and Republican conceptions of freedom in English political thought', *Journal of History of Ideas*, 66:1 (2005), pp 37–58. 10 M. Johnson, *An archaeology of capitalism* (Oxford, 1996). 11 T. Hamling & C. Richardson, *A day at home in early modern England: material culture and*

Allied with enclosure, house-building and large-scale dislocation, ancestral memory experienced a hard stop from the English state, delivered with a severity that never happened in Ireland. The Reformation created 'a great cultural hiatus, which had dug a ditch, deep and dividing, between the English people and their past'.[12] The state launched a hostile takeover of the parish in England, as it acquired new and overlapping legal, civil and religious competencies.

Protestant Reform in England was never a clear-cut, once-and-for-all process: rather it offered at best an equivocal progression: 'a premature birth, a difficult labour and a sickly child'.[13] The strength and integrity of late medieval Christianity and post-Reformation Catholicism is now acknowledged: far from being a spent force, deservedly collapsing under the weight of its corruption, the late medieval church was embedded in the lives and affections of ordinary people. The English parish endured as a cohesive social and cultural system, even when assaulted by the state. In Ireland, a buildings-based study concluded that 'the late medieval church in Meath was healthy and indeed vibrant'.[14]

In Ireland, the Protestant Reformation and state formation were not separate but linked processes.[15] In 1606, the Munster president, Henry Brouncker (1550–1607), recognized that only the presence of Protestant communities in the cities and towns would convert the rural population because the cities were as 'lanterns to the country round about'.[16] There was never a Reformation from below in Ireland, as there were simply no Irish-born Protestants in numbers at the start or the heart of this project. By 1600, there were only 120 Irish-born Protestants on the whole island,[17] a mere twenty Irish-born attended Protestant service in Dublin (out of a total population of 10,000), and only five attended in Cork city in 1595.[18] The ex-Carmelite John Bale (1495–1593) complained plaintively that in Kilkenny 'helpars I founde none': he baled out and abandoned his flock permanently.[19] No word for Reformation even appeared in Irish until

domestic life, 1500–1700 (New Haven, 2017). Post-medieval urban houses had a narrow street frontage, three to four stories high, two rooms deep, with the finest room on the first floor and the ground floor room serving as a workshop or shop. These house types are clearly visible in Van Der Hagen's landscapes of Waterford and Londonderry *c.*1730. **12** This is the conclusion of the classic study by the Dundalk-born historian Eamon Duffy in his *The stripping of the altars: traditional religion in England, 1400–1580* (New Haven, 1992). **13** C. Haigh, *English Reformations: religion, politics and society under the Tudors* (Oxford, 1993). **14** O'Neill, 'Medieval parish churches of Meath', p. 46. **15** D. MacCulloch, *The Reformation: Europe's house divided, 1490–1700* (London, 2003). **16** 'Concerning reformation of religion in Ireland' [1606], *CSPI, 1603–6*, pp 543–5. **17** *CSPI, 1600*, p. 295. **18** H. Jefferies, 'Elizabeth's Reformation in the Irish Pale', *Journal of Ecclesiastical History*, 66:3 (2015), pp 524–42. **19** E. Boran, 'Persecution and deliverance in sixteenth-century Kilkenny: the *Vocacyon of Johan Bale* 1553', *Old Kilkenny Review*, 69 (2017), pp 71–92. Bale's flight is understandable given that five of his servants were murdered in a brutal fashion on 8 Sept. 1553 at Holmes Court near the town: he names his English servants but not the Irish groom and maid servant who were among the slain.

Ó Raiftearaí in the 1820s.[20] That foundational anorexia ultimately made all the difference.

Ireland experienced not so much the Protestant Reformation as an English Protestant Reformation (Henry VIII's 'rebranding of a failed cross-channel state as an island kingdom')[21] imposed from outside and above by a violently coercive state on 'Irish Papists' defined by a double taint. Gaelic society resisted the Protestant Reformation, because its leaders like the O'Donnells, in the late sixteenth-century words of the Donegal poet Gofraidh Óg Mac an Bhaird, remained 'i seilbh bhar sean' (in possession of your ancestral lands), 'tugais aná[i]l don eaglais' (breathed life into the church) and accordingly 'do chongbháil cáig 'na ccreideamh' (everyone kept the faith).[22] This commitment to Catholicism would also prevent Ireland helplessly succumbing to anglicization, of becoming a 'Saxa óg' (little England), in the words of the late sixteenth-century Ulster Franciscan poet Eoghan Ó Dubhthaigh.

Impotent to impose or enforce uniformity, the English (later British) state was forced to content itself with clamping a precautionary lid on the religious heats simmering away in the Irish colonial cauldron. When British Protestantism sought to assert its hegemony on Catholic Ireland, it could only congeal a fragile consensual crust, and the magma beneath, retaining its high temperature, could easily burst through at moments of weakness or international tension, as in the revolutionary decades of the 1640s, 1690s, 1790s, 1910s and 1960s.

TITHES UNTIL 1800

Despite its minority status (hovering around ten per cent of the population), the Church of Ireland was supported by universally imposed and state-enforced tithes. A ramshackle system was cobbled together as a gallimaufry rather than as a transparent and consistent legally based modus. Tithes were wildly variable, province by province, parish by parish, incumbent by incumbent. Ulster had a fixed 'Tything Table' since 1629, whose prices were never adjusted upwards, and the anglican clergymen there, cowed by unremitting Presbyterian pressure, were forced to keep tithes lower than elsewhere. It was virulent Dissenter wrath in the Presbyterian areas of Antrim and Derry that launched the first major commotion against tithes with the Oakboy movement of the 1760s.[23]

20 M. MacCraith, 'Do chum glóire Dé agus an mhaitheasa phuiblidhe so/For the glory of God and this public good': the Reformation and the Irish language', *Studies*, 106:424 (2017–18), pp 476–83. **21** D. MacCulloch, *All things made new: writings on the Reformation* (London, 2016). **22** E. Mac Cárthaigh, 'Gofraidh Óg Mac an Bhaird ceccinit: Do dúiseadh gaisgeadh Ghaoidheal', *Ériu*, 66 (2016), pp 77–110. **23** E. Magennis, 'A Presbyterian insurrection?: reconsidering the Hearts of Oak disturbances of July 1763', *IHS*, 41 (1998), pp 165–87.

The Dissenters regarded themselves as suffering under the collusive impositions of landlord and parson, 'oppressed by extortive rents, rectors' small dues, land cesses, and taxes for highways and bridges, charging rents for commons, boggs and mosses'.[24] An English judge regarded Irish Presbyterians in 1759 as 'more troublesome to the clergy of the Church of England with regard to the payment of tithes than the papists'.[25] In 1766, the rector of Killeeshil (Co. Armagh), where the Hearts of Oak had originated, described Dissenters there as 'the spawn of the Scottish Covenanters, avowed enemies to all civil and religious establishments, and the most virulent and furious prosecutors of the established clergy during the late turmoil in the north of Ireland'.[26] In 1772, the Steelboys accused the landlords and rectors of having 'reduced us to such a deplorable state by such grievous oppressions that the poor is turned black in the face and the skin parched on their back'.[27]

The highest tithes were imposed in Munster and south Leinster (especially Kilkenny) where tithe was levied on the potato, the staple of the poor. By contrast, the agistment adjustment in 1735 removed tithes on dry and barren cattle (beef cattle) but retained it on dairy cattle. This was a boon for the rich and a burden on the poor, as the English journalist William Bingley pointed out in the 1780s:

> By the present mode of taking tythes, the richest Protestants pay the least towards the support of their own religious establishment; for, in order that they may contribute as little as possible to the maintenance of their own clergy, and the augmentation of livings, they prefer occupying vast tracts of land with stock not tytheable; leaving the laborious tillagers of all denominations to groan under the ponderous weight of the English.[28]

Tithes bit ever harder in the dairying regions of the south, where the tithe on potatoes already constituted a major grievance. As agricultural prices soared from the mid-eighteenth century, pressure piled on the small tillage farmers, exacerbated by efforts to impose tithes on turf and furze – the poor man's fuel. A complicated outsourcing system had evolved, where the clergyman sold his rights to tithes through 'canting' (selling them off to the highest bidder) to tithe farmers, who then tried to squeeze more from the actual tithe payers. Tithe farmers tended to be substantial farmers (mostly Catholic). Locally knowledgeable proctors (universally reviled and labelled 'vultures' in parliament in the 1780s) assessed and managed the tithes on behalf of the tithe farmer or the clergyman if he collected them personally.

24 *A true copy and contents of the Hearts of Oak's general petition* (Dublin, 1764). 25 Kelly (ed.), *Willes*, p. 38. 26 NAI, MS 652, IA/46–9. 27 Address to Lord Lieutenant, *FJ*, 24 Mar. 1772. 28 W. Bingley, *An examination into the origin and continuance of the discontents in Ireland* (London, 1799), p. 11.

The Whiteboy and Rightboy movements spread earliest and fastest in the areas where tithes were levied on the potato. However the exclusively Protestant parliament dug in its sectarian heels ever deeper over even the most obvious of reforms, spooked by the aftermath of the successful and universally supported separation of church and state in America. The Church of Ireland had long considered itself as the squeezed middle, uncomfortably situated between the Dissenting north and the Catholic south and west: the English controversialist Revd Peter Heylyn (1600–62) described Ireland in 1658 with 'the papists prevailing on the one side and the puritans on the other, getting so much ground that the poor Protestants seemed to be crucified in the midst between them'.[29] According to the bishop of Cloyne, Richard Woodward (1726–94), the 'North American plan', where everyone supported their own clergy but only them, would wipe out the Church of Ireland in Connaught, Munster and most of Leinster (with the exception of 'a few great towns').[30] The brilliant Cork artist James Barry (1741–1806) warned the earl of Shannon in 1778 that an eruption would occur if Irish Protestants continued to insist on their right 'to despoil, distress and torment the great majority consisting of more than three-fourths of the inhabitants', 'keeping them as sauntering, ragged skeletons to scare the crows away'.[31] And these conditions fuelled resentment, as condensed in a celebrated aphorism by the Kerry poet Eoghan Rua Ó Súilleabháin (1748–82): 'Ní insan ainnise is measa linn bheith síos go deo ach an tarcaisne do leanas sin' (it is not always being sunk in hardship that is the worst but the contempt that it attracts).[32]

Archbishop King showed sympathies to the Irish Catholics in 1721, including a phrase that may have sparked Jonathan Swift's *A modest proposal* of 1729:

> They have already given their bread, their fish, their butter, their shoes, their stockings, their beds, their furniture and houses to pay their landlords and taxes. I cannot see how any more can be got from them except we take away their potatoes and buttermilk or flay them and sell their skins.[33]

John Ferrar (1740–1800), another well-informed Protestant commentator later in the century, noted succinctly that 'long pinned in neglected poverty', 'the [Catholic] poor were treated worse than horses'.[34] By contrast, the Catholic

---

29 P. Heylyn, *Respondet petrus* (London, 1658), p 386.   **30** M. Bric, 'The tithe system in eighteenth-century Ireland', *PRIA*, 86, C (1986), pp 271–88.   **31** J. Barry (London) to earl of Shannon, 4 Jan. 1778, Special Collections, University College Cork, MS U 333.   **32** B. Ó Conchúir (eag.), *Amhráin Eoghan Rua Ó Súilleabháin* (Baile Átha Cliath, 2009), p. 66.   **33** Archbishop W. King on the taxation of Ireland [1721] in J. Wooley (ed.), *Jonathan Swift and Thomas Sheridan,* The Intelligencer (Oxford, 1992), pp 228–9.   **34** J. Ferrar, *The prosperity of Ireland displayed in the state of 54 Charity Schools in Dublin* (Dublin, 1796), p. 41.

Bishop Thomas Hussey (1746–1803) urged his priests in 1797 to remember that 'the poor were always your friends, they inflexibly adhered to you, and to their religion, even in the worst of times'.[35] That same year, the French traveller Jacques-Louis De La Tocnaye (1767–1823) described Anglican bishops (he was in Derry, presumably with the very strange Earl-Bishop in mind) as 'the spoiled children of fortune, rich as bankers, who enjoyed good wine, good cheer and pretty women'.[36]

THE CATHOLIC REFORMATION

The Catholic Reformation revitalized the inherited sacred landscape rather than prising people away from it.[37] Within Irish Catholicism, an informal truce was worked out between the Tridentine and the traditional.[38] Expelled from their inherited ecclesiastical buildings, Irish Catholicism sacralized an extensive landscape. For example, the 'turas' or 'stations' ritual at venerated sites, an Irish expression of the Stations of the Cross, was largely post-medieval in date. This late medieval concept and practice was exclusively associated with the Franciscans, and intensified with the Catholic Reformation.

In England, religious practice was driven into the gentry houses (with their recusant gentry and priests' holes),[39] and in the Netherlands into *schuilkerken* (hidden churches)[40] and *schuurkerken* (barn churches). In Ireland, the Catholic Reformation infiltrated itself into the sympathetic wider landscape. Catholic practice in Ireland became more creative because it was forced to adapt quickly and under brutal pressure. Weak central authority favoured the local but so did the inability of a harried Irish episcopacy to implement the strict edicts of the Council of Trent (1545–63).

Seeming weakness generated a flexibility that provided a lifeline for Irish Catholicism in the longer term, conferring a resilience that was less apparent in states where the Tridentine decrees were rigidly enforced. Irish bishops could tailor their parochial system to suit current needs, whereas the state church was

35 T. Hussey, *A pastoral letter to the Catholic clergy of the united dioceses* [sic] *of Waterford and Lismore* (Dublin, 1797), p. 7. **36** [J. De La Tocnaye], *A Frenchman's walk through Ireland 1796–7*, ed. J. Stevenson (Belfast, 1917), p. 201. **37** A. Walsham, *Catholic Reformation in Protestant Britain* (London, 2014), p. 162. **38** S. Meigs, *The Reformations in Ireland: tradition and confessionalism, 1400–1690* (Dublin, 1997). **39** A. Hogg, *God's secret agents: Queen Elizabeth's forbidden priests and the hatching of the Gunpowder Plot* (London, 2005). **40** In Amsterdam, more than thirty Catholic churches were built between 1578 and 1853. They were inserted in high but narrow galleried halls, hidden in the upper stories of the fabric, and lacked exterior architectural expression. The seventeenth-century *Ons' Lieve Heer op Solder* ('Our Lord in the Attic') is open to the public. B. Kaplan, 'Fictions of privacy: house chapels and the spatial accommodation of religious dissent in early modern Europe', *American Historical Review*, 107 (2002), pp 1031–64.

constrained by the outmoded structures that underpinned the parish-based tithe system, causing, for example, endless problems with impropriation. In 1622, there were 2,492 parishes in Ireland, of which 1,289 (fifty-two per cent) were impropriate.[41] That same year, the Protestant clergy of Killaloe threw up their hands in despair, requesting that:

> ye office of p'senting recusants may not be imposed on them any longer, but on ye churchwardens of ye severall parishes, who are best at leasure in time of divine service to observe who are absent; and who are best acquainted wth ye inhabitants; yt ye clergy by avoyding of that office may ye better win ye love of theyr parishioners, and avoide that danger wch ye malice of their Popish adversaries is well known to plot against them.[42]

With the advent of the Catholic Reformation, the Catholic parochial network was extensively reworked, especially in the south-east.[43] Following the re-establishment of a Catholic episcopacy in 1618, re-organization accelerated in the 1630s, creating an effective shadow system in Dublin city. This wave then washed out over the surrounding countryside. By 1689, there were twenty chapels in the country districts of Dublin diocese for the first time in a century. A functioning infrastructure of priests, chapels and parishes was emerging. While respecting the boundaries of earlier civil parishes, the newer Catholic versions grouped these into larger units that better matched the rapidly changing geography of the seventeenth century.[44]

In Ossory, Bishop David Rothe (1573–1650) rationalized the Catholic parochial network after he was appointed bishop in 1615, and an average of six civil parishes were absorbed into each new Catholic one in his streamlined system.[45] In the neighbouring diocese of Ferns, Bishop John Roche (1584–1636) reported in 1631 that 'the parochial districts are everywhere well defined and pastors may be readily found for the administration of the Sacraments, and the exercise of their ecclesiastical functions'.[46] Thirty priests served seventy Catholic parishes (reduced from 150 civil parishes) in Ferns and consolidation

---

41 W.D. Killen, *Ecclesiastical history of Ireland*, 2 vols (London, 1875), i, p. 130. **42** P. Dwyer, *The diocese of Killaloe from the Reformation to the close of the eighteenth century* (Dublin, 1878), p. 146. **43** Three excellent atlas treatments of dioceses are [T. Morris], *Pobal Ailbe: atlas of the diocese of Cashel and Emly* (Thurles, 1971); P. Duffy, *Landscapes of south Ulster: a parish atlas of the diocese of Clogher* (Belfast, 1993); E. Culleton, *On our own ground: Co. Wexford parish by parish, volume 1* (Wexford, 2013). **44** P. Power, 'The bounds and extents of Irish parishes' in S. Pender (ed.), *Féilscríbhinn Torna: essays and studies* (Cork, 1947), pp 218–24. **45** Map in Nolan & Whelan (eds), *Kilkenny*, p. 201. For the background, see C. Lennon, 'Political thought of Irish Counter-Reformation churchmen: the testimony of the *Analecta* of Bishop David Rothe' in H. Morgan (ed.), *Political ideology in Ireland, 1541–1641* (Dublin, 1999), pp 181–202. **46** Hore, *Wexford*, vi, p. 314; P.F. Moran, *History of the Catholic archbishops of Dublin since the Reformation* (Dublin, 1864), p. 325.

was proceeding apace in terms of delivering an amalgamated system. By contrast with the south-east which had been densely settled from the medieval period onwards, lightly settled Ulster civil parishes were substantially bigger initially: there was accordingly much less need for dramatic post-Reformation surgery.[47] Here too the Catholic parish system was in place by 1630 as the Protestant bishop William Bedell (1571–1642) reported from Kilmore: 'Every parish hath its priest and some two or three a piece; so their masshouses also'.[48]

Already in 1612, the Protestant Bishop was arguing against Ferns as a suitable site for a bishopric:

> The cathedral of Fernes, which having been burnt by Feagh McHew [Fiach Mac Aodh Ó Broin (1534–97)] in the time of Rebellion, is so chargeable [costly] to re-edify, that the Deane and Chapter are not able to compasse that work; neither is it indeed fitt that the Cathedral Church sho[u]ld be at Fernes, being now but a poor country village, but either at Wexford or at New Rosse, being both incorporate townes, very populous of themselves, especially Wexford, and of much resort by strangers.[49]

By 1564, the papacy had requested a feasibility study on transferring cathedrals to neighbouring towns where Mass could be more conveniently celebrated.[50] In 1630, the Catholic Bishop John Roche moved decisively to switch the Catholic episcopal seat from Ferns to Wexford town.[51] The Church of Ireland remained stuck with the old seat at Ferns.

Ironically, Catholicism could exhibit flexibility because it had been forcibly detached from the tithe revenue stream tied tightly to the older system. The Protestant clergy in Ossory acknowledged in 1622 that 'the masse priest proceed in their office securely, with boldness, enjoying their demanded dueties … not answering anie lawe ecclesaistical or civill'. They were all too aware that if they enforced the recusancy laws, 'they incurre the hatred of the people'.[52]

Catholics proved to be masters of sly resistance. The most eminent men of Waterford city, forced to attend Protestant service in 1585, displayed their

47 See the useful summary map 'Medieval parish boundaries lost in the creation of the modern Catholic parish network' in W.J. Smyth, *Mapmaking, landscapes and memory: a geography of colonial and early modern Ireland, c.1530–1750* (Cork, 2006), p. 369. 48 Monck Mason, *Life of William Bedell*, p. 170. 49 Hore, *Wexford*, vi, p. 261. 50 P.J. Corish, 'An Irish Counter-Reformation bishop: John Roche', *Irish Theological Quarterly*, 25 (1958), pp 14–32, 101–23; 26 (1959), pp 105–16, 313–30. In 1774, Luttrell Wynne described Ferns as 'a miserable little town', 'though it is the see of a Bishop', *Ireland Illustrated* database [unpaginated] https://ttce.nuigalway.ie/irelandillustrated/; G. Gelléri, 'An unknown "creator" of picturesque Ireland: the Irish sketches and notes of Luttrell Wynne', *Irish Architectural and Decorative Studies*, 18 (2016), pp 44–65. 51 Pius IV to D. Wolf SJ and R. Creagh, 13 July 1564, in J.M. Rigg (ed.), *Calendar of State Papers relating to English affairs preserved principally at Rome in the Vatican Archives and Library, 1558–1578*, 2 vols (London, 1916–26), i, pp 166–9. 52 Ó Fearghail, 'Wheeler's visitation', p. 196.

recalcitrance: 'if they come to church, they walk round like mill horses, chopping, changing, making merchandise, so that they in the quire [choir, ie around the altar] cannot hear a word, and these not small fools but the chief of the city'.[53] The men-only detail is significant; women and children were not subject to the recusancy laws and never attended service. This proved to be a major flaw, as the Englishman Fynes Moryson (1566–1630) pointed out: 'if some of them [men] uppon hypocriticall dispensation went to church commonly, their parents, children, kinsmen and servants were open and obstinate papists'.[54]

In Ireland, this period saw a remarkable efflorescence of holy wells. In the early medieval period, baptism had occurred at wells and springs, requiring portable equipment like buckets, rather than fixed stone fonts.[55] Dry-stone mortared superstructures and well 'houses' (stone canopies) emerged in the post-Reformation period. Humble holy wells were not subjected to the same state invigilation as churches, and escaped unscathed and even revivified. Holy wells should be regarded as an active response to the Protestant Reformation rather than as a passive residue left over from an earlier period. While some sites were undoubtedly older, post-Reformation conditions prompted enhanced Catholic attention to wells.[56] These locations, less subject to scrutiny by church and state, allowed more informal practices to flourish.[57] In 1660, the Synod of Tuam decreed that 'dancing, flute playing, singing in harmony, intermingling and other such abuses are all forbidden during the visitation of wells and other holy places'.[58]

Even the barest recitation of dated structures tells its own story in relation to the strength of the culture of holy wells: 1622 Toberacht (Co. Sligo);[59] 1625 Brideswell (Co. Roscommon);[60] 1625 Brigid's well, Roscrea (Co. Tipperary);[61]

---

53 W. Brady (ed.), *State Papers concerning the Irish church in the time of Queen Elizabeth* (London, 1868), p. 99. **54** G. Kew (ed.), 'The Irish sections of Fynes Moryson's unpublished itinerary', *Anal. Hib.*, 37 (1998), p. 43. **55** M. Pepperdene, 'Baptism in the early British and Irish churches', *Irish Theological Quarterly*, 22 (1955), pp 110–23; N. Whitfield, 'A suggested function for the holy well?' in A. Minnis & J. Roberts (eds), *Text, image, interpretation: studies in Anglo-Saxon literature and its insular context in honour of Éamonn Ó Carragáin* (Turnhout, 2007), pp 495–563; H. Pike, *Medieval fonts of Ireland* (Greystones, 1989). The 1143 Synod of Cashel and the 1186 Synod of Dublin mandated a stone font in every parish church. At least 110 medieval examples survive (AAI, i, p. 324). **56** Walsham, *Catholic Reformation in Protestant Britain*, p. 461. **57** Barnaby Rich (1540–1617) devoted an entire chapter to them: 'Of the superstitious conceit that is holden by the Irish about certaine wells' in B. Rich, *A new description of Ireland* (London, 1610), pp 51–7. W. Brenneman *&* M. Brenneman, *Crossing the circle at the holy wells of Ireland* (Charlottesville, 1994); M. Carroll, *Irish pilgrimage: holy wells and popular Catholic devotion* (Baltimore, 1999), pp 19–35, 55–8, 72–9, 101–24. **58** Carroll, *Irish pilgrimage*, p. 45. **59** W. Wood-Martin, *The history of Sligo county and town, from the close of the Revolution of 1688 to the present time* (Dublin, 1895), p. 367. **60** A coat of arms over the doorway bears the inscription, 'built by the Right Honourable Sir Randal Mac Donnell, first Earl of Antrim, 1625': I. Weld, *Statistical survey of Roscommon* (Dublin, 1832), p. 515. **61** Meigs, *Reformations in Ireland*, p. 120.

1684 Tobar Mhuire, Rosserk (Co. Mayo);[62] 1696 Balla (Co. Mayo); 1696 Duncormick (Co. Wexford);[63]1710 Creevaughbawn (Co. Galway);[64] 1730 Legan (Co. Longford),[65] 1731 Killone (Co. Clare), and 1772 Aglish (near Kilcooley, Co. Tipperary).[66] Wells continued to attract new functions well into the late nineteenth century, providing holy water for emigrants about to embark on the Atlantic crossing, for example, at St Fiacre's holy well at Ullard (Co. Kilkenny). These wells have a distinct if scruffy landscape expression. In Connemara, carefully chosen smooth rounded stones were prioritized, which stand out ostentatiously from the profusion of irregular stones that litter the west of Ireland landscape. Gabriel Beranger described the celebrated stones on Inishmurray in 1778 as 'round stones like Dutch cheeses'.[67] Modern examples of these distinctive stones include those at two St Fechin's wells at Omey Island and Ross (Co. Galway). On less stony ground, holy wells were often marked by lone trees, notably whitethorn and ash. Holy wells are frequented to the present day, albeit a fast-fading force.[68]

The sceptical humanist strand sought to cleanse religion of magical accretions, superstition and paganism. An iconoclastic nihilism violated the proprieties of holy places.[69] The medieval sacralized landscape was dismembered in countries where the Protestant Reformation prevailed but it acquired a particular urgency in Puritanizing Britain.[70] What was once regarded as holy was now assailed as folly. Monasteries were dissolved, relics burned, crosses smashed and churches stripped by 'a decidedly Protestant

62 Tobar Mhuire holy well is 800m from Rosserk Friary, 6km north of Ballina (Co. Mayo). The well house was built in 1684 and rebuilt or repaired in 1799. A plaque bears the inscription 'This chapel was built in honour of the Blessed Virgin, in the year of Our Lord 1799 by John Lynott of Rosserk'. Beneath this is a motto 'Peace and Love' with the figure of a Dove. Two slabs bear Latin inscriptions (*OS letters, Mayo*, p. 25). These can be translated as follows: (1) 'Be warned and learn to be righteous and not despise the divine: I do not fear death which is at our door. I would leave the world like a shadow of the sun'; (2) 'Father Moriartus Crehn had me erected in honour of Almighty God, the Blessed Virgin conceived without sin, and all the saints of the Heavenly Choir'. 63 Clomaun's well has a stone with the inscription 'R.C. 1696'. 64 *OS letters, Galway*, p. 34. 65 Our Lady's well had an adjoining thatched chapel, 'built by John Farrell of Ardcandra in honour of BVM 1730': *Teathba* (1992), p. 186. 66 C. O'Dwyer, *Archdiocese of Cashel and Emly* (Strasbourg, 2008), p. 136. 67 Tour through Connacht 1779, RIA MS 12 1 9, f. 15. 68 D. Ó Giolláin, 'Revisiting the holy well', *Éire-Ireland*, 40:1–2 (2005), pp 11–41; A. Rackard & L. O'Callaghan, *fishstonewater: holy wells of Ireland* (Cork, 2001); S. Connolly & A. Moroney, *Stone and tree sheltering water: an exploration of sacred and secular wells in Co. Louth* (Drogheda, 1998); R. Foley, *Healing waters: therapeutic landscapes in historic and contemporary Ireland* (Farnham, 2010); F. McCormick, *Struell wells* (Downpatrick, 2011); G. Branigan, *Ancient and holy wells of Dublin* (Dublin, 2012); E. Broderick, *Patterns and patrons: the holy wells of Waterford* (Waterford, 2015). 69 D. Gimster & R. Gilchrist (eds), *The archaeology of Reformation, 1480–1580* (London, 2003). 70 Huldrych Zwingli (1484–1531) launched a purging of images in Zürich in 1524, but gave the Catholics time to transfer all objects associated with their families into their private houses, ensuring that a surprising amount of pre-Reformation ecclesiastical materials survived in the most Reformed city of them all.

contempt'.[71] The ancient relics of Christ Church Cathedral were dumped on the street at Skinners' Row in 1537, including the most venerated of Irish relics, the Bachall Íosa (Patrick's crozier), and incinerated ostentatiously by the English-born Archbishop George Browne (*ob.*1556).[72] The statue of Mary at Trim (Co. Meath) suffered the same fate in 1538.[73]

Erasing the Irish religious past proved notoriously difficult. The Catholics were confident that the Reformation would soon be overturned, as can be felt in the remarkable confidence displayed by Donncha Ó Maonaigh OFM (Donatus Mooney) as late as 1616. This encouraged the Catholics to secrete objects with trusted laymen, as with the possessions of Donegal Friary still in the possession of the Ballyshannon merchant Thaddeus Coan in 1698.[74] The arch-iconoclast Bishop John 'Bilious' Bale suffered repeated anguish as Catholic objects reappeared in the 1550s under Mary.[75] Carefully hidden objects were sometimes later recovered, as at Sheephouse (Co. Meath),[76] Lismore (Co. Waterford),[77] Dunnamaggin and Black Abbey (Co. Kilkenny),[78] Cashel and Derrynaflan (Co. Tipperary) and Rathawilladoon (Co. Clare).[79] The magnificent set of Waterford vestments were hidden in 1650 and rediscovered in 1773 when the medieval cathedral was demolished.[80] Another set of sixteenth-century vestments, long preserved at the Plunkett's house in Portmarnock (Co. Dublin), are now in Stoneyhurst.[81] A chalice with the inscription 'Convent of the Friars Minor of Timoleague' was secreted in Cape Clear (Co. Cork) until the early twentieth century: a box containing the chalice and vestments (which disintegrated once exposed) was given to a priest at a station Mass on the island.[82] A communion

71 Walsham, *Catholic Reformation in Protestant Britain*, p. 563.   72 AFM, v, pp 1447, 1449; M.V. Ronan, *The Reformation in Dublin, 1536–1558* (Dublin, 1926), pp 116–18.   73 'The very miraculous image of Mary which was in the town of Trim, in which all the Irish people believed for a long time previously, which healed the blind, the deaf and the lame, and every other ailment, was burnt by the English; and the Bachall Íosa, which was in Dublin, working numerous prodigies and miracles in Ireland from the time of Saint Patrick to that date, and which had been in Christ's own hand, was similarly burned by the English; and not alone this, but there was not a holy cross, or a figure of Mary, or an illustrious image in Ireland, that was not burned where their power reached' [translation] (Annals of Loch Cé, 1538, CELT). AFM sub. 1444 elaborated on its virtues.   74 K. Smith, 'An investigation of the material culture of Donegal Franciscan friaries in the late sixteenth and seventeenth centuries', *Donegal Annual*, 63 (2011), pp 96–104.   75 P. Happe & J. King (eds), *The vocacyon of Johan Bale* (New York [1593], 1990).   76 C. Armstrong, 'Processional cross, pricket candlestick and bell, found together at Sheephouse, near Oldbridge, Co. Meath', *JRSAI*, 95 (1915), pp 2–31. These may have belonged to Mellifont Abbey.   77 The Book of Lismore and the Lismore crozier were found in 1814 behind a blocked up doorway at Lismore Castle.   78 W. Carrigan, *The history and antiquities of the diocese of Ossory*, 4 vols (Dublin, 1905), iv, p. 38: H. Fenning, *The Black Abbey: the Kilkenny Dominicans, 1225–1996* (Kilkenny, 1996), p. 12.   79 E. Lenihan, 'Bronze medieval crucifix: a recent important find', *The Other Clare* (1989), pp 18–20.   80 Now on display at the Treasures of Waterford Museum.   81 This seventeenth-century house, containing a private chapel, was destroyed by a fire in 1953.   82 IFC Schools Manuscripts, Scoil Molaga, Timoleague (Co. Cork).

Fig. 8 This powerfully designed 1740 crucifixion stone was found in a sealed secret compartment in a farmhouse at Summerhill (Co. Meath) in 1950. The instruments of the passion are shown: coiled rope, cock and pot, miniaturised sun, crescent moon, ladder, two dice, Veronica's veil, a scourge, three nails, hammer and pincers in a basket and the temple of Jerusalem (E. Prendergast, 'Crucifixion stone from Summerhill, County Meath' in C. Manning (ed.), *Dublin and beyond the Pale* (Bray, 1998), pp 253–5) (NMI).

set (vestments, chalice, paten) was recovered in 1922, buried in a wooden box in a ruined house in Cong (Co. Mayo) near the kitchen fireplace: the chalice dated to 1663 was from the Augustinian priory at Ballinrobe.[83]

83 T.B. Costello, 'Chalice etc recently found at Cong', *JRSAI*, 52 (1922), pp 177–8.

While they remained in local circulation, these religious objects attracted intimate styles of veneration; the personal touch – touching, kissing, handling – was a central act, often performed amid loud prayers, chanting, and as part of processions and crowds. The removal of these religious icons to the hushed glass-cased sterility of museums inflicted a wound on local communities. The Catalunyan artist Joan Miró (1893–1983) observed that 'un museo tiene algo de cementerio' (a museum emits a whiff of the graveyard).[84] Apprised of the existence of the bell of Saint Colman on Inishbofin, George Petrie (1790–1866) shockingly instructed John O'Donovan to 'steal or buy it'.[85] The Reformation and the spread of literacy promoted a different and more privatized version of devotional practice, stressing a new kind of quiet interiority.

Catholic religious objects survived because they remained in the custody of the ordinary people. Coarbs, erenaghs and priests comprised multi-generational gatekeepers who cherished these objects: the O'Healys, erenaghs of Donoughmore (Co. Cork), looked after the Lámh Lachtáin until 1639, the O'Gormans of Malin (Co. Donegal) preserved the 'holy stone of Malin' into the nineteenth century, the Gillans of Ballinascreen retained a hand bell into the early nineteenth century,[86] the O'Doweys of Culdaff and McEnhills of Drumragh kept bells into the late nineteenth century, St Manchan's Shrine is still protected by Mooneys of the Doon (Co. Offaly),[87] the Keanes of Scattery Island (Co. Clare) preserved the Clogán Óir, the Psalter of St Caimín was held by the Ó Bruidheadha of Tearmann Caimín at Inis Cealtra (Co. Clare).[88] The 'fragment of the True Cross' from Holy Cross (Co. Tipperary) was carefully handed down through the old Catholic families.[89] The 1631 Synod of Tuam

---

84 *Joan Miró: esculpturas/sculptures, 1938–1983* (Santander, 2018), p. 257. 85 G. Petrie to J. O'Donovan, 12 June 1838 (*OS letters, Mayo*, p. 76). 86 Jefferies, 'Derry diocese', pp 181–2. 87 AAI, i, p. 291. In 1979, the Mooney family, who still live at Doon, granted permission for the shrine to be displayed on the altar at Clonmacnoise when Pope John Paul celebrated Mass there. 88 AAI, i, p. 248. This was gifted to Micháel Ó Cléirigh by the Mac Bruidheadha family, who still lived on Caimín's termon lands at Moynoe in the early seventeenth century (T. O'Neill, *The Irish hand: scribes and their manuscripts from the earliest times* (Cork, 2014), p. 34). 89 'Declaration of Mrs Margaret Butler of Ballyragget. This portion of the Holy Cross was deposited in the hands of Doctor Fennell by Walter, Earl of Ormonde in the year 1632. By him it was handed over to James, 2nd duke of Ormonde, who in the year 1691 deposited it in the hands of Valentine Smith esq of Carrick-on-Suir who according to the direction received by him from the said Duke, gave it to Helen Butler of Kilcash, relict of Colonel Butler of Westcourt, Callan, who left it at her death to Mrs Margaret Kavanagh, of Borris, wife of Richard Galway Esq., of Kilkenny, who gave it to Mrs Mary Kavanagh, of Borris, wife of George Butler, Esq., of Ballyragget, who delivered it into the hands of the Right Rev. Francis Moylan, Roman Catholic Bishop of Cork to be disposed of by him according to the intentions of the first possessor. Signed by me Mary Butler of Ballyragget, this 18th day of May 1801'. Moylan presented the 'portion of the Holy Rood in a silver case, which we received in a green plush bag' to the Ursuline convent in Cork in 1801. J. Coleman, 'The relic and reliquary of the Holy Cross in the Ursuline Convent, Blackrock', *JCHAS*, 3 (1894), pp 45–68 [quotation at p. 47]. The nuns returned it to Holy Cross in the 1970s.

explicitly instructed that sheela-na-gigs be hidden, but not destroyed.[90] In 1735, the Stowe Missal was discovered by the Catholic middleman John O'Kennedy in the wall of Lackeen Castle near Lorrha (Co. Tipperary).[91] The Mac an Fhirléinn (Killerlean) family, coarbs of Drumcliff (Co. Sligo), retained a shoe gifted them by Columba, with an associated promise of a cure for cattle ailments and general prosperity: the shoe was lent to 'a man of the North, who had cattle sick; it was never returned', 'leaving the Killerleans of the Rosses as poor as their neighbours'.[92]

The loss, survival and recovery of portable and fragile objects like manuscripts proved notoriously complex.[93] The 2006 discovery of the Fadden More psalter, still legible after spending more than a millenium in a Tipperary bog, demonstrated the unparalleled longevity possible in even the most apparently dismal of conditions.

Irish Catholics formulated complex strategies of thwarting, opacity, compliance and accommodation to the emerging British Protestant state between the 1530s and 1580s. The colonial state's surveillance ran foul against obdurate cultural techniques for ensuring impenetrability. A common religious disaster compacted class and social solidarity among the Catholics, pressing priest and people into a closer community. The clergy, and their sheltering congregations, proved adept at derailing the efforts of the state to terminate their ministry. One strategy was to encourage women and children to lead the opposition: on Stephen's Day in 1629, the Carmelite chapel in Cook Street (Dublin) was violently ransacked:[94]

> On ther comming in the pepell [people] were in an ubproare, the Maior had the pickterr pulled down and the Lord Archbishop pulled down the pulpett; the sowlders and the peopell weare by the heres [ears] one with another, and the pickteres were all brocken and defaased [defaced], and they toke within five sutts of vestments and one chales [chalice].[95]

The resistance was orchestrated by Widow Nugent from Winetavern Street who incited other women in the congregation to scratch and thump the soldiers so hard that they 'were glad to hasten out of doores', fleeing ignominiously through the streets, the retreat led by the mayor (Christopher

---

90 AAI, i, p. 71. Of 159 known Irish sheela-na-gigs, about one-third are now missing. B. Freitag, *Sheela-na-gigs: unravelling an enigma* (London, 2004). 91 O'Neill, *Irish hand*, p. 18. 92 T. O'Rorke, *The history of Sligo town and county, volume I* (Dublin, 1889), p. 483. This 'shoe' was presumably a relic shrine like the extant example of St Brigid (NMI). 93 R. Sharpe, 'Medieval manuscripts found at Bonamargy friary and other hidden manuscripts', *Studia Hib.*, 41 (2015), pp 49–85. 94 M. Empey, 'We are not yet safe, for they threaten us with more violence': a study of the Cook Street riot 1629' in W. Sheehan & M. Cronin (eds), *Riotous assemblies: rebels, riots and revolts in Ireland* (Cork, 2011), pp 64–79. 95 Events at the Franciscan [sic] chapel in Dublin, 4 Jan. 1629 in B. Jennings (ed.), *Wadding papers, 1614–38* (Dublin, 1953), p. 330.

Forster, 'a great puritan')[96] and the Protestant archbishop (Lancelot Bulkeley (1568–1650) an Englishman), while being pelted with stones and dog shit by women, boys and apprentices.[97] The state response was to arrest 'six prime papistical' aldermen, and enforce humongous bonds of 1,000 pounds on each of them to close personally all ten Catholic mass houses in Dublin and deliver the keys to Dublin Castle.[98]

When Francois de la Boullaye le Gouz (1623–68), the French traveller, visited Wexford town in May 1644, he observed the leading role of women:

> Au pied de ce chateau sont plusieurs ruïnes des Eglises anciennes, entr'autres de la Saincte Trinité, où les femmes vont en grande devotion, & y font une maniere de procession, la plus âgée marche la premiere, & les autres la suivent, puis tournent trois tours autour des ruïnes, & font une reverence aux vestiges, & s'agenoüillent, & recommencent cette ceremonie plusieurs fois, je les ay observées dans cette devotion trois & quatre heures.[99]

Irish Catholics were infinitely better educated in the school of historical hard knocks than their upholstered Rees-Moggian English counterparts, who were generally drawn more from the upper class. The English dramatist's Alan Bennett's aphorism on observing a red-faced Irish nun was 'I could never be a Catholic because I am such a snob'.[100] The battle-hardened and worldly-wise Irish evolved ways of evading the dictates of a remote state.[101] Abstract legal rights remained subordinate to the stubborn facts on the ground, and this created a fertile repertoire of recalcitrance, ranging from 'sly civility'[102] to outright violence.[103] The 'reputed priest-catcher' John Garzia[104] was observed

---

96 Bishop John Roche (Wexford) to Luke Wadding (Rome), 6 Jan. 1630 in Jennings (ed.), *Wadding papers*, p. 332. 97 BL, Harley MS 3888, ff 109–10. 98 R. Boyle to Viscount Dorchester, 9 Jan. 1630 in HMC, *Twelfth report*, appendix 1, p. 398. 99 [F. de La Boullaye le Gouz], *Les voyages et observations du sieur de La Boullaye Le Gouz* (Paris, 1653), p. 455. 'At the foot of this castle, there are many ruins of old churches, among others that of the Holy Trinity, for which the women have great devotion, and form there in a kind of procession. The eldest walk first, and the others follow; then take three turns around the ruins, make a reverence to the remains, genuflect, and repeat this ceremony many times. I have noticed them continue this devotion three and four hours'. 100 A. Bennett, *Writing home* (London, 1994), p. 86. 101 McCafferty, 'Irish Franciscan responses to the Dissolution of the Monasteries'. 102 The concept is from Homi Bhabha, *The location of culture* (London, 1993). 103 C. Tait, 'Riots, rescues and 'grene bowes': Catholics and protest in Ireland 1570–1640' in T. Ó hAnnracháin & R. Armstrong (eds), *Insular Christianity: alternative models of the church in Britain and Ireland, 1570–1700* (Manchester, 2013), pp 66–87. 104 **John Garzia** (*ob.* 1744) was a Spanish priest who fled the Spanish Inquisition, moved to Ireland, converted to Protestantism, married and was ordained. In 1724, he was assigned to the colony of Virginia, where he served for nine years before moving in 1733 to remote Bath, North Carolina. He died there in 1744 after being thrown from his horse. The church of Saint Thomas in Bath retains a silver chalice, just over nine inches high, inscribed 'D. D. Johannes Garzia, Ecclesiae Anglicanae Presbyter' (Revd

entering a house in James Street in Dublin in 1718. The Jesuit schoolmaster Michael Murphy gained access, taunted Garzia as 'a rogue, rascal and priest-catcher', and incited an angry mob to assault him.[105] The defensive strategy of Irish Catholicism was to dig in deep, seeking to weather an adverse climate. Clandestine and fugitive vernacular arenas emerged, where neither state nor indeed ecclesiastical invigilation could readily be exercised. In 1674, the friars of New Ross (Co. Wexford) were ostentatiously deported but they landed quietly at Ballyhack ten miles downriver and slipped back into the town.[106]

In the seventeenth century and uniquely in Europe, Ireland's organizational jurisdiction was designated by the papacy as being *in partibus infidelium,* as this designation previously applied to areas of the globe that lay outside Catholic states.[107] To adapt to operating in a Protestant state, Propaganda Fide promoted an episcopal ecclesiastical model in Ireland after 1618. Sixteen new bishops were appointed between 1622 and 1630 and the subsequent performance of outstanding bishops like David Rothe and John Roche cemented Catholic identity.[108] A shadow church adjusted to Ireland's unique circumstances was steadily if stealthily coming into existence.

Catholics adroitly deployed the weapons of the weak,[109] oscillating between opportunistic but ephemereal compliance, regret, resignation, resentment, resistance and repudiation. In 1589, the Munster-based agriculturalist Robert Payne observed that 'the Irish would gladlye haue their publike masse againe: but they had rather continewe it in corners, then to heere it openlye in fetters and chaines as the poore Indianes do'.[110] We can never minimize their scalding

---

John Garzia, priest of the Anglican church). Garzia was accused of stealing a chalice from a Catholic church in Dublin just before he sailed to America so it is possible that this is the chalice. B. Jones, *The life and times of John Garzia* (Bath, NC, 2005). The entry in *DIB* is unaware of this American phase. **105** *The whole tryal and examination of Richard Barnwell, Patrick Burk, Patrick Brien, Thomas McLoghlen, John Bridges, Felim and Margaret McAnally, John Levin, Henry Chinton, Jacob Connor, Patrick Burn and Bryan Swiney, all of which were tried at a commission of Oyer and Terminer, at the Tholsel of the city of Dublin on the 9th and 11th days of August 1718, before the Right Honourable The Lord Chief Justice Whitsed, Lord Mayor, Recorder and the rest of His Majesty's Justices of the Peace for the county and City of Dublin* (Dublin, 1718) [TCD Hib. o 718: 6]. **106** B. Millet, 'Survival and reorganization 1650–1695' in P. Corish (ed.), *A history of Irish Catholicism,* 6 vols (Dublin, 1968), volume 3, part 7, p. 52. **107** T. Ó hAnnracháin, *Catholic Europe, 1592–1648: centre and peripheries* (Oxford, 2015). **108** T. Ó hAnnracháin, 'The bishop's role in two non-Catholic states: the cases of Ireland and Turkish Hungary considered', *Church History & Religious Culture,* 95:2–3 (2015), pp 245–55. **109** This celebrated concept was developed by James Scott to understand asymmetric power. Scott analyses subtle everyday forms of resistance – 'foot-dragging, evasion, false compliance, pilfering, feigned ignorance, slander and sabotage'. Scott emphasizes linguistic adroitness, by making use of prescribed roles and language to resist the abuse of power – including 'rumour, gossip, disguises, linguistic tricks, metaphors, euphemisms, folktales, ritual gestures, anonymity'. J. Scott, *Weapons of the weak: everyday forms of resistance* (New Haven, 1985). **110** R. Payne, *A briefe description of Ireland made in this year 1589* (London, 1589) [CELT].

anger at their sorrow-stung experience when stranded on the wrong side of history, internal exiles in their own land, supping the sour thin gruel of dispossession. The dislocation when ancient sites were lost to Catholic worship is captured in a verse.

A Dhoireagáin, a Dhoireagáin	Little Derry, little Derry
Mo chrú-choill agus m'áilleagán	My hazelnut and my jewel
Mo chrádh go bhfuil se i ndán	It is my affliction that fate
Do na Gallaibh bheith 'na gcónuí	Has decreed that foreigners
Astuigh i lár mo Dhoireagáin.[111]	Will live in the heart of my little Derry.

In 1578, 'Corck O'Coely' [Cormac Ó Cadhla], a New Ross surgeon, wrote from Tinnaranny in adjacent south Kilkenny: 'Neither is there given respect or honour to any holy house since [Elizabeth] attained power'. He accused the English of being the most arrogant people in the whole European continent ('is uaibhrighe san roinn Eorpa co huilidhi').[112] Elizabeth entered the unforgiving folk memory of Ireland as 'Éilis a' mhorta' – 'Elizabeth of death'. Among the charges against Brian Ó Ruairc (executed in 1591) was that:

> Sir Bryan, contrary to the lawes of the Churche of Englande and Irland, did selebrate and keepe the feaste of the Natyvitie of our Lord God according to the Romishe and Popishe computation; and moste trayterously and wickedly caused a woman's pycture to be drawne and draged after a horsse tayle through his owne towne, where then he kept his Xpmas, in the very pudle and myre and like most fylthy places, and did publishe and declare to the voulgare people that the same was her highnes pycture, and that he caused the same to be soe used in despighte and contempte of her Ma[ty], tearmynge her highnes the mother and nurse of all herisies and heretiques.[113]

Tales of swift retribution on perpetrators and their families dogged those who violated Catholic holy objects. A statue of the Blessed Virgin at the chapel of St Mary's in Mullaghmore (Co. Derry) attracted pilgrimage: it was burned at the instigation of the Protestant bishop Brutus Babington in 1611, and his untimely death in the very same year was ascribed to his sacrilege.[114] At St Breagh's chapel at the Burrow in Rosslare parish (Co. Wexford), a local priest reported that 'where latelie miraculous accidents happened, God demonstrating his indignation with signal severity against

111 É. Ó Tuathail, *Sgéalta Mhuintir Luinigh/Munterloney folktales: Irish traditions from Co. Tyrone*, trans. S. Watson (Dublin, 2015), p. 249.   112 P. Walsh, *Gleanings from Irish manuscripts* (Dublin, 1933), p. 160.   113 *The Egerton papers: a collection of public and private documents, chiefly illustrative of the times of Elizabeth and James I, from the original manuscripts*, ed. J. Collier (London, 1840), p. 148.   114 J.B. Leslie, *Derry clergy and parishes* (Enniskillen, 1937), p. 6.

the contemners & scoffers of his beatified servants & profane violators of things and places dedicated to divine service, to the confusion & immediate chastisement of impious blasphemers'.[115] A lurid fate was reserved in popular memory for the Davis family, who were accused of drowning the Dominicans of Cloonshanville (near Frenchpark, Co. Roscommon) in a pool called Poll na mBratháir. Whenever descendants of the family were buried in the family vault adjoining the ruined abbey, the vault was engulfed by fire on the following night when the Devil came to carry them off 'and the Davis's being fat men, their lard holds burning a long time for as soon as the devil touches any corpse, it takes fire'.[116] Similarly misfortune was believed to follow the Piers family of Tristernagh (Co. Westmeath) following their disturbance of the graveyard at the nearby abbey.[117]

From the Franciscan friary in Athlone (Co. Westmeath), Séamus Carthún (1607–76) composed 'Deorchaoineadh na hÉireann' ('Ireland's tearful lament'), where the churches are described as 'without an altar, without Mass or genuflection,/used as stables, a story that stinks/or left without a stone upon a stone'.[118] Aodhagán Ó Rathaille (1670–1726) in Kerry lamented: 'Tá an Eaglais ruaighte ó chuantaibh imill na gcríoch/'s gach mainisteár uaigneach le mórsmacht fhuinnimh an dlí' ('the church banished from its havens to the margins of territories/and every monastery desolated through the oppressive energy of the law').[119] A mid-eighteenth-century sermon by Revd Séamas Mac Poilín of Co. Down bewailed the condition of the sacred places of Ulster, 'without abbot, church, priest, altar or worship'.[120]

Religious orders in Ireland were not annihilated as happened in England: some went west, others to the Continent. The post-Reformation dissolution of the monasteries in Ireland was later and less drastic than that visited on England and Wales. The first commission for suppression of monasteries was completed in 1539–40, with 'voluntary' surrenders of thirty-eight monastic communities. Only one in five of Irish mendicant houses were affected, leaving relatively meagre pickings for the state from the fifty-one suppressed monasteries.[121] The Old English of the Pale were granted properties within the Pale and its borders. More exposed positions, however, were frequently allocated to New English, especially those with a military background: abbies offered large living quarters

115 H.F. Hore (ed.), 'An account of the barony of Forth, in the county of Wexford, written at the close of the seventeenth century', *Kilkenny & South-East of Ireland Archaeological Society Journal*, new series, 4:1 (1862), pp 53–84. 116 *OS letters, Roscommon*, p. 50. 117 Note by L. Melia of Templeacross to F. Murtagh of Kilmacnevin, Upton papers, RIA, MS 22/5. 118 C. Mhág Craith, *Dánta na mBráthar Mionúr* 1 (Baile Átha Cliath, 1967), p. 252. 119 P. S. Dineen & T. O'Donoghue (eds), *Dánta Aodhagáin Uí Rathaille/The poems of Egan O Rahilly*. Second edition revised & enlarged by B. Ó Buachalla (London, 2004), p. 48. 120 C. Ó Maonaigh (eag.), *Seanmónta Chúige Ulaidh* (Baile Átha Cliath, 1965), pp 36–7. 121 Ó Clabaigh, *Friars in Ireland*, p. 328. Detailed records are available in N.B. White, *Extents of Irish monastic possessions, 1540–1541* (Dublin, 1943).

useful for garrisons. Some monasteries were transformed into dwelling places for the New English: Tintern (Co. Wexford) by Colclough,[122] Molana (Co. Waterford) by Harriott,[123] Tralee (Co. Kerry) by Denny, Tracton (Co. Cork) by Grenville, Dunbrody (Co. Wexford) by Etchingham,[124] Bective (Co. Meath) by Agard,[125] Mellifont (Co. Louth) by Moore,[126] Tristernagh (Co. Westmeath) by Piers, Rathmullan (Co. Donegal) by Knox,[127] and Dungiven (Co. Derry) by Doddington.[128] It was much easier to find takers for the Pale properties; those in the west and north were broadly scorned. The lawyer John Davies (1569–1626) revealed in 1612 that allegedly dissolved abbies in Tyrone, Donegal and Fermanagh remained continuously in the possession of the Catholic church until the accession of James 1 to the throne.[129]

From a Catholic perspective, all of this disruption was painful in the extreme. Oliver Lambert (*ob.*1616), governor of Connaught in 1601, used the Franciscan chalices from Donegal Friary as 'common drinking cups'. Captain Guest, one of his officers, reported that 'since he hath the command of Connaught, he is become altogether intolerable', oppressing the country, injuring the soldiers, selling protections and enriching himself through 'the preys taken from the enemy' which 'he divideth like Aesop's lion'.[130]

Sir Edward Moore of Mellifont (Co. Louth) later draped the religious statues from there in 'scarlet, clapped muskets on their shoulders and, transforming them into British grenadiers, placed them to do duty in his hall'.[131] A Cistercian monk from Holy Cross (Co. Tipperary) cuttingly observed that the Dissolution of the Monasteries violated long-standing Christian practice, by favouring the rich over the poor:

> Hoc nostrum de Sancta Cruce coenobium nec ab angustiis, vexationibus, suppressionibus, multiplicibusque (uti caetera omnia) calamitatibus

122 B. Colfer, *The Hook peninsula, Co. Wexford* (Cork, 2004), pp 70–2, 115–16; A. Lynch, *Tintern Abbey, Co. Wexford: Cistercians and Colcloughs: excavations, 1982–2007* (Dublin, 2010). 123 J. Lyttleton, 'Molana Abbey and its New World master', *Archaeology Ireland*, 24:4 (2010), pp 32–5. 124 G. Stout, 'The Abbey of the Port of St Maria, Dunbrody, Co. Wexford: an architectural study' in I. Doyle & B. Browne (eds), *Medieval Wexford: essays in memory of Billy Colfer* (Dublin, 2016), pp 97–123. 125 G. Stout & M. Stout, *The Bective Abbey project, Co. Meath: excavations 2009–2012* (Dublin, 2016), pp 65–7. 126 G. Stout, R. Loeber & K. O'Brien, 'Mellifont Abbey, Co. Louth: a study of its post-dissolution architecture 1540–1727', *PRIA*, 116, C (2016), pp 191–226. 127 *AAI*, iv, p. 316. 128 N. Brannon, 'A lost seventeenth-century house recovered: Dungiven, Co. Londonderry' in A. Hamlin & C. Lynn (eds), *Pieces of the past: archaeological excavations, 1970–1986* (Belfast, 1988), pp 81–4; N. Brannon, 'Archaeological excavations at Dungiven Priory and Bawn', *Benbradagh*, 15 (1986), pp 15–18. 129 J. Davies, *A discovery of the true causes why Ireland was never entirely subdued* (London [1612], 1786), p. 202. 130 Cited in 'Sir Olive Lambert (*d.*1616) of Southampton, later of Co. Cavan, Ireland' in P.W. Hasler (ed.), *The history of parliament: the House of Commons 1558–1603* (London, 1981). 131 Smith, 'Material culture of Donegal Franciscan friary'; R. Armstrong, 'Mellifont Abbey', *Dublin Penny Journal*, 32:1 (1833), pp 249–52.

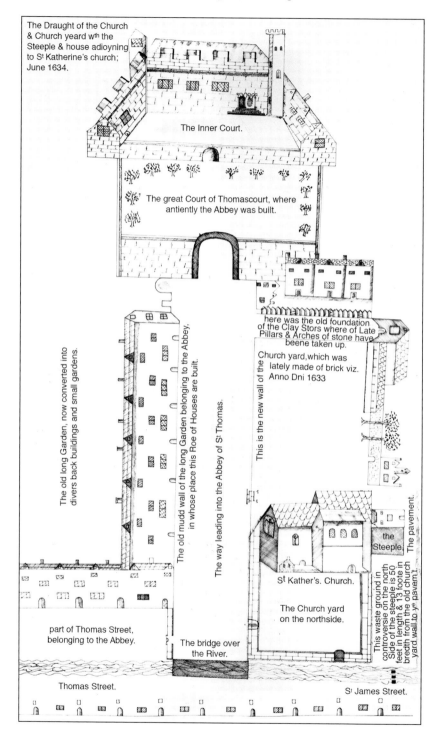

The Draught of the Church & Church yeard wᵗʰ the Steeple & house adioyning to Sᵗ Katherine's church; June 1634.

The Inner Court.

The great Court of Thomascourt, where antiently the Abbey was built.

The old long Garden, now converted into divers back buildings and small gardens.

The old mudd wall of the long Garden belonging to the Abbey, in whose place this Roe of Houses are built.

The way leading into the Abbey of Sᵗ Thomas.

here was the old foundation of the Clay Stors where of Late Pillars & Arches of stone have beene taken up.

This is the new wall of the Church yard, which was lately made of brick viz. Anno Dni 1633

Sᵗ Kather's. Church.

The Church yard on the northside.

the Steeple.

The pavement.

This waste ground in controversie on the north Side of the steeple is 50 feet in length & 13 foote in bredth from the old church yard wall to yᵉ pavemᵗ.

part of Thomas Street, belonging to the Abbey.

The bridge over the River.

Thomas Street.

Sᵗ James Street.

Fig. 9 (*opposite page*) Thomas Court in Dublin 1634. The lands and revenues of the Abbey of
Saint Thomas fell into the grasping hands of the carpetbagger William Brabazon (*ob.*1552).
The Englishman Brabazon came to Ireland as Thomas Cromwell's eyes and ears and he
lined his pockets and those of his cronies through insider trading. This drawing–cum–map
shows the monastic precincts being transformed into urban fabric after the Dissolution of
the Monasteries. Early terraces of row houses are depicted in the old garden of the abbey.
The roof of Saint Catherine's Church still appears to be shingled while the new houses are
slated. Older mud walls are giving way to brick ones: a new brick wall is shown around the
churchyard of Saint Catherine's. The houses exhibit unusual fenestration and there is as yet
no sign of the highly symmetrical piercing that was to characterize the Georgian period. The
original drawing has been reoriented to make it more legible (NLI, 16 9 15 (35)).

immune fuit. Quid memorem de quindecim argenteis deauratis calicibus de
preciosis ac variis hujus ecclesia ornamentis e tela aurea argentea et serica,
idque genus alia. Sacrilegorum sane manus prophanavit, et irreverenter
non pauperibus sed divitibus dispersit, ita ut uni versum monasterium olim
sancta conversationis monachorum Cisterciensium habitaculum non aliud
quam spelunca latronum, hara, equile, bovile, et brutorum quid simile.[132]

The gradual transformation of suppressed monasteries in Dublin converted
All Hallows into a university, St Mary's into an arsenal, St Saviour's into an
Inns of Court and St Thomas's into a private house. Medieval churches were
turned into a tennis court, tippling rooms, a communal oven, and private houses
for the Aungiers, Moores and Brabazons.[133] Archdeacon John Bramhall (1594–
1663), just arrived from England, was shocked by what he first encountered in
Dublin in 1633:

> In Dublin alone one church is used as the Deputy's stable, another as a
> nobleman's house, and the choir of the third as a tennis court where the vicar
> officiates as keeper. The vaults under Christ Church, the principal church in
> Ireland, whither the Lord Deputy and Council repair every Sunday, are let for
> tippling-houses for beer, wine, and tobacco, and these are frequented by Papists:
> so that although there is no chance of the assembly overhead being blown up, they
> may very likely be poisoned with the fumes. The table for the administration of
> the Divine Sacrament is used as a common seat for maidens and apprentices.[134]

132 'Our monastery of Holy Cross, like all others, has not been immune from hardships,
vexations, suppressions, and many similar calamities. Why should I not speak of the fifteen
silver-gilt chalices, of the precious and varied church ornaments made of gold, silver and
precious stones, and other similar possessions? Sacrilegious hands profaned them, and
irreverently disposed of them not for the benefit of the poor but for the rich, and so the
entire monastery, formerly the home of the spiritual life of Cistercian monks, was reduced
to a den of thieves, a sty, stall or cowshed fit only for beasts' [my translation]. [J. Hartry],
*Triumphalia chronologica monasterii Sanctae Crucis in Hibernia de Cisterciensium Hibernorum
viris illustribus*, ed. D. Murphy (Dublin, 1891), p. 72. 133 N. McCullough, *Dublin: an urban
history: the plan of the city* (Dublin, 2007), p. 30.

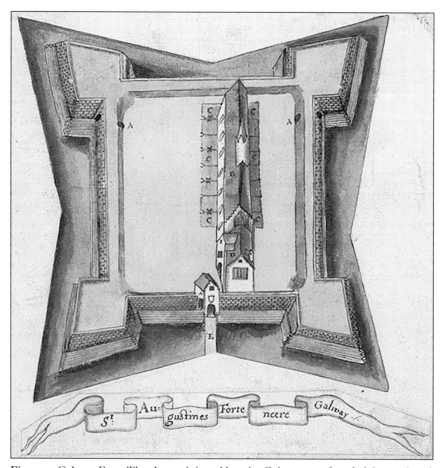

Fig. 10 Galway Fort. The Augustinian abbey in Galway was founded in 1506 and converted into a fort in 1603. This 1611 plan by the English military engineer Josias Bodley (1550–1618) showed the fort as a square structure with a segmental bastion at each corner. The internal buildings (named via an alphabetical key) included a church and lodgings for soldiers and their captain. In 1643, it was briefly returned to the use of the friars who repaired it. It was pulled down in 1652 lest it be fortified against the town (Trinity College Dublin).

Buildings were amputated in the Reformation transformation, and their melancholy limbs lie buried under the Georgian city. The spectral footprint of All Hallows still governs TCD's courtyard[135] while Ormond Quay was built up with the debris of St Mary's Abbey.[136]

134 J. Bramhall to bishop of London, 10 Aug. 1633, *CSPI, 1633–47*, p. 17. 135 L. Simpson, 'The priory of All Hallows and the Old College: archaeological investigations in Front Square, Trinity College Dublin' in S. Duffy (ed.), *Medieval Dublin XIII* (Dublin, 2013), pp 246–316. 136 AAI, i, p. 89.

RUINS

The desecrators exposed a void at the heart of iconoclasm, unwittingly releasing a transgressive power as fresh ruins were resanctified as venerable. The Irish sense of the past manifested itself in place as much as in time, in locations as much as in dates. A memory field, reinforced by both the literati and the locals, hovered over the old holy sites. The views of the learned were not estranged from those of the locals, as can be seen in the writings of Ruaidhrí Ó Flaithbheartaigh (1629–1718) in Co. Galway,[137] Tadhg Ó Rodaighe (1614–1706) in Co. Leitrim[138] and Seán Ó Gadhra (1648–1720) in Co. Sligo. Curating memories involved a complex collaboration with the ordinary Irish people and their store of inherited vernacular knowledge.[139] This is evident in the Annals of the Four Masters,[140] in the seventeenth-century choreographic surveys, in the nineteenth-century Ordnance Survey memoirs and letters,[141] and in the twentieth-century work of the Irish Folklore Commission.[142]

The fabric of ruins reflected the rupture in the landscape, condensing maximum meaning into minimal forms. The dissolution of the monasteries in the 1530s, followed by the Puritan drive to flense older churches, spawned a new generation of ruins. The effect of ruins in Ireland was noticeably more potent than in England. Dugdale's *Monasticon Anglicanum* was published between 1655 and 1673 but Archdall's Irish equivalent appeared over a century later in 1786, suggesting a delayed appreciation of ruins in Protestant Ireland, where the Papist threat had not yet waned sufficiently to afford the necessary aesthetic distance. As late as 1822, the earl of Rosse was warning that Protestants might yet pay a heavy price for having allowed their castles to become ruins if the Catholics rose again:

> No man can be sure that they will not. If they should, this time will be as memorable for the massacre of Protestants as 1641. Then the Protestants lived in the castles which we see everywhere in ruins and therefore they could often protect themselves much better than now.[143]

137 R. Sharpe, *Roderick O'Flaherty's letters to William Molyneux, Edward Lhwyd and Samuel Molyneux, 1696–1709* (Dublin, 2013).   **138** J. Logan, 'Tadhg O'Roddy and two surveys of Co. Leitrim', *Breifne*, 4:14 (1971), pp 76–81; J.H. Todd (ed.), 'Autograph letter of Thady O'Roddy', *Miscellany of the Irish Archaeological Society*, 1 (1846), pp 112–25. He was 'the lineal representative' of the O'Roddys, coarbs of the monastery of Fenagh (p. 113).   **139** John O'Donovan advised his field workers to 'walk through the parish from one end to the other', and 'seek old men who speak Irish' (*OS letters, Roscommon*, p. 15). He himself liked to assemble and consult 'a little parliament of old men' (*OS letters, Roscommon*, p. 23).   **140** B. Cunningham, *The Annals of the Four Masters: Irish history, kingship and society in the early seventeenth century* (Dublin, 2010).   **141** G. Doherty, *The Irish Ordnance Survey: history, culture and memory* (Dublin, 2006).   **142** D. Ó Giolláin, *Locating Irish folklore: tradition, modernity, identity* (Cork, 2000); M. Briody, *The Irish Folklore Commission, 1935–1970: history, ideology, methodology* (Helsinki, 2007).

Fig. 11 'View of the Seven Churches [Glendalough] with a procession of the Catholics at Christmas' [1777?] by Peter Van Lerberghe (British Library, Maps K.Top.55.53).

The religious controversialist Ceasar Otway (1780–1842) noted in the 1830s:

> In almost every religious ruin I have ever visited, the neighbouring people, besides telling you of the original destruction by bloody Bess or cursed Cromwell with his copper nose, always have some more recent instances to narrate of Protestant mischief-doers. The children have got these stories at their fingers' ends: it seems part of a system by these means to preoccupy the minds of the young Roman Catholics with deep and hateful prejudices against their Protestant countrymen.[144]

The nationalist politician William O'Brien (1852–1928) lectured the Cork Young Ireland Society in 1885:

143 Ross to Redesdale, 19 Apr. 1822, PRONI, T 3030/13/2.   144 Caesar Otway, *A tour in Connaught, comprising sketches of Clonmacnoise, Joyce Country and Achill* (Dublin, 1839), p. 308.

When the framers of the penal laws denied us books, and drew their thick black veil over Irish history, they forgot that the ruins they had themselves made were the most eloquent schoolmasters, the most stupendous memorials of a history and a race that were destined not to die. They might give our flesh to the sword, and our fields to the spoiler, but before they could blot out the traces of their crimes, or deface the title deeds of our heritage, they would have to uproot to their last scrap of sculptured filigree the majestic shrines in which the old race worshipped; they would have had to demolish to their last stone the castles which lay like wounded giants through the land to mark where the fight had raged fiercest.[145]

As late as 1930, it was noted that 'There is not a great estate in Ireland owned by one of Cromwell's settlers which had not always had a ghostly other owner in the memory of the common people'.[146]

In 1622, Fennanstown [Ballyfinnan/Fennorstown] near Kilkenny was considered 'a prophane place', where the new proprietors had 'turned the same to their own use': 'ye churche made a barne to put cattell in' by Robert St Leger.[147] Of 122 churches and chapels in the diocese of Ossory in 1622, forty-three were already ruined. By the end of the century, the situation had dramatically deteriorated: over ninety per cent of churches in the sprawling diocese of Meath were ruined in 1697.[148] In 1709, at Kilconnell Abbey (Co. Galway), the churchyard had become a theatrical killing field, surrounded by a wall of dead men's sculls and bones 'pil'd very orderly, with their faces outwards, clear round against the wall to the length of 88 foot, about 4 high, and 5 feet 4 inches broad, so that there may be possibly here to the number of 50,000 sckulls. Within they shew you Lord Gallway and other great men's heads kill'd at Aghrim'.[149] At Aughrim itself, 'dead men's sckulls lye scatter'd in ye fields, ye remains of ye battle there fought in ye troubles' (a very early use of this term).[150] A Dutch priest in 1716 was struck by the circumstance that 'on this island, everything appears to be destroyed and knocked'.[151]

Ecclesiastical ruins in Ireland were animated by a numinous afterlife, fostering an imaginative preoccupation with the preceding world and a strong

---

145 W. O'Brien, *Irish ideas* (London, 1893), p. 4.   **146** H.V. Morton, *In search of Ireland* (London, 1930).   **147** F. Ó Fearghail, 'Bishop Wheeler's visitation of Ossory 1622', *Ossory, Laois & Leinster*, 6 (2016), p. 148.   **148** 'State of the diocese of Meath 1693' in M. O'Neill (ed.), *Episcopal visitations of the diocese of Meath, 1622–1799* (Dublin, 2017), pp 55–140. Bishop Dopping proposed that 'not all of them' be rebuilt, as that would create 'too great a burden' and elicit 'much murmur' (p. 137).   **149** A memorandum on a fly leaf supplied the measurements of 'the wall of heads round the churchyard' as 33 lengths of Molyneux's 2 foot 8 inches long cane – 1½ high and 2 broad ('Molyneux tour', p. 40).   **150** 'Molyneux tour', p. 46.   **151** J. Mitchell, 'The ordination in Ireland of Jansenist clergy from Utrecht 1715–16: the role of Fr Paul Kenny O.D.C.', *JGAHS*, 42 (1990), pp 1–29, 43 (1991), pp 46–81.

desire for reconnection to it. Ruined churches continued to attract burials, and big crowds on patron days.[152] A knowledgeable commentator described the patron in 1804.

> An Irish patron resembled, in some manner, the old English wake: probably they both sprung from the same origin. It was a large assemblage of people from all parts within a distance of ten or twenty miles, collected together round a sacred fountain dedicated to and called after the name of the Saint, in honour of whom this festival was celebrated. In the morning or forenoon the priest of the parish performed mass on a large stone, which was called an altar. Several old men and women at the same time performed penance round the well. Here were all sorts of hawkers, mountebanks, conjurers and itinerant musicians: and tents and booths were erected chiefly for the sale of liquor.[153]

Depending on their outlook, some magistrates saw these patterns as threatening events, others as a harmless social outlet. In August 1828, William Grainger of Causestown (Navan, Co. Meath) publicly berated his Meath fellow magistrates (Robert Bourke of Hayes and Revd T.D. Hamilton of Navan) for banning a long-established patron at Stackallen Bridge on the Boyne. Grainger argued that it was 'an ancient custom, held on the first Sunday of the harvest, where farmers and labourers amuse themselves after the fatigues and privations of the summer' and that it would 'encourage tranquillity and harmony if the gentry attended these rustic sports'. By contrast, Bourke regarded it as 'a scene of drunkenness, debauchery and excess', all the more obnoxious for taking place on 'the Lord's Day'.[154]

A 1697 Act laid down that 'none shall bury in suppressed monasteries not used for divine service' (9 William III, c. I, s. vi) but it was utterly ignored by both Protestants and Catholics. The German traveller Hermann von Pückler-Muskau (1785–1871) observed in 1826:

---

152 K. Whelan, 'Reading the ruins: the presence of absence in the Irish landscape' in Clarke, Prunty & Hennessy (eds), *Surveying Ireland's past*, pp 263–94.   153 R. Bell, *A description of the condition and manners of the peasantry of Ireland* (London, 1804), p. 21. Another description came from Saint Peter's parish in Athlone (Co. Westmeath): 'the collection of peasantry called patterns, more properly denominated patrons, being originally assemblies of people met together with their priest for prayers and the religious adoration to be paid to the saints who are considered the patrons of the places where these patterns are held; at which there is necessarily some holy well or other local object tending to call forth the attendants' devotion ... At these places are always erected booths or tents, as in fairs, for selling whiskey, beer, and ale, at which pipers and fiddlers do not fail to attend, and the reminder of the day and night (after their religious performances are over and the priest withdraws), is spent in singing, dancing and drinking'. The local patrons frequented were Brides Well and Saint John's (Co. Roscommon) and Clonmacnoise (Co. Offaly) (W. Shaw Mason, *A statistical account or parochial survey of Ireland*, 3 vols (Dublin, 1814–19), iii, pp 72–4).   154 CSO/RP/1828/1198.

Ireland is teeming with the vestiges of ruins of ancient castles and monasteries more than any other country in Europe, although these ruins are not on the same scale as, for example, those in England. Most of the old ruins (many are new, unfortunately) now serve as graveyards, a poetic notion, that is, I believe, peculiar to these people. They never erect tasteless modern monuments as one finds in English churches but are content with a simple mound of earth or at most a stone on the grave, something that heightens rather than profanes the affecting aura of earthly transience.[155]

In these varied ways, apparently abandoned sites remained alive in the Irish landscape. In 1609, for example, vast gatherings at Monaincha (Móin Inse Cré, near Roscrea, Co. Tipperary) and Inis Cealtra on Lough Derg attracted official mistrust.[156]

These ruins conferred legitimacy on Catholicism as the ancient religion of Ireland, conveying the sense that Catholicism was rooted in Ireland for 'time out of mind'. Consider the contrast between the Franciscan Colleges on the Continent, especially Rome and Prague, and their ruined foundations at home.[157] Rome created a virtual reality of an imagined Ireland in the late nineteenth-century illustrations of ruined Franciscan friaries in the refectory and chapter hall of S. Isidoro. The visual prompt was designed to stiffen the resolve of the seminarians of the present.

THE CATHOLIC REFORMATION IN THE PALE

A counterfactual to ponder is what might have happened to the failed project of making Ireland British if it had prioritized an anglicizing rather than a Protestantizing agenda. When the New English Protestants contemptuously repudiated any sense of affiliation with the Old English, the Old English were forced to reach out to the Gaelic Irish as heirs to their threatened religious tradition, elevating their Catholicism over their anglicity. That sense of a common Catholic purpose consolidated after the decisive English break with the papacy in 1534. The tentative coming together of the hitherto antagonistic Old Irish and Old English was signalled by the neologism of the inclusive term 'na hÉireannaigh' (the Irish) – shared dwellers in the náisiún/land of Éire/Ireland.[158]

---

155 *Letters of a dead man: Prince Hermann Fürst von Pückler-Muskau*, ed. & trans. L. Parshall (New York, 2016), p. 487. **156** *CSPI, 1608–10*, pp 240–1. **157** There is a pioneering treatment of the 1672 fresco cycle in San Isidore's in Carroll, *Exiles in a global city*, pp 89–143. **158** The animus directed by the Mac An Mhaoir family at Oliver Plunkett laid bare the ugliness. The MacMoyer family had lived at Ballymacmoyer since the fourteenth century and were custodians of the Book of Armagh. In 1681, Finghin Mac An Mhaoir (Florence MacMoyer) pawned the manuscript for five pounds to fund his travel

The Armada survivor Francisco De Cuellar (*ob.* 1606), shipwrecked off the Donegal coast, had improvised communications with the locals in which it was clear that they were if anything hyper-conscious of nationality, and the relative bearings of Irish, English and Spanish.[159] The French traveller Francois de la Boullaye de Gouz noted in 1644 that the ordinary Irish called themselves 'Ayrenake' (Éireannach), a neologism that had entered common speech as a way of transcending the divisive Gael/Gall distinction:

> Les naturels sont connus des Anglois sous le nom d'Iriche, des François sous celuy d'Hibernois que l'on tire du Latin, ou d'Irois que l'on tire de l'Anglois, ou d'Irlandois que l'on tire du nom de l'Isle, parce que Land signifie terre, ils se nomment Ayrenake, ce qu'il faut apprendre par la practique, parce qu'ils n'escrivent point leur langue, & n'apprennent le Latin que sur le pied de l'Anglois.[160]

Their well-developed consciousness of their national identity differentiated the Irish poor from their European counterparts, who generally had to await the intrusion of centralized nation states before advancing to this stage. That precocious national consciousness emerged out of their historical circumstances. Those who were the butt of adverse perceptions were inevitably politicized as a result. The lived experience of Irish Catholics was dignified by being so richly amenable to biblical interpretation, softening the harsh experience of oppression.[161] As late as 1839 when a new Catholic church was dedicated at Ferns (Co. Wexford), the preacher commented:

> The beautiful words of the inspired David on the calamities of the Jewish people bear a striking application to the condition and circumstances of the people of this country; and the Sion of his cares and hopes was as

to London (with his cousin, Friar John MacMoyer) to testify against Plunkett. Florence, imprisoned after his return to Ireland, was unable to redeem the Book of Armagh, which passed to the Brownlow family in 1707, and he died in 1713, alone, despised and destitute. The remaining family members changed their name to Maguire to hide their connection to him. T. Ó Fiach, 'The fall and return of John Mac Moyer (and his connection with the trial of Blessed Oliver Plunkett)', *Seanchas Ardmhacha*, 3:1 (1958), pp 50–86.   **159** Francisco De Cuellar, 'Carta de uno que fué en la Armada de Yngaletera y cuenta la jornada' in P. Gallagher & D.W. Cruickshank (eds), *God's obvious design: papers from the Spanish Armada symposium, Sligo* (London, 1990), pp 201–21.   **160** [Boullaye le Gouz], *Voyages et observations*, p. 456. 'The natives are known to the English as Irish, to the French as Hibernois (derived from the Latin), or Irois (derived from English), or Irish (derived from the name of the island, because 'land' means terre). They call themselves Ayrenake, which must be learned by being heard, because they do not write their language at all, and learn Latin only through the prism of English'. For the general backdrop, see M. Mac Craith, 'Litríocht an 17ú h-aois: tonnbhriseadh an tseanghnáthaimh nó tonnchuthú an nuaghnáthaimh?', *Leachtaí Cholm Cille*, 26 (1996), pp 50–82.   **161** B. Ó Buachalla, *Aisling ghéar: na Stíobhartaigh agus an t-aos léinn, 1603–1788* (Baile Átha Cliath, 1996).

Fig. 12 The Babylonian captivity was a recurring metaphor used by Catholics during an droch-shaol (the troubled times). This drawing of Jeremiah lamenting under a tree in Sion was made by the scribe William Lynch of Dublin in 1686. It illustrated the poem published in C. O'Rahilly (ed.), *Five seventeenth-century political poems* (Dublin, 1952), pp 50–1 (British Library, Egerton MS 187).

Ireland in ours. The people of this country were persecuted for their allegiance to heaven and were made captives in their native land.[162]

The Catholic Reformation announced itself first in the Pale and stiffened dramatically after 1580. The 1614 Synod of Dublin contented itself that sufficient priests were already assigned to adjacent unprovided parishes, and that a redesigned parochial network was functioning smoothly. In 1630, sixty of 150 civil parishes (forty per cent) in County Dublin were impropriate[163] of which thirty-five remained in Catholic hands (one-quarter of the total).[164] The Pale lords –

---

162 J. Sinnott, *Sermon preached in Ferns cathedral on its dedication October 2 1839 by the Rev. John Sinnott, President of St Peters College Wexford* (Wexford, 1839), p. 4. **163** **Impropriation**, in English ecclesiastical law, assigned the tithes (and sometimes the right of clerical nomination) of an ecclesiastical benefice to a layman, who was obliged to provide and maintain a cleric to serve the parish. **164** M. Ronan (ed.), 'Archbishop Bulkeley's visitation of Dublin 1630', *Archiv. Hib.*, 8 (1941), pp 56–98; C. Ó Fearghail, 'The evolution of Catholic parishes in Dublin city from the sixteenth to the nineteenth centuries' in F.H. Aalen & K. Whelan (eds), *Dublin, city and county from prehistory to present* (Dublin, 1992), pp 63–71.

Fig. 12 Dunsoghly Castle (Co. Dublin) was built *c*.1450 by Sir Thomas Plunket (*c*.1440–
1519), chief justice of the Irish Common Pleas, and it remained continuously occupied by the
same family for four centuries until *c*.1870. The Pale lords often had Catholic chapels annexed
to their castles, as in this 1573 example. The plaque on the chapel shows the instruments of
the passion and reads I.P.M.D.G.S. 1573, which can be read as Iohannes (John) Plunket,
Miles (Knight = Sir) of Dunsoghly, and his wife Genet Sarsfield. John Plunkett also endowed
a chantry chapel at St Margarets: 'Joannes Plunkett de Dunsoghlia miles capitalis quondam
justiciarius regii in Hibernia banci hoc struxit sacellum' (John Plunkett of Dunsoghly,
Knight, former chief justice of the Irish Bench, constructed this chapel) (RSAI).

Talbot of Malahide, Cheevers of Monkstown, Plunkett of Dunsoghly, Luttrell of
Mulhuddard, Fagan of Feltrim, Barnewall of Turvey, Preston of Gormanstown
– sheltered priests, hosted Masses and thwarted Protestant reforms.[165] In 1612, the
English-born Bishop Thomas Ram (1564–1634) of Ferns and Leighlin claimed
that the 'poorer sort' were less wedded to Catholicism than 'gentlemen and those
of the richer sort': he found that the richer Catholics were always 'very obstinate,
which have proceeded from the priests resorting unto their houses and company,
and continuall hammering of them upon their superstitious anvell'.[166] In 1606,
Sir John Davies, on circuit in Munster, claimed that 'priests live in the houses of
gentlemen under the name of surgeons and physicians'.[167]

165 C. Lennon, 'Mass in the manor house: the Counter-Reformation in Dublin 1560–1630'
in J. Kelly & D. Keogh (eds), *History of the Catholic diocese of Dublin* (Dublin, 2000), p. 123.
166 P.H. Hore, *History of the town and county of Wexford*, 6 vols (London, 1900–11), vi, p.
259. 167 *CSPI, 1603–6*, p. 476.

Fig. 14 Gormanston was the long-established home of the Prestons, classic Pale lords. The drawings show the building from the back and the front. (Front) 'North-west view of the castle of Gormanston in the county of Meath in Ireland the residence of Preston Viscount Gormanstown 1700'. (Back – facing the Delvin river) 'South-east view of the castle of Gormanston in the county of Meath in Ireland the residence of Preston Viscount Gormanstown 1700'. The then owner was Jenico Preston (1640–1700), eighth Viscount Gormanston. The 1687 chapel is shown to the side of the castle, with its Y-shaped tracery windows and its formal door. Above the door was a date plaque, a distinctive carving featuring a skull, and the Preston coat of arms. The roof has a bell on one end and a crucifix on the other. The chapel remained in use until 1947 when the Franciscans bought the estate. They promptly and shamefully demolished this chapel with its roots twining right back through the history of Catholic Ireland (courtesy of Magda Loeber).

These families had long exerted a leadership role. For example, the Plunketts in Meath acted as church patrons in the mid-to-late fifteenth century, as at Killeen, Dunsany, Rathmore, Duleek and Stackallan. In the late medieval period, a diffusion of architectural fashions from the city to the country can occasionally be traced. Early fifteenth-century architecture in Meath was dominated by the three Plunkett churches of Killeen, Dunsany and Rathmore, which carried design elements from Dublin into the wider Pale. Killeen and Dunsany, with their twinned towers, copied from the west front of Saint Patrick's in Dublin, were remodelled between 1370 and 1400.[168]

Fonts were common in Cork, Kilkenny and Meath (Kilcarne, Rathmore, Crickstown, Dunsany, Clonard).[169] Wayside crosses in Meath were maintained by the Plunketts, Cusacks, Nangles and Dowdalls.[170] Shrines were erected by the Catholic elite at holy wells, notably in Dublin, Meath, Cork and Kilkenny. The rising status of the concept of purgatory[171] promoted an efflorescence of chantries across Europe.[172] Wooden and stone wayside crosses appeared, especially at road junctions, and the ornate family tomb re-emerged, with a heartland in Kilkenny and Tipperary.[173] In the late sixteenth and seventeenth centuries, the O'Tunney and Kerins ateliers produced magnificent signed carvings featuring the Instruments of the Passion.[174] The Callan-born

---

168 O'Neill, 'Parish churches of Meath'. **169** AAI, i, p. 324. **170** H. King, 'Irish wayside and churchyard crosses 1600–1700', *Post-Medieval Archaeology*, 19:1 (1985), pp 13–33; H. King, 'Late medieval Irish crosses and their European background' in C. Hourihane (ed.), *From Ireland coming: Irish art from the early Christian to the late gothic period and its European context* (Princeton, 2001), pp 333–50. **171** C. Tait, *Death, burial and commemoration in Ireland, 1550–1650* (Basingstoke, 2002). **172** C. Lennon, 'The chantries in the Irish Reformation: the case of St Anne's Guild Dublin 1550–1630' in R. Comerford, M. Cullen, J. Hill & C. Lennon (eds), *Religion, conflict and co-existence in Ireland* (Dublin, 1989), pp 6–25. The Guild of St Anne, founded in 1430, established its chantry chapel at St Audoen's Church in Dublin, and this survived until 1693. 'Benetbrygge' (Bennettsbridge, Co. Kilkenny) had a 'free chapel' (presumably a chantry chapel) dedicated to the Blessed Virgin on its medieval bridge. The bridge and chapel were both swept away prior to 1743 (Carrigan, *Ossory*, iii, pp 46–7). The 'Bennett' in the placename presumably derived from 'Benoit', a middle French word for 'blessed'. A 1470 chantry at Waterford cathedral was demolished in 1770: M. Byrne, *Waterford 1470: Dean John Collyn and the chantry chapel of St Saviour* (Drogheda, 2013). A chantry chapel at St Mary's in Youghal (Co. Cork) was invaded and privatized by the *nouveau-riche* Robert Boyle (1556–1643) as a space to erect his blingy alabaster monument. In 1641, according to a petition by the Protestant discoverer Thomas Lowe, there were three chantries (St Anne's guild, St Sythe's [Osgyth] guild, Corpus Christi) in Dublin and one in Drogheda (HMC, *Fourth report*, p. 56). **173** H. King, 'Late medieval crosses in Co. Meath c.1470–1635', *PRIA*, 84, C (1984), pp 79–115. **174** M. Phelan, 'The O'Kerin school of monumental sculpture in Ossory and its environs in the sixteenth and seventeenth centuries', *JRSAI*, 126 (1996), pp 167–81: J. Hunt, 'Rory O'Tunney and the Ossory tomb sculptures', *JRSAI*, 80:1 (1950), pp 22–8; E.C. Rae, 'Irish sepulchral monuments of the later Middle Ages: Part II: the O'Tunney atelier', *JRSAI*, 101 (1971), pp 1–39. Presumably the actual name of Rory O'Tunney (*fl.* 1541–52) was Ruaidhrí Ó Tuine. He described himself as the son of Pádraig (*et ego Ruoricus Otyuny filius Patricii*

artist Tony O'Malley (1913–2003), who was inspired to become an artist by contemplation of these tombs when he was growing up, judged that the O'Tunneys 'understood stone' and accordingly exercised 'power over abstract forms': 'they drew a hammer, it was carved in the stone, it was still a stone but it was also a hammer – it retained the two qualities'.[175]

The Fagans of Feltrim sponsored the heavily visited St Doolagh's well (near Balgriffin, Co. Dublin). Redecorated in the 1660s, it was described in 1678 as 'beautiful with an arch erected over it, painted in the concave thereof with the scheme of heaven, representing the sun and the moon and the stars of that celestial fabrick'.[176] In the mid eighteenth-century, it was described as:

> a well of most lucid and delightful water, enclosed and arched over, and formerly embellished at the expense of Peter Fagan, brother of the late John Fagan, of Feltrim, Esq., with decorations of gildings and paintings. The descent of the Holy Ghost on the Apostles was represented on the top, with the figures of St Patrick, St Columb, and St Brigid, much after the manner they are engraved in Messingham's title-page of his *Florilegium Sanctorum Hiberniae*, as also of St Dolough, in a hermit's habit.[177]

In 1745, the topographer Isaac Butler visited the 'excellent well' at Mulhuddard (Co. Dublin):

> It is carefully walled & several large trees about it. Here on 8th September a great patron is kept with a vast concourse of all sexes & ages from many miles; upwards of eighty tents are pitched here furnished with all kinds of liquors & provisions for the reception & refreshment of the company.[178]

---

scripsi) on the William and Margaret Cantwell tomb at Kilcooley (Co. Tipperary). The family was likely from Callan (Co. Kilkenny). The name may ultimately derive from Ó Maoltuile > Ó Tuile > Ó Tuine. The name Flood (Ó Maoltuile) was still in Callan in Griffith's Valuation. **175** T. O'Malley, 'Inscape: life and landscape in Callan and south Kilkenny' in W. Nolan & K. Whelan (eds), *Kilkenny: history and society* (Dublin, 1900), p. 630.   **176** Kelly & Keogh (eds), *Catholic diocese of Dublin*, p. 131.   **177** Cited in T. Wall, 'An 18th century life of St Patrick' in *Reportorium Novum*, 3, 1 (1961–2), p. 123. This account also described what happened to **Sir Richard Bulkely** (1660–1710) of Old Bawn 'who greatly defaced and disfigured the decorations of this well, but his profanation escaped not unpunished, for not long before his death, which happened in April, 1710, he was strangely misled by a visionary set of people, who pretended to be prophets, and had promised to make him strai[gh]t, he being a crooked-backed man'. These 'French prophets' also promised him supernatural protection if he burned Old Bawn and walked through the flames. When Bulkely sought to sell his estates and give the proceeds to these prophets in 1710, he was declared *non compos mentis*. His estate then passed to William Worth, who had married both Bulkely's stepmother and his widow.   **178** I. Butler, A journey to Lough Derg [CELT]. In 1754, the Catholic clergy, to stop 'scandalous excesses at the well near Mulahedard, commonly called Lady's Well, have prevailed on landholders contiguous thereto not to permit any tents or booths to be erected', gave public notice to prevent disappointment to publicans (*FDJ*, 15 Aug.

Overall the wider Pale (Dublin, Kildare, Meath, Louth, south Down) and the older Anglo-Norman areas (Kilkenny, south Tipperary, south Wexford) 'after so great shakings and changes'[179] were still densely populated in the mid-seventeenth century, with many thatched buildings dotting its tillage fields.[180] Pale scholar Richard Stanyhurst (1547–1618) praised Old English families in Fingal, 'gripping with their tallants [talons] so firmly that warm nest', that they were never ousted by the Irish or the New English.[181] The medieval triad of castle, church and mill anchored this settled landscape: they were often surrounded by a cabin cluster, and this is the situation recorded on contemporary maps and surveys.[182]

The barony of Forth in south Wexford was described in 1680:

> They are generally zealous in their religious profession, having very many remarkable monuments extant of the pious zeal and devotion of their progenitors, in the aforesaid narrow extent of that barony; wherein ancientlie were erected, and the precints and walls yet extant visiblie, of churches and chappells, first firmelie builded and richlie adorned for divine service, in the several peeces or parishes ... There were very many crosses in publique roads, and crucifixes, in private houses and churches in the said barony kept, builded of stone, timber, or metal, representing the dolorous passion of our Saviour Jesus Christ, which, wherever found, were totally defaced, broken, or burned by Cromwellian soldiers ... The direption [disruption] and demolition of the aforesaid churches and chapells were perpetrated, and their sacred ornaments profaned, since and during the late usurper's government.[183]

Of these chapels and churches in the barony of Forth, twenty-one (more than half) were at towerhouse locations (thirty-three chapels, eighteen churches, two

1754). The *Postchaise Companion* (1786) commented on this 'very handsome well, supplied with a remarkably fine spring of water, and dedicated to the Virgin Mary, whose statue in miniature is set up in a niche of the building, in the form of a small house round the well'. It was connected to the church of Mary via the historical Order of the Guild of the Blessed Virgin Mary. This Order, founded by Henry VI, was entrusted with the upkeep of various shrines, including this holy well. Mulhuddard remained the preferred cemetery of Dublin Catholics in the eighteenth century. The cemetery was 'remarkable for the number of tombs' (L. Price (ed.), *An eighteenth-century antiquary: the sketches, notes and diaries of Austin Cooper (1759–1830)* (Dublin, 1942), p. 65). It survives remarkably well considering recent suburbanization.   **179** Treatise on the state of the churches in Britain & Ireland [*c.*1650?], University of Sheffield, Hartlib papers, MS 17/18/1A-4B.   **180** Horner, 'Through the fractured lens of the Civil Survey'.   **181** L. Miller & E. Power (eds), *Holinshed's Irish chronicle* (Dublin, 1979), p. 13.   **182** This type of landscape is depicted on the 1655 map of Castletown (Co. Louth) (*Atlas of Irish rural landscape*, p. 260), the 1702 map of Clondalkin (Co. Dublin) (*Atlas of Irish rural landscape*, p. 204), and the 1737 map of Forth (Co. Wexford) (*Atlas of Irish rural landscape*, p. 76).   **183** H.F. Hore (ed.), 'An account of the barony of Forth in the county of Wexford written at the close of the seventeenth century', *Kilkenny & South-east of Ireland Archaeological Society Journal*, 4:1 (1862), p. 69.

convents, one religious hospital). The implication is that private chapels were located within the towerhouses. In the following centuries, the densely settled and overwhelmingly Catholic baronies of Forth and Bargy supplied the priests who backboned the re-emergence of Catholicism in the diocese of Ferns.[184]

The sheer density of population and the settlement maturity in these areas made them unavailable to be colonized with New English in the seventeenth century.[185] In 1598, County Kilkenny had 'the most show of civility of any other of the border counties, in respect of the fayre seats of houses, the number of castles and the Inglysh manner of inclosure of their grounds'.[186] In staunchly Catholic but innovative Fingal in north Dublin, new mansions and stone houses ('a fair stone house' in the Civil Survey signifies a non-castellated house), with avenues, orchards and ornamental trees, had already replaced castles by the time of the Civil Survey. Wyanstown, Kenure, Malahide and Howth are examples.[187] These cores were surrounded by well-enclosed and quicksetted farmland, studded with mills (162 in Co. Meath) and with an evolved road network, as revealed in the detailed verbal thumbnails of over 300 townlands in the Trustees Survey of 1700–2.[188] Estate cores also hosted villages: the old Fitzgerald village at Portlester was still intact in 1700 with '18 cott[i]ers houses in ye town';[189] Upper Culmullin had 'four good farm houses', one of stone, three mud-walled and thatched, 'and 18 cabins'.[190] Manor courts were still functioning at Swords, Lusk and Balrothery, as recorded in the Civil Survey.

There was notable continuity of settlement and cultural patterns on the surviving Catholic and crypto-Catholic estates; for example, the Butlers of Ormonde (Kilkenny and Tipperary), the Kavanaghs of Borris (Co. Carlow), the Mastersons of Monaseed, Colcloughs of the Duffry, and Devereuxs of Carrigmenan (Co. Wexford), the Plunkett and Taaffe estates (Co. Louth) and the Daly, Burke and Lynch estates (east Co. Galway).[191] In Leinster, it only proved possible to insert durable colonies in wooded, hilly or boggy regions,

184 K. Whelan, 'The Catholic community in eighteenth-century Co. Wexford' in T. Power & K. Whelan (eds), *Endurance and emergence: Catholics in Ireland in the eighteenth century* (Dublin, 1990), pp 156–78. 185 R. Loeber, *The geography and practice of English colonization in Ireland* (Athlone, 1991). 186 *Description of Ireland and the state thereof as it is at this present in anno 1598*, ed. E. Hogan (Dublin, 1878), p. 65. 187 **Wyanstown** was a large stone house, with two gate houses, a pigeon house and several office houses, two bawn walls and a base court wall (all of lime and stone), three thatched houses, an orchard, a garden, ornamental ash trees, groves and hedgerows. It had a Catholic owner, Thomas Conran (R.C. Simington (ed.), *The Civil Survey AD 1654–1656: County of Dublin* (Dublin, 1945), pp 155–6). The details for Kenure are on p. 60, Howth on p. 169, and Malahide on p. 195. 188 A. Horner & R. Loeber, 'Landscape in transition: descriptions of forfeited properties in Counties Meath, Louth and Cavan in 1700', *Anal. Hib.*, 42 (2011), pp 59–180. 189 Horner & Loeber, 'Landscape in transition', p. 116. 190 Horner & Loeber, 'Landscape in transition', p. 157. 191 The Galway Catholic gentry are well treated in P. Melvin, *Estates and landed society in Galway* (Dublin, 2013). On the settlement impact, see J. Burtchaell, 'The south Kilkenny farm villages' in Smyth & Whelan (eds), *Common ground*, pp 110–23.

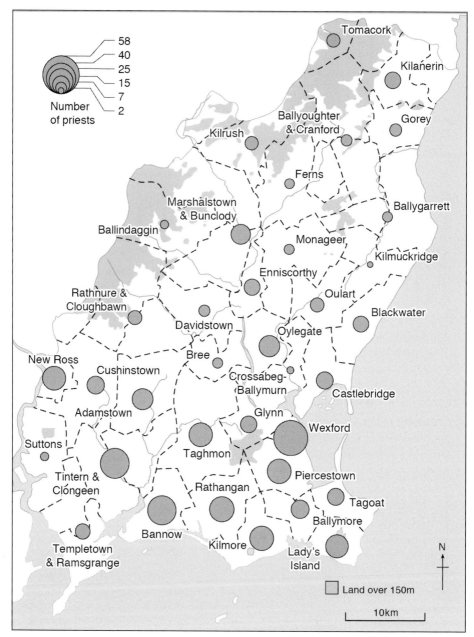

Fig. 15 The birthplaces of Catholic priests in the diocese of Ferns, 1700–1900. The map is based on 914 known priests, of whom the birth places of 587 (64%) were identified. The parishes are shown as they existed in 1800. Castletown (Dublin diocese), Annacurra and Killaveney (Co. Wicklow) are omitted. Only twelve priests were born outside Co. Wexford.

formerly lightly settled. North Wexford, Wicklow and parts of Laois and Offaly attracted new settlements.[192] Formed in the wake of significant woodland clearance, the north Wexford plantation proved successful.[193] The massive Wentworth (later Fitzwilliam) estate in south Wicklow was the most glamorous 'Protestant' settlement in the south of Ireland. The Wandesfordes developed a viable colony based on coalmining on the bleak Castlecomer plateau, the only example in Co. Kilkenny.[194]

VILLAGES

Medieval villages disintegrated in the second half of the seventeenth century. The late medieval village system depicted on Lythe's map of 1563[195] was shattered by the cumulative impact of the Reformation, landownership changes and economic restructuring. The older institutional foci of castle and parish church were superseded, as the manor gave way to the estate, the individual lease dissolved feudal communal obligations, enclosure consolidated the open fields, and villages decomposed. Rocque's maps of the vast Fitzgerald estates in Co. Kildare in the 1760s showed this withering process in an advanced state.[196] The stripping of the medieval churches, the displacement of the old landowning élite and their dependents, and the new commercialized, pastoralist-orientated agriculture truncated established settlement roots, and culminated in their shrivelling away. The labour-intensive tillage that once surrounded the old villages yielded to extensive pastoralism and with that transition came the scattering of the labour force away from the old cores, to be reconstituted as a potato-dependent cottier class, dispersed to the margins of newly consolidated individual tillage farms.[197] One major result was to erode the Irish village tradition, setting it on a radically different trajectory to its European counterparts. W.B. Yeats (1865–1939), surveying the ruin-studded landscapes of east Galway and Clare, surmised that without the negative impact of colonialism: 'It might be now like Bayeux or like Caen/Or little Italian town amid its walls'.[198]

A geography of revolutionary transformation implanted a radically new settlement system. At Carton (Co. Kildare), many townlands were

192 Chapter on 'Village and countryside: landlord and settler' in L.M. Cullen, *The emergence of modern Ireland, 1600–1900* (London, 1981). **193** R. Loeber & M. Stouthamer-Loeber, 'The lost architecture of the Wexford plantation' in K. Whelan (ed.), *Wexford: history and society* (Dublin, 1987), pp 173–200. **194** W. Nolan, *Fassadinin: land, settlement and society in southeast Ireland, c.1600–1850* (Dublin, 1979). **195** A modern version of Lythe's map is in *Atlas of Irish rural landscape*, p. 260. **196** A. Horner, 'Retrieving the landscapes of eighteenth-century Co. Kildare: the 1755–60 maps of John Rocque', *Archaeology Ireland*, 31:2 (2017), pp 19–23. **197** K. Whelan, 'The modern landscape: from Plantation to present' in *Atlas of Irish rural landscape*, pp 73–103. **198** In his play, *The dreaming of the bones* (1919).

quicksetted when the commonage was divided in the 1670s and the estate village of Maynooth replaced the abandoned village at the demesne core.[199] Rathmore (Co. Meath) had a motte, a towerhouse, and a fifteenth-century church sponsored by the Plunketts. After the Cromwellian Blighs took over, the village was deserted, and a 1767 estate map depicted a demesne landscape incorporating the abandoned features.[200] Irish demesnes often incorporated lost villages as at Dunsany, Dowth, Loughcrew[201] and Newtown Platten (Co. Meath), Strokestown (Co. Roscommon)[202] and Tintern (Co. Wexford).

This phase of decline, desertion and loss was especially evident in the midlands (a triangle linking counties Meath, Roscommon and Tipperary), the zone most affected by pastoralization and its concomitants – privatization, population movements and the narrowing of the social spectrum to a binary of graziers and herdsmen. Two zones of middle Ireland were most affected by these changes. The first ran from mid-Kilkenny through south Tipperary to Limerick. There are 100 deserted sites in Co. Tipperary alone.[203] The second zone sprawled across the north midlands from Louth to Roscommon.

While towerhouses surrounded by cabin clusters were still the hub of settlements in the Down and Civil Surveys, the Cromwellian onslaught forced their disintegration. Spectral villages haunt many demesnes, with the diagnostic remnants of forsaken parish church and castle. In contrast to their European equivalents, the gaunt carcasses of church and castle are now all that remains of dismembered Irish villages. The cabins, built of dissolveable organic materials like mud and thatch, faded quickly into invisibility. Irish deserted sites belong to the traumatic seventeenth century, not to the late medieval period as in England. This unravelled fabric struck contemporary observers like Luke Gernon (1580–1672) in 1620:

> When I look about I cannot but bewayle the desolation which cyvill rebellion hath procured. It lookes like the latter end of a feast. Here lyeth an old ruyned castle like the remaynder of a venyson pasty, there a broken forte like a minced py [pie] half subiected, and in another

199 Horner, 'Through the fractured lens of the Civil Survey', p. 235. **200** S. Rheinisch, 'Uncovering an Anglo-Norman manor and deserted medieval village', *Archaeology Ireland*, 27:3 (2013), pp 32–5. **201** In the bone-dry summer of 2018, the outlines of the long-lost old house could be traced in the abandoned village at Loughcrew (*Irish Times*, 6 Aug. 2018). **202** *OS letters, Roscommon*, p. 134. The village was moved out of Beál na mBuille (Strokestown) demesne to Lisroyne townland. The old church was converted to a mauseoleum for the Mahon family in 1686. 'Under this monument lie the bodies of Captain Nicholas Mahon of Strokestown who dyed the 10th of October 1680 in the 60th year of his age and of his dearly beloved wife Magdalen Mahon alias French who dyed the 13th of March 1683 in the 50th year of her age in whose memories their eldest son John Mahon of Strokestown esq caused this monument to be erected Anno Domi. 1686'. **203** I. Leister, *Peasant openfield farming and its territorial organization in County Tipperary* (Marburg, 1976).

place an old abbey with some turrets standing like the carcase of a goose broken up.[204]

The Reformation discontinuity etched itself into the Irish countryside. The older parish centres became ivy-engulfed ruins, where the graveyard endured as the only living force.[205] Protestant landlords promoted what they regarded as the tightly bound conjunction of English civility and Protestantism by developing exemplary new settlements as the centrepiece of their estates. In 1733, Henry Maule (*ob.*1758), bishop of Cork, Cloyne and Ross, contrasted the 'fair little Protestant village composed of a church, an English school and a house for a Protestant clergyman' with a Catholic landscape of 'miserable huts and cottages and a mass house'.[206] Such conceptions were inscribed into the contested ground of Ireland. A century later, the political scientist Alexis de Tocqueville (1805–59) homed in on the same contrast in Co. Galway: 'At the top of the hill, the hovels of the village [clachan] and the little home of the priest were on one side. On the other were the mansion, the demesne, and the smoke, rising above the trees that surround the house of the minister'.[207] The poet Austin Clarke (1896–1974) later gave this memorable expression: 'The house of the planter is known by the trees'.

204 C.L. Falkiner (ed.), *Illustrations of Irish history and topography mainly of the seventeenth century* (London, 1904), pp 355–6. 205 E. Costello, 'Medieval memories and the reformation of religious identity: Catholic and Anglican interactions with parish church sites in County Limerick, Ireland', *Post-Medieval Archaeology*, 51:2 (2017), pp 332–53. 206 D. Dickson, *Old world colony: Cork and south Munster, 1630–1830* (Cork, 2005), p. 212. 207 *Alexis de Tocqueville's journey to Ireland, 1835*, ed. E. Larkin (Dublin, 1990), pp 128–9.

CHAPTER FOUR

Death in the Irish Landscape

POST-MEDIEVAL GRAVEYARDS

GRAVEYARDS TEEMING WITH SEDIMENTED LIFE remain among the most ubiquitous and least regarded elements in the Irish settlement pattern. There are remarkably scanty treatments of them aside from recording gravestones primarily for genealogical purposes. Very few areas even have preliminary listing of graveyards.[1] This continuity of burial requires to be explored and understood. In the medieval period, the *communio sanctorum* had bound together tightly the dead and the living, time and eternity. By transforming death into a starkly individual reckoning with a predestined doom or salvation, 'Protestantism stripped religion of mediation and intimacy with the dead' and desacralized the graveyard.[2] Calvinists barred burial in the church: the 1609 Melville mausoleum in Collessie (Fife, Scotland) exhorted: 'Defyle not Christ's kirk with your carrion'. The most Calvinist of the Dublin churches, Saint Werburgh's, did not permit church burial in the early seventeenth century, as indicated by the absence of wall memorials.[3] All Irish Quaker headstones were designed to be exactly the same, an egalitarian pattern that remained unbroken until 1860.[4]

The extravagant Catholic lamentations at funerals disgusted reformers. In Waterford in 1552, Bale complained that: 'Then wayled they over the dead with prodygouse howlyings and pateryings [pater-noster/our father], as th[o]ugh their sowles had not been quyeted in Christe'.[5] Two centuries later in 1784, the German Kurt Küttner (1755–98) while tutoring at Curraghmore (Co. Waterford) noted that only Catholics keened their dead and that 'respectable [i.e., Protestant] people

---

1 'List of old churches and graveyards Tuam and Annaghdown' in H.T. Knox, *Notes on the early history of the dioceses of Tuam, Killala and Achonry* (Dublin, 1904), pp 228–42: D. Corry, 'Ancient church sites and graveyards in County Fermanagh', *JRSAI*, 9 (1919), pp 35–46; 10 (1920), p. 183. 2 C. Eire, *Reformations: the early modern world, 1450–1650* (New Haven, 2016), p. 754. 3 R. Loeber, 'Sculptured memorials to the dead in early seventeenth-century Ireland: a survey from Monumenta Eblanae and other sources', *PRIA*, 81, C (1981), pp 267–93. 4 AAI, iv, p. 321. 5 Happe & King (eds), *Vocacyon of Johan Bale*, p. 104.

bury their dead in silence usually in the very early morning, and send only their servants to accompany the corpse'.[6]

The English antiquarian Thomas Dingley (*ob.*1685) in 1681 lamented that Protestant contempt for funerals had lowered their tone in Ireland:

> So that dayly not onely there but here nobles and gentry of eminent condicion & offices are either secretly convey'd to their sepulture in the dark, or with the light as it were of a dark lanthorne or niggardly buried in the day time, scutcheon'd by some daubing countrey painter, without the attendance of any Officer of Arms, whose dependance formerly used to be upon the performance of funeral rites and exequies (and the sordid opinion in some people already that tombs and monuments with epitaphs relish of Roman superstition and Popery, having most sacrilegiously pict out, eraz'd, and stol'n away, for the metal's sake, most of the inscripcons, epitaphs, arms, pedigrees, & history of families upon the goodly tombes of our worthy ancestors).[7]

The Reformed church transformed graveyards through the sanctioning of individual designated family plots belonging to the deceased and their family in perpetuity. In Ireland, this innovation occurred earliest in the areas of seventeenth-century Scottish settlement.[8]

The effort by Protestants to control Catholic burial services was resented. In 1608, the Court of Castle Chamber heard a case brought by Thomas Meredythe, Church of Ireland clergyman of Balrothery (Co. Dublin), against James Barnewall of Turvey House, the leading local Catholic family. He had intruded himself at the burial of Barnewall's mother (presumably at Lusk, their ancestral burial ground) but the Barnewalls 'having resolved to bury the said corpse after a superstitious and idolatrous fashion' entered the church, pulled his beard, struck him in the face, knocked the Book of Common Prayer from his hand and trod it 'disdainfully' under foot.[9] James Barnewall and some of his comrades were heavily fined and jailed. Presumably the Barnewalls as Pale lords considered Meredythe as a trifling insignificant little blow-in upstart.

6 Cited in E. Bourke, *'Poor green Erin': German travel writers' narratives on Ireland* (Frankfurt, 2011), p. 42. 7 E.P. Shirley (ed.), 'Extracts from the journals of Thomas Dineley [Dingley] Esquire giving some account of his visit to Ireland in the reign of Charles II', *JRSAI*, 5 (1858–9), pp 30–1. 8 F. McCormick, 'Reformation, privatization and the rise of the headstone' in A. Horning, R. Ó Baoill, C. Donnelly & P. Logue (eds), *The post-medieval archaeology of Ireland, 1150–1850* (Bray, 2007), pp 355–70; H. Mytum, 'Popular attitudes to memory, the body and social identity: the rise of external commemoration in Britain, Ireland and New England', *Post-Medieval Archaeology*, 40:1 (2006), pp 96–110. 9 HMC, *Egmont*, i, p. 33. Barnaby Rich commented on this fracas (Rich, *New description of Ireland*, p. 317). The Barnewalls of Turvey (Donabate) had sheltered the English recusant Edmund Campion in 1571, and their relative Sir Patrick Barnewall of Trimleston had been jailed as a recusant in 1606–7 (Lennon, *Lords of Dublin*, pp 142–3).

If Dissent placed less emphasis on the theology of death, Catholics hyper-sacralized it, doubling-down on the dogma, rituals and institutional practices rejected by the Reformation. In Ireland, burial in the older sites outlasted formal ecclesiastical use, the mediation of the saints in connecting the dead and the living was emphasized, especially that of the three great Irish saints, Patrick, Brigid and Colmcille, who were upgraded in the aftermath of the Reformation.[10] Ostentatiously ornate Catholic tombs emerged in the late sixteenth/early seventeenth century, precisely in the region that became the Catholic heartland for the following three centuries, with a concentration in Kilkenny, Tipperary and Waterford. Marmaduke Middleton (*ob.*1593), bishop of Waterford and Lismore, was infuriated in 1580 by the prevalence of Catholic funeral rituals: 'ringing of bells and praying for the dead, and dressing their graves divers times in the year with flower pots and wax candles'.[11] Bishop John Rider (1562–1632) in Killaloe complained in 1622:

> There are divers abbies or monasteries dissolved in my dioces, wherein yet ye people do bury theyr dead out of ye ordinary place of christian buriall to ye contempt of religion and maintenance of theyr superstition. And besides that, to these places many friars and priests doe ordinarily resort and sometimes in ye yeare a great concourse of people publikely: as in ye abby of Quin in ye county of Clare: and abby of Inshinameoh [Inis na mBeo, Monaincha] in ye county of Tipperary: and in Inishgealtragh [Inis Cealtra] or ye Band of Seven Altars [Clonmacnoise] standing in ye midst of ye river of Shanan bordering on ye county of Galway.[12]

His clergy's noses were equally out of joint that these burials avoided parochical charges: 'so many burialls are used in abbies, monasteries, old chappells and places where rectories and vicarages are both imppriat [impropriate], whereby they are defrauded of theyr duties due to them in such cases'.[13]

Irish Catholics resented any disruptive presence in their ancestral communal graveyards. Plumptre commented in 1814 on the tenacity with which Catholics clung to their burial sites:

> The attachment of the Irish Catholics to particular places of interment has been noticed: they are so tenacious of these spots that they will not on any account suffer a stranger to be intruded into them. If the thing is attempted, they will even take the coffin up, carry it to a proper distance from the sacred ground, and there leave it exposed.[14]

10 T. Massingham, *Florilegum insulae sanctorum seu, vitae et acta sanctorum Hiberniae* (Paris, 1624). Luke Wadding (1588–1657), highly regarded in the Vatican, masterminded this elevation.   11 Brady (ed.), *State Papers concerning the Irish church*, p. 40. The bishop excoriated the 'stiff-necked, stubborn, papistical and incorrigible people of the city of Waterford' (p. 41).   12 Dwyer, *Diocese of Killaloe*, p. 142.   13 Dwyer, *Diocese of Killaloe*, p. 142.   14 Plumptre, *Tour*, pp 455–6.

Edmund Sexton, Anglican mayor of Limerick city between 1606 and 1623, described how his grandfather's corpse was disinterred and strung up by the heels above St Mary's Cathedral.[15] Protestant corpses were ejected from churches that once were Catholic, with episodes spiking in Ulster in 1641. In Enniskillen (Co. Fermanagh), rebels exhumed the recently interred archdeacon of Killaloe.[16] In Limerick, the Protestant bishop was dug up a few days after his burial in Munchin's church.[17] In Clonmel (Co. Tipperary), the corpses of 'English and Protestants buryed in the church and church yard', were cast 'into a ditch', following which the Catholics 'newe consecrated their church againe'.[18]

Disinterrment was not just a Catholic phenomenon. The rector Revd John Kearney (*ob.*1771) of Loughgilly (Co. Armagh) was livid that his fees had not been paid when a Presbyterian was buried in 'his' churchyard and 'ordered the dead body to be taken up': 'it lay above the ground until it putrified and became very offensive in so much that it occasioned the people to rise in a mass: they reinterred the corpse and drove the doctor from the parish'.[19] At Monamolin (Co. Wexford), the body of James Redmond (executed for the murder of Revd Robert Burrowes, the Protestant clergyman at Kyle), was exhumed from its grave on 3 August 1801 and propped up on the scalán (or temporary shelter) on the site of the incinerated chapel, so that Catholics attending Mass the following morning could not avoid this gruesome spectacle.[20]

In 1828, the corpse of David Burke, a Protestant and Orangeman (master of Drumnan Orange Lodge, Co. Antrim), was disinterred and hung from a pine tree at Drumswords churchyard (Co. Fermanagh). The incident occurred during disturbances between Orangemen and Ribbonmen in the Clones area.[21] Philip Duffy of Drumenan (Killevan, Co. Monaghan) identified twenty locals responsible for 'raising of David Burk out of his silent grave and hanging him to a tree exposed to publick view for malises porpase' [malicious purposes], and 'rob[bing] him of his dead cloth[e]s'.[22]

15 C. Lennon 'The shaping of a lay community in the Church of Ireland, 1558–1640' in R. Gillespie & W. Neely, *The laity and the Church of Ireland, 1000–2000: all sorts and conditions* (Dublin, 2002), p. 64. 16 Deposition of Riccard Bourk, TCD, MS 835, ff 238–9. 17 Deposition of Ursula Lory, TCD, MS 829, f. 180; Deposition of Michael Swainton, TCD, MS 829, ff 381–2. 18 Deposition of Hugh Croker, TCD, MS 820, f. 56. 19 Bingley, *Discontents in Ireland*, p. 14. 20 E. Hay, *History of the insurrection of the County of Wexford, AD 1798* (Dublin, 1803), p. 301. 21 CSO/RP/OR/1828/111. 22 CSO/RP/1829/27. Duffy, who had served in the Royal Navy, was willing to testify against these men but sought a position in the constabulary for so doing (CSO/RP/1828/1200).

CILLÍNI AND LEACHTÁI

Cillíni proliferated with the renewed emphasis on Purgatory.[23] Bishop Richard Pococke (1704–65), a proto-anthropologist, provided one of the earliest references in 1752: 'They have a way in this country of burying children in some little plot near the house, when they are at a distance from the church, and such a burial place I saw'.[24] There are currently 1,444 known cillíni, of which 954 are in Counties Kerry, Galway and Mayo, a distribution that is pronouncedly western. Cillíni belong to the early modern period, and faded after new burial regulations were imposed in 1863. Their post-Reformation dating and western distribution were influenced by Franciscan teaching, emphasizing the Catholic Reformation theology of unbaptized children. The sixteen excavated sites are all post-medieval in date, containing graves outlined with small stones around their edges, wooden coffins, and the presence of quartz pebbles. At Tonybaun (Co. Mayo), there were 248 burials while Carrowkeel (Co. Galway) yielded 158 burials.[25] Infanticide was common in the west, according to one informed if hostile observer.[26]

The west of Ireland was festooned with leachtaí (wayside cairns).[27] They generally marked the precise spot where a person had died suddenly through an accident or violence – they were not grave markers. 'It is the custom in this part of Ireland to raise a heap of stones not only where a person was killed or fell suddenly dead but also on every spot where they lay down a corpse when carrying it to the churchyard'.[28] Passerbys added a stone to the leacht, and said a traditional prayer, as at Tuosist (Co. Kerry):

Mo chloch sa leacht	My stone on the leacht
agus mh'fhleasc im dheárnain,	and my wreath in my hand
Beannacht dhílis Dé	Special blessing of God

---

23 S. Ó Súilleabháin, 'Adhlacadh leanbhaí', *JRSAI*, 69:3 (1938), pp 143–51; A. O'Connor, *Child murderess and dead child traditions* (Helsinki, 1991); E. Dennehy, 'Children's burial grounds', *Archaeology Ireland*, 15:1 (2001), pp 20–3; E. Dennehy, 'Dorchada gan phian: the history of ceallúnach in Co. Kerry', *Kerry Archaeological & Historical Society Journal*, 2 (2003), pp 5–21; N. Finlay, 'Outside of life: traditions of infant burial in Ireland from cillíní to cist', *World Archaeology*, 31:3 (2000), pp 407–22; C. Donnelly & E. Murphy, 'The origins of cillíní in Ireland' in E. Murphy (ed.), *Deviant burial in the archaeological record* (Oxford, 2008), pp 191–222.   **24** Pococke, *Tour*, p. 95 [CELT].   **25** J. Nolan, 'Excavation of a children's burial ground at Tonybaun, Ballina, Co. Mayo' in J. O'Sullivan & M. Stanley (eds), *Settlement, industry and ritual* (Bray, 2006), pp 89–101; S. Lalonde & A. Tourunen, 'Investigating social change through the animal and human remains from Carrowkeel, east Galway', *Archaeology Ireland*, 21:4 (2007), pp 36–8.   **26** Otway, *Tour in Connaught*, p. 354.   **27** M. Mac Néill, 'Wayside death cairns in Ireland', *Béaloideas*, 15 (1946), pp 49–63; M. ac Cordhuibh, 'Ros Dumhach Erris [Kilcummin (Co. Mayo)]: leachtaí cloch', *Béaloideas*, 16 (1946), pp 64–71; T. Robinson, *Mementos of mortality: cenotaphs and funerary cairns of Árainn* (Roundstone, 1991).   **28** *OS letters, Mayo*, p. 72.

le h-anam m'athar is mo mháthar
Agus go spesialta le h-anam
an té cailleadh san áit seo.[29]

on the souls of my father and mother
Especially for the soul of the person
who died in this place.

The leachtaí could function as a resting place for a coffin, at a time when coffins had to be carried over long distances by pedestrians on shoulder-mounted 'bearers' to ancestral graveyards (the bearers were broken in the graveyard). A *c*.1760 painting of Devenish (Co. Fermanagh) clearly depicted this mode of carrying the coffin to the grave.[30] Coffins were carried on bearers for as much as six miles, and it was traditional to take the longest route possible. Walking funerals were only displaced by horse-drawn hearses in the early twentieth century.[31] Coquebert De Montbret (1755–1831), a careful observer, noted at Rathass (Co. Kerry) that coffins were borne by four men, often over long distances, because each family had its own burial place: carrying the coffin 'is a service of the poor to the poor'.[32] The pauses while the coffin carriers rested created an obvious time for keening to occur. An example is at Ard Chianáin (Ardkeenan, Co. Roscommon): O'Conor Don funerals wending their way to Clonmacnoise marked this spot with keening because the ancient monastic site first hove into view there.[33] Similarly, Tisara (Co. Roscommon) was anglicized from Teach Srathara (the house of the straddle). It derived its name because corpses were waked here for one night, while being carried on biers between two horses from Uí Mhaine (Hy Many) to Clonmacnoise to be interred.[34]

The tradition of leachtaí was recorded by Dunton in 1698, by Molyneux in 1709 and by Pococke in 1752:[35] 'They have a custom of raising heaps of stones called here laktch, in other parts *cairns*, to the memory of the dead, mostly in the shape of sugar loaves,[36] which are kept up as long as their friends remain, and are raised commonly not far from the church, in the way to and from the house; some are built with mortar and have inscriptions on them'.[37] Near Cong (Co. Mayo), there were prominent leachtaí in the townland of Creggaree. A

---

29 Cited in Mac Néill, 'Wayside death cairns', p. 53. 30 This painting is still in Florence Court (Co. Fermanagh); reproduced in A. Crookshank & Knight of Glin, *Ireland's painters, 1600–1940* (New Haven, 2002), p. 46. 31 A. Ridge, *Death customs in rural Ireland: traditional funerary rites in the Irish midlands* (Galway, 2009), pp 106–7. 32 [De Montbret], 'A new view of eighteenth-century life in Kerry, ed. S. Ní Chinnéide', *Kerry Archaeological & Historical Society Journal*, 6 (1973), p. 93. 33 Ridge, *Death customs in rural Ireland*, p. 114. 34 *OS letters, Roscommon*, p. 8. 35 Dunton in E. MacLysaght, *Irish life in the seventeenth century* (Cork, 1939), p. 326; Molyneux in 1709 observed: 'All along, as we travell'd thro' ye county of Gallway, I observ'd a very great number of heaps of stones rais'd into a piramide, some with lime, generally without, along the road, in memory, as I am told of burialls that have pass'd that way' ('Molyneux tour', p. 42). 36 Refined sugar was sold in the form of a **sugarloaf** (a tall cone with a rounded top) until the late nineteenth century, when granulated and cube sugars were introduced. Ironically, the Sugarloaf mountain (Co. Wicklow) is not the proper shape of an actual sugarloaf. 37 Pococke, *Tour*, p. 94 [CELT].

1712 specimen was dedicated to John and Mary Joyce, another one was called 'Leacht Mháire Óg', and the rest were nameless, 'though each family recognize and name their own after the person for which they erected them'.[38] An 1855 description described these same leachtaí:

> Another strange superstition of the good people of this neighbourhood is connected with a rocky piece of ground near the westward road leading to Bealnabrack and Cornamona. This is chosen for some reason as a locality suited for the erection of cenotaphs, or cairns on a small scale, consisting of pyramidal heaps of stones, of which a considerable number may be noticed. These belong to the different families of the district, and when a funeral passes, a stone is added to the funereal heap of that particular family. They keep count in the families of the number of stones, and when one of these slip off the pile, a soul is supposed to be released out of purgatory.[39]

The Scottish traveller Mary Anne Grant commented in 1804:

> We passed one of those pyramids of stones, which superstition places to commemorate a murder committed on that particular spot; they do not form a regular building, but are merely thrown together in a heap, by travellers; it is considered the indispensable duty of every Roman Catholic to contribute one to the number.[40]

GRAVESTONES

Gravestones are the most ubiquitous, most clearly dated and most ignored of Irish field monuments. They evolved through variations of style. From earlier unsigned low grave markers and flat slabs, upright flat headstones bearing the name of the deceased appeared in the late seventeenth century. Only eighteen gravestones predated 1700 from a sample of 731 pre-1800 examples in thirty-seven burial grounds in north Wexford and south Wicklow.[41] The semi-circular-topped tomb followed in the 1720s. From the 1760s onwards, the innovative sculptor Dennis Cullen (*ob.*1798) of Monaseed (Co. Wexford) produced hundreds of high quality and varied memorials across north Wexford and south Wicklow, ninety-five per cent within a thirty-kilometre radius of Monaseed, stretching from Rathnew (Co. Wicklow) to Gorey (Co. Wexford).

---

38 *OS letters, Mayo*, p. 215.   39 J. E. Howard, *The island of saints or Ireland in 1855* (London, 1855), p. 45. Note the emphasis on Purgatory.   40 M. Grant, *Sketches of life and manners with delineation of scenery in England, Scotland and Ireland* (London, 1804), p. 239.   41 E. Grogan, 'Eighteenth-century headstones and the stone mason tradition in Co. Wicklow: the work of Dennis Cullen of Monaseed', *Wicklow Archaeology & History*, 1 (1998), pp 41–63.

Fig. 16 'Geata na gcoirp', Drum (Co. Mayo). An ingenious hole in the wall allowed coffin bearers to slide the coffin more easily towards the path leading to the ancient graveyard (photograph by Hubert Knox, *c*.1900) (RSAI).

Cullen, the first craftsman to sign his gravestones, excelled at crucifixion scenes in semi-relief, with confidently executed horsemen, shown in anachronistic eighteenth-century military costume, knee breeches, and pointing guns (inspired by the Volunteers?).[42] Cullen was a master of vivid details such as precise nail holes in the hands and feet. He was equally a master of three-dimensional lettering, created through skillful chisel work and (presumably) stencils, and exhibiting a remarkable command of shadows.[43] His distinctive vernacular art emerged in the 1760s, reflecting a resurgent Catholicism in the public sphere, with renewed confidence and aspirations, and featuring iconographically Catholic elements like rosary beads, even in mixed graveyards (they are absent in exclusively 'Protestant' graveyards like Abbeylands (Arklow, Co. Wicklow).[44] From the 1780s and 1790s onwards, named headstones surge.[45] Rarely used prior to 1800, townland names proliferated on tombstones in the first decades of the nineteenth century.[46]

---

42 Cullen is known to have worked with the Grogan family of Monaseed and Johnstown Castle, and he may have attended Volunteer reviews in the 1780s. According to Miles Byrne, Cullen, 'a very able sculptor, and a very enlightened man, fell a victim to the rage of his fellow yeomen when the insurrection broke out, for his being a Catholic' but this is not mentioned in the various articles on Cullen. The implication is that Cullen was a United Irishman (Byrne, *Memoirs*, i, p. 27). **43** G. Thomson, *Lettering on gravemarkers in Britain and Ireland* (Bray, 2011). **44** A.K. Longfield, *The eighteenth-century memorials by Dennis Cullen of Monaseed* ([Dublin], 1958); C. Corlett, *Here lyeth: the eighteenth-century headstones of Co. Wicklow* (Wicklow, 2015). **45** H. Mytum, 'A long and complex plot: patterns of family burials in Irish graveyards from the eighteenth century', *Church Archaeology*, 5–6 (2004), pp 31–41. **46** M. Timoney, *Had me made: a study of grave memorials of Co. Sligo from 1650 to the present* (Sligo, 2005).

THE FUNERAL

Edward Wakefield (1774–1854) was struck by the 'warmth of attachment' to traditional graveyards:

> An extraordinary veneration prevails among them for their places of burial, and persons of the poorest class frequently carry their dead to a great distance, that they may be deposited with their kindred. I have heard that many of them believe that the gates of Heaven will be shut against those whose remains are not committed to the earth of the same churchyard where the rest of their family have been laid. [47]

In 1814, the English traveller Anne Plumptre (1760–1818) saw a vast funeral of a priest heading from Sackville Street to Mulhuddard:

> An immense concourse of people, walking two-and-two, wearing white linen scarfs and hatbands, preceded and followed the hearse; after them came a long train of carriages, coaches, and chariots, and last of all an almost equally long train of jaunting cars and jingles. The priest was a man extremely beloved among his flock, and they had united to do honour to his memory by making this splendid funeral. The persons walking and riding in the procession could scarcely be less than five hundred, and a vast concourse of people besides kept company with them. The carriages were filled with persons going unbidden, merely for the sake of doing honour to their pastor; but the walkers must have been from two to three hundred. [48]

It was already a commonplace by the early nineteenth century to note that the Irish were adepts of funerals. Vast throngs customarily attended the funeral of 'an opulent farmer': 'everyone who meets the procession turns to accompany it, let his haste be ever so great, for a mile or two, as nothing is accorded more unlucky or unfriendly than to neglect doing so'. [49] An 1830s description, noting that more than 2,000 men and women could take part in funerals, captured the essence of that distinctive tradition.

> The peasantry everywhere are wonderfully eager to attend the funerals of their friends and relations, and they make their relationships branch out to a great extent. The proof that a poor man has been well beloved during his life is his having a crowded funeral. Even the poorest people have their own burying places, that is spots of ground in the churchyards,

---

47 E. Wakefield, *An account of Ireland statistical and political*, 2 vols (London, 1812), i, p. 807. 48 A. Plumptre, *Narrative of a residence in Ireland during the summer of 1814 and that of 1815* (London, 1817), p. 54. 49 T. Crofton Croker, *Researches in the south of Ireland* (London, 1824), pp 171–3.

which are situated sometimes in the wildest parts of the mountains, their situation indicated by some remnant of a ruin, and a few scattered tombstones and the low green hillocks of the graves. Here, they say, their ancestors have been buried ever since the wars of Ireland; and, though these burial places should be many miles from the place where a man dies, his friends and neighbours take care to carry his corpse thither.[50]

A 1754 description from the Rosses (Co. Donegal) describes a curragh funeral flotilla:

> Wrapped in a coarse woollen cloth called by them ebed [aibíd, a shroud], the corpse was put into a curragh, the feet and legs hanging over the stern, and (with it) a man with a paddle to conduct the whole train to the isle of Aran [Aranmore], where their burial ground was: this curragh was followed by that which carried the priest; next him went the relations of the deceased in the order of their proximity in kindred; and then as many as had curraghs and of these Mr N.... saw sixy or eighty in a train.[51]

In 1768, the American Quaker Samuel Fisher observed a funeral in Clonmel (Co. Tipperary):

> A coffin covered with black cloth is brought out and laid upon a carr in the middle of the street, where the men with white handkerchiefs in their hats and the women with the same tyed about their heads stand making a dismall halloo for some time. When they move, they continue their noise to the place of internment, more like a mob than anything else.[52]

Fights over funerals were not uncommon, especially over the burials of wives: a 'bloody battle' erupted in Kilkenny city in 1774:

> The place of internment was the scene of contention. The Muintiree,[53] that is to say the kindred and friends of the deceased woman, on both her mother's and father's side, stopped short at a certain spot which led to their respective places of burial. One party cried out and contended that the corpse should be brought this way; the other party insisted to the contrary and to it they fell with shillelaghs in hand with as much eagerness, violence and asperity as the Irish clans in days of yore fought

---

50 'The Irish funeral cry: the ullaloo, keeners and keening', *Dublin Penny Journal*, 26 Jan. 1833, p. 243.   **51** 'An account of the customs, manners and dress of the inhabitants of the Rosses on the coast of the County of Donegal', J.C. Walker, *An historical essay on the dress of the ancient and modern Irish* (Dublin, 1778), p. 148.   **52** Samuel Rowland Fisher, Philadelphia, Historical Society of Pennsylvania, MS 2019.   **53** 'Muintiree' most likely represents muinteartha (belonging to a household or community; associated, familiar), a substantive form of muintir (kinfolk, household, community).

the quarrels of their respective lords. A great deal of blood was spilled before the mayor ended this bloody quarrel.[54]

The Hamburgh merchant and expert on poverty Caspar Voght (1752–1839) reported a row at Innisfallen (Co. Kerry) in 1794:

> Der mann war aus einer der alten grossen Irländischen familien, die in den ehemaligen unruhen alle ihre güter verlohren haben, hier aber unter dem volke sehr geachtet werden. Einige seiner wohlhabenden verwandten wollten nicht erlauben, daß er hier begraben werden solle, weil er arm war. Darüber entstand ein sehr lebhafter streit, von dem wir nichts verstehen konnten, weil er in der Irländischen sprache, die hier durchgängig gesprochen wird, geführt wird. Je unglüklicher der mensch lebt, desto wichtiger wird ihm das sterben; da tröstet ihn der gedanke, daß er wenigstens hier wieder in gleiche Rechte mit seinem unterdrüker tritt, und hoft [auf] eine zeit wo die lage sich umkehren wird.[55]

However, there was a sectarian and political dimension as well. In 1732, John Loveday observed a Catholic funeral at Golden (Co. Tipperary): 'in ye morning their priest comes, & performs some ceremonies, & then they carry ye dead to its grave, ye priest attending to ye churchyard gate'.[56] 'Whilst we were in ye churchyard, a child was attended to its grave with ye Irish howl; it surpris'd us to see it put in ye ground & cover'd up, without any burial service, ye company returning home; upon enquiry, it was ye child of a Catholic, & ye Protestant service is never read over them in this Kingdom'.[57] Catholic priests were prohibited from entering the graveyard, as Coquebert De Montbret noted at Rathass (Co. Kerry) in 1791: 'no prayers are allowed to be said by the priest in the cemetery itself'.[58] Instead the priest blessed clay at the wake house and it was this 'cré na cille' (graveyard clay) that was subsequently cast by the bereaved family onto the coffin once it was lowered into the grave.[59] Catholics also had to pay a fee to the Protestant clergyman for burial, and this was 'due to [the] minister irrespective of where buried in the parish'.[60] In Limerick city in 1700,

---

54 *FLJ*, 6–9 Apr. 1774.   55 'A corpse was brought here according to the custom of the country, with great shouting and howling. The man was from one of the old great Irish families who lived in the area, having been deprived of all their estates, but who are still greatly respected among the people. Some of his wealthy relatives would not allow him to be buried here because he was poor. This gave rise to a very lively dispute, of which we could understand nothing, because it was conducted in the Irish language, which is spoken here. The more unhappily a man lives, the more important is his death. The thought of having at least the same rights with his oppressor comforts him, and suggests a time when their situations will be reversed'. C. Voght, 'Schilderung von Irland, bruchstücke aus dem tagebuche eines reisenden im herbst 1794' in *Der genius der zeit*, 8 (1796) pp 566–653 [quotation at p. 607] [CELT].   56 Loveday, *Diary of a tour*, p. 44.   57 Loveday, *Diary of a tour*, p. 44   58 [De Montbret], 'Kerry', p. 92.   59 Ridge, *Death customs in rural Ireland*, p. 93.   60 A. Browne, *A compendious view of the ecclesiastical law of Ireland* (Dublin, 1803), p. 89.

13*s.* 4*d.* was claimed for each burial in the chancel, 7*s.* 6*d.* in 'the body of ye church' and 3*s.* 6*d.* 'in ye churchyard', of which 4*d.* was due to the sexton.[61]

A busy graveyard was a revenue earner, a principal reason why Catholic burials were tolerated in the old cemeteries. These attracted thousands of burials over the centuries. In 1797, there was 'hardly earth enough to cover the dead' in Muckross Abbey (Co. Kerry).[62] In Kinsale (Co. Cork), St Multose's Church was full of burials.[63] In 1858, when 'the aisle of the church was excavated to a depth of about four feet, the entire area beneath was a series of stone cists, containing skeletons (all the remains were swept out)'.[64] Kilcrea Abbey (Co. Cork) was packed cramful of graves.[65] The profusion of burials in ancient graveyards testify to the transmission of burial rights tenaciously asserted across many generations by local families.[66] From Co. Clare, Westropp noted that the 'horrible habit of digging out all the contents of the grave' resulted in the piling up of skulls, bones and coffins in ancient graveyards with traditions of continuous burial (Quin, Killone, Dromcreehy, Kilmacrehy, Doora, Tomfinlough):

> A consequence of this fearful overcrowding is that no old graveyard is free from coffin planks and plates, bones, and fragmentary or whole skulls. Those who saw Quin 'Abbey' before 1879 will remember the enormous heap of skulls (even then, however, much diminished), heaped round a tree near the graveyard gate. At Tomfinlough the bones and skulls were neatly stacked in a recess, at Kilmacreehy they were heaped on a sort of side altar in the chancel, and in other churches (Coad etc.) I have seen single skulls staring out of holes in the wall.[67]

These multiple burials built up the ground surface in the graveyards: a step down is often required into an old church, as at Corcomroe (Co. Clare), the suitable setting 'among great rocks on the scarce grass' and the 'haunted stones' for Yeats's great play *The dreaming of the bones* (1919). A rule of thumb is that the bigger the height differential inside and outside the cemetery walls, the

---

61 R. Wyse Jackson, 'Lewis Prytherch's manuscript', *NMAJ*, 4 (1945), pp 143–51 [quotation at p. 148]. 62 [De La Tocnaye], *Frenchman's walk through Ireland, 1796–7*, pp 101–2. 63 J. Lindsey Darling, 'St Multose's Church, Kinsale', *JCHAS*, 2 (1893), p. 74. 64 R. Day, 'The ancient and present state of the county and city of Cork', *JCHAS*, 1 (1892), p. 230. 65 R. Cochrane, 'Notes on the structures in the County of Cork vested in the Board of Works for preservation as ancient monuments', *JCHAS*, 18 (1912), pp 60–2. 66 See the chaotically crowded plan of burials there by R. Cochrane, 'Kilcrea Franciscan friary, County Cork', *JCHAS*, 18 (1912), p. 58. 67 T.J. Westropp, *A folklore survey of County Clare*, website of Clare County Library. **Westropp** (1860–1922), conducting his extensive survey of the field monuments of Clare, became fascinated by, and started collecting, popular history. Between 1910 and 1913, he published thirteen articles in *Folk-Lore: Transactions of the Folk-Lore Society*, which are conveniently assembled on the website.

older the burial site. And while choosing a representative sample is obviously subjective, a defining characteristic of the Irish landscape is atmospheric graveyards, as at St Mullins (Co. Carlow), Ardmore (Co. Waterford), Aghowle and Glendalough (Co. Wicklow), Monasterboice (Co. Louth), Kilsheelan (Co. Tipperary), Derrynane (Co. Kerry), Knockbreda (Co. Down), Slane (Co. Meath) and Omey island (Co. Galway).

THE POLITICS OF FUNERALS

Catholics had very long memories of injustices perpetrated on them, and could wait in the long grass. Four years after Fr Nicholas Sheehy (1728–66) had been judicially murdered, a man was scheduled to be executed for murder at Philipstown (modern Birr, Co. Offaly):

> During the execution the mob (which was very great) were remarkably quiet but as soon as it was over they stoned the hangman to death and the body lay for two or three days under the gallows. This unfortunate creature was the person who hung Sheehy the priest.[68]

The Convention Act of 6 November 1796 declared public gatherings, including funerals, illegal, 'in consequence of the disaffected having adopted a practice of marching in military array and assembling in large bodies, in some instances to the number of several thousands ... under various pretences such as funerals, football meetings etc with a view of displaying their strength, giving the people the habit of assembly from great distances'.[69] The 1790s saw the development of the republican funeral. Closely modelled on classical precedent, and building on the Volunteer paramilitary funeral, a republican genre of public death ritual emerged in the 1790s. This was secular; it emphasized merit rather than birth and it fused the exemplary greatness of the republican hero with his representativeness of the wider community.[70] The carefully choreographed funeral of the Presbyterian martyr William Orr (1766–97) at Templepatrick (Co. Antrim) in 1797 was the finest but by no means the only example of such a republican event in the 1790s. In the 1790s, the older eighteenth-century 'gallows speech' mutated into an explicitly political form.[71] The informer

---

68 *Sleator's Public Gazetteer*, 18 Sept. 1770.   **69** *Report from Committee of Secrecy of the House of Commons of Ireland* (London, 1798), p. 6.   **70** A. Ben-Amos, *Funerals, politics and memory in modern France, 1789–1996* (Oxford, 2000).   **71** These political versions are inexplicably excluded from J. Kelly, *Gallows speeches from eighteenth-century Ireland* (Dublin, 2001). It is precisely this innovation that distinguished the Irish versions from the British genre and which also became the precursor to the 'Speeches from the Dock' versions of the nineteenth century.

Leonard McNally (1752–1820) noted in May 1798 that the 'great severity' of the military created:

> sullen, silent rancour, and revenge will be a consequence. It would astonish you to hear the vindictive language and bitter curses of the carmen on the subject. Executions are now considered martyrdoms and when the procession for an execution commences, those within doors to whose knowledge it comes go to prayers.[72]

Wexford magistrates 'unanimously agreed' to request that the body of the slain rebel James Corcoran (*c.*1770–1804) should ideally be hung 'in chains as a public spectacle': alternatively, he should be 'interred in the gaol yard' as 'it would be highly injurious to the public tranquillity to have his body delivered to his friends'. Dublin Castle ordered that Corcoran be interred in the usual way 'for convicted malefactors in the most private manner'.[73]

In 1819, John Carson (sub-sheriff of Co. Roscommon) reported an escape attempt in which John Standish (the deputy gaoler) had been murdered by Patrick O'Hara and John Burncan, two prisoners sentenced to death. He sought government permission that their bodies should be buried at the gaol following their execution, because of his 'apprehension of something serious happening at the wakes and funerals of these men as they have an immensity of friends and connexions in the county who have threatened to bring the dead bodies to the houses of the prosecutors'.[74]

In 1821, at Rathkeale (Co. Limerick), two insurgents involved in a clash with police were killed. They were hastily 'buried on a common near the police barracks & quick lime thrown upon them'.[75] Major Richard Going, the local magistrate who had ordered this burial in a 'croppy hole', was assassinated in October 1821 and threatening letters soon predicted that the same fate awaited others who proposed similar disrespectful burials: 'Captain Rock' warned Leake, another Limerick magistrate, that he would use 'the same restrictions with you as you have done so inhumanely and unchristianly ordered into a croppy hole in the manner of Rathkeale & and for so doing you may be sure of sharing the same fate of your comrade Major Going'.[76] By contrast, 'Matilda, a female loyalist' from the same town, urged quick executions: then, 'stick their heads in public places as examples, while their bodies are consuming with quick lime in the croppies hole'.[77] James Connery of Ballyduff (Co. Kerry) complained in 1823 at the hesitation of police magistrate Major Samson Carter in acting on two arms depots, one 'in a grave yard', and another in a coffin. Carter argued that his caution was justified,

72 NAI, Rebellion Papers, 620/10/121/155.   **73** NAI, State of the Country Papers, 1030/96; Waller (Wexford) to Chief Secretary, 13 Feb. 1804, NAI, State of the Country Papers 1030/97.   **74** CSO/RP/1819/164.   **75** CSO/RP/SC/1821/656.   **76** S. Gibbons, *Captain Rock, night errant: the threatening letters of pre-Famine Ireland, 1801–45* (Dublin, 2004), p. 110.   **77** CSO/RP/SC/1821/27.

as the arms were concealed among 'the ashes of the dead' and he wanted to avoid fomenting 'animosity'.[78] In 1825, the police in Belturbet (Co. Cavan) reported a funeral attended by a large procession of Ribbonmen 'decked with paper and green ribbon', 'dressed with white scarves' with 'white wands in their hands', and led by a standard bearer carrying a garland of green and white. The funeral march was allegedly for Conlon (a Ribbonman), whose coffin was carried from Drummully (near Belturbet) to a cemetery at Wattlebridge (Co. Fermanagh). The police suspected that the coffin 'did not contain a corpse'.[79]

Rodolphus Greene of Dungarvan, sub-sheriff of Co. Waterford, was making arrangements for the execution of William Fitzgerald on 31 March 1823, and sought advice on the disposal of his body. Henry Joy (1766–1838), Solicitor General, advised him to bury the body instantly within the county jail:

> The Crown has the right of disposing of the bodies of malefactors who have been executed. In times of disturbance it has been most frequently deemed prudent not to give up the body to the friends of the criminal as they are in the habit of having a wake at which many are sworn in & many plans formed for committing outrages & for destroying the witnesses on whose testimony the criminal was convicted.[80]

Dr Edward Trevor, supervisor of convict transportation, reported on a violent escape from the hulk *Essex* at Kingstown in 1825. Thomas Cullen, a convict convicted for trade union combination, was shot by the guards; another convict escaped by jumping overboard; a third was thought to have perished in the water. Cullen's family had requested Trevor to release the body to them. The Attorney General (W.C. Plunket, 1764–1854) instead advised that Trevor should organize that Cullen be 'quietly but decently interred' in some graveyard, the 'object of the application evidently being to have a grand procession in Dublin and to excite the combined workmen by such a procession'.[81]

FUNERAL ROWS

Other disputes emerged from mixed marriages: in 1828, a police subconstable John Gilbert was accused of assaulting Ellen Styles at the funeral of her father Edward Styles at Aghowle (Co. Wicklow).[82] Revd James McGhee, magistrate and Protestant clergyman, had ordered Gilbert to prevent the burial in 'his' churchyard, unless conducted by a Protestant clergyman using Protestant rites. McGhee claimed that Styles was a Protestant and that his eldest son wished for him to be buried accordingly, although his daughter was adamant that he died

78 CSO/RP/1823/2425.   79 CSO/RP/SC/1825/108.   80 CSO/RP/1823/559.   81 CSO/RP/1825/1310.   82 CSO/RP/OR/1828/203.

a Catholic.[83] In neighbouring Wexford in the same year, Revd Edward Bayly, rector of Horetown, withdrew from the Protestant funeral service of Thomas Cooper of Tullicanna, after he was disrupted by Catholics who attended the service. Bayly had been requested to officiate by Edward Cooper of Kilgarvan, a Protestant, and he alleged that the interference was orchestrated by the dead man's illegitimate Catholic daughter.[84]

Disputes over Catholic burials intensified dramatically in the 1820s, when Catholics became more assertive. In 1824, Revd John Edgar (curate), James Lee (church warden), and Thomas Blake (sexton) of Castlelyons parish (Co. Cork) reported an unsanctioned funeral service on church property conducted by Fr Daniel Donovan, the local Catholic curate. Donovan approached the graveside and took 'from his pocket a large ribbon or tippet [stole] which he put round his neck and down his shoulders and which hung below both his knees, at the same time, having a book in his hand out of which he read some kind of service or prayers in a language [Latin] unknown to me'.[85] In 1823, Revd Hume Lawder, rector of Devenish (Co. Fermanagh), reported a Catholic funeral in the churchyard of Monea, objecting to the priest praying and sprinkling holy water at the graveside.[86] In 1824, Revd Fitzgibbon, the rector of Saint John's in Limerick, interrupted the funeral of Captain Durack.[87] In the same year, Richard Wolfe of Forenaghts (Co. Kildare) reported the consecration of a new graveyard by James Doyle (1786–1834), the Catholic bishop of Kildare and Leighlin; 'they have left in the field four crosses and it is thought performed Mass there'.[88] In 1828, Revd James Martin of Kilmurry (Co Clare) complained that the local Catholic priest conducted a funeral rite for a deathbed convert to Catholicism to 'triumph over and insult the established religion and its ministers'.[89] In 1829, Revd Richard Hood reported Catholic funeral ceremonies involving a priest in the graveyard at Kilmacduagh (Co. Galway).[90]

Funerals in Ireland observed many protocols derived from tradition. One was the clay pipes smoked at the wake, and then broken while saying 'Lord have Mercy'. This custom was often repeated at the graveside where the broken pipes were laid on the grave. So embedded was this custom that a workshop to make them went into operation at Knockcroghery (Co. Roscommon). By 1832, eight kilns were producing up to 500 boxes of pipes per week.[91] By 1890, 57,000 pipes were manufactured weekly at the factory operated by the Curley family. The 1901 census listed sixteen people (in 1911, nine) employed in pipe making. Production terminated in 1921 when the village was burned by the Black and Tans. These pipes consistently surface in graveyards as new graves are dug.

83 CSO/RP/OR/1828/244.   84 CSO/RP/1828/1938.   85 CSO/RP/1824/132.   86 CSO/RP/1823/2054.   87 26 Feb. 1824, CSO/RP/CA/1824/10.   88 CSO/RP/1824/1516. 89 CSO/RP/1828/762.   90 CSO/RP/OR/1829/352.   91 Weld, *Roscommon*.

CATHOLIC CEMETERIES: GOLDENBRIDGE AND GLASNEVIN

An orchestrated incident in Dublin in 1823 escalated Catholic discontent. The sexton William Dunn made an affidavit concerning the recent funeral in Saint Kevin's churchyard of Arthur D'Arcy, from the Catholic mercantile family that operated the Anchor Brewery (founded by Edward Byrne on Usher Street in 1740, and acquired by Arthur in 1818), the second largest brewery after Guinness's, and purveyors of 'D'Arcy's Dublin Porter'. Arthur's brother John became lord mayor of Dublin in 1852 so the D'Arcys were a high-profile Catholic family. [92] As always there was a nasty sectarian element, as Guinness was considered a Protestant beer, and D'Arcys a Catholic one. Instructed to act by William Magee (1821–91), the newly consecrated archbishop of Dublin, Dunn 'was sorry to be obliged to interfere' to prevent the distinguished priest, Archdeacon Michael Blake (b.1775), from officiating at the graveside, because the laws 'prevent any priest from reading his prayers or performing any service in a Protestant church yard'. The archbishop considered Blake's presence as a provocative innovation: previously the priest always 'performed their funeral service before the corpse was removed from the house'. Magee, who participated robustly in contemporary politics, was severely criticized for interfering and leading Catholics warned that 'millions of them were not to be trampled on nor insulted by a few, nor would they endure it any longer'.[93]

The Catholic Association instantly ramped up its campaign on the injustice of Catholics being forced by law to pay to be buried in Protestant churchyards and the prohibition on any prayers being said. On 24 January 1824, it proposed house-to-house collections for its burial committee, which had examined and found appropriate cemetery sites 'in and near Dublin' by 7 February.[94] Fundraising would be needed.[95] On 29 January 1826, O'Connell described the Burial Bill [Burial (Ireland) Act, 1824], as 'a new penal statute' in its restriction of Catholic burial rites.[96] The Commitee sought the repeal of the law requiring Catholic priests to obtain the permission of Protestant clergymen prior to the performance of burial rites.[97] On 15 September 1827, the burial committee reported on the best means of securing burial grounds for Catholics 'without their remains being liable to insult' and noted that the new Catholic Archbishop Daniel Murray (1768–1852) of Dublin was willing to consecrate a suitable plot.[98]

The pivotal breakaway from parochial churchyards was legally facilitated by the 'Act of Easement of Burial'. In 1828, the Catholic Association purchased

92 The Dublin Brewing Company currently brews an IPA called 'D'Arcy's Dublin Beer'. 93 CSO/RP/1823/1451. 94 7 Feb. 1824, CSO/RP/CA/1824/8. 95 18 Feb. 1824, CSO/RP/CA/1824/10. 96 CSO/RP/CA/1826/15. 97 14 Jan. 1826, CSO/RP/CA/1826/2. 98 15 Sept. 1827, CSO/RP/CA/1827/12.

three acres for £600, located two miles from the city at Goldenbridge (Inchicore). Goldenbridge cemetery was consecrated in 1829, the earliest dedicated Irish Catholic cemetery.[99] It was one of the first purpose-built burial grounds, unattached to an extant place of worship. It was inspired by the informal garden style of Père-Lachaise in Paris in 1805[100] and was the first landscaped garden cemetery opened in Ireland or Britain. These new cemeteries were typically large (forty-eight hectares at Père-Lachaise) and they were designed to avoid the horrors of burial in old city graveyards, which were hemmed-in, crammed with coffins piled in a disorderly fashion on top of each other in narrow shafts and considered to be disease-ridden, given the inevitable constant displacement of older tombs. The architect George Papworth (1781–1855) exhibited a design at the Royal Hibernian Academy in 1832 for a major national cemetery in the Phoenix Park, 'to be erected for the prevention of the danger and inconvenience of burying the dead within the metropolis'.[101]

Goldenbridge had a formal layout with specimen tree and box-hedge planting. At its centre was a formal setpiece by Patrick Byrne (1783–1864), an open Ionic temple built as a mortuary chapel (1834–5).[102] Its open plan was innovative, since existing mortuary chapels were closed structures. The building faced an open-air congregation space, a low rectangular podium with large ashlar granite edge stones. The basement vault, used as a watch room to impede body snatchers, was lit by small windows in the plinth: these are now blocked as is its access stairs. Before burial, the coffin would briefly rest in the portico, while the elevated priest prayed over it from a raised podium space in the sanctuary.[103] Newly built Catholic churches around this time installed their own burial vaults, notably at the Pro-Cathedral in 1826 and St Andrew's (Westland Row) in 1834.

Goldenbridge pioneered the establishment of larger graveyards outside the city, being quickly followed by Glasnevin in 1832 and Mount Jerome (designed by George Papworth) in 1836.[104] Patrick Byrne was also the architect for

---

99 P. Thorsheim, 'The corpse in the garden: burial, health and the environment in nineteenth-century London', *Environmental History*, 16 (2011), pp 38–68. **100** J.S. Curl, *Death and architecture* (Stroud, 2002); AAI, iv, p. 325. **101** Royal Hibernian Academy Exhibition (1832), No. 254, 259 and 267. A print of No. 267 is in Irish Architectural Archive, MS 95/5. **102** L. Hurley, 'Death in the garden: Patrick Byrne's mortuary chapel at Goldenbridge Cemetery, Dublin', *Irish Architectural and Decorative Studies*, 19 (2017), pp 76–89. **103** It was closed to fresh burials in 1869. By the 1990s, it had become a derelict drug haunt. It was refurbished in 2010. **104** V. Igoe, *Dublin burial grounds and graveyards* (Dublin, 2001), p. 123; W. J. Fitzpatrick, *History of the Dublin Catholic cemeteries* (Dublin, 1900); *The Dublin Cemeteries Act, 1846 and bye-laws for the management and maintenance of the cemeteries at Golden Bridge, and Prospect, Glasnevin in the city and county of Dublin respectively and rules and regulations made in pursuance thereof: illustrated with a folding plan of the cemetery* (Dublin, 1901); J. Langtry & B. Fay, 'Mount Jerome cemetery of Dublin' in S. Carmen Giménez (ed.), *Arte y arquitectura funeraria / Arte e architettura funeraria / Funeral art and architecture XIX–XX* (Madrid, 2000), pp 106–91.

Glasnevin from 1831 to 1860, designing the entrance lodge and gates, temple, chapel, the Finglas Road gate (1845), and the O'Connell Circle.[105] J.J. McCarthy (1817–82) added the Romanesque mortuary chapel between 1872 and 1879.[106] Graveyards, surrounded by high walls surmounted by spiked railings, sought to deter body snatchers through defensive architecture. Both Goldenbridge and Glasnevin (Co. Dublin) were enclosed within high limestone walls, with entrance via an iron gateway. In 1828, the marquis of Donegall gifted an acre (which doubled its size) to the ancient and exclusively Catholic burial ground at Friar's Bush, just outside Belfast.[107] Consecrated in 1829, it was surrounded by an eight-foot high wall, with a Gothic gate lodge for the caretaker, and entered via a carriage arch. It became overcrowded as the Belfast Catholic population soared (from 4,000 in 1816 to almost 20,000 by 1837 and to over 40,000 by 1861) and it was closed to new burials in 1870 when Catholic burials were transferred to the new Milltown cemetery.[108] Timothy Hevey (1846–78) was commissioned by Patrick Dorrian (1814–85), Catholic bishop of Down and Connor, to design the new cemetery with its gateway and boundary wall.[109]

THE KEEN: LANDSCAPE AS SOUNDSCAPE

Death in the Irish arena was presided over by women for long centuries. Women cared for the dead body, cleansed it, laid it out, watched and waked it, and managed the chief tasks of mourning. It was women who orchestrated the sophisticated keening ritual.[110] In 1809, Lady Louisa Lansdowne was treated to an emotional display of public grief a few weeks after the untimely death of Silvester Mac Fhinín Duibh O'Suilleabháin at Kilmakilloge (Co. Kerry), twenty-first in the line of the Mac Fhinín Duibh chieftains.

> The moment our boat reached the land, all the inhabitants of the bay, who had assembled themselves on some high ground near the shore, began to howl and lament McFinnin and continued to bewail him the

105 C. Connell, *Glasnevin cemetery Dublin, 1832–1900* (Dublin, 2004). Incongruously given its later dominance by Irish-style gravestones, the cemetery contains the magnificently Roman Republican tomb of the lawyer **John Philpott Curran** (1750–1817). The 1834 design by John Thomas Papworth proposed a 'richly sculpted granite Doric sarcophagus' 'modeled on the tomb of Scipio Barbatus at Rome'. This splendid tomb was erected in 1840 (W.J. Fitzpatrick, *History of the Dublin Catholic cemeteries* (Dublin, 1900), pp 26–31). **106** J. Sheehy, *J.J. McCarthy and the Gothic Revival in Ireland* (Belfast, 1977), p. 67. **107** *Northern Whig*, 28 Feb. 1828; *Belfast News Letter*, 11 Aug. 1829. **108** E. Phoenix, *Two acres of Irish history: a study through time of Friar's Bush and Belfast, 1570–1918* (Belfast, 1988). **109** *Irish Builder*, 1 July 1870. **110** P. Lysaght, 'Old age, dying and mourning' in E. Biagini & M. Daly (eds), *The Cambridge social history of Ireland* (Cambridge, 2017), pp 282–6; P. Lysaght, 'Caoineadh os cionn coirp: the lament for the dead in Ireland', *Folklore*, 108 (1997), pp 65–82.

whole time we staid and till our boat was well out of sight. The howl is a most wild and melancholy sound and impresses one with the idea of real sorrow in the people. As we heard it at Kilmacaloge echoed by the rocks and softened by the distance, nothing could be more striking and affecting.[111]

In the same year, the botanist Joseph Woods (1776–1864) encountered the keen at a Protestant funeral at Muckross (Co. Kerry):

After a child has exhausted itself in the first paroxysms of rage or grief, it will frequently continue a sort of measured cry and if any person will conceive that multiplied by perhaps two hundred or three hundred voices, he will have no bad idea of an Irish howl. The coffin is not shut up on a hearse but laid on a sort of car, which is not inelegant and a female sitting at each corner seems lost in the profoundest grief, at intervals leading the oo loo low. This is called keening, the performers are not paid for their sorrow and do it to be neighbourly. The men never keen except for near relations.[112]

While Irish culture was still vibrant and intact, two styles of caoineadh co-existed. One was formal and literary, composed retrospectively, utilizing a long line containing a regular number of natural speech stresses.[113] These intricate and sophisticated versions had a venerable literary genealogy. The superlative 'Caoineadh Airt Uí Laoghaire' immediately entered the veins of Gaelic Munster. The French traveller Coquebert de Montbret encountered it in north Kerry in 1790, where it was 'praised above all others' as a lamentation.[114] The second style of caoineadh was more informal, improvised extempore, using a simple metre with one stress per line.[115] By the mid-nineteenth century, the literary tradition had collapsed, and only the oral caoineadh survived.

The caoineadh furnished formal and public acknowledgements of women's responsibility for death as well as for birth. It functioned as a transition ceremony, a cathartic, therapeutic theatre of death, which explored both the

111 Diary, 4 Oct. 1809, cited in G. Lyne, *The Lansdowne estates in Kerry under W.S. Trench 1849–72* (Dublin, 2001), p. 531. He was killed by a fall from his horse. His family held 2,000 acres as middlemen on the estate in 1795. For the family background, see G. Lyne, 'The Mac Finín Duibh O'Sullivans of Tuosist and Berehaven', *Kerry Archaeological & Historical Society Journal*, 9 (1976), pp 32–67.　112 G. Lyne & M. Mitchell (eds), 'A scientific tour through Munster: the travels of Joseph Woods, architect and botanist, in 1809', *NMAJ*, 27 (1985), pp 30–1.　113 B. Ó Buachalla, *An caoine agus an chaointeoireacht* (Baile Átha Cliath, 1995); B. Ó Madagáin (eag.), *Gnéithe den chaointeoireacht* (Baile Átha Cliath, 1978); S. Ó Coileáin, 'The Irish lament: an oral genre', *Studia Hib.*, 24 (1984–8), pp 97–117.　114 [De Montbret], 'Kerry', p. 92.　115 A. Bourke, 'The Irish traditional lament and the grieving process', *Women Studies International Forum*, 11 (1988), pp 287–91; A. Bourke, 'Performing not writing', *Graph*, 11 (1991), pp 28–31; A. Bourke, 'Caoineadh na marbh', *Oghma*, 4 (1992), pp 3–11.

emotional experience of loss and the necessary continuity of the surviving community. The carnivalesque quality of the wake responded to this liminal ambiguity. Far from being the 'wild and inarticulate uproar' heard by outsiders,[116] the caoineadh was structured, rhythmic and orchestrated, utilizing iterative procedures drawn from a formulaic repertoire, composed in performance and adhering to a strict if simple metre. While the pre-existing compositional vocabulary structured it, there was flexibility of improvisation within it.

The keen created a distinctive soundscape. In 1856, an American visitor to Milltown (Co. Kerry) 'heard in the distance a wild and plangent strain of music. We started for there was in it something strange and unearthly. It swelled and died away as if borne upon a fitful breeze. Presently appeared a funeral procession and the keeners were keening over the departed'.[117] This dramatic effect, with its baroque ostentation, was noted in a Mayo account from 1876: 'The cry and clapping of hands rose higher and higher, piercing into every room and corner of the house; through the open windows and doors, it floated outside to the farmyard and on the midnight breeze, it was carried and heard at two miles distance'.[118] The American traveller Asenath Nicholson (1792–1855) was highly affected by a caoineadh that she heard at Muckross Abbey (Co. Kerry): 'The pounding upon the coffin, the howling and the shovelling of earth from the grave made together sounds and sights strange if not unseemly'.[119]

There could be expressions of emotional tenderness, as in a lament for a dead brother from Mitchelstown (Co. Cork):

A dhriothair óig a rúin,	My beloved young brother
Mo chreach is mo bhuaidhreamh	it is my desolation and my burden
Is ní bheidh do thuairisc	that the only news we will get of you
Feasta againn ach mar	from now on will be like
chaithfidhe cloch i bpoll	stones flung into a hole,
Ná mar d'imtheoch cubhar le habhainn	or like foam fading on the river,
Ná mar bheadh sméara dubha ann	or like the blackberries
Idir fhéile Mhichíl is Samhain	between Michaelmas and Halloween
San t-am ná bíonn siad ann.	when they are no longer there.[120]

Exchanges between priests and women keeners are frequently recorded. In a Kerry example, the keening women had been rudely pushed aside by a posse

116 T. Crofton Croker, *The keen of the south of Ireland* (London, 1844), p. 173.   117 G. Haskins, *Ireland* (Boston, 1856), p. 70.   118 T. Ó hAílín, 'Caointe agus caointeoireacht', *Feasta* (Eanair, 1971), p. 8.   119 A. Nicholson, *Ireland's welcome to the stranger or an excursion through Ireland in 1844 & 1845 for the purpose of personally investigating the condition of the poor* (Dublin, [1847], 2002), p. 290.   120 T. Ó hAílín, 'Caointe agus caointeoireacht', *Feasta* (Feabhra, 1971), p. 6.

of priests making for the coffin of one of their brethren, with the dismissive imprecation 'Druideadh siar, a chailleacha' (Stand back, you hags).[121] While robust encounters between poets and priests were frequent in the eighteenth century, a sense of intimacy existed between the two in the Gaelic tradition.[122] However, once the church began to distance itself from the tradition and once the Devotional Revolution took hold, the clerical distance from the people dramatically widened. A Waterford woman, loudly keening her only son, was counselled by a priest to restrain her immoderate grief, and to trust in the will of God. She replied:

Éist, a shagairt agus seasuigh díreach,	Shut up, priest, and stand up straight.
léigh an tAfreann is gheobhaidh tú díol as.	Read the Mass and you will be paid for it.
Níor thug sé trí raithe in imeall do chroí agat,	He never spent nine months near your heart,
ná naoi mbliana déag ar fuaid an tí agat.	nor nineteen years around your house.[123]

Fr Matthew Horgan (1775–1849) of Blarney (Co. Cork) launched a vendetta against wakes:

> Irish wakes, I say, are synonymous with everything profligate, wicked, wasteful, and disgraceful to a Christian people, and every lover of religion, morality, and good order should co-operate to abolish such a foul stain on the Irish character. As I was well aware of the difficulty of rooting out old customs and prejudices, I earnestly proceeded to the task for the good of the people whose governor I am. I cursed in the chapel those who allowed wakes and those who frequented them, knowing their business there was neither sorrow or sympathy, but to have a glorious night's fun, in eating, drinking, and smoking nasty tobacco, and I found that those who frequented wakes, like executions, became hardened villians who could not be trustworthy. I have so well succeeded that the people are grateful and unanimous in their suppression. For this I had a facility which few others could boast of: in the building of my round towers, I left a vault of ten feet in diameter in the base, to which, as soon as a coffin is procured, the body is conveyed to remain there for a time.[124]

The Famine altered the tradition of grieving the dead. The sheer frequency of deaths inured people towards it. In County Clare, a police constable claimed in 1850 that the ordinary people eventually 'thought no more of the life of a fellow creature than they would of that of a dog'.[125] Archdeacon John O'Sullivan (1806–74) recorded the abandonment of the dead in the streets of Kenmare

121 P. Ferritéar, 'Bean chaointe a cosaint féin', *Éigse*, 3 (1939), p. 222.   122 T. Ó Fiaich, 'Irish poetry and the clergy', *Leachtaí Cholm Cille*, 4 (Má Nuad, 1975), pp 30–56: A. Partridge [Bourke], *Caoineadh na dtrí Maire: teáma na paise i bhfilíocht bhéil na Gaeilge* (Baile Átha Cliath, 1983).   123 Ó hAilín, 'Caointe', p. 10.   124 RIA, MS 12 M 11, f. 395.   125 S. Osborne, *Gleanings in the west of Ireland* (London, 1850), p. 25.

(Co. Kerry) in March 1847: 'Nothing is more usual than to find four or five bodies in the street every morning. They would remain so and in their houses unburied until putrefaction would ensue, had we not employed three men to go about and convey them to the graveyard'.[126]

In these appalling circumstances, death itself died – the social significance of death. Considering the demise of the caoineadh (keen), the antiquarian Francis Keane observed that 'especially since the Famine of 1848, the practice has not been much in use'. He ascribed that change to 'the innumerable deaths which at that time had daily taken place, together with the hunger and destitution which prevailed throughout the country deprived the people in fact of that natural feeling and regard which they were wont to have for the dead'.[127] A similar shift was noted by Edmund Fitzmaurice Donnelly (1830–87) at Kenmare (Co. Kerry) during the Famine: 'We had famished and spectral human beings crawling about from door to door; we had the trap coffin or the black van performing its never ceasing journeys to "Old Kenmare" and Kilmakallogue, unaccompanied by friend or neighbour of the plaintive Munster caoine'.[128]

As the institutional church's assault on the keen intensified, the Catholic middle class internalized the new value of restraint. Asenath Nicholson witnessed an incident at Roscrea (Co. Tipperary) in 1845, when an old woman was admonished by another to desist: 'Stop, ye are going to do what nobody does now. Get up and stop the bawling'. A man told her: 'Ye can't bring him back and what's all this bawling about?'[129] John O'Donovan commented in 1849: 'All decent half-civilized people now laugh at these elegies and hence the better class of farmers have entirely given them up'.[130] Fr Ulick Bourke (1829–87) in Galway noted in 1879 that the clergy preferred 'prayers to keens, kneeling to mourning',[131] while the bookseller John Fleming (1815–95) claimed in the same year that in County Waterford, 'once famous for its keeners, the caoine has seldom been heard for the last sixty years'.[132]

In a moment that symbolized the stark transition from female to male ownership of the grieving process (consider the simultaneous ascendancy of male professionals over the traditional midwives in birth procedures), the folklorist Seán O Súilleabháin (1903–96), described a funeral scene in the parish of Tuosist in south Kerry in the early decades of the twentieth century.

> As the coffin was being taken in a cart to the local graveyard at Kilmakillogue, three women keeners sat on top of it, howling and wailing at intervals. The parish priest, on horseback, met the funeral near Dereen,

126 O'Sullivan, Diary, 26 Mar. 1847, courtesy of Gerry Lyne.   127 RIA, MS 12 Q 13, f. 10. 128 *Nation*, 12 Dec. 1857.   129 Nicholson, *Ireland's welcome to the stranger*, p. 139.   130 J. O'Donovan, 'Elegy on the death of Rev. Edmond Kavanagh by the Rev. James O'Lalor', *Journal of the Kilkenny and South-East of Ireland Archaeological Society* , n.s., 5 (1858–9), pp 131–2.   131 RIA, MS 12 Q 13, f. 19.   132 RIA, MS 12 Q 13, f. 40.

a few miles from the graveyard, and rode at its head along the road. As soon as he heard the three women howl loudly, he turned his horse about and trotted back until he reached them, where they sat on the coffin. He started to lash them with his whip, as the cart passed by, and ordered them to be silent. This they did, but on reaching the graveyard, they again took up their wailings, whereupon the priest forced them down from the coffin with his whip. They were afraid to enter the graveyard to howl at the graveside. This put an end to the hiring of keening women in that parish.[133]

The keen occupied a prominent position in attacks on Gaelic culture – 'the counterfeit and barbarous clamour of howling savages that would disgrace the funeral of a Hottentot or the obsequies of a native of Otaheite [Tahiti]'.[134] Free food, drink and tobacco attracted people to funerals and wakes to which 'they flock together like crows after carrion'.[135] An observer estimated that half a million pounds was lost annually due to time profligately spent at funerals: 'to attend a neighbour's funeral is a cheap proof of humanity but it does not cost nothing'.[136] From Athlone (Co. Westmeath) in 1819, another adverse commentator observed:

That barbarous custom, the Irish cry at wakes, is still kept up here in all its savage howl of discordant sounds, calculated to shock the ears of any civilized member of human society; a custom which requires only to be heard to decide that it is derived from a barbarous people. It can certainly pretend to no Christian authority. Such barbarous customs are a most incontestible proof of the absence of sorrow, for grief disdains the form which such a savage howl affects; it does not submit to rules for expressing what it feels; instead of publishing its sorrows to the world, it shuns ostentation, and seeks retirement.[137]

The keen's affront to the canon of polite taste was all the more unsettling in that it had a formulaic, ritualistic and even professional dimension (in the case of keening women). Its theatrical performance of emotion was opposed to Protestant privacy and inwardness in response to grief. An English traveller congratulated himself in 1852 when he first heard the keen: 'When we saw the wringing of hands and heard the wailings, we became aware, for the first time perhaps, of the full dignity of that civilization which induces control over the expression of emotions'.[138]

The keening tradition transferred to the American wake. Jeremiah O'Donovan Rossa (1831–1915) reported on the scene when his family was emigrating to the United States, leaving him behind:

133 S. Ó Suilleabháin, *Irish wake amusements* (Cork, 1967), p. 143.   134 *Wexford Herald*, 29 Nov. 1792.   135 Ibid.   136 'Irish funerals' [by a modern English author] in *Walker's Hibernian Magazine*, Feb. (1801), p. 104.   137 'The parish of St Peters (Athlone)' in Shaw Mason, *Statistical survey of Irish parishes*, iii, p. 77.   138 H. Martineau, *Letters from Ireland* (London, 1852), pp 139–40.

The cry of the weeping and wailing of that day rings in my ears still. That time it was a cry heard every day at every crossroads in Ireland. I stood at Renascreena cross till this cry of the emigrant party went beyond my hearing. Then I kept walking back towards Skibbereeen looking at them till they sank from my view over Mauleeyregan hill.[139]

The American escaped slave Frederick Douglass (1818–95) pronounced himself 'much affected' in 1845 when he heard these Irish 'wailing notes' because they carried personal echoes of the 'wild notes' of sorrowful slave songs.[140]

139 J. O'Donovan Rossa, *Rossa's recollections* (New York, 1898), pp 142–3. **140** F. Douglas, *Narrative of the life of Frederick Douglass, an American slave* (New York, [1845], 1973), p. 106.

CHAPTER FIVE

Vernacular Religion and its Landscape Expression

HE VERNACULAR CHURCH REMAINED ROOTED in the Irish landscape
and the Irish language.[1] A biting traditional quatrain ridiculed the new
church: 'Ná trácht ar an mhinistéir gallda/ná ar a chreideamh gan beann gan
brí/mar níl mar bhuan-chloch dá theampuill/ach magarlaí Aonraí Buí' (Don't
talk of the foreign minister/nor his faith without rhyme or reason/because
the foundation-stone of his churches is only/the balls of Yellow Henry).
Resilience and embeddedness hallmarked the old church but this was never
an uncomplicated narrative of age-old continuities. Vernacular knowledge
surfaced in the official world in laminated, braided and occult ways, and formal
theological teaching percolated into a cultural landscape steeped in an aura of
ancient efficacy.[2]

The vernacular imagination deployed its own creative cartography in
articulating its surrounding world.[3] The west created its distinctive pattern
of clachans,[4] and the lack of resident authority figures (landlords, priests)
opened a space for tradition bearers, including women. It conferred room for
improvisation within a surging population and settlement expansion onto fresh
land. This conferred an unusual degree of social and cultural freedom within
one of the most autonomous and self-contained rural cultures of Europe.

Tradition-bearing women were elevated as the cultural arbiters of religious
observance, valued for their inherited practical know-how. The Mayo poet
Riocard Bairéad (1740–1809) composed the humorous song 'Giolla na Péice',
pitting an Erris bean ghlúine (midwife) against the priest and the surgeon
over relevant skills and prerequisites: the midwife Sally O'Malley asserted

1 The abundant Irish language material is crucial here. There is a survey chapter on
'Faith' in V. Morley, *The popular mind in eighteenth-century Ireland* (Cork, 2017), pp 68–
93. 2 Beneath its bland title, there is a treasure trove of scholarship in D. Ó hOgáin,
Myth, legend, & romance: an encyclopaedia of the Irish folk tradition (London, 1990). 3
Suggestive studies include L. Taylor, *Occasions of faith: an anthropology of Irish Catholics*
(Dublin, 1995); A. Bourke, *The burning of Bridget Cleary: a true story* (London, 1999); G.
Ó Crualaoich, *The book of the cailleach: stories of the wise-woman healer* (Cork, 2003). 4 K.
Whelan, 'Clachans: landscape and life in Ireland before and after the Famine' in Duffy &
Nolan (eds), *At the anvil*, pp 453–75.

that her skilled fingers were more effective than any learned anatomy, and accordingly should be better recompensed than the light labours of the priest. The agriculturalist Patrick Knight in 1839 observed that the midwife's lines assumed 'all the dignity of her office and totally despising the book learning and jargon of the whole college of surgeons with their instruments as compared to her natural ones'. Similarly she was paid (and was entitled to be paid) more than a priest who sauntered in after all the hard work was done. [5]

The landscape became an experimental laboratory of the imagination, peopling an otherworld brimming with life. The Icelander Jón Ólafsson was astounded on seeing the countryside around Youghal (Co. Cork) come alive with Midsummer fires in 1625.

> On the road, as we travelled back, the Irish country folk kindled great fires on high mountains every night, with much dancing round the fires by great multitudes both of men and women, with junketings and merrymaking. This is the old custom of the Irish people, which they have observed from the most ancient times, maintaining that all goes better with them if they continue it, than if they should let it drop. This is, as it were, their faith, and though the English have tried to wean them from the custom, and sternly forbidden it, the Irish have obstinately refused to give up their fires and dances, which have become the custom and habit of the countryside. [6]

The countryside was animated by strongly felt but invisible presences, the everyday capable of being suddenly impregnated with the enchanted. A magic realist sensibility permeated the stories that were told, many of them precisely set in specific locations. Haunted ground included boundaries, bridges, standing stones, lone bushes, raths, hills (in Donegal, the sídhe were called 'bunadh na gcnoc' – the hereditary dwellers of the hills) and other 'lonesome' (uaigneas in Irish) places. [7] In a single townland in Kilgalligan (Erris, Co. Mayo), forty places with supernatural resonances were identified. [8] Specific locations like An Aill Eidhneach at Trá Bhán in Leitir Mór in Conamara were considered to be haunted. From these places, enchanted music issued, like the still popular tune 'Port na bPucaí'. [9]

---

5 N. Williams (eag.), *Riocard Bairéad amhráin* (Baile Átha Cliath, 1978), pp 77–8.   6 J. Olafsson, *The life of the Icelander Jón Ólafsson*, p. 233 [CELT]. A similar scene is described almost two centuries later in Connaught: C.J. Woods (ed.), 'Johan Friedrich Hering's description of Connacht 1806–7', *IHS*, 25:99 (1987), pp 311–21.   7 S. Ó hEochaidh, *Síscéalta ó Thír Chonaill/Fairy legends from Donegal*, trans. M. Mac Néill (Dublin, 1977).   8 S. Ó Catháin & P. O'Flanagan, *The living landscape: Kilgalligan, Erris, Co. Mayo* (Dublin, 1975). See the map of 'supernatural areas', p. 62.   9 R. Uí Ógáin & T. Sherlock, *The otherworld: music and song from Irish tradition* (Dublin, 2012), p. 114. Seamus Heaney's poem 'The given note' drew on this tradition to anchor a meditation on the enigmatic nature of the gift [fis] of poetry and music.

The lonesome inarticulate keening of the bean sí was an eerie sound emanating from the Irish landscape. The bean sí (banshee, badhbh, bow, bean chaointe), the supernatural female death messenger attached to specific ancient families, was a consoling creation of the Irish imagination as it contemplated death.[10] The insistence that the bean sí only deigned to follow the ancestral families (the O's and the Mac's) established a comforting distance from the settler population. O'Donovan recorded the Roscommon tradition: 'Whenever any of the O'Flynns of Ballinlough are on the point of death, a banshee is heard most plaintively lamenting on the banks of the lough' [Loch Uí Fhloinn].[11]

In a famished landscape ravaged by death and emigration, and founded on disappearance, the presence of absence could be overwhelming. The fóidín mearbhaill was a sod of ground that once stepped on set the affected person astray, disoriented and unable to find a way home. Similarly, the féar gortach (hungry grass) imparted hunger pangs, as it marked the spot where a person had died during the Famine. This was the readily recognized quaking grass (*briza media*), its triangular loose clusters of flowers quivering and shivering in the summer wind.

The pioneering American ethnographer Jeremiah Curtin (1835–1906) was struck by attitudes on the Corca Dhuibhne peninsula (Co. Kerry) in the late nineteenth century: 'I find a remarkable freedom of intercourse between the visible and the unseen worlds, between what we call the dead and the living – a certain intimate communion between what has been and what is'.[12] There was a 'seamless continuity of community between the dead and the living', and 'the thin veil between this world and the otherworld can be parted, especially at certain times of the year and in certain places'.[13] The restless or marginalized dead (suicides, child murderers, abortionists, priest's lovers) were doomed to roam the earth. The revolutionary Ernie O'Malley (1897–1957) described these beliefs in Co. Mayo: 'The dead walked around, there was an acceptance of their presence, no horror and little dread, the wall was thin between their living and their dead'.[14]

The fairies prompted 'accounts of their shapes and the clothes worn, their fear of iron, and the prayer when a sudden, unexpected swirl of dust [sí gaoithe/sídhe gaoithe][15] is seen, for 'they're surely in it'.[16] An account from Laois in 1870 reported:

10 P. Lysaght, *The banshee: the Irish supernatural death messenger* (Dublin, 1996). 11 Edmond, 'chief' of the O'Flynns of Newborough, 'still holds a few townlands in fee tail' and he knows 'every bush in the parish of Kiltullagh' (*OS letters, Roscommon*, pp 41–2). 12 J. Curtin, *Tales of the fairies and of the ghost world collected from oral tradition in south-west Munster* (Boston, 1895), p. 16. 13 A. O'Connor, 'Perspectives on death from Irish folklore' in S. Ryan (ed.), *Death: a miscellany* (Dublin, 2016), p. 179. 14 E. O'Malley, *On another man's wound* (Cork, [1936] 2013), p. 122. 15 This term is an abbreviated form of sitheadh (rush, dash, swoop, gust), so sí gaoithe originally meant 'a gust of wind'; its meaning was later reinterpreted as being associated with the fairies. 16 O'Malley, *On another's man's wound*, p. 122.

On alighting at, or departing from, a particular spot, their rapid motion, through air creates a noise somewhat resembling the loud humming of bees, when swarming from a hive. Sometimes, what is called shee gaoithe, anglicé, a whirl wind, is supposed to have been raised by the passing fairy host.[17]

Rather than regarding these beliefs as a superstitious residue from earlier belief systems, it is more accurate to understand them as expressing a vigorous exchange between vernacular beliefs and Catholic theology.[18] The formative influence of the Franciscans must be acknowledged here. They exerted a powerful mediating role between Catholic Reformation thought and the Gaelic world in the seventeenth century (Old English Catholics were unwilling or incapable of creating that synthesis) when they produced an array of gifted scholars and preachers trained on the Continent but steeped in the Irish tradition. Flaithrí Ó Maol Chonaire (1560–1629), Aodh Mac Aingil (1571–1626) and Giolla Bhríde Ó hEoghusa (*ob*.1614) (Bonaventure O'Hussey) were committed to both theology and the pastoral mission, while Luke Wadding (1588–1657), John Punch (1603–61) and Bonaventure Baron (1610–96) involved themselves more in the intellectual and political realms.[19] Defined and sustained by their experience of, and allegiance to, a universal church, Irish priests returned to their own patch and infused this fresh thinking into their local communities.

A network of pilgrimage sites encouraged movement through a sacralized landscape.[20] Pilgrimage escaped the confines of the parish system, assuming a fluid rather than a fixed form. In 1593, the Catholics of Barra in Scotland went on pilgrimage to Croagh Patrick (Co. Mayo).[21] In 1812, 20,000 persons climbed the reek:

The great season is about the latter end of September. At that time there are seen for several days, the great roads leading to it, crowded: day and

17 [J. O'Hanlon], *Irish folklore: traditions and superstitions of the country* (Glasgow, 1870), p. 34. 18 A. O'Connor, 'To hell or to purgatory? Irish folk religion and post-Tridentine Counter-Reformation Catholic teachings', *Béaloideas*, 80 (2012), pp 115–41. 19 None of them returned to minister in Ireland. E. Bhreathnach, J. MacMahon & J. McCafferty (eds), *The Irish Franciscans, 1534–1990* (Dublin, 2009); E. Bhreathnach, 'The mendicant orders and vernacular Irish learning in the late medieval period', *IHS*, 37:147 (2011), pp 357–75. The Franciscans also produced rumbunctious mavericks like the Clare man Antonious Bruodin: L. McInerney, 'A "most vainglorious man": the writings of Antonius Bruodin', *Archiv. Hib.*, 70 (2017), pp 202–83. 20 L. Nugent, 'Gatherings of faith: pilgrimage in medieval Ireland' in F. Beglane (ed.), *Gatherings: past and present* (Dublin, 2017), pp 20–30: M. Nolan, 'Irish pilgrimage: the different tradition', *Annals of the Association of American Geographers*, 73:3 (1983), pp 421–38. 21 Sir Richard Bingham (1528–99), Elizabethan Governor of Connacht, reported this event, presumably for fear that it might conceal covert movements by gallowglasses (*CSPI, 1592–3*, p. 129). For the wider backdrop, see J. Campbell, 'The McNeils of Barra and the Irish Franciscans', *Innes Review*, 5 (1954), pp 33–8.

night they proceed, with anxious looks and hasty steps. There is at this time a pattern, or sort of fair, held at its foot, chiefly for food and drink.[22]

The geometrical certitude of Croagh Patrick aided its popularity, as it was visible over a surprisingly wide vista to a mapless and appless people moving on foot.

Further north in Donegal, Lough Derg also exerted a regional pull. Five thousand pilgrims attended annually by the 1720s and this number had doubled a century later. In 1824, the Master of Portora school reckoned that between 50,000 and 60,000 annually participated.[23] Lough Derg had its trademark stylized 'penal crosses', with their date range from 1702 to 1830, and their primarily north-western distribution. Of 129 examples in one sample, 111 had a provenance north of a Dublin/Galway line.[24]

BALLA (CO. MAYO): A PILGRIMAGE SITE

Balla tooks its name from the Balla Álainn (beautiful wall) that encircled the monastic site of its founder Crónán (Mo-Chua). Antiquities include a round tower (of which only the stump survives), a tenth-century grave slab, a church (the ruin was extant into the early nineteenth century), a graveyard and the holy well Tobar Mhuire.[25] It was located on the Tóchair Phádraig[26] and an Irish saying elevated the arduous reek over Balla on the limestone lowlands: 'Turas na cruaiche naoi n-uaire go Balla' (one pilgrimage to Croagh Patrick is worth nine to Balla).[27] The church was coarbial and its tearmann comprised twenty-four townlands, according to Giolla Íosa Mór Mac Firbisigh in 1417: 'Tearmann Balla fán binn cluig/Fond bláth do bheadoigh Padraig' (The ecclesiastical territory of Balla under the sound of it sweet bell,[28] the flowery land that Patrick blessed).[29] At the centre of the site was Tobar Mhuire and a major 'pattern' occurred here every September. The pattern was described in 1812:

> Here, on what is called the Great Lady Day, in September, there is an immense assemblage; and here, as in the other place, the most abominable immorality is indulged amidst their devotions. The place is resorted to by fiddlers, pipers, etc and drunkenness and lewdness prevail. It is a

22 *Evangelical Magazine*, 20 (1812), p. 73.   **23** Glassford, *Three tours*, p. 95.   **24** A.T. Lucas, *Penal crucifixes* (Dublin 1958).   **25** E. Rynne, 'The round tower, evil eye, and holy well at Balla, Co. Mayo' in C. Manning (ed.), *Dublin and beyond the Pale: studies in honour of Paddy Healy* (Bray, 1998), pp 177–84. An earlier treatment is Knox, *Tuam, Killala and Achonry*, pp 134–9.   **26** O Maille, *Seanfhocla*, p. 134.   **27** Knox, *Tuam, Killala and Achonry*, p. 140.   **28** A seventh- to tenth-century bell from Balla survives and is illustrated in Waldron, *Tuam*, p. 13.   **29** *OS letters, Mayo*, p. 302.

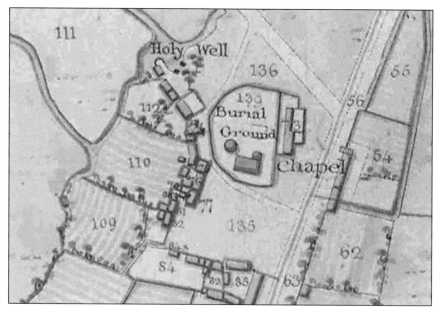

Fig. 17   Balla (Co. Mayo) in 1811. The graveyard boundary suggests that a circular ecclesiastical enclosure once delimited the site. The Catholic chapel of 1754 was replaced in 1913, after strong fundraising in the US and England (maps of Sir Robert Lynch-Blosse estate in the barony of Clanmaurice 1811 by Sherrard, Brassington and Greene, Dublin, 1811, Mayo County Council).

harvest of gain to the priest of that place, who raises contributions from the devotees. This meeting lasts about three days.[30]

An extant 1696 slab erected over the well by the parish priest of Balla bears the Latin inscription: 'Sub tuum preaesidium confugimus/sancta Dei genetrix & parrochus Fontis de Ballah me apponi curavit 25 Mar: 1696'.[31] There were also two small (now lost) stone crosses on the leacht, both dated to 1733 and both bearing English inscriptions.[32]

Balla featured prominently in the Irish language poetry of Mayo, notably in a celebrated line by the blind poet Antóin Ó Raifteirí (1779–1835) which has him heading to the pattern in Balla: 'Féach anois mé 's m'aghaidh ar Bhalla/Ag seinm ceoil do phocaí folamh' (Look at me now heading to Balla/playing music to empty pockets). Ó Raifteirí also spoke of taking to the road in spring, and beginning to carouse in Balla: 'I gClár Chlainne Mhuiris/A bhéas mé an chéad oíche,/Is i mBalla taobh thíos de/A thosóidh mé ag ól' (I will be in Claremorris the first night/and I will start drinking in Balla).[33] In another poem, he is 'ag

---

30 *Evangelical Magazine*, 20 (1812), p. 73.   **31** *OS letters, Mayo*, p. 301. The Latin uses phrases from the Litany of Loreto.   **32** *OS letters, Mayo*, p. 302.   **33** N. Ó Muraile (eag.), *Amhráin agus dánta Raifteараí le Dúghlas de Híde* (An Spideál, 2018), p. 363.

Fig. 18 Charles Green, 'An Irish Pattern at Balla, Co. Mayo; the Long Station', engraved by Eugène Froment (*The Graphic*, 23 Jan. 1875).

trial go haonach Balla dom/'is mo chos ar lár an bhóthair (heading to the fair in Balla/with my feet in the middle of the road).[34] In 'Bríd Véasaigh', he praised Balla and Bohola: 'Is da mbéim ar bláth na h-óige/i mBalla nó i mBothóla/ní fhágamais go deireadh fhóghmair é/acht ag spórt 's ag déanamh grinn' (if I was in my flower of youth in Balla or Bohola, I wouldn't leave either of them until the autumn, just enjoying myself and and having the craic).[35]

In an anonymous Mayo poem, 'Nóirín mo mhian', the composer situated himself in Balla: 'A' dul thrí shráid Bhalla dom lá Fhéil' Muire Mór/ag díol mo chuid earraidh a's gha roinnt le mo stór/nuair fhiafruigheas bean na leann diom/Cia bhfuil luach na mbróg?/Chuir mé le hanam na marbh é atá i dteampull Mhuigheó (Going through the street of Balla on Lady Day/selling my goods and sharing them [the proceeds] with my sweetheart/when the porter woman asked me 'what is the price of the brogues'?/I put it to the souls of the dead in Mayo graveyard).[36]

Overnight, Balla lost its long-standing popularity in 1879 with the apparition at neighbouring Knock. The ancestral Muire na nGael gave way to a

<hr>

34 'An potaire ag moladh uisce beatha' (The drunkard extolling whiskey) in Ó Muraile (eag.), *Amhráin*, pp 201–3. 35 E. Mhic Choisdealbha, *Amhráin Mhuighe Séola: traditional songs from Galway and Mayo* (Baile Átha Cliath, 1918), p. 57. Mág Seóla is the barony of Claregalway and these 'songs of the people' were collected there by the Tuam-dwelling Englishwoman Eileen Costello (1870–1962). 36 Mhic Choisdealbha, *Amhráin Mhuighe Séola*, p. 139.

Fig. 19 The unroofed walls of 'the little chapel over the well' (Hubert Knox), which sheltered the lame and the blind that frequented Balla on patron day (photograph by Hubert Knox, *c.*1900) (RSAI).

gaudy Frenchfied version. Local reports of the apparition of the Blessed Virgin at Knock in 1879 noted that she was silent.[37] In the midst of a community in headlong transition between two languages, in which should she have spoken? In the Mayo of that time, it was not uncommon for monoglot Irish-speakers to have grandchildren who were monoglot English speakers. In a vivid anecdote, Douglas Hyde (1860–1949) captured the confusion of the period:

> About two or three miles west of Ballaghdereen [Co. Roscommon], I chatted with a little 'gossoon' [garsún, boy] who ran beside my car. And as I spoke to him in Irish, he answered me in English. At last I said: 'Nach labhrainn tú Gaedhlig?' [Don't you speak Irish?]. His answer was: 'And isn't it Irish I'm spakin'? [38]

37 J. White, 'The Cusack papers: new evidence on the Knock apparition', *History Ireland*, 4:4 (1999), pp 39–43. 38 Douglas Hyde, 'My memories of the Irish Revival' in W. Fitzgerald (ed.), *The voice of Ireland* (Dublin, 1922), p. 455. Hyde's own early notebooks offer a vivid example of the linguistic flux in Ireland in the post-Famine period. Aged thirteen in 1873, among his copperplate exercises in Latin, Greek, French and English are jotted down what appears to be an extraordinary farrago of nonsense or gibberish words. Closer study reveals a preliminary attempt to transcribe phonetically the words of an Irish-language poem by Ó Raifteirí (Introduction by Dominic Daly to Douglas Hyde, *Songs ascribed to Raftery* (Shannon, 1973), p. vii).

Fig. 20 Oileán Mhic Dara (Co. Galway): Pilgrimage Day, 16 July 1943 (Fáilte Ireland).

NARRATING THE LANDSCAPE

Stories are a permanent sediment sieved from the fleeting flow of real life. The tales of accomplished seanchaí were constructed in terms of a vernacular magic realism, a non-literal fidelity to the world that transmitted what should not be forgotten, a stylization of lived and felt experience generated by and for those who needed it, especially when the Irish experience fell, as it so often did, outside conventional representational bounds. In this sense, the Irish attraction to the Gothic as a representational form was expressed as much through oral culture as in precocious literary experimentation. The Gothic as a genre emerged when strict boundaries between inner identity and the external world were breached or perforated, as it navigated the disquieted intersection of past and present, or absorbed the lacerating shock of injustice.[39]

Traditional narrators balanced an earned familiarity with lived realities against liberation from stinted circumstances, releasing an exotic geography of desire. Their stories deftly handled the capricious uncertainty of the lives of the Irish rural poor, operating within that taken-for-granted world because they were composed from inside the culture, without any compulsion

---

39 E. Weber, 'Fairies and hard facts: the reality of folktales', *Journal of the History of Ideas*, 42:1 (1981), pp 93–113.

to explain or contextualize, an obligation that a realist novelist would feel.[40] Seanchaí offered compressed narratives, with little or no attention to interiority, motivation or mindsets, but with precision regarding the location of the story, and a sharp attention to action. At the same time, these storytellers possessed the capacity to think beyond the constraints of immediate experience through an imaginative mode of shaping cognition. Telling stories became a form of thinking with words, an expression of vernacular intelligence.[41] Farmers, fishermen and artisans typically had no master but experience but their earned ways of knowing made them masters of reality. Through their stories, a culture became audible to itself, establishing a fixed density to the fluidity of life.[42] Cultures shape stories to fathom the fearful strangeness of the world, its malign power to pierce and disturb lives, its power and its grip, its fascination and its emotional weight. Storytelling is a form of self-defense, a way of enclosing, domesticating or containing that which threatens life as it is lived.[43]

Consider how stories of the Famine relay telling details: potato thieves working stealthily at night, their spades muffled with cloth, the mantraps in the Mayo fields, the eerie cortège of curious sheep who follow the orphaned child with his mother's coffin in west Cork.[44] Sometimes, as in a comment from Eyeries (Co. Cork), there is a piercing aphorism: 'Dá neosfainne dhuitse cá bhfuil uaghanna daoine atá curtha, ní raghfá thar dhoras istóiche' (If I told you where all the people were buried, you wouldn't stir out of doors at night).[45]

Seanchaí dignified hardship, suffering, injustice and dislocation by establishing a narrative moral framework that conferred meaning on these otherwise inexplicably painful experiences. The Irish popular mind cherished a clear vision of an ideal order based on egalitarianism, human decency and Christian charity, immersed in supportive networks of mutual dependence and reciprocity. Shared values were perpetuated by stabilizing and transmitting experience in inherited stories. A rupture ensued when this moral equilibrium was disturbed by external violation. These difficulties could be elicited by individuals behaving badly: 'Colliton's stone' in Cloghprior parish (Co.

40 A. Bourke, 'The virtual reality of Irish fairy legend', *Éire-Ireland*, 31:1–2 (1996), pp 7–25; A. Bourke, *Voices underfoot: memory, forgetting and verbal art* (Hamden, CT, 2016). Master storytellers included Éamon a Búrc (1866–1942), a tailor from Aill an Brón, Cill Chiaráin in Connemara, Seán Ó Conaill (1853–1931), a farmer-fisherman from Cill Rialaigh in Iveragh (S. Ó Duilearga, *Leabhir Sheain Í Chonaill* (Baile Átha Cliath, 1948); translated 1981), Pádraig Ó Crualaoí (1861–1949), a tailor from Baile Mhuirne in Cork, Stiofáin Ó hEalaoire (1858–1944), a small farmer from Doolin (Co. Clare), Peig Sayers (1873–1958) who married into An Blascaod Mór (Co. Kerry) and Colm Ó Caoidheáin of Glinsce (Cárna, Co. Galway). 41 H. Glassie, *Passing the time in Ballymenone*, second edition (Bloomington, 1995); G.-D. Zimmerman, *The Irish storyteller* (Dublin, 2001). 42 R. Cashman, *Storytelling on the Northern Irish border: characters and community* (Bloomington, 2011). This is a contemporary study of Aghyaran (Co. Tyrone). 43 W. Benjamin, 'The storyteller' in *Illuminations* (London, 1973), p 83–107. 44 C. Ó Gráda, *An drochshaol: béaloideas agus amhráin* (Baile Átha Cliath, 1995); C. Poirtéir, *Famine echoes* (Dublin, 1995). 45 IFC, MS 1188, ff 256–7.

Tipperary) derived its name from a man who lived in Ballycollitons House in the 1740s. John O'Donovan recounted the local story:

> On an evening when he was from home, a woman came to his wife as she was milking and requested some milk for a child she had in her arms; she refused her and the child began to cry; the woman told her not to cry, that she would give it Colliton's blood that evening. Colliton fell from his horse (on his return home) on this stone and the mark of the saddle is in it ever since.[46]

An Irish poem in wide circulation imagined the emaciated ghost of a named recently deceased rich person encountering a living person that had been wronged: the revenant was asked 'cad a chaolaigh do chosa? (what shrivelled your legs?). The answer was that his punishment derived from making money 'le allas lucht an tsaothair/is a bheith go daor ar na boicht' (from the sweat of workmen and being hard on the poor).[47] In east Galway, a fisherman met a ghastly revenant (or 'fetch') on the banks of the river and inquired what the problem was and was answered:

> The grazing of two sheep made my two legs thin/The sweat of workmen and overcharging the poor;/I trampled on the weak, and helped nobody/ And I will not get to the right hand of God./Doing my penance is all I care about,/Just as your fishing basket is all you care about.[48]

In Doolin (Co. Clare), a notorious landlord figure reappeared as a skeleton 'covered with skin only, the fat all burned away' and led by a devil with chains as reins to warn Claremen about the future of those who led 'lives of luxury and cruelty'. Behind him walked the jeering spectres of those he had mistreated: 'widows, starved orphans'. His jeremiad commenced: 'Cad a chaolaigh mo chosa? Allas lucht saothair/is gan a bheith báidheamhail do'n bocht' (What shrivelled my legs? The sweat of working folk and not being kind to the poor).[49]

This deeply ingrained interpretative framework could be readily adjusted to incorporate both colonialism and the Protestant Reformation as disruptive pressures within the Irish moral economy, external adversarial forces that pressed down with heavy insistence on individual lives. In 1813, Matthew O'Connor (1773–1844) of Mount Druid (Co. Roscommon) commented on Irish Catholics:

> The constant degradation lowered them in their own estimation, and rendered them crouching and pusillanimous. Sorrow and dejection were stamped in their foreheads; their timid gait and cautious reserve marked

46 RIA, Ordnance Survey namebooks, Co. Tipperary. 47 Ó Máille, *Seanfhocla Chonnacht*, p. 468. 48 S. Mac Giollarnáth, 'Seanchas fola: folklore from east Galway', *JGAHS*, 64 (2012), p. 118. 49 S. Fenton, *It all happened: reminiscences of Seamus Fenton* (Dublin, 1948), pp 319–20.

their abject condition. They did not dare to look a Protestant in the face, they avoided the side of the street he walked on, just as the slave evades the countenance of the master.[50]

The wealthy Catholic merchant John Keogh (1740–1817) put it succinctly: 'Our grievance is that many men beneath us in birth, education, morals and fortunes are allowed to trample upon us'.[51] In 1817, J.B. Trotter was informed by 'a very respectable and intelligent Catholic' in Dublin that 'a cloud hangs over us which extinguishes us whenever we raise our heads'.[52]

An 1835 broadsheet on the Cork election by James O'Brien linked broader politics to personal circumstances:

's is fada dhom ghéagaibh féin dá sníomh	My own limbs are long wrecked
a' gráfadh 's a' réabadh 's a' déanamh claí	grubbing, rooting, digging ditches
a bodaigh an Bhéarla 's a scaipeadh mo shaothair	for the English-speaking boors who waste my labour
agus miste go céasta ón sáfaigh.	and I tormented from handling the spade.[53]

The post-Reformation west of Ireland remained overwhelmingly loyal to the old religion, an outcome aided by the strong survival of Catholic gentry there. In the longer term, Catholicism here was well served by its distinctive clerical provision. The barest statistical recital tells that tale. In 1834, when reliable island-wide figures first became available, eighty-one per cent of the population was Catholic, eleven per cent Church of Ireland and eight per cent Presbyterian. In 1749, an Elphin census turned in ninety per cent Catholic, Co. Clare was ninety-four per cent Catholic in 1766 and Galway city was ninety-six per cent Catholic in 1770.[54] It is a distortion to exaggerate the lack of formal religion in the west of Ireland, as, for example, when Mass attendances were

---

50 M. O'Connor, *The history of the Irish Catholics from the settlement in 1691, with a view of the state of Ireland from the Invasion by Henry II to the Revolution: part I* (Dublin, 1813). John O'Donovan described him as 'the greatest historical sceptic I ever met with' (*OS letters, Roscommon*, p. 53) but 'a very clever man, an excellent lawyer, an acute critic and a very worthy man' (*OS letters, Roscommon*, p. 57).   **51** *Sketch of a speech delivered by John Keogh esq at a meeting of the Catholics of Dublin* (Dublin, 1807), p. 10. Keogh caused a sensation by buying back almost 1,000 acres of ancestral Keogh lands in the parish of Killukin, barony of Boyle (Co. Roscommon): Ballindrehid (51 acres), Ballyculleen (175 acres), Deerpark (69 acres), Drumercool (163 acres), Lodge (203 acres), Mullaghmore (180 acres), Rock (25 acres) and Tawlaght (84 acres) – a total of 954 acres.   **52** J.B. Trotter, *Walks through Ireland in the years 1812, 1814 and 1817: described in a series of letters to an English gentleman* (London, 1819), p. 527.   **53** P. Holohan, 'Two controverted Cork parliamentary elections and a broadsheet poem in the Irish language', *JCHAS*, 113 (2008), pp 114–30 [quotation at p. 124].   **54** M.L. Legg (ed.), *The census of Elphin 1749* (Dublin, 2004), p. xxvii: Clare had 37,154 Catholics and 2,475 Protestants in 1766 (S. Ó Cillín, *Travellers in Co. Clare, 1459–1843* (Galway, 1977), p. 26). Galway city in 1770, with a total population of 14,000, contained only 350 Protestants (P.F. Moran, *The Catholics of Ireland under the penal laws in the eighteenth century* (London, 1900), p. 67). In 1808, Mary Beaufort reported that Galway's population was 26,000, but that there were 'only 800–1000 Protestant. No other sects. No Presbyterians or Methodists' (TCD, MS 4035).

calculated in the 1830s.[55] As the population in the west of Ireland ballooned, the priest–people ratio soared with it: the eclipse of the friars who had been most prevalent in Connacht, the escalating population, the deepening immiseration that militated against chapel building (due to the dearth of sponsors given the paucity of a middle class), and the lack of towns which were the hubs of the renewal elsewhere lay behind that novel situation.

On the whole, this distinctive expression of Catholicism nourished its people well outside the Tridentine template in the centuries after the Protestant Reformation. Its spiritual culture integrated lived and felt experience with abstract theological thought. No one who visited the area ever thought of Connacht as insecurely grounded in Catholicism. Even in the grip of an existential crisis (one in four of its population died during the Famine), the old religion, indelibly watermarked into the texture of daily lives, easily held its ground under opportunistic Protestant challenge.

BIDDY EARLEY: BEAN FEASA

Biddy Earley (1798–1874) was a bean feasa (wise woman), a herbal healer, a clairvoyant and a medium.[56] She herself claimed: 'My gift, such as it is, is a purely natural gift. It was born with me: it is a part of me, like the hair on my head'.[57] An only child, she was born in Lower Faha (Co. Clare) between Feakle and Gort, and she came from the poorest substratum of pre-Famine society – the beo-bocht Irish-speaking agricultural labourers. She spoke both Irish and English. In 1814, her father died. While still a vulnerable teenager, her family was evicted in 1816 (ever after, she retained a visceral dislike of those who evicted) and she was forced to take to the roads to beg. To avoid the rigours of a life on the road, she eventually admitted herself to Ennis Poorhouse, where her pride and glory – her red hair – was shorn off. She married an old man, Pat Malley of Gurteenreagh, presumably to get herself out of the workhouse. After his death, she married her stepson, who also died soon after from alcoholism in 1840. She then married a much younger husband, a labourer who held conacre land at Kilbarron near Feakle, overlooking the lake. Here he erected a bothan scóir (conacre cabin)[58] – a two-roomed thatched mud-walled

55 D. Miller, 'Landscape and religious practice: a study of Mass attendance in pre-Famine Ireland', *Éire-Ireland*, 40:1 & 2 (2005), pp 90–106.   56 M. Ryan, *Biddy Early: the wise woman of Clare* (Cork, [1978], 1991).   57 Ryan, *Biddy Early*, p. 83; D. Stewart, 'Biddy Earley' in *Limerick Chronicle*, 3 Oct. & 10 Oct. 1953; J. Rainford, 'Feakle's Biddy Early: a victim of moral panic?', *History Ireland*, 20:1 (2012), pp 28–31.   58 **Conacre** was a system of letting land in small patches for tillage, primarily to grow potatoes. Conacre was let on an eleven-month system, sufficient to sow and harvest a crop but without creating a legal relationship between landlord and tenant. Rent was paid in cash or more commonly

house. Her third husband died in 1868 and the following year, when she was over seventy, she married a man thirty years younger than her. He died the following year, leaving her a widow for the fourth time. When she herself died in 1874, she was buried in an unmarked grave.

Her magic bottle, always believed to be a gift from the sídhe, was filled with a dark healing liquid and she used it for divination and mixing herbs.[59] She used a magic mirror into which she encouraged her visitors to gaze – a powerful aid to autosuggestion. An astute reader of character, she was compassionate ('she was as good or better to the poor as to the rich'),[60] and a shrewd observer of human nature: 'It's a thing you never should do, to beat a child that breaks a cup or bowl'.[61] Mediating disputes in families or between neighbours, she counselled 'Be as one and ye can rule the world'.[62]

As her fame spread, she was assailed equally by the state and by various irate priests, to whom she stood up vigorously – ('the priests were so set against her'):[63] she was accused of complicity in the Moonlighters, charged with witchcraft and pilloried as 'a witch or sorceress'.[64] Like many intelligent women born into the humiliations of poverty, Biddy Earley despised male authority figures: priests, landlords, doctors, police, judges ... Yeats astutely commented on her ability to generate 'a second life', a vivid, imaginative interior life that served as a coping mechanism, releasing her to soar above and away from her external constrained circumstances.[65]

An incident at Burren (Co. Clare) in 1825 showed how vulnerable to victimization poor lower-class women could be. Revd Timothy Gahagan, parish priest of (Cormcomroe) Abbey and Aughtamma (Oughtmama), forcibly expelled Mary Donelan and her family, destroying her cabin, furniture and potato store. When a neighbour helped her by erecting a temporary covering, Gahagan destroyed that too. A local magistrate, Walter Molony of Gort (Co. Galway), consulted locals, and confirmed that the 'cabin has been levelled literally to the ground' but justified it by the local opinion that Donelan was 'of loose character & had several bastard children'.[66] In Castlebar (Co. Mayo), the local curate (Revd James Hughes) and two 'respectable' parishioners (John Maguire and Robert Sheridan) were charged with 'violently assaulting Catherine Geraghty', 'a woman of bad

---

in labour. In commercial tillage areas, conacre was widely used to keep a tied but flexible agricultural labour force. It was common for a cabin (a bothán scóir) to be constructed on the conacre patch. C. Ó Danachair, 'The bothán scóir' in E. Rynne (ed.), *North Munster studies* (Limerick, 1967), pp 489–98. **59** Her son Pat, a handy hurler, was credited with acquiring the bottle as a gift for taking part in a fairy hurling game near Feakle. **60** Ryan, *Biddy Early*, p. 39. **61** Ryan, *Biddy Early*, p. 35. **62** Ryan, *Biddy Early*, p. 37. **63** A. Bourke et al., (eds), *The Field Day anthology of Irish writing, volume IV: Irish women's writing and traditions* (Cork, 2002), p. 1,438. **64** *Limerick Chronicle*, 29 July 1869. **65** *Bealtaine*, i (1899), p. 14. **66** CSO/RP/SC/1825/596.

character'. Hughes lashed her with a horsewhip and a cudgel, 'flogging her before him for above a mile of ground', and then shearing off her hair.[67] In 1826, Revd Denis O'Donnell and Revd Patrick Quirk, two priests of Tallow (Co. Waterford), horsewhipped an alleged prostitute Margaret Hogan and then cut off her hair.[68] An aggressive Irish-language sermon in 1820 by Revd Patrick Wall of Clonea (Co. Waterford) targeted a named local woman as a 'striapach' [whore].[69]

The local priest had been determined to prevent people visiting Biddy Earley: 'He'd be dressed in a frieze coat with a riding whip in his hand, driving away the people from going to her'.[70] Locals were forbidden to give directions to her house or to provide lodgings for those who sought her out. But people in dire straits still consulted her in droves: 'who wouldn't go to hell for a cure if one of his own was sick?'[71] A woman told the bishop: 'Do what you like with me, but I'd walk the world for my son who was sick'.[72] After her death in 1874, Biddy Earley's dark bottle was flung into Kilbarron Lake by Fr Andrew Connellan, parish priest of Feakle, marking a decisive break between vernacular and Roman Catholicism.

There were many other similar wise women, not exclusively Catholic either. Known mná feasa (wise women) include Moll Anthony from Co. Kildare,[73] Éibhlín Ní Ghuinníola [Kennelly?] from Baile Bhoithín (Dingle, Co. Kerry), Brídín Cúileann from Co. Galway, Máire Cáitlín Conway from Co. Wicklow, Mary Doheny from Carrick-on-Suir (Co. Tipperary)[74] and Mary Butters (1770–1850), from Carnmoney (Co. Antrim). It was believed that Butters had the power to cure afflicted cows. On an August night in

67 *Limerick General Advertiser*, 26 Oct. 1819.   68 CSO/RP/OR/1826/316.   69 'Irish sermons by the Rev Patk Wall, PP of Stradbally and Ballylonin in the county of Waterford 1822–1829', RIA, MS 23 H 17, f. 171.   70 Ryan, *Biddy Early*, p. 34.   71 Ryan, *Biddy Early*, p. 39.   72 Ryan, *Biddy Early*, p. 46.   73 '**Moll Anthony**, lived near the Red Hills, at the 'chair of Kildare', an antiquarian object of curiosity, within this county. Her reputation as a possessor of supernatural knowledge and divination drew crowds of distant visitants to her daily, and from the most remote parts of Ireland. In various instances, these were furnished with a bottle, containing some supposed curative liquid. They were then directed to return homewards, without falling asleep on their journey. The bottle given was filled with water, darkly coloured with a concoction of herbs gathered, with certain incantations, near a rath, which afforded the customary *materia medica* of the fairy doctors, for the cure of special diseases, regarding which consultation was required' (O'Hanlon, *Irish folklore*, p. 50).   74 'A Mrs Mary Reeves was her victim. Death had been busy with the family, two sisters, a child, and her father had been numbered amongst the dead; a younger child was ailing, and to cure her, the 'wise woman', **Mary Doheny**, was called in. For ten months Mary Doheny attended the sick child, and in that time, doubtless, she ascertained the mental power of the child's parents. At last she told Mrs Reeves that all the dead of her family were coming home again. Adopting a popular superstition she said that at present they were confined in Ballydine Moat. There was in the moat also one Captain James Power, who had died, but who undertook to write letters from the dead to the living. A great number of letters came from the moat, but they all contained references to comforts anything but ghostly ...

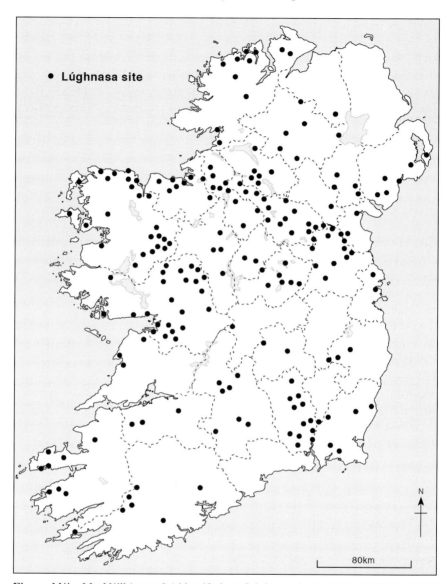

Fig. 21 Máire MacNéill (1904–87) identified 195 Lúghnasa sites in Ireland (M. Mac Néill, *The festival of Lughnasa* (Dublin, [1962] 2008), pp 652–6). There are two striking erasures: one in the Pale, where the Norman impact eroded Gaelic influence in the densely settled areas, the second in east Ulster, where the Plantations exercised a similar obliteration. The sapping of Gaelic influence in the Pale helps explain an otherwise puzzling feature of Ireland's cultural geography – why hurling, the great game of the limestone lowlands, failed to flourish there.

1807, she worked a charm to return the butter to the milk of a cow belonging to Alexander Montgomery, a tailor in Carnmoney. Her charm consisted of a pot of needles, pins, and crooked nails, mixed with milk and boiled over the Montgomery's hearth.[75] Butters ordered that all openings 'which would admit air' were to be sealed. Three people subsequently died of suffocation: Montgomery's wife (Elizabeth), their son, and an old woman (Margaret Lee). Butters was imprisoned in Carrickfergus, and when discharged lived there until her death in 1850.

CLOCHA BREACA ('CURSING STONES')

Clocha breaca[76] (translated as 'speckled stones' as early as 1603) were round stones, sometimes now called 'cursing stones'. Petrie in 1849 described specimens in Aran and Connemara as 'roundish, but never perfectly globular, of a flattened convex form on their upper and under faces; not unlike the case of a watch, and in diameter from two inches and a-half to about five inches'.[77] The antiquarian Hubert Knox (1845–1921), a careful observer, described 'the commonest' as 'smooth, round, or egg-shaped, or oval and flat-sided, such stones as may be picked up on any shingle beach of the sea or large lake. Differing in size and shape, they are alike in being smooth and more or less rounded'.[78] These stones were placed on stone altars – hence the term 'leac' sometimes associated with them.

These 'maledictive stones'[79] were typically associated with early medieval ecclesiastical sites, and releasing their powers involved the invocation of

---

– potatoes, wine, whiskey and tobacco were obtained by Mary Doheny, for the dead, every evening for four months. At last the 'wise woman' offered to show Mary Reeves her father; and the strangest part of the story is that Mary Reeves, on the trial swore 'she did see him sitting on a chair in the kitchen, near the door, wearing a blue coat, knee breeches, and a hat, and leaning on a stick'. A child's voice, too, was heard 'outside the door', which Mary Reeves 'believed' was her child's voice. The husband of Mary Reeves confirmed the main parts of this extraordinary story, and adds, that he, too, saw his father-in-law. His son also was seen and he remained in view for 'five minutes' (*Irish Times*, 25 Oct. 1864). **75** *Belfast Newsletter*, 21 Aug. 1807. **76** They are called 'clocha breacha' in *OS letters, Mayo*, p. 92. **77** W. Stokes, *The life and labours in art and archaeology of George Petrie* (London, 1868), p. 295. **78** Knox, *Tuam, Killala and Achonry*, p. 178. **79** Samuel Ferguson's poem 'The Burial of King Cormac' included the lines (after King Cormac has renounced paganism and foretold the arrival of Christianity and the druids are planning their revenge): 'They loosed their curse against the king;/They cursed him in his flesh and bones;/And daily in their mystic ring/They turned the maledictive stones'. Ferguson added his own note on 'maledictive stones' in his *Lays of the western Gael* (London, 1865), p. 240, which was largely recycled by Stokes in his *Life of Petrie*. As usual, Joyce picked up on this (*Ulysses*, annotated by Sam Slote (London, 2012), p. 720).

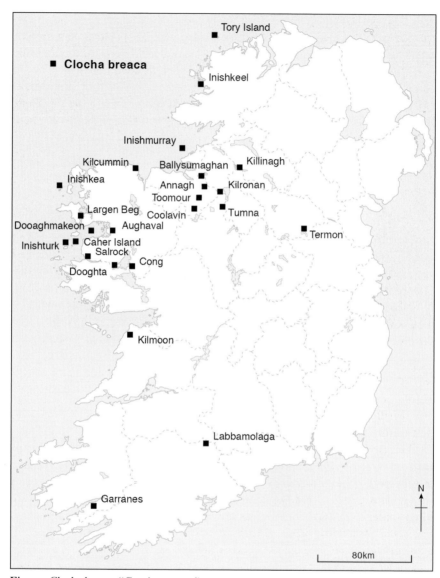

Fig. 22 Clocha breaca ('Cursing stones').

Christian saints. Petrie observed that the stones were also used for 'healing sicknesses' and 'for swearing on' as well as for malediction.[80] Deploying them to redress a perceived evil involved ritual turning of the stones in an anti-clockwise or against the sun direction – known in the Irish language and tradition as deiseal. Knox noted that turning was 'essential' and that the many stones 'are

80 Stokes, *Life of Petrie*, p. 295.

Fig. 23 Carefully hidden clocha breaca ('cursing stones') at Labbamolaga (Co. Cork).

used to keep count of prayers or curses and are taken in the hand or turned round'.[81] This practice may have originated in early medieval excommunication rituals, as the nineteenth-century descriptions stressed that turning the stones was usually preceded by ritual fasting, recitation of traditional prayers, and performing 'rounds'.[82]

The ritual around these stones closely resembled the well-known use of bells and relics for swearing oaths, and saints were believed to intervene directly to protect their own.[83] Their ecclesiastical origins is suggested by the fact that the stones were associated with and named after a local saint, and that they were often under the guardianship of hereditary keepers – described as erenachs or maors – who gave access to them and who may also have transmitted the appropriate rituals. The correct sequencing and placing of the multiple stones was an arcane secret. The sixteenth-century 'Beatha Maedoc' [Mo Aodh Óg, Mogue, Aidan] stressed that the O'Connolly family were appointed by the saint himself as erenachs to 'protect and maintain' his church at Killybeg (Co. Fermanagh), and that he left his stone in their possession to be used by them by

---

81 Knox, *Tuam, Killala and Achonry*, p. 178.   82 C. Corlett, 'Cursing stones in Ireland', *JGAHS*, 64 (2012), pp 1–20.   83 M. Johnson, '"Vengeance is mine": saintly retribution in medieval Ireland' in S. Throop & P. Hyams (eds), *Vengeance in the Middle Ages: emotion, religion and feud* (Abingdon, 2016), pp 5–50; K. Overbey, *Sacral geographies: saints, shrines and territory in medieval Ireland* (Turnhout, 2012).

turning it deiseal against 'whoever shall do wrong of injustice to the erenaghs or tenants of this church', 'as the wise men of that land and territory agree'.[84] Petrie was clear that when these stones were turned, 'their order [is] changed by the inhabitants'.[85] The known evidence for these stones comes from the west and north-west although it is likely that they were once more widespread. The presence of similar stones at many sites with no recorded tradition of incantation suggests that this is the case.

These stones gained psychological potency when incantationary rituals summoned and released their latent energy. A crucial feature is that the power recoiled on an inappropriate or untruthful meddler. The use of these stones was a classic weapon of the weak, an answering back to vulnerability and injustice, as in the widow's curse. Westropp supplied an example from the 'cursing stones' at Kilmoon, between Killeany and Lisdoonvarna (Co. Clare).

> They lie on a dry-stone wall under an old wind-bent tree at the holy well, adjoining the ruin in the field to the west of the church, and were brought to more than local knowledge some fifteen or sixteen years ago [c.1897]. A farmer was prosecuted by a beggar woman for beating and laming her. He put forward as his defence (at petty sessions, I think, at Corofin), that 'she swore to turn the stones of Kilmoon' against him. It was believed that, if a person went fasting to the place and did seven rounds 'against the sun' [deiseal], turning each stone in the same unlucky direction, the mouth of the person against whom the stones were turned would be twisted under his ear, and his face permanently distorted. It is said that the magistrate, in consequence of the strong local belief in the possibility of such injury, regarded the farmer's act as one of bona fide self-defence, and advised him to end the grievance by satisfying the damaged would-be practitioner of the black art with a sum of money.[86]

These stones formed part of a highly developed repertoire of informal justice within Irish vernacular culture, ranging from threatening letters,[87] to faction fights to secret societies.

---

84 C. Plummer, *Lives of the Irish saints* (Oxford, 1922), p. 241.   85 Stokes, *Life of Petrie*, p. 296.   86 Westropp Folklore Survey, Clare.   87 Gibbons, *Captain Rock, night errant*. Of 483 location-specific examples, the leading counties were Cork (58), Tipperary (56) and Limerick (54). Munster had 43 per cent, Leinster 42 per cent while Connaught had 10 per cent and Ulster 5 per cent (p. 43).

CHAPTER SIX

Irish Protestantism from the
Reformation to Partition

THE EARLY SEVENTEENTH CENTURY witnessed the initiation of significant English and especially Scottish settlement in Ulster.[1] Dissenting congregations rose from fifty in 1660 to 100 in 1702 (following the surge in immigration in the 1690s), and reached 250 by 1790, comprising half a million adherents. Antrim, Down and east Derry were heavily populated by the Scottish, but they were equally plentiful in the area of the official plantation, especially along the Bann valley, and in the Laggan area south of Derry city – 'the most fertile, best inhabited and improved [land] is that part of the champaign region centred on the barony of Raphoe'.[2] English settlers were concentrated in Fermanagh, mid-Armagh and in a crescent stretching from there back along the Lagan valley towards Belfast. Severe differences existed between the Scottish and the English, in social origins, cultural disposition, political attitudes and settlement patterns but above all in religion, for while the English belonged to the Established Church, the Scots were Presbyterian, cleaved to Calvinist theology, and sought no truck with bishops or church hierarchy. English-dominated areas in Armagh and Fermanagh were village-based, centred around supportive landlords and a social hierarchy. Dissenting communities were farm-based and socially homogeneous, with Scottish-style fermtouns, clachans and rundale, and they were led by their ministers rather than by their landlords.

The sombre Dissenting theology, with its foreboding sense of imputation,[3] contrasted with the studied blandness of Anglicanism. Irish Presbyterians, well schooled in the porcupine politics of the grudge, felt cheated by their exclusion from the fruits of the Williamite victory in Ireland, despite what they regarded as their pivotal input in achieving it. This fomented an Ulster-

---

1 A. Gailey, 'The Scots element in North Irish popular culture', *Ethnologica Europeae*, 11:1 (1975), pp 2–22. 2 J. McParlan, *Statistical survey of the county of Donegal* (Dublin, 1801), p. 21. 3 **Imputation** was the pessimistic theological concept that Adam's sin was transmitted unredeemed to his descendants and accordingly that all humans were born sinful, and could only be saved by being born again. 'Precondamned' is Joyce's witty version in *Finnegans wake* (FW, 418.30).

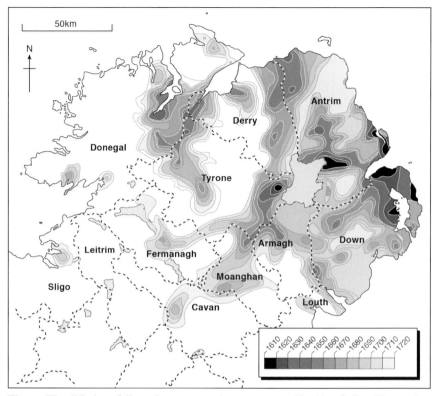

Fig. 24 The diffusion of dissenting congregations was mapped by Alan Gailey. The surging wave dissipated eventually in the drumlins and mountains of south Ulster. The spread was influenced by a combination of culture, economics, topography and environment.

Presbyterian culture of grievance, potent in a covenanted community, tightly knotted by kinship, geographically condensed and with a spur to maintaining a distinct sectarian and ethnic identity through their juxtaposition with English-Anglican and Irish-Catholic communities. Dissenters disagreed vigorously over what they actually stood for but they were utterly convinced about what they opposed. The Ulster Presbyterian John Gamble (1770–1831) observed in 1810: 'It would appear incredible how pertinaciously they retain the customs and usages of their ancestors, were it not considered that they were settled among a people they detested'.[4]

Dissenting was never a monolithic phenomenon and careful attention needs to be paid to its internal varieties, social composition and spatial variegations. Non-Subscribers, Covenanters, Seceders, Burghers, Anti-Burghers, New and Old Light represented the enormously fissile tendencies within the intensely

4 J. Gamble, *Sketches of history, politics and manners taken in Dublin and the north of Ireland in the autumn of 1810* (London, 1811), p. 128.

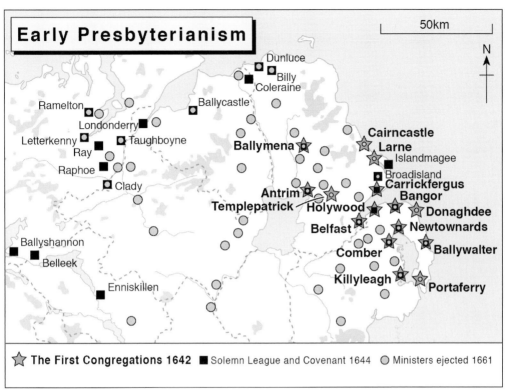

Early Presbyterianism

50km

N

Dunluce
Billy
Coleraine
Ramelton
Ballycastle
Londonderry
Letterkenny
Taughboyne
Ray
Cairncastle
Raphoe
Ballymena
Larne
Islandmagee
Clady
Broadisland
Carrickfergus
Antrim
Bangor
Templepatrick
Holywood
Donaghdee
Belfast
Newtownards
Ballyshannon
Comber
Ballywalter
Belleek
Killyleagh
Enniskillen
Portaferry

☆ The First Congregations 1642   ■ Solemn League and Covenant 1644   ○ Ministers ejected 1661

Fig. 25   The geography of seventeenth-century Irish Presbyterianism, 1642–61 (Presbyterian Historical Society of Ireland).

democratic world of Presbyterianism, but this atomization should not be judged as weakness. Popular ministers with a reputation for excellent preaching could easily break away and found new congregations. The result was a multiplicity of meeting houses in areas dominated by Presbyterianism: Newtownards (Co. Down), for example, currently has seven. In 1809, the tiny town of Cootehill (Co. Cavan) had seven churches: two Presbyterian, Anglican, Methodist, Moravian, Quaker and Catholic. Proliferation was a sign of vitality not of degeneration, and Dissent fed a lively vernacular intellectual tradition. One commentator concluded that 'the ruling elders of the Presbyterian congregation are generally small farmers but of no ordinary theological attainments'.[5] Theology ruled the realm of political ideas and sophisticated spiritual disputes revealed an advanced level of debate, sustained by close links to Scotland.

Presbyterianism became a theologically literate and ramifying set of sects rather than one big church. It incubated a democratic congregational spirit,

5   A. Shafto Adair, *The winter of 1846–7 in Antrim with remarks on outdoor relief and colonization* (London, 1847), p. 64.

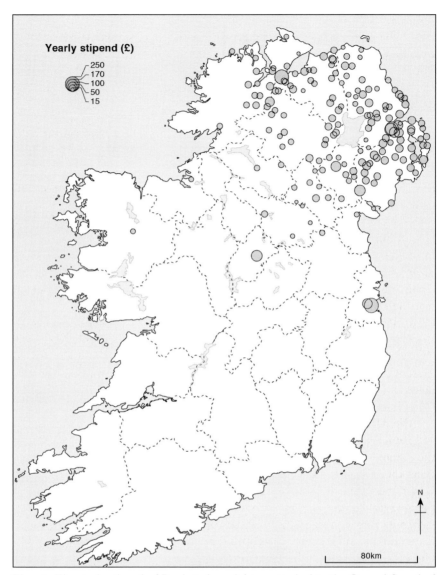

Fig. 26 The yearly stipend of Presbyterian ministers attached to the General Synod of Ulster, 1799 (*Castlereagh correspondence*, iii, pp 167–71).

with a spiky resentment and aggression, defined by its anti-establishment and anti-deferential ethos. Jonathan Swift (1667–1745) long smarted from his traumatic stint in Kilroot (Co. Antrim) in 1695–6, among 'cursed Scottish hell-hounds', 'that discontented brood/who always loudest for religion brawl'.[6] A

---

6 Swift argued that that the Scots in Ireland have 'come over full fraught with that spirit which taught them to abolish Episcopacy at home': J. Swift, *A letter from a member of the*

surge of dissenting energy was displaced from Scotland towards the end of the seventeenth century, and it coursed through Ulster subsequently, seething with democratic vigour. Contempt for inherited institutions animated 'the auld church, the cauld church, the church without a steeple'. The actor Woody Harrelson compares being raised Presbyterian as opposed to Catholic: 'half the ritual, double the guilt'.[7]

PRESBYTERIAN CHURCHES

Reformed churches advocated a stark setting to focus on a word-based rather than a ritualized liturgy, a marked refusal to merge the container (the church) with the content (the Church), and to attempt to corral God within a merely human building of walls and stone. In 1619, David Calderwood, a Scottish Presbyterian, preached that 'the sacraments are not tied to the materiall kirks made of dead stones but the kirke made of living stones'.[8] They rejected any architectural expression of hierarchy or decorative exuberance in the belief that their aloof Calvinist God would be unimpressed by such idle trumpery. Ulster Presbyterians favoured severe, even dour boxes, shorn of images, with altars downsized to a plain table, and the pulpit elevated to pride of place. The church as the theatre of God's word should prioritize preaching by gathering hearers within range of the pulpit, while clergy were judged primarily on their powers of preaching. This emphasis favoured an architectural solution where the pulpit was positioned on the long rather than the short wall.

After 1661, Presbyterians were barred from attendance at Anglican churches and from then on were disposed to build their own distinct churches. Unlike the Catholics and the Anglicans, they were free to make a radical break from the geographical and architectural traditions of the established denominations. In Ulster, their preferred models were Scottish precedents that focused worship on the long wall, with T-shaped plans and wrap-around galleries that maximized proximity to the preacher. In 1676, the Armagh Presbyterian meeting house featured three large galleries and a central pulpit arrayed against a long wall.[9] However, early eighteenth-century examples were typically modest, 22m x 7m in the excavated example at Ramelton (Co. Donegal).[10] The thatched church at Malin (Co. Donegal) was stilted below the high water mark in 1711 because of

House of Commons in Ireland to a member of the House of Commons in England concerning the Sacramental Test in *Prose works*, ed. H. Davis et al., 14 vols (Oxford, 1939–68), ii, p. 116. For the background, see C. Fox, 'Swift's Scotophobia', *Bullán*, 6 (2002), pp 43–65. **7** Interview in *Financial Times*, 27 May 2018. **8** Walsham, *Catholic Reformation in Protestant Britain*, p. 90. **9** AAI, iv, p. 446. Regrettably demolished in 1970. **10** J. Carroll, 'The excavation of the old Presbyterian meeting house at Ramelton, Co. Donegal', *Archaeology Ireland*, 3:2 (1989), pp 61–3.

hostility from the landlord, with early graves higgly-pigglied into the adjacent sand dunes at Lagg.

A stream of churches vernacular in style and appearance followed: Coagh (1711[?]), Co. Tyrone), Ballee (1721, Co. Down), Armagh 'New' (1722), Corboy (1729, Co. Longford), Downpatrick (1729, Co. Down), Magherally (1734, Co. Down), Killinchy (1739, Co. Down), Clondermot (1743, Co. Derry), Ballynahinch (1751, Co. Down), Dunmurry (1779, Co. Antrim), Rademon (1787, Co. Down), Randalstown (1790, Co. Antrim) and Tyrone's Ditches (1797, Co. Armagh).[11] The Covenanters, disparaged for their poverty as 'mountain men',[12] built a suite of sturdy churches in the second half of the eighteenth century following their break from the General Synod in 1760: Kellswater (1760, Co. Antrim), Knockbracken (1776, Co. Down), Bready (1786, Co. Tyrone), Creevagh (1789, Co. Monaghan) and Faughan (1790, Co. Derry).[13] This Presbyterian-style architecture influenced Catholic chapels in the province.[14] These were likely constructed by the same set of mobile master builders.[15] The impetus accelerated after the rise of the Volunteers in the 1780s. This can be seen in the extraordinary support given to the building of Catholic chapels in Ulster in the 1780s. The Volunteers financially sponsored chapels at Dromore, Saul, Saintfield, Ballynahinch, Ballee and Portaferry (all Co. Down),

---

11 J. Curl, *Classical churches in Ulster* (Belfast, 1980). Some of the later ones are possibly by the enigmatically gifted Roger Mulholland (1740–1818), who certainly designed the superb Rosemary Street church in Belfast in 1783: C. Brett, *Roger Mulholland: architect of Belfast* (Belfast, 1976).   12 'We, the members of the Reformed Church, called Presbyterian Dissenters (reproachfully called Mountain Men) hold it our duty to step forward from conscience ... Done in the name of the Reformed Church in the counties of Antrim and Down' (*Northern Star*, 10–14 Oct. 1796). Three decades later, Covenanters were 'contented to purchase conscience with poverty' (Glassford, *Three tours*, p. 112).   13 A valuable set of early photographs of these evocative churches can be found in S. Ferguson, *Brief biographical sketches of some Irish Covenanting ministers* (Londonderry, 1897). In 1824, William Bell, moderator of the Seceders, observed that 'The number of people entrusted to the supervision of the Seceding ministers in Ireland is around 100,000'. Bell claimed credit for their loyalty in 1798: 'no Minister of this Communion was punished in any way for fomenting the spirit of disloyalty and insurrection' (CSO/RP/1824/1634). As late as 1901, the *Church of Ireland Gazette* could poke gentle fun at the Covenanters: 'A quaint and empty ceremony was gone through in the town of Ballymoney on 2nd and 3rd July, when a few ministers of the little sect of Covenanters – numbering about 3,000 in County Antrim – met together and renewed the solemn league and covenant of 1649. It appears that this performance was last gone through by them in 1853; but the weather being fine and the holiday season arrived, it was deemed a suitable occasion for another 'renovation'. The Pope and the "Prelatic Church" came in for their usual hard words, all present swore and uplifted hands to "endeavour the extirpation of Popery and Prelacy"; and then dined amicably together in the Temperance Café, and went peaceably home' (*Church of Ireland Gazette*, 19 July 1901).   14 F. McCormick, 'Mass houses and meeting houses: Catholic and Presbyterian church design in eighteenth-century Ireland' in Lyttleton & Stout (eds), *Church and settlement in Ireland*, pp 208–28.   15 Anthony O'Flaherty is an example of a master builder: he signed his 1763 church at Lough Derg (Co. Donegal).

Glendermot and Londonderry (both Co. Derry), and Belfast and Lisburn (both Co. Antrim).[16]

In the early nineteenth century, upwardly mobile Presbyterianism, enriched by the linen boom,[17] embraced the classical temple, as at Banagher (1825) and Ballykelly (1827) in Co. Derry. The Presbyterians presumably chose Greek Revival because it was a style equally underplayed by the Church of Ireland and Catholicism. There followed a fine series in this style by the Belfast architect John Millar (1811–76): Third Belfast, Rosemary Street (1829–31, demolished 1941), Castlereagh (1834–5), First Antrim (1834–7) and Portaferry (Co. Down) (1839–41). Two other fine Greek Revival churches in Co. Down are First Presbyterian, Banbridge (1844–6) and Killinchy Non-Subscribing (1846). By mid-century, Irish Presbyterianism embraced the Gothic, notably in Dublin at Rathgar (1860–2), Dún Laoghaire (1863), Findlaters's (1862–4), and the Non-Subscribing (later Unitarian) church on Stephen's Green (1861–3). Belfast gained many Scottish-Baronial Gothicized churches from the 1870s onwards, mostly by the favoured local firm of Young and MacKenzie.

Ulster Presbyterianism remained in close connection with Scotland. An example is the flurry of corpse houses that were built in east Antrim at Donegore, Ballylinney, Rashee and Kilbride in the early 1830s in response to the Scottish panic over body snatching for the medical schools. The gallows were the only legal source of medical cadavers, incentivizing graverobbing. Other graveyards employed paid nightwatchmen. The Anatomy Act of 1832 made pauper bodies available (to be poor was to be criminalized in death as in life) and this closed down the resurrection men.

MOUNTAINS AND LOWLANDS: SECTARIAN LANDSCAPES

The Presbyterian wave had surged up the Lagan, Bann and Foyle valleys, before its momentum dissipated among the drumlins, bogs and lakes of watery south Ulster. A pronounced religious frontier was accentuated by topography along the ragged southern border of Ulster, where the small-farming and protoindustrial linen world of the drumlin belt petered out. This was the breán tír (sour land), poorman's country, with a clear divide separating it from the fat farm areas of Meath and the midlands.

In south Ulster, a predominantly Catholic swathe of territory stretched from south Down through south Armagh, into Cavan, and then on to south Fermanagh and south-west Donegal. In 1801, a local landlord Charles Coote (1738–1800), the first earl of Bellamont, described Co. Cavan: 'It is all acclivity and declivity,

16 P. Rogers, *The Irish Volunteers and Catholic Emancipation: a neglected phase of Ireland's history* (London, 1934), p. 153.   **17** K. Rankin, *The linen houses of County Antrim and north County Down* (Belfast, 2012).

without the intervention of one horizontal plane: the hills are all rocks and the people are all savages'.[18] This sentiment was echoed by Thomas Bell in 1809: 'the Alps or Pyrenees could not be more difficult than the Cavan hills'.[19] The poorest, most isolated and most homogenous communities in Ireland lingered here, bearing the crushing weight of their defining defeat in the seventeenth century. A detailed case study of Strabane barony (Co. Tyrone) showed that the native Irish in 1622 were 'concentrated in less accessible upland areas'.[20] Plantation officials produced a list of mountainous townlands 'most fitt and convenient' 'to be graunted and let to the inhabitants and mere natives of this country'.[21]

In Glenfinn (Co. Donegal), John O'Donovan encountered 'remnants of the men of Moy-Iha [Maig Íotha, the plain beside the river Finn, later called the Lagan], who were driven to the mountains by the dominant party of James 1'.[22] South of Lough Neagh, in the area known as the Montiaghs in north Armagh, Catholics were 'refugees from the planted lowlands in the vicinity who sought the shelter of the Moyntiaghs, which at that time was almost isolated by vast bogs, as they are even to this day by winter floods'.[23] In Co. Down, 'when the Catholics were driven off the territories granted to the Hamiltons and Montgomerys, to make room for Scotch settlers, they found a place of refuge in Lecale, where the descendants of the early English colonists were Catholics'.[24] On the bleak north-facing slopes of Omeath (Co. Louth), the ancestral memory was of being uprooted from north Armagh and east Derry.[25]

In County Mayo, Ulster refugees were still called na hUltaigh (or more cuttingly 'na h-Ultaigh bradacha')[26] as late as the 1830s, when they still spoke Ulster Irish. In Ballycroy and Ballymunelly, the northern families included MacSweeney, O'Cleary, O'Gallagher, Conway, MacManamin, Friel and Monelly. They arrived there around 1638, when Ballycroy was still wooded.[27] Their 1830s leader Manus Sweeney could trace six generations back to Lochlainn Garbh Ó Dónaill, the first of the family that came to Ballycroy.[28] Similarly Cú Choigcríche Ó Cléirigh (Cucogiry O'Clery), from Kilbarron near Assaroe (Co. Donegal), led his family to Ballycroy.[29] The Derry O'Cahans arrived around 1630 with Niall Garbh O Dómhnaill.[30]

18 *Walker's Hibernian Magazine* (1801), p. 42.   **19** S. Ó Loingsigh (ed.), 'An excursion to Co. Cavan 1809', *Breifne*, 8 (1965), p. 498.   **20** G. Farrell, *The 'mere Irish' and the colonization of Ulster, 1570–1641* (London, 2017), p. 178.   **21** Farrell, *'Mere Irish' and the colonization of Ulster*, p. 183.   **22** *OS letters, Donegal*, p. 81.   **23** J. Smyth, 'Hearth money roll' [Aghagallon parish], *Down & Connor Historical Society Journal*, 6 (1934), pp 52–4. Tradition then held that 'whatever Protestants are in the Moyntiaghs are the descendants of '98 refugees'.   **24** J. O'Laverty, *An historical account of the Diocese of Down and Connor, ancient and modern*, 5 vols (Dublin, 1878–95), i, p. 115. The sheltering effect of the Catholic Savages was crucial to this survival on the Ards peninsula.   **25** T. Jones Hughes, 'Landholding and settlement in the Cooley peninsula of Co. Louth', *Irish Geography*, 4:3 (1961), pp 149–74.   **26** *OS letters, Mayo*, p. 115, p. 137. Bradacha means scoundrelly or thieving.   **27** *OS letters, Mayo*, p. 137.   **28** *OS letters, Mayo*, p. 55.   **29** *OS letters, Mayo*, p. 118.   **30** *OS letters, Mayo*, p. 132.

Within Protestant-dominated lowland Ulster, some dominantly Catholic pockets survived as 'the retreat of the ancient inhabitants'[31] in the Mournes, the Sperrins and the Glens of Antrim. John Gamble observed about the Sperrins that they:

> were the asylum of those unfortunate people, and they were not dispossessed of them, probably because no other people would live in them. Into these mountains, they were driven and pent up like sheep, and left upon black bog, and dun heath, and barren rock to mourn over their fallen greatness, their fertile vales, their flocks and their fields.[32]

In 1714, the Catholic bishop of Clogher diocese Hugh MacMahon (1660–1737) diagnosed poverty as the defining problem for Ulster Catholics: 'this province is worse off than the rest of the country, because Presbyterians from neighbouring Scotland are arriving here daily in large groups of families, occupying the towns and lowlands, seizing the farms in the richer parts of the country and expelling the natives'. The result was that 'the Catholic natives are forced to erect their cabins in mountainous or boggy country'.[33]

Differential leasing policies spawned segregation in areas of heavy immigration. These patterns acquired an inbuilt topographic dimension with Protestant tenants steered to the better lands while Catholics were gradually squeezed out to the marginal lands. Bargaining power, sectarian and social cachet, and ease of access to decision makers permeated the leasing system. Because of the frequent juxtaposition of good and poor land, a leasing system operating within these sectarian parameters assigned Catholics upslope and Protestants to the richer lowlands.

Once established, this association held at various scales (from counties through parishes to townlands) and times: the earlier patterns remained remarkably consistent, and there is evidence of conversion to the dominant religion by the minorities. For example, the main belt of planter settlement in south Derry ran through the lowlands from Moneymore through Magherafelt, Castledawson and Bellaghy to Kilrea, a pattern evident in sources from 1631, 1660, 1663, 1740 and 1831.[34] A stable pattern emerged in the early seventeenth century, followed by a secondary expansion after the 1690s. In 1740, half the planter families were still in their original core area after half a century of accelerating demographic expansion.

---

31 J. Dubourdieu, *Statistical survey of the county of Antrim* (Dublin, 1812), p. 260. **32** J. Gamble, *Views of society and manners in the north of Ireland* (London, 1819), pp 318–19. **33** P. Moran (ed.), *Spicilegium Ossoriense, being a collection of original letters and papers illustrative of the history of the Irish church from the Reformation to the year 1800*, 3 vols (Dublin, 1874–84), ii, p. 470. **34** W. MacAfee, 'The colonization of the Maghera region of south Derry during the seventeenth and eighteenth centuries', *Ulster Folklife*, 23 (1977), pp 70–91.

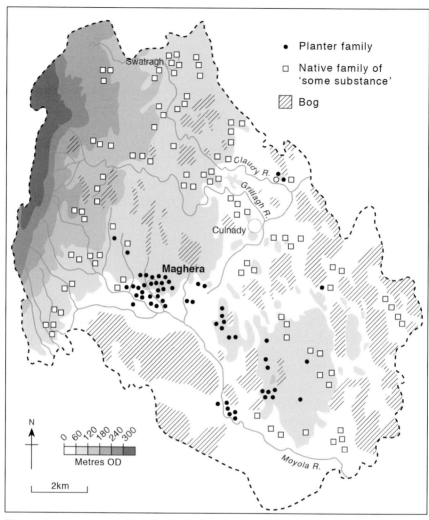

Fig. 27 Protestants and Catholics in the Maghera area (Co. Derry), 1663 as mapped by William Macafee from the Hearth Money Rolls.

Within the Maghera area, a strikingly concentrated planter belt formed as a wedge between the Moyola boglands to the south and Irish-dominated areas to the north. Planter-dominated townlands were associated with better quality arable land, surrounded by relatively poorer Irish areas on three sides. Plantation regulations to remove the natives were flouted because Catholics proved willing to pay higher rents, and the sectarian distribution was constrained within the leasing pattern. Even at the micro-level of the townland, self-segregation ruled. In Gorteade in 1831, planters and native Irish were more or less split by the road that bisected the townland. Remarkably, as late as the 1970s, the old pattern in south Derry had assumed an even more concentrated form.[35]

As early as 1667, it was claimed in Ulster that the 'mountainous, boggy and coarse lands [are] inhabited only by natives'.[36] In 1674, Archbishop Oliver Plunkett commented that in Ulster 'all the good land is in the hands of Protestants and the poorer Catholics occupy the mountains and the uplands'.[37] By 1714, Bishop MacMahon had reduced the situation to an aphorism: 'Throughout Ulster, the towns and the fertile lands were occupied by the planters; the Catholics were left nothing but the mountains and bogs'.[38]

Preaching in the open air in Derry on 21 March 1725, a young Catholic called William Smith[39] claimed that 'the Romans were depressed and obliged to go to the ditches and glens to celebrate Mass' and lamented that 'the Church of Rome was so much under' in Ulster.[40] A Derry priest in 1736 observed that the penal laws had forced itinerant friars and priests in Ulster to assemble furtive congregations in the fields for Mass and teaching.[41] Anthony Coyle, bishop of Raphoe (1782–1801), reported in 1786: 'Although they are the majority, Catholics are settled in the mountains, while the heretics, equal in number, occupy the plains and towns'.[42] From Cavan, James Connery lamented in 1832: 'All the rich valleys in his dear Cavan were occupied by Protestants exclusively while the Catholics were forced to live in the highlands or mountainous districts', where they were reduced to mere 'hewers of wood and drawers of water' to the Protestants.[43] The same sentiments permeated the Irishtowns on the edge of urban settlements, as, for example, the Bogside huddled under the walled shadow of Londonderry.

Throughout Ulster, 'Catholic' townlands were typically upslope of 'Protestant' ones. The United Irishman Charles Teeling (1778–1850) described the Catholics in the late eighteenth century as 'the segregated sons of Ulster in a land of persecution', 'a distinct and separate people'[44] who had been decimated in the seventeenth century and who endured now as feral 'children of the wild':

> The scattered and impoverished few derived security from their own weakness, and those who still cleaved with a lingering fondness to the sod of their ancestors were suffered to draw a precarious subsistence

---

35 MacAfee, 'Maghera region', p. 86.   36 J.P. Prendergast, *Ireland from the Restoration to the revolution, 1660–1690* (London, 1887), p. 99.   37 Hanly (ed.), *Letters of Oliver Plunkett*, p. 411.   38 Cited in Moran (ed.), *Spicilegium Ossoriense*, ii, p. 470.   39 P.J. Larkin, '"Popish riot" in south Co. Derry 1725', *Seanchas Ard Mhacha*, 8:1 (1975–6), pp 97–110.   40 Deposition of Walter Bell, 5 Apr. 1725, NLI, MS 9,612, f. 60.   41 F.D. Brullaughan, *Opusculum de missione et missionariis tractans* (Metz, 1747). The original (and extremely rare) edition was entitled *Vade mecum missionariorum* (Louvain, 1736).   42 Cited in Moran, *Catholics of Ireland under the penal laws*, p. 15.   43 J. Connery, *The reformer* (London, 1836), p. 59.   44 C. Teeling, *Observations on the history and consequences of the Battle of the Diamond* (Belfast, 1838), p. 113.

from their laborious allure of the sequestered mountain or in the unwholesome fen of the deep morass.[45]

The English commentator Edward Wakefield observed the solidifying effect of such circumstances on the Ulster Catholic community in 1812: 'The persecuted and proscribed form a compact body distinct from their oppressors and the union which common misery produces is firm and lasting'.[46]

Outside Ulster, notably in north Wexford and Wicklow (forty-eight per cent Protestant in 1731), Protestants and Catholics were also segregated by slope. By the eighteenth century, it was well-established that 'there is a Protestant price for land and a Popish price for land'.[47] The complicated pattern can be seen from the sprawling parish of Rathdrum in 1766 (forty per cent Protestant in 1831). In 1766, the religious groupings were allocated by townland and a typical south Wicklow/north Wexford pattern of alternating townlands solidified, some Protestant, some Catholic. The lowland area around the town itself was dominantly Protestant, while the more marginal upland areas were dominantly Catholic. An inbuilt topographic dimension juxtaposed pockets of Catholics cheek by jowl with pockets of Protestants. On the Powerscourt estate near Enniskerry (Co. Wicklow) in the 1830s, the Protestants were said to 'hold the best part of the lands, the Catholics being principally located on the mountainsides, and in the rugged bottoms of Glencree'.[48] In south Munster, Tadhg Gaelach Ó Súilleabháin (1715–95) contrasted 'garbhchnoic fraoigh na líog do chráigh me' (the rough stony heathery hills that torture me) to 'machairí míne sioda 's na mbanta sróill' (silky satiny smooth plains).[49]

These perceptions went deep in popular culture. Sectarian signatures could all too easily be read into the landscape, which was also moralized. Abraham Hume in 1853 mapped upland/lowland areas in Ulster against religion and concluded that Ulster Protestants occupied the lowlands because 'The natural position of the white, like that of the Protestant, is on the higher steps of the social pyramid'. He noted that 'The line of the English settlers is the line of orchards in the north of Ireland to this hour, and if the people and the names are blotted out, their history would be partially written in the trees which they planted'.[50] Ian Paisley claimed that 'Our ancestors cut a civilization out of the bogs and meadows of this country while Mr Haughey's ancestors were wearing pig skins and living in caves'.[51]

---

45 Teeling, *Observations*, pp 13–14.   **46** Wakefield, *Ireland statistical and political*, ii, p. 645.   **47** *Seasonable advice to Protestants containing some means of reviving and strengthening the Protestant interest*, second edition (Cork, 1745), p. 21.   **48** *OS letters, Wicklow*, p. 28. **49** Cited in Mac Mhurchaidh, *Lón anama*, p. 245.   **50** A. Hume, *Origin and characteristics of the people in the counties of Down and Antrim*, (Belfast, 1874), p. 12.   **51** In a 1981 TV programme, John Hume once asked Paisley: 'if the word "no" were to be removed from the English language, you'd be speechless, wouldn't you?' Paisley's reply was: 'No, I wouldn't'.

PROTESTANT VILLAGES AND THE LINEN INDUSTRY

The eighteenth century saw an attempt to spread Protestantism by creating linen colonies in new towns south and west of the main Ulster protoindustrial[52] region. Early examples include Listowel (1709, Co. Kerry),[53] Churchill (1720, Co. Fermanagh),[54] Manulla (1733, Co. Mayo),[55] Ballyhaise (1735, Co. Cavan), Dunmanway (1740s) and Inishannon (1750s, both Co. Cork), Mountshannon (1740s, Co. Clare), Ballymote (1750s, Co. Sligo),[56] Monivea (1750s, Co. Galway) and Villierstown (1750s, Co. Waterford).[57] Later linen villages of the 1760s included Fintona (Co. Tyrone), Castlewellan (Co. Down), Emyvale (Co. Monaghan) and Collon (Co. Louth), while among belated examples was Newtown Bellew (Co. Galway) in the 1780s. For landlords, the great attractions

---

52 **Protoindustrialization** was an earlier phase in the development of modern industrial economies that preceded and paved the way for fully-fledged industrialization. It was marked by the increasing involvement of rural families in domestic but market-oriented production, especially in the highly labour-intensive weaving and spinning required in the linen industry before it became town- and mill-based. **53** The Listowel linen colony comprised 'several English families from the north' ('Molyneux tour', pp 64–5). **54** 'Churchill, County Fermanagh: These are to give notice, that the Right Honourable Sir Gustavus Hume Baronet designs to set up and establish a linnen manufactory at the town of Church Hill in the county of Fermanaugh, where he hath already built a good inn, and several good houses of stone and lime fit for tradesmen, and where there is a weekly market on every Saturday, and three fairs in the year, viz. on the third of May, and nineteenth of August, and the nintenth of November, within three miles of Iniskilling, and 12 miles of Ballyshannon, two considerable market towns and places of good trade; And for the encouragement of the same will give leases for 21 years or three lives, of ground sufficient for houses and gardens, at 12 pence per annum to persons that will build the same with stone and lime, the quarry for stone and limestone being within a quarter of a mile of the said town, and good turf for firing at the same distance; The said Sir Gustavus will build a bleach yard at a convenient distance from the said town, at a proper place well watered, and the better to carry on the said manufactory will lend to any undertakers the sum of £500 at 3 per cent for the first 2 years, and 4 per cent for the next 2 years, and 5 per cent for the 3 years more, said undertakers giving good security for the repayment of the said money at the end of the said 7 years, with interest as aforesaid in the mean time, and imploying the said money in carrying on the said manufactory and improving the said town. Any undertakers or tradesmen that have a mind for parks for graising or sowing flax may be supplied with any quantity of land near the said town they think proper for 21 years or 3 lives at reasonable rent' (*Dublin Courant*, 10 Jan. 1718–19). **55** 'A mile further brought us to Manilla, a poor small town situated on a rising ground to the west of a rivlet: It is chiefly a colony of Protestants, settled here as freeholders by Mr Brown of the Neal, who founded a Charter School here for 12 boys and 12 girls, by giving 10 acres for ever and twenty [acres] at five shillings an acre': Pococke (1752), p. 82 [CELT]. **56** Lord Shelburne in 1760 'contracted with people in the north to bring Protestant weavers and establish a manufactory' in Ballymote. 'He lost £5,000 by the business, with only seventeen Protestant families and twenty-six or twenty-seven looms established for it' (A. Young, *A tour in Ireland with general observations on the present state of that Kingdom made in the years 1776,1777 and 1778*, 2 vols (Dublin, 1780), i, pp 223–31). **57** Young also reported on Monivea (*Tour*, i, p. 272); D. Cronin, *A Galway gentleman in the age of improvement: Robert French of Monivea, 1716–1779* (Dublin, 1995).

of linen were that it was regarded as a 'Protestant' industry, that it gave a fillip to fairs and markets, that it exercised a powerful monetizing effect, and that it enjoyed considerable government support. As one booster described the linen colonies: 'The Protestant religion as well as the linen manufacture would be hereby extended into the Popish parts of Ireland, which would greatly strengthen and promote the Protestant interest'.[58]

In 1767, when Thomas Maude (1727–77) began his estate village at Dundrum (Co. Tipperary), he advertised for 'Protestant manufacturers' who would be eligible for leases for three lives set in units of five to ten acres on a total of 270 acres.[59] These linen colonies suffered a high degree of failure at centres like Creevenully[60] and Fuerty (both Co. Roscommon),[61] Drumersnave (Co. Leitrim) and Gortboy (Co. Leitrim) (established by Nathaniel Clements to attract Protestant weavers, lured by pre-built houses, workshops and looms),[62] Kilsellagh (Co. Sligo), Barry (Co. Longford),[63] Collinstown (Co. Westmeath), Grangegeeth (Co. Meath), Clonmore (Co. Louth) and Mullafarry (Co. Mayo). The attrition rate proved high:

> [Colonies] in the Popish parts of *Ireland*, were so weak, that they have not been able to stand their ground, against the natives of the country, who imagine it their interest to discourage them. It is, indeed, to be feared, that such colonies will never be successful until the gentlemen of those parts universally find their interest in tillage. Whenever that comes to pass, northern Protestants will be transplanted into the Popish countries of the south in such numbers, as will give them strength; and it will then become the common interest of the gentlemen in the country to support and protect them.[64]

A successful zone of industrial and mill villages developed only in the north-east, where earlier plantation settlements were subsumed into the linen economy in the eighteenth and nineteenth centuries. Mill villages, common in Armagh, Antrim, Down and Tyrone, maintained the distinctive

---

58 *Some thoughts on the tillage of Ireland* (Dublin, 1741), p. 33.   **59** *FJ*, 10–14 Feb. 1767. There was 'great encouragement for Protestant tenants at James Agar's of Brandon Park near Graigue [Graiguenemanagh (Co. Kilkenny)] who will come and reside there or in the town of Graigue' (*FLJ*, 18–21 Jan. 1769).   **60** *Belfast Newsletter*, 24 Apr. 1770.   **61** 'Thomas Mitchell, of Castlestrange, in the County of Roscommon, Esq; will give great encouragement to common weavers to come and settle in the town of **Fuerty**, where he has built a number of good houses, and intends building more this summer, which he will give free, with good plots, with other advantages; and constant work and the highest price given in the kingdom. He also has a great number of choice looms already made, which he will also give free. N. B. Great convenience of fire and water to the town of Fuerty, and in the midst of a fine, plentiful country' (*Dublin Journal*, 20–3 Feb. 1762)   **62** *Belfast Newsletter*, 6 Feb. 1770.   **63** In 1759, a linen village to be set only to Protestant tenants was planned at Barry (Co. Longford): three leases of five acres for weavers Robert Harman, John Ledford and James Oates are extant (*Teathbha* (2016), p. 320).   **64** *Some thoughts on the tillage of Ireland*, p. 34.

Ulster Protestant ethos. These formed Irish outliers of the British industrial tradition, encompassing Sionmills,[65] Darkley, Milford, Gilford, Shrigley, Drumaness, Ligoniel, Mossley, Whitehouse[66] and Donaghcloney. Such towns were dominated by Presbyterians and non-conformists, and the proliferation of the churches of the different sects was a diagnostic feature. Their vitality continued throughout the nineteenth century when landlord-sponsored settlements elsewhere in the island lost their dynamism. Their origins led to strong links between workers and industrialists and a consequent close sectarian solidarity. The industrialization of these towns revitalized east Ulster, adding a vigorous new impetus to the tradition initiated by the seventeenth-century plantation towns, an impetus which faltered, faded and died elsewhere on the island.

TITHES AFTER 1800

Forcing Catholics to support an alien church fuelled seething resentment. John Jebb (1805–66), bishop of Limerick, concluded that ultimately there were only two strategies available to control Irish Catholics: 'hold them in, like rough beasts, with bit and bridle' or 'draw them in with the cords of a man, with the bonds of love'.[67] The 'rough beast' strategy had long been the preferred one. Charles Boyle (1674–1731), fourth earl of Orrery, noted in 1692: 'The English Protestants are the conquerors, the Irish papists the conquered and ancient as well as modern experience has made it appear the conquered never did (some think morally never will) love the conqueror'.[68] He recommended harsh treatment of the natives because they were a 'nationally violent' people'.[69] 'The beast if pamper'd will kick, if kept low, obey'.[70] The Protestants, rather than desiring the extermination of 'even the worst principled of the Irish papists', simply wanted them to be 'hewers of wood and drawers of water' for them.[71] These attitudes in turn contaminated the law itself, as the French political

---

65 J. Hamill, *The Herdman family and Sion Mills* (Belfast, 2017).   **66** W. Grimshaw, *Incidents recalled or sketches from memory of the cotton manufacture in Ireland, the Irish Volunteers, the rebellion of 1798 & the Irish parliament* (Philadelphia, 1848). The Grimshaws had founded Whitehouse as a mill village in the 1780s and this little-known book offers a detailed description of the family.   **67** I. Whelan, *The Bible war in Ireland: the 'Second Reformation' and the polarization of Protestant–Catholic relations, 1800–1840* (Dublin, 2007), p. 75.   **68** [Orrery], *An answer to a scandalous letter lately printed and subscribed by Peter Welsh* (Dublin, 1692), p. 10.   **69** Orrery, *Answer*, p. 3.   **70** Orrery, *Answer*, p. 58.   **71** Orrery, *Answer*, p. 65. From Kanturk in Cork in 1746, another Protestant observer concluded of the Catholics 'that they and their descendants are like to continue little better than hewers of wood and drawers of water' (D. Dickson, 'Jacobitism in eighteenth-century Ireland: a Munster perspective', *Éire-Ireland*, 39:3–4 (2004), p. 51). The original phrase 'hewers of wood and drawers of water' is derived from the Bible (Joshua 9:21).

scientist Gustave de Beaumont (1802–66) concluded in 1839: 'Where the strong exterminated the weak in the name of justice and the laws',[72] it created contempt, accounting for the anarchy of the law in pre-Famine Ireland: 'the words penalty, punishment and Ireland are synonymous: they are marked in blood on the margin of their statutes'.[73]

The motive was largely financial. The German atheist republican Jakob Venedy (1805–71) concluded in 1843 that 'The Protestant church in Ireland is a speculation on the stock market of the Catholics'.[74] An example shows what he meant. In 1818, the bishop of the Church of Ireland diocese of Meath conducted a census that counted 3,769 Protestant families in eighty-seven parishes. On the basis of these figures, only the parishes of Tullamore and Mullingar could have realistically contemplated building or maintaining their own churches and their own clergy out of their own resources. Without cesses and tithes collected from the Catholics, the Church of Ireland was simply unsustainable everywhere else. Of eighty-seven recorded parishes in 1818, two (Cruicestown, Moymet) had no Protestants at all, and twenty-three had ten or less Church of Ireland families (Agher, Almoritia, Assey, Ballygarth, Ballymaglasson, Castlerickard, Clonmacnoise, Donaghpatrick, Drakestown, Galtrim, Innishmott, Kilbrew, Kilmainhamwood, Kilmessan, Knockmark, Moorechurch, Moyglare, Moyvore, Newtown, Rathbeggan, Rathcondra, Rathkenny, Ratoath). And yet thousands of pounds were extracted from the Catholic poor to be spent on churches, glebe houses and clergy in these ghost parishes. In 1818, Revd Ponsonby Gouldsbury of Tullamore (Co. Offaly) claimed and was paid three pence from the parish fund 'for two brass hooks to hang up Mr Gouldsbury's cane over the reading desk'.[75]

Tithe proctors attracted continual opprobrium, as in this example of a threatening letter from Co. Wexford in 1811:

> Every tythe proctor rascal that will walk into a man's field and he will say, you will have so many loads of hay oats barley with that, it now wont do without the cow. A scab proctor that never tilled a field he will swear all this to get to walk about like a gentleman of consequence.[76]

By the 1820s, with strong political cover from O'Connell, a powerful grassroots campaign spearheaded from south Leinster and east Munster forced a fairer settlement on tithes. Tithes on potatoes was a major grievance for the poor as they were not tithed north of a line from Arklow (Co. Wicklow) to Galway. The 1830s movement started in Graiguenemanagh (Co. Kilkenny), a county with a

72 G. De Beaumont, *Ireland: social, political, and religious*, ed. T. Garvin & A. Hess (Boston [1839–42], 2006), p. 158.   73 Beaumont, *Ireland*, p. 101.   74 J. Venedy, *Ireland*, 2 vols (Leipzig, 1844), ii, pp 95–6.   75 RCB, Tullamore Vestry Minutes Book, 26 Feb. 1816, f. 111.   76 A.H. Jacob (Enniscorthy) to Dublin Castle, 22 Feb. 1811, cited in Gibbons, *Captain Rock, night errant*, p. 60.

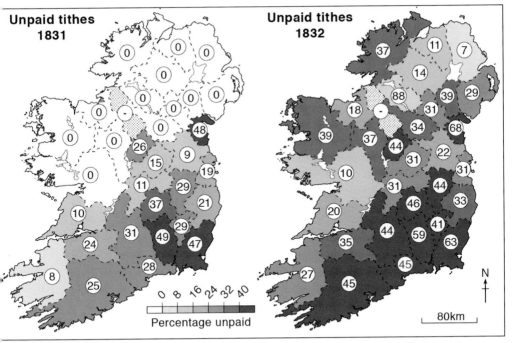

Fig. 28 Mapping the Tithe War, 1831–2. The maps depict the percentage of tithes unpaid as a percentage of the total tithes demanded for each county in each year.

vibrant Whiteboy tradition. When tithes initially surfaced as an issue in the Irish parliament in the 1780s, Kilkenny was the first county to present a petition.[77]

When the anti-tithe movement matured into a non-payment campaign in 1831, the civil parishes committed to the campaign were led by Kilkenny (90), Tipperary (53), Wexford (30) and Waterford (16), followed by Cork (11), Limerick (10), Louth (10), Laois (5), Carlow (3) and tailing off to one each in Offaly, Meath and Kerry. Connaught and Ulster remained uninvolved. Only in the summer of 1831 did the tithe agitation spread outwards from Kilkenny, Wexford, Carlow and Laois.[78]

Like Catholic Emancipation, electoral reform and slavery,[79] tithes formed a pillar of the anti-democratic basis of Irish society, which was swept away by the early 1830s: only a generation earlier, many thousands of Irish people lost their live striving to achieve those reasonable democratic aims. The failure of the 'Protestant Ascendancy' advocates to embrace even minimal or incremental reform inflicted long-term damage on their church from which it never recovered.

77 W. Tighe, *Statistical observations relating to the County Kilkenny* (Dublin, 1802), p. 599. 78 P. O'Donoghue, 'Opposition to tithes payment in 1830–1831', *Studia Hib.*, 6 (1966), p. 75. 79 Belfast in particular was a hub of anti-slavery agitation. Slavery was only abolished in the British Empire in 1833.

Such circumstances generated a specific, historically based and adversarial political consciousness, as in this speech by the activist Jeremiah O'Connor at an anti-tithe meeting in Tralee (Co. Kerry) in 1832:

> Táimíd féin is ár máithreacha romhainn le trí chéad bliain nach beag faoi chrúba na ministrí. Is le hallas ár mailí do shaothraíomar an deachú dóibh chun iad a choimeád i ngradam agus in árdréim, ag imeacht 'na gcóistí ag fiach, ag sealgaireacht, ag imeacht go Sasana agus go tíortha eile thar lear, ag caitheamh ár gcuidne airgid mar do scaipfeadh cáith le gaoith, ár bhfágan féin agus ár gclann ag treabhadh 's a' fuirse dóibh faoi shrathar na h-ainnise ó bhliain go bliain, gan de bhia againn ach lumpers agus an ní nach fiú leis na ministrí d'ithe.[80]

A notice was posted on Dungarvan church (Co. Kilkenny) on 30 August 1831 about the 'The Church of Bayonets':

> The Catholic inhabitants of Dungarvan who are compel[l]ed by a bad law to support the above gorgeous iniquity whose sanctified and self-denying priesthood (the followers and servants of a barefooted and poverty-loving master) revel in princely luxury, faring sumptuously every day in a country whose wretched peasantry have been for months dragging out a miserable existence on boiled sea weed and nettles. Those Catholics are informed that an ecclesiastical parliament commonly called a vestry will assemble on Wednesday (to Mon[day]) to make laws taking money out of the pockets of the people for the decoration of this temple of Baal on whose altars nineteen victims were lately immolated at Newtown Barry, those nineteen lives being far less precious than a parson's tithe heifer.[81]

In 1832, a visitor to Kilrane (Co. Wexford) was amazed at an effigy hanging on a tree:

> I approached and found it to be an effigy of a parson's jackal – an unfortunate proctor. It was indeed a ludicrous caricature: it was formed of old ragged clothes stuffed with straw (the proctor's favourite article of trade), the head was capped with an old tattered caubeen having a stout cabbage stalk for its cockade; the proctor's neck was even allowed

---

80 'Ourselves and our ancestors have been under the hoof of the ministers for nearly three centuries. It is with the sweat of our brows that we earn their tithes, to keep them in luxury and ascendancy, heading off in their coaches to hunt and to fish, going to England and other countries overseas, spending our money like chaff in the wind, leaving ourselves and our families ploughing and harrowing for them under the halter of hardship from year to year, with only lumpers for our food, which the minister himself would disdain to eat'. S. Ó Mórdha, 'An anti-tithe speech in Irish', *Éigse*, 9 (1958–61), pp 233–6. I have modernized the orthography. His speech [NLI, MS G 702] landed O'Connor in jail for a month.   81 Gibbons, *Captain Rock, night errant*, p. 223.

the ordinary compliment of culprits ie a hempen rope to swing in. His rope was also made of straw; his poor mouth that often swore to recover his master's tithes was gagged by a wisp of straw. To the chest was tacked in a tailor-like style the *Wexford Herald* having two patches of white print stuck thereon, one of which had printed on it in large letters 'The last end of an unfortunate proctor'. On the other patch appeared Lusty Old Nick telling all who passed by 'you need not pray for him, he is mine, I have plenty of these lads'. Some farmers work boys treated the poor proctor thus out of gratitude for having, by issuing tithe tickets, deprived their masters of the means of affording them more bread to eat. I was so awed at this spectacle that I would rather go to the treadmill or the hulks rather than accept the hated title of tithe proctor.[82]

THE CHURCH OF IRELAND

The overall texture of religious experience in the Irish public sphere in the long eighteenth century (1690–1829) is well-tilled ground.[83] It is useful to consider in turn the divergent settlement impact of the three main groups, Protestants, Dissenters and Catholics.

The chancel/nave distinction was rendered redundant in Protestant service: the preference (until the nineteenth-century ecclesiological revival) was for an auditory church, favouring a single cell, as opposed to more complex articulated interiors.[84] Accordingly, the post-Reformation Church of Ireland generated an architecture of disjunction.[85] Owing to demographic circumstances, and the resultant financial pressures, it proved difficult to sustain viable Protestant congregations and to maintain so many churches. In 1622, Oliver Mather, the non-resident Protestant minister of Killelagh (Co. Derry), visited the ruined church there: 'sometimes (as once in three months), he resorteth to the church where no man cometh at him, the whole parish consisting of Irish recusants'.[86] Almost two centuries later in 1809, the melancholy condition of churches in Waterford city was apparent: 'It is not unusual to see the church walls grown green on the inside; and the clergyman, dressed in a surplice covered with iron-mould spots, which, perhaps, had not

82 A barony of Forth visitor, Wexford, 14 Mar. 1832, *Wexford Herald*, 21 Mar. 1832. 83 There is a succinct summary in D. Hempton, *The church in the long eighteenth century* (London, 2011). The Irish material is at pp 170–7. 84 A. Rowan, 'Irish Victorian churches: denominational distinctions' in B. Kennedy & R. Gillespie (eds), *Ireland: art into history* (Dublin, 1994), pp 207–30; R. Usher, *Protestant Dublin, 1660–1760: architecture and iconography* (Basingstoke, 2012), 'Churches and cathedrals', pp 49–95. 85 McCullough, *Palimpsest.* 86 PRONI DIO/4/23/1/1. I owe this reference to William Roulston, 'The provision, building and architecture of Anglican churches in the north of Ireland 1600–1740' (PhD, QUB, 2003).

Fig. 29   The Middle Church, Ballinderry (Co. Antrim), is one of the few surviving seventeenth-century churches in Ireland. It was built in 1668 by the accomplished spiritual writer Revd Jeremy Taylor (1613–67). It is comprised of a single-cell rectangular interior 71 x 29 feet (22 x 9m). The walls are three feet thick, pierced by oak windows with mullions and circular heads, and lit by lancet clusters. In 1827, when a new parish church was built at Ballinderry Upper, the Middle Church fell into decay. The indefatigable antiquarian F.J. Bigger (1863–1926) prompted a major restoration in 1902. Many original fittings have survived, notably the three-tier oak pulpit, the communion table and chairs, the box pews and the long-handled collecting pans. The church still lacks electricity and only intermittent services are currently held (photo: Robert Welch).

been washed for twelve months, delivering a discourse to a congregation, composed of from two to six persons'.[87]

In Ireland, the architectural constraints imposed by the auditory requirement were reinforced by practical considerations of the Irish weather: shivering congregations withdrew into the chancel because smaller spaces were so much easier to heat. In long-established ecclesiastical practice, parishioners were held responsible for the building and upkeep of the nave, while the clergyman was expected to maintain the chancel from his tithe income.[88] Long medieval

87 Wakefield, *Ireland statistical and political*, i, p. 265.   88 'The rector (or impropriator) is only bound to repair the chancel – abroad, the incumbent repairs the whole church' (Browne, *Ecclesiastical law of Ireland*, p. 176). 'The parishioners are bound to repair the

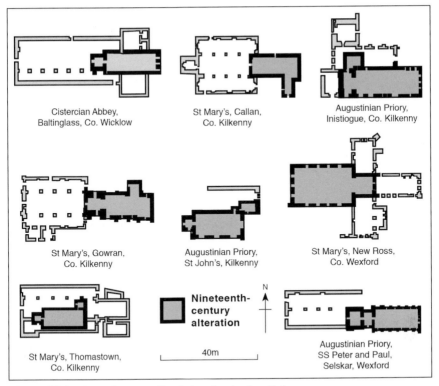

Fig. 30 Eight plans of post-medieval churches by Ana Dolan.

churches contracted into buildings with only a single space (whether nave or chancel), especially in the Catholic-dominated south-east and east. Naves were shorn of their aisles at, for example, St Mary's in Kilkenny. Some congregations retained their chancels and unroofed their naves, for example, parish churches at Gowran (Co. Kilkenny) and Athenry (Co. Galway). A smaller new building could be condensed within a more elaborate medieval one, as at Thomastown (Co. Kilkenny).[89] At Tullaherin (Co. Kilkenny), the date 1616 appears on an archstone above the chancel, presumably marking the conversion to Protestant

whole church except the chancel, which, by the custom of England, is to be repaired by the parson and also except such private [a]isles or chapels, as belonging to private persons are to be repaired by them. The parishioners are also bound to fence and keep in good order the church-yard, but if the owners of lands adjacent have used time out of mind to repair so much of the fence as adjoined to their ground, they may be compelled to do it' (Browne, *Ecclesiastical law of Ireland*, p. 181). This division of responsibilities was explicit in Ireland as early as the legislation of the Provincial Council of Cashel in 1453 (D. Wilkins (ed.), *Concilia Magnae Britanniae et Hiberniae, AD 446–1717*, 4 vols (London 1737), iii, p. 565).   **89** A. Dolan, 'The large medieval churches of the dioceses of Leighlin, Ferns and Ossory: a study of adaptation and change', *Irish Architectural and Decorative Studies*, 2 (1999), pp 26–65; N. Nic Ghabhann, *Medieval ecclesiastical buildings in Ireland 1789–1915* (Dublin, 2015).

Table 2: State of Church of Ireland cathedrals, 1611

'Standing and not ruined'

Cashel	Leighlin
Cork	Limerick
Christ Church [Dublin]	Ossory [Kilkenny]
St Patrick's [Dublin]	Waterford

'Now ruined to be re-edified'

Ardagh	Killaloe
Ardconnarah [Achonry]	Kilmacow [Kilmacduagh]
Armagh	Lismore
Clogher	Roscarberry
Clonfert	Ardfert [to be moved to Dingle]
Clo[y]ne	Connor [to be moved to Carrickfergus]
Derry	Dromore [to be moved to Newry]
Down [at Downpatrick]	Ferns [to be moved to either the Priory
Elphin	there or to Selskar (Wexford town)]
Emly	Kilmore [to be moved to Cavan]
Kildare	Raphoe [to be moved to Donegal]
Killala	Tuam [to be moved to Galway]

use.[90] This practice generated discordant buildings, partially derelict, partially roofed, that exhibited the scars of history.

In Ossory in 1622, eleven churches were ruined, except for their chancels (Blackrath, Clara, Donaghmore, Dungarvan, Ennisnag, Illud, Kells, Kilbeacon, Kilderry, Owning (Bewley) and Tubbridbritain).[91] Such dead-and-alive buildings featured prominently in eighteenth-century sketches of the Irish landscape, for example, by Gabriel Beranger (1725–1817), Francis Grose (1731–91), Austin Cooper (1759–1830) and Daniel Grose (1766–1838).[92]

Housing for the bishops proved a problem. The lord deputy put pressure on the archbishop of Canterbury in 1613 to encourage bishops to reside in their 'mansion houses, if any there were or to build new where none is' because they were currently residing in borrowed houses or in thatched cabins 'unbecoming

90 Carrigan, *Ossory*, iii, p. 480.   91 Ó Fearghail, 'Wheeler's visitation'.   92 F. Grose, *The antiquities of Ireland*, 2 vols (London, 1791–7); R. Stalley (ed.), *Daniel Grose (c.1766–1838): the antiquities of Ireland* (Dublin, 1991); P. Harbison (ed.), *Beranger's antique buildings of Ireland* (Dublin, 1998); P. Harbison (ed.), *Cooper's Ireland: drawings and notes from an eighteenth-century gentleman* (Dublin, 2000); P. Harbison, *'Our treasure of antiquities': Beranger and Bigari's antiquarian sketching tour of Connacht in 1779* (Bray, 2002); P. Harbison, *William Burton Conyngham and his Irish circle of antiquarian artists* (New Haven, 2012).

their dignity'.[93] John Bramhall complained in 1634 that the church and bishop's palace in Killaloe had been built on the 'meanest bank of the Shannon' 'for no end that I can find but for the conveniency of weirs for catching eels'.[94] In 1635, the house of the bishop of Dromore, the Englishman Theophilius Buckworth (1580–1652), was just 'a little timber house of no great state'.[95]

In 1611, nine cathedrals were 'standing and not ruined' while twenty-three were 'now ruined [and] to be re-edified'.[96] Many post-Reformation cathedrals were abandoned (Cashel was unroofed as late as 1748)[97] or downsized (Clonfert, Ferns, Down and (later restored) Kildare); others were allowed to become ruins (Clonmacnoise, Elphin, Kilmacduagh), or shoehorned into ruined carapaces (Raphoe, Dromore, Lismore, Killala, Clogher, Leighlin). The cathedrals at Ardfert, Ardagh and Achonry were relegated to parish churches. In another slight to these cathedrals, episcopal palaces had money and architectural ambition lavished on them, as, for example, at Ferns,[98] Raphoe and Cashel.

---

93 R.D. Edwards, *Church and state in Tudor Ireland: a history of penal laws against Irish Catholics, 1534–1603* (London, 1935), p. 85. **94** HMC, *Hastings*, iv, p. 58. **95** [W. Brereton], *Travels in Holland, the United Provinces, England, Scotland and Ireland, 1634–1635*, ed. E. Hawkins (Manchester, 1844), p. 129. Buckworth fled his diocese in 1641and never returned. **96** 'An Act for the re-edifying and repairing of cathedral and parochial churches, wherein it may be provided that the cathedral churches which are standing and not ruined, viz., Christchurch and St Patrick's in Dublin, the cathedral churches of Laughlin, Ossory, Kilkenny, Waterford, Cashill, Corck and Limrick, be repaired by the several bishops, deans, &c., of the several churches; and that the cathedral churches which are not ruined and not standing be re-edified at the charge both of the clergy and the laity of every diocese, the charge or contribution to be rated by this Act. The cathedral churches now ruined to be re-edified are those of Kildare, to be erected at Kildare; Ferns, at Wexford, either in the priory there or in the church of Selskar; Lismore, at Lismore; Emly, at Emly; Clone, at Clone; Roscarberry, at Roscarberry; Ardfert in Kerry, at Dingly Chuse; Killalowe, at Killalowe; cathedral of Tuam, at Galwaye in the church of the college there; Clonfert, at Clonfert; Elphin, at Elphin; Killmacow, at Killmacowe; Killala, at Killala; Ardconnorath, at Ardconnorath; Armagh, at Armagh; Kilmore, at the Cavan, in the priory there; Ardagh, at Ardagh; Clogher, at Clogher; Derry, at Derry; Rapho, at Dunegall, in the priory thereof; Downe, at Downe Patrick; Connor, at Carigfergus; Dromore, at the Newry House'. *CSPI, 1611–14*, pp 188–9. **97** R. Loeber et al. (eds), *Art and architecture of Ireland, volume 4: architecture 1600–2000* (New Haven, 2014), p. 311 (henceforth AAI, iv). **98 Ferns** was an expensive building costing over £10,000 (AAI, iv, p. 317). 'The palace is a noble building erected a few years since [1785] by the late Doctor Cope [*ob.*1787], then bishop. The houses and offices are the completest and best finished of any episcopal building in Ireland, and what is singular the house is covered with copper, the first attempt of its kind in this kingdom' [1790 Tour of Wexford]. The aged Bishop Thomas Ram in 1630 had built an episcopal palace at Old Leighlin which would pass to his successors: there he erected the famous punning stone subsequently moved to Ramsfort, the family seat at Gorey (Co. Wexford) in 1781): 'This house Ram built for his succeeding brothers/ thus sheep bear wool not for themselves but others'. At Ferns, the cathedral was formed from the thirteenth-century church built over Aidan's original church. It had been burned by the O'Byrnes in 1575 (the 1615 visitation noted that it 'was destroyed formerly by rebells and yet remains waste'), was restored in the 1680s, and enlarged in 1817. The architect J.F. Fuller (1835–1924) restored it between 1901–3. His excavations showed that the medieval church was 180 feet (54.9m) in length, while the modern cathedral retreated into a severely shrunken footprint in the central aisle of the nave (Leslie, *Ferns*, p. 28).

In the 1630s, Bishop John Leslie (1571–1671) erected his palace at Raphoe (Co. Donegal), 'one of the architecturally innovative glories of the plantation', while his patched-up cathedral languished.[99] Nearby Clogher (Co. Tyrone) was described in 1709 as 'most miserable'.[100] Bishop Spottiswoode in 1628 claimed that Clogher had only twelve poor people living in it in wattled cabins while Bishop Bedell described Kilmore (Co. Cavan) as 'but a meer village of good large bounds but so thinly inhabited that nowhere in the whole parish was any street or part of a street to be found'.[101]

Archbishop William King (1650–1729) complained in 1712 about rapacious Englishmen sent to Irish dioceses, singling out Charles Hickman (1648–1713), bishop of Derry, and Edward Wetenhall (1636–1713), bishop of Kilmore: 'As to those clergymen who are sent us from England, I believe it will not be pleaded that they are the brightest generally speaking though I confess to my observation they seem notably dexterous and industrious to make money for their wives and children'.[102] In 1718, he penned an icily polite but stinging letter to the archbishop of Canterbury when his English superior sought to delay the passage over to Ireland of the new bishop of Derry:

> A man may govern over a country diocess in Ireland as well if he live in London as in Dublin, that he may live as cheap there as here, & houses are cheaper that he will have so many and strong precedents to justify him in the practice that he need not fear any condemnation from the world for his absence, most of his brethern being examples to justify him in it. If an act of parlement be cheaper than a journey into Ireland he may I doubt not procure one for taking the oaths there as well as so many civil offices and so without any trouble of giving himself the pain of visiting a miserable country, he may gett two thousand pounds per annum instead of 8 or 900£. This will in my opinion be a piece of very commendable frugality & very gratefull to his family as well as to your Grace, who will thereby have the benefit of his advice & assistance. As for the diocess of Derry, I see no reason why it may not do as well without a resident bishop for 15 years to come as it did for ye 15 years last past. Your Grace sees by this how heartily I come into your measures and how sollicitous I am to gratify you.[103]

---

99 R.J. Hunter, *Ulster transformed: essays on plantation and print culture, c.1590–1641* (Belfast, 2012), p. 74. There is a plan of Raphoe palace in M. Craig, *The architecture of Ireland from earliest times to 1880* (London, 1982), p. 116. **100** 'Molyneux tour', p. 32. **101** H. Monck Mason, *The life of William Bedell D.D., lord bishop of Kilmore* (Dublin, 1843), p. 824. **102** W. King to A. Charlett (Oxford), cited in Henry, *Upper Lough Erne*, pp 11–12. **103** W. King (Dublin) to W. Wake, archbishop of Canterbury, 25 Mar. 1718 in Christ Church, Oxford University, Wake MS, XII, ff 248–9. King later said that William Nicolson (1655–1727) since his translation to Derry 'had given about £2000 in benefices to English favourites and relations'. Nicolson, heedless of the fact that their tithes kept himself and his

Swift complained in 1732 that the English clergy regularly appointed to fill Irish bishoprics were more committed to social climbing than religion, and came 'all bedangled with their pert illiterate relations and flatterers'.[104] The classical facelift applied to Armagh in the last quarter of the eighteenth century by Primate Richard Robinson (1709–74) demonstrated what was feasible had the will been there.[105] The overall assesment was bleak. Joseph Cooper Walker (c.1762–1810) concluded that Irish Protestant churches 'when compared to those of Britain and the continent are rather mean'.[106] An English military officer in 1662 was appalled by the condition of the church in Arklow (Co. Wicklow): 'mud walls, thatched roof, hogsty shape, the seats like partitions for pigs'.[107]

By the mid-eighteenth century, more active bishops commissioned entirely new churches. Early Georgian specimens were intended to be virile, rational and assured; their inspiration was classical rather than Christian. John Perceval (1683–1748), first earl of Egmont, criticized Henry O'Brien (1688–741), eighth and last earl of Thomond, for remarking to him in 1730: 'If God Almighty tread on his toes, he would never forgive him'.[108] After the enlightenment, architectural innovation across Europe migrated to the secular realm, and ecclesiastical buildings favoured venerable forms, initially neo-classical in inspiration and (following the French Revolution) Gothic revival.[109]

The architecturally awkward junction of steeple, portico and rectangular box was eventually worked out satisfactorily in the late eighteenth century after many steeple disasters.[110] The favoured solution was to append a more stable tower to the plain rectangular box. A Protestant church without a

---

seven children in luxury, considered the local Catholics to be 'sorry slaves': 'these animals are bigotted papists and we frequently met them trudging to some ruin'd church or chapel, either to mass, a funeral or a wedding, with a priest in the same habit with themselves' (Moran, *Catholics under the penal laws*, p. 9). **104** J. Swift to J. Barber, 11 Sept. 1732 in D. Wooley (ed.), *The correspondence of Jonathan Swift, D.D.*, 4 vols (Frankfurt, 1999–2005), iii, p. 126. **105** A.P.W. Malcolmson, *Primate Robinson, 1709–94* (Belfast, 2003). **106** J.C. Walker, *On the rise and progress of architecture in Ireland* (Dublin, 1818), p. 239. **107** Col. Edward Cooke (Dublin) to Lord Bruce, 12 Nov. 1662 (HMC, *Fifteenth report*, app. vii, p 168). **108** *Diary of Viscount Percival afterwards First Earl of Egmont, volume 1, 1730–1733* (London, 1920), pp 120–1. **109** H. von Achen, 'Fighting the disenchantment of the world: the instrument of medieval revivalism in nineteenth-century art and architecture' in H. Laugerud & S. Ryan (eds), *Devotional cultures of European Christianity, 1790–1860* (Dublin, 2012), pp 131–54. **110** The steeple of Belturbet (Co. Cavan) collapsed in 1664 (Belturbet Corporation records). On 30 June 1701, the 1683 steeple at Blessington (Co. Wicklow) had to be repaired, when ten pounds was paid to John Ellis for 'picking, pointing and dashing the walls of the steeple throughout'. Further repairs, including slating, were necessary on 17 May 1703 (Blessington Vestry Minutes books, courtesy of Rolf Loeber). At New Ross (Co. Wexford), 'A steeple was built and handsomely finished in the year 1769, but in the following year it fell on a level with the roof occasioned, I suppose, by its being constructed with bad materials' ('Tour in Wexford 1790', p. 485). The spire of Kilcoleman church (Co. Mayo) collapsed following a lightning strike in 1828, killing two women (CSO/RP/1828/1790).

steeple or tower resembled a 'cow without horns', according to Archbishop King in 1716.[111] He had encouraged the newly appointed Jonathan Swift to build a steeple at Saint Patrick's Cathedral in 1713, 'which kind of ornament is much wanting in Dublin'.[112] Bishop Frederick Hervey (1730–1803) helped Tamlaghtfinnan, Ballyscullion and Banagher (Co. Derry) to add towers and spires to their earlier plain stone boxes. The gothicized hall and tower plan was first worked out satisfactorily at Ballymakenny (1774, Co. Louth) by the London-born architect Thomas Cooley (1742–84), who was employed by Richard Robinson after he became archbishop of Armagh in 1765 on his building projects in the city and diocese of Armagh.[113] Cooley's successful design became the Board of First Fruits template for late eighteenth/early nineteenth-century Protestant churches.

Several villages were dominated by their churches set atop a drumlin, as at Tynan, Killylea and Richhill (Co. Armagh) or on a hill, as at Waringstown (1681) and Hillsborough (1663), both in Co. Down.[114] It was also common for clear sectarian zones to exist in the towns. Belturbet (Co. Cavan) in 1739 had 'a large church which is generally crowded, all the inhabitants within the corporation being Protestants'.[115] In 1748, Isaac Butler observed that 'no Roman Catholic is allowed to live on the east side of the bridge'.[116] Ulster landlords, including Abercorn at Strabane and Chichester at Dungannon (both Co. Tyrone), Balfour at Lisnaskea and Cole at Enniskillen (both Co. Fermanagh), and Grandison at Tanderagee (Co. Armagh), sponsored

---

111 Cited in E. McParland, *Public architecture in Ireland, 1680–1760* (New Haven, CT, 2001), p. 45.   112 W. King (Chester) to J. Swift (London), 16 May 1713 (W. King & C. King, *A great archbishop of Dublin: William King, D.D., 1650–1729* (London, 1906), p. 153). Swift's predecessor had designed a 120 feet (36.6m) high brick spire to be added onto the steeple that was 'twenty-one feet [6.4m] in the clear wide where the spire is to stand.' King advised that scaffolding would be the principal cost but that this was 'pretty cheap in Dublin'. However the lack of skilled workmen would be the problem. Swift replied on 23 May that the spire would cost more than the proposed £200 because 'no bricks made in that part of Ireland will bear being exposed so much to the air': marking King's card about the superiority of England, Swift advised King that he would seek architectural advice in London.   113 Cooley supplied an album of twelve church designs to Robinson (Armagh Public Library, MS P001923591). 114 G. Camblin, *The town in Ulster* (Belfast, 1951), p. 97.   115 Henry, *Upper Lough Erne*, p. 19.   116 In 1745, Isaac Butler described **Belturbet** as 'pleasantly situated upon the bank of Lough Earne. Entring the main street, the town arranges in a strait line which with the market house, church & steeple form a pleasant prospect. The barracks are neatly built at the north entrance of the town & have the lough in front. The church is at the south end on a rising ground from whence appears a beautifull prospect of the country & lough. At the north end of the bridge Lord Lanesborough has a house, a large quadrangular building. The gardens behind the house are well laid out on the banks of the Lough. The bridge of 5 arches is in the West Street, here are several boats & lighters, which take in goods & passengers for Eniskillen & several parts of the country. This town is a borough & a rectory & vicarage in Kilmore diocess. No Roman Catholic is allowed to live on the east side of the bridge. Here are 4 yearly fairs' (Isaac Butler, Lough Derg). [CELT].

churches for their new towns. A favoured disposition was to place the church at the opposite end of the street from the landlord's fortified residence. At Newtownstewart (Co. Tyrone), the pre-1641 church faced down the street towards the plantation castle. At Killyleagh (Co. Down), the main street ran directly between Hamilton's castle and the church originally built in 1640. A similar layout once existed at Strabane (Co. Tyrone). A conveyance of land in Moira (Co. Down) specified that the new church must be built opposite to the avenue leading to Sir John Rawdon's demesne.[117]

Archbishop Michael Boyle (1615–1702), primate of Ireland (1679–1702), was among the first to appreciate the charms of living under the Wicklow Mountains, for centuries regarded as a wild, dangerous location, especially as a relief from crowded, noisy, smelly Dublin. In 1678, he talked of 'stepping into his coach' to go to Blessington (Co. Wicklow) 'to take a little ayre this weeke as physicke [medicine] to prepare me against the next terme' [of parliament].[118] He had built an open-arcaded brick mansion in 1672 (designed by Thomas Lucas), 106 feet [32m] long by sixty feet [18m] wide (1,360 square feet [576 m²]), then a garden that contained the first hothouses in Ireland.[119]

Boyle built a church (dedicated 24 August 1683) and then an early estate village. According to a stone in the church, Boyle founded and erected it at his own expense and he furnished the communion table, silver flagons, cups, patens and other ornaments. He also supplied an elegant steeple with a greatly admired ring of six musical bells. In 1779, the 'very neat and well kept' church had 'a sweet ring of bells, a thing not commonly met with in this kingdom'.[120] A royal warrant dated 5 June 1682 had permitted Boyle to 'transport to Ireland a ring of six bells which has been cast here [London] and the frame etc, for hanging the same which has been made here: all for a steeple which he has built at his own cost to the church of the town'.[121] Around this time, the English bookseller John Dunton (1659–1733) had observed that bells 'are a great rarity in all the country churches here'.[122]

Boyle created a perfect church-avenue alignment. Luckombe in 1779 described the 'elegant, neat and well furnished' house 'at the end of an avenue to the left of the road with a noble large terrace walk a quarter of an English mile in length that leads to the church in the town across the road which faces

---

117 PRONI MIC/1/79. This topic is handsomely treated in W. Roulston, 'Places of worship of the Established Church in Ireland, 1550–1688' (forthcoming). 118 Archbishop Boyle (Dublin) to Orrery 20 May 1678 (E. MacLysaght (ed.), *Calendar of the Orrery papers, 1620–1689* (Dublin, 1941), p. 200). 119 J.C. Walker, *Essay on the rise and progress of gardening in Ireland* (Dublin, [1791] 1818), p. 170. 120 [P. Luckombe], *A tour through Ireland in 1779* (Dublin, 1780), pp 66–7. 121 *Calendar Treasury Papers*, vii, part I, 1681–5, p. 503: see also *Cal. State Papers, Domestic, 1682*, p. 230. 122 MacLysaght, *Irish life in the seventeenth century*, p. 328.

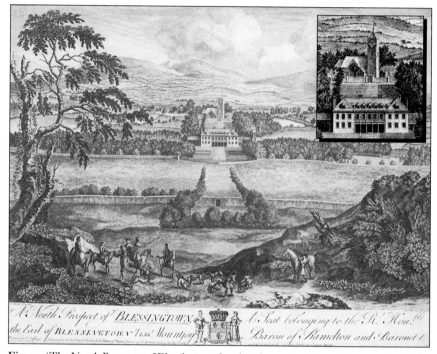

Fig. 31 'The North Prospect of Blessington showing the garden front of the mansion'. The engraving is from a painting by Joseph Tudor (*ob.*1759). The eleven-bay house was burned and permanently abandoned in 1798.

the house'.[123] The alignment was well publicized through a later engraving that stressed the nexus.[124]

> About Blessingtown the land is very mountainous and wild yet here the late Primate Boyle built one of the finest seats in Ireland. It is now enjoyed and kept in good order by his son the Lord Blessingtown.[125] The house and furniture are very great and beautifull particularly the chappel.[126] All manners of conveniencies, out houses and offices with a very handsome, noble garden; wilderness, greenhouses, fishponds, a

123 [Luckombe], *Tour,* pp 66–7. Early greenhouse and garden paths were revealed by excavation to be composed of red brick, pebbles, limestone and mortar (V. Costello, *Irish demesne landscapes, 1660–1740* (Dublin, 2015), p. 141). **124** B. De Breffny, 'The building of the manor at Blessington 1672', *Irish Arts Review* (1988), pp 73–7; E. Malins & Knight of Glin, *Lost demesnes: Irish landscape gardening, 1660–1845* (London, 1976), pp 126–7. Relevant illustrations are reproduced in P. Butler & M. Davies, *Wicklow through the artist's eye: an exploration of County Wicklow's historic gardens, c.1660–c.1960* (Bray, 2014), pp 32–40. **125** Murrough Boyle (1648–1718), first Viscount Blessington. The estate passed out of the Boyle family in 1696 following an earlier marriage to a Mountjoy of his daughter Anne (eventually the sole heiress). **126** A detailed description of this chapel in 1779 is in Luckombe, *Tour,* p. 67.

noble large park and paddocks, and is in short much beyond any seat in all respects that I have seen in this kingdom and, as I am told, would make no bad figure in England.[127]

CHURCH OF IRELAND CHURCHES AFTER THE ACT OF UNION

The Church of Ireland massively overbuilt in the first quarter of the nineteenth century. Its confidence had been shattered by the 1798 rebellion, which had forced it back into a defensive crouch. When the new Bishop Charles Lindsay (1760–1846) of Kildare visited the church at Rathangan (Co. Kildare) in 1804, he found it still 'a kind of citadel' with 'the windows half-built up with loopholes for firing upon an attacking populace'. He concluded that 'as yet the remembrance of the treason is too fresh to be overruled by reason and decency'.[128] This mindset intensified under the lash of O'Connell's vituperative and unsettling campaigns. In 1825, John Young of Ballingarrane (Rathkeale, Co. Limerick), identifying himself as a descendant of Protestant Palatine families who could no longer live amid an inflamed Catholic population, felt affronted that his favourable lease had not been renewed: as a result, the Palatines, 'cast abandoned on the world', were 'compel[l]ed to emigrate to a foreign land'.[129]

In 1824, the Scottish educationalist James Glassford (1771–1845) concluded that Protestant landlords and clergymen 'while this exclusion continues will be always inclined to trust more to their monopoly and to the shield and power of the law which gives them a preference and a peculiar protection than to the effect of their own conduct and measures'.[130] Henry Beresford (1772–1826), second marquess of Waterford, from the celebrated Waterford family, was disgruntled to find that the government intended that in any future disputes between Catholics and Protestants 'the offending and offended parties are left undistinguished and are to be treated precisely as if both were offenders equally'.[131] A generation later, Colonel George Keogh of Kilbride (Co. Carlow) had answered the question posed by Captain George De La Poer Beresford (1826–65), son of the bishop of Kilmore, as to what the Church of Ireland was for: 'I have come to the conclusion that it was established solely for the benefit of the Beresford family'.[132]

127 'Molyneux tour', p. 68. **128** R. Refaussé, 'Visitation notebook of Charles Lindsay 1804–1808', *Journal of the Kildare Archaeological Society*, 17 (1987–91), p. 133. **129** CSO/RP/1825/632. **130** Glassford, *Three tours*, p. 106. **131** CSO/RP/SC/1826/10. Beresford complained about violent breaches of the peace on the commonage of Slievegrine which emboldened the 'lower orders' to believe that their 'system of intimidation' could be continued with impunity (CSO/RP/SC/1826/8). **132** J.F. Fuller, *Omniana: the autobiography of an Irish octagenarian*, second edition (London, 1920), p. 202. The congenial and worldly-wise Fuller (1825–1924) was the go-to architect for the Church of Ireland in the post-Famine period: 'Mr Fuller must, from the frequency with which we meet with his

The hyperactive building of new churches represented an emphatic statement of claim in this unsettling landscape. The Board of First Fruits initially stipulated that older churches must be unroofed for sixteen years before a grant would be advanced, thereby creating a strong incentive to allow them to degrade or simply to demolish them. Only in 1808 did the Board relax this stipulation – too late for most surviving pre-Reformation churches.

In the two decades after the Union, and especially after its funding and remit were vastly expanded from 1808 (48 George III, c. 65) to 1823, the Board of First Fruits expended £800,000 in grants to purchase 193 glebe lands, construct 550 glebe houses, and build, rebuild or enlarge 697 churches. The scale of its intervention can be gauged from calibrating these figures against the total of 1,396 Church of Ireland benefices in 1830, and from the fact that there had been only one glebe house in the entire diocese of Cashel in 1779 and only two in Emly.[133] Less than half of Church of Ireland clergy were actually living in their parishes in 1806.[134] The Cashel clergy were 'well paid for doing nothing', according to another observer.[135]

Board of First Fruits church plans tended towards the flat-pack variety, with squat towers decorated by spiky towerlets, diminutive buttresses, hood mouldings, mullioned windows with Y-tracery window bars or diamond-shaped lead lattices. The surgeon William Wilde (1815–76) excoriated 'the barn-like churches erected by small builders and master carpenters, under boards of penurious commissioners and tasteless rectors'.[136]

A local Protestant, Richard Ruxton of Black Castle (Co. Meath), objected in 1823 that 'several of the parishes are burthen'd with enormous church rates for the most expensive & fanciful decorations & improvements in churches on a scale far beyond the income or wants of the parishes'.[137] Agreeing and collecting vestry cesses proved a constant vexation, because both Catholics and Dissenters could participate (but not vote) in vestry meetings, and understandably they often combined to minimize excessive expenditure on church buildings. However, according to the law, 'No Papist [can] vote at a vestry for repairing or rebuilding'[138] and 'The consent of the majority of Protestant parishioners in vestry is sufficient to assess a rate for building the new church on notice three Sundays before'.[139]

name in connexion with church work, have built over half of Ireland' (*Irish Ecclesiastical Gazette*, 1 Jan. 1877, p. 16). Fuller built at least fourteen churches, worked on at least eighty more, and 'restored' the medieval cathedrals of Waterford (1870s), Limerick (1877–80), Lismore (1878), St Patrick's Dublin (1882–6), Killaloe (1887), Kildare (1890), Tuam (1896), Clonfert (1896–1900) and Ferns (1901–3). **133** A. Malcomson, *Archbishop Charles Agar: churchmanship and politics in Ireland, 1760–1810* (Dublin, 2002), p. 209. **134** E. Brynn, *The Church of Ireland in the age of Catholic Emancipation* (New York, 1982), p. 27. **135** J. Gough, *A tour in Ireland in 1813 and 1814* (Dublin, 1817), p. 42. **136** W. Wilde (ed.), *Memoir of Gabriel Beranger and his labours in the cause of Irish art and antiquities from 1760 to 1780* (Dublin, 1880), p. 253. **137** CSO/RP/1823/451. **138** Browne, *Ecclesiastical law of Ireland*, p. 183. **139** Browne, *Ecclesiastical law of Ireland*, p. 173.

In 1826, the forty-five landowners of the parish of Moymet (Co. Meath) protested against proposals to erect a new church because there were no Protestant parishioners with the sole exception of the rector's own family.[140] Similarly there were complaints in the same year about a church cess levied on the poor Catholics of the parishes of Drum and Moore (Co. Roscommon) for the erection of a church in Moore, despite the lack of Protestants.[141] In 1828, an anonymous member of his 'small' congregation criticized Revd Morgan Jellett, rector of Tullycorbet (Co. Monaghan), for holding a furtive vestry meeting behind the back of his parishioners at which it was decided to commission a new church: their existing church was adequate and it would be 'a hard matter for us to build a church in the situation the world is in at present: the half of them is broak [and] not able to pay any [cess]'.[142]

In 1830, the people of Errismore near Clifden (Co. Galway), led by the chief tenant Con King, violently resisted police efforts to distrain their livestock to pay the vestry cess.[143] Three decades later in 1860, the German traveller Julius Rodenberg (1831–1914) observed that around Clifden 'the entire area is Catholic and only a few Protestant families – I heard the number is five – live in the town; these are however prosperous and powerful and they have built their place of worship on the highest hill so that it dominates the town'.[144]

Frequently these Protestant churches stood isolated in the countryside but conveniently located to suit the local landlord family, who retained the right to appoint the rector until as late as 1870. In 1825, forty-one inhabitants of Derrybrusk (Co. Fermanagh) petitioned the lord lieutenant to prevent their new church being located by their rector on a distant site to facilitate the landlord, who wished it to be 'contiguous to his castle and demesne' (presumably Castle Archdale). Despite having earlier agreed a more central site with the churchwardens and the parishioners, the rector was persuaded to change his mind 'under pretence of removing it from floods' in the winter.[145]

Protestantism had two other spasms of intense activity, largely London-driven proselytism in the west of Ireland in the 'Second Reformation' in 1820s, and in the west of Ireland from the 1830s in Achill (Co. Mayo) and Dingle (Co. Kerry), but particularly in the aftermath of the Famine, when activities in Connemara attracted heated debate. Louisa Beaufort (1781–1863) commented on efforts on the Blaskets (Co. Kerry) in the 1840s:

> I had a little conversation with Connor the Blasket reader and learnt from him that now the Romish priest visits the islands every month or two. He used to go only once in two years, when he held a station and collected his two years dues, with which he loaded his boat: corn, butter,

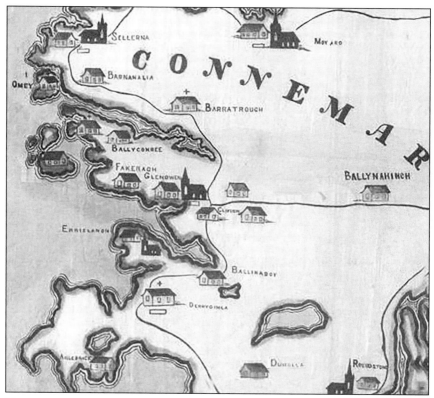

Fig. 32 Extract from 'Irish Church Missions map of west Galway 1858' (NLI, PD 2197 TX 6).

calves, sheep and whatever he could get. He held an auction of them on
the mainland and often made a large sum. A priest is now going to reside
on the great Blasket, and two days ago was there, said mass and cursed
all the converts from the altar. But they don't mind it now, and even
the Roman Catholics are now shocked and disgusted at this violence.
All outrage on their part has ceased in spite of the priest's exhortation.
Lately he told them he would not advise them to do it, but that the
reader ought to be tied neck and heels and thrown into the deep sea.[146]

A distinctive pictorial map of 'Irish Church Missions[147] map of west Galway
1858' depicted the infrastructure of schools, churches and orphanages that sprang

---

146 At Dunquin, a new schoolhouse was erected for the converts, of whom there were
between eighty and ninety adults plus 'a multitude of children'. In Dingle church, the
transept gallery was used to accommodate 'only converts of all classes': M. Loeber & R.
Loeber, 'Louisa Beaufort's diary of her travels in south-west Munster and Leinster in 1842
and 1843', *Anal. Hib.*, 46 (2015), pp 152–3. 147 The 'Irish Church Missions to the Roman
Catholics' was founded and funded in 1849 chiefly by English Anglicans, although with the
support of Church of Ireland clergy and bishops.

Fig. 33 Ballyburly church, near Edenderry (Co. Offaly), photographed by Rolf Loeber in 1973, just before it was obliterated completely. Elgy Gillespie described it as a 'pretty church with its latticed windows and beamed gallery' in 1975, when it still contained two remarkable stone monuments (*Irish Times*, 3 Feb. 1975). The stone above the door carried the arms of John Wakely quartered with those of his wife Elizabeth, daughter of Oliver Lambert of Painstown. Underneath was the inscription 'Joannes Wakely edifida has aedes anno secundo regni regis Jacobi Secundi anno domini 1686' (John Wakely built this house in the second year of the reign of King James II 1686). (E. Hickey, 'The Wakelys of Navan and Ballyburly: a discussion of a sixteenth-century family', *Ríocht na Midhe*, 5:4 (1974), pp 3–19). Ballyburly House, described as 'a fine old mansion in the Elizabethan style roofed with bog oak' and with five-feet thick walls, was razed by an accidental fire in 1888 (*King's County Chronicle*, 28 June 1888). It may have been designed by Thomas Burgh (R. Loeber, *A biographical dictionary of architects in Ireland, 1600–1720* (London, 1981), p. 39). A new house was built by 1890 (the architect was the ubiquitous J.F. Fuller) but it too was burnt – this time deliberately – during the Civil War in 1923. The Wakeley family commissioned a new house in 1924 from Joseph Bruntz (*Irish Builder*, 3 May 1924), but ultimately abandoned the area. Captain John Wakeley had been granted land seized from the O'Connors on the edge of the Pale. Inside the church, a monument represented in relief the family arms and the effigy of a spade-bearded Elizabethan warrior in full military costume – ruff, doublets, padded hose, holding a cavalry sword and a lance. The monument, perhaps by the sculptor John Cusack, also displayed an obviously Gaelic decapitated head. Erected by Thomas Wakely post-1617, it stated that Thomas was son of 'Jo[h]n Wakely of Navan, Esq.', Captain of 'a 100 horse and 100 foot in the beginning of Queen Elizabeth's reigne, of famous memory' who 'govern'd them to the advancement of Her Highness's service'. The two stones are now in storage in the National Museum. (Courtesy of Magda Loeber).

up in the post-Famine decade. [148] These missions generated so much controversy that they even generated their own tour book.[149] The Dublin slums were also the pitiful arena for acridly competitive proselytism in the mid nineteenth century.[150]

When the Irish Church Act of 1869 disestablished the Church of Ireland, a key objective was to prevent coveted ancient buildings from falling back into the eager Catholic grasp. This was achieved by creating the category of 'National Monument' for any churches deemed worthy of preservation, which were then vested in the Board of Works.[151] On 1 January 1871, the Church of Ireland – no longer state-funded and suddenly dependent on its own diminished resources – found itself responsible for 1,630 churches, 1,400 graveyards and 900 glebes. By 1917, 1,061 unions remained functioning and these were rationalized into 422 unions in 1925. In a further curtailment exercise in 1965, 144 more churches were closed, with 743 retained.[152] Wider social and political changes weakened Church of Ireland communities especially in the towns. The Ferns Diocesan Synod in 1927 reported on 'the change in the centre of gravity which had taken place in the Diocese':

> While the town parishes, Wexford, Enniscorthy, Gorey and New Ross, had lost more than half of their Church population in the last few years, many of the country parishes had hardly suffered at all. In County Wexford, the Protestant farmers were the backbone of the Church.[153]

The sustained hollowing out of the Church of Ireland since disestablishment has resulted in a proliferation of abandoned towers and roofless naves in the Irish landscape, especially in the midlands, the south and the west.[154]

GLEBE HOUSES

As well as First Fruits churches, architecturally distinctive glebe houses left a lasting imprint on the Irish landscape.[155] In 1801, there were 2,436 parishes, arranged in 1,123 benefices, but there were only 436 glebe houses.[156] A glebe

---

148 NLI, PD 2197 TX 3.   149 A. Dallas, *A mission tour-book in Ireland: showing how to visit the missions in Dublin, Connemara, etc.* (London, 1860).   150 J. Prunty, *Dublin slums, 1800–1925: a study in urban geography* (Dublin, 1998), 'Church charities respond: women and children 1850–1900', pp 234–73.   151 H. Shearman, *Privatising a church: the disestablishing and disendowment of the Church of Ireland* (Lurgan, 1995).   152 M. Maguire, 'Churches and symbolic power in the Irish landscape', *Landscapes,* 5:2 (2004), pp 91–113.   153 *Church of Ireland Gazette,* 7 Oct. 1927.   154 An insider's perspective is offered by R.B. McCarthy, 'The Church of Ireland in south Tipperary in the twentieth century', *Tipperary Historical Journal* (2007), pp 145–52.   155 W. Roulston, 'Accommodating clergymen: Church of Ireland ministers and their houses in the north of Ireland, 1600–1870' in T. Barnard & W. Neely (eds), *The clergy of the Church of Ireland, 1000–2000* (Dublin, 2006), pp 106–27.   156 T.L. O'Beirne, The state of the church in Ireland & provisions for the Roman Catholic clergy, Apr. 1801, PRO MS 30/9/163, f. 161.

house was a residence provided in each parish (or union) for the clergyman and his family. The word glebe (Middle English, from French *glèbe*, Latin *gleba*, land or soil) designated land within a parish set aside in perpetuity to support a clergyman. Glebelands varied in size, and were sometimes scattered. Initial provision had been scarce to non-existent. In the Ulster Plantation, sixty from every 1,000 acres from plantation grants were to be assigned as glebelands. In 1622, the Killaloe clergy reported that they 'either must live in some poore naked cabin in danger of theyr lives, or in a victualling house not answerable to theyr calling: or be non-resident in repairing to some well peopled towne for safety and habitation'.[157]

In 1626, the state decreed that each incumbent granted 120 acres within two miles of a parish church must 'build a sufficient mansion of stone, thirty feet [9m] in length, twenty [6m] in height and eighteen [5.5m] in breadth, English standard measure, within the walls'.[158] Stipulations regarding building materials were made in 1724 (12 George I, c.10) and 1727 (1 George II, c. 15). The glebe house 'must be of stone and lime, or brick and lime, and timbered in the roof and the floors of such dwelling house with oak or fir timber (bog oak excepted) and covered with slate, shingles or tiles; except livings under £100 per year, on which such houses or buildings may be covered with thatch'.[159] Living conditions were often tenuous enough. In the diocese of Meath in 1801, the incumbent of Dunboyne described his house as 'an old cabin'. Another at Loughcrew refused to live in the 'very wretched thatched cabin' in which his predecessor had resided.[160]

A fine seventeenth-century glebe house survives at Graffan (Co. Offaly), there is a 1691 example at Hezlett House (Co. Derry),[161] an early eighteenth-century one at Clonegal (Co. Carlow)[162] and a more grandiose 1739 specimen at Oakfield, near Raphoe (Co. Donegal). The eighteenth-century style is well illustrated.[163] Beaufort mapped 363 glebe houses in 1792,[164] and the number climbed quickly to 436 by 1805, 768 by 1829 and 829 by 1832.[165]

---

157 Dwyer, *Diocese of Killaloe*, p. 146.   **158** J. Morrin, *Calendar of the patent and close rolls of chancery*, 3 vols (Dublin, 1863), iii, pp 176–7.   **159** Browne, *Ecclesiastical law of Ireland*, p. 133.   **160** J. Healy, *History of the diocese of Meath*, 2 vols (Dublin, 1908), ii, pp 140–1.   **161** This is a single-storeyed thatched long house with cruck roof-timbers located at Castlerock near Coleraine.   **162** R. Loeber & K. Whelan, 'An early eighteenth-century house: Clonegal Rectory, Co. Carlow', *Wexford Historical Society Journal*, 13 (1990–91), pp 135–41.   **163** J. Payne, *Twelve designs of country-houses, of two, three and four rooms on a floor, proper for glebes and small estates* (Dublin, 1757). Revd John Payne, himself a rector, primarily considered the design and layout of glebe houses.   **164** D.A. Beaufort, *A new map of Ireland civil and ecclesiastical* (London, 1792). There is a *c.*1779 vignette of the neat and still extant glebe house at Ardmore (Co. Waterford) in Harbison (ed.), *Beranger's Views of Ireland*, p. 72.   **165** S. Brown, 'The New Reformation movement in the Church of Ireland, 1801–1829' in S. Brown & D. Miller (eds), *Piety and power in Ireland, 1760–1960: essays in honour of Emmet Larkin* (Belfast, 2000), pp 180–208.

Parish of Grange Gorman Glebe House, 1836.

Rev.ᵈ Arthur Smith Adamson. A.M.   Incumbent.
Samuel Allen Daly   )
Thomas Haslam Es.   ) Church Wardens.

Fig. 34 Grangegorman (Co. Dublin) glebe house in 1836. It was designed for the Board of First Fruits by John Semple Sr (1763–1840) and his son John Semple (1801–82) in 1827. It is a compact box-Georgian house set in a miniature villa-style parkland (RCB).

Early nineteenth-century drawings emphasized the integration of house, rear enclosed yard and offices (stables, coach house, dairy, barn, outhouses).[166] This reflected the importance of horse and coach and the assumed self-sufficiency

166 The RCB Library holds seventy sets of drawings (280 drawings in total), of which twenty-eight sets are twentieth century, mainly from the 1960s. The bulk of the remainder are from the first three decades of the nineteenth century.

associated with farming glebe land. The initial construction spurt was from 1771 to 1790; a second followed from 1808 to 1820. Two-thirds of glebe-houses in Down and half of those in Kilmore diocese emanated from this period, but the hey-day of glebe building was over by 1823, once Board of First Fruits funding was drastically curtailed.[167] The poet John Betjeman (1906–84) captured their geographic ambience: 'The Protestant glebe house by beech trees protected/ Sits close to the gates of his Lordship's demesne'.

By the mid-nineteenth century, the diocese of Armagh had spent £84,000 on glebe houses and only £80,000 on churches.[168] It was common for the glebe house to be architecturally more distinguished than its church. Being a clergyman was a respectable middle-class occupation and many long-tailed 'clerical' families flourished in Protestant Ireland.[169] All eight children of Revd Samuel Skene (1839–1919), rector of Ballyvaldon (Co. Wexford), served 'in the ministry of the Church of England'.[170]

OTHER PROTESTANT DENOMINATIONS

Quakers
Following its arrival in Ireland in 1654, Quakerism had 800 adherents in Ireland by the 1680s, 2,500 by 1760[171] and 6,000 by 1812, as reported by the English Quaker Thomas Shillitoe (1754–1836), at a time when there were 22,000 British Quakers.[172] The first documented Friends Meeting was held in 1654 in Lurgan (Co. Armagh), but the low-decibel Quakers did not eventually flourish in the shouty bellicose world of Ulster religion. The severely religious Robert Willis (1713–91) of Philadelphia, an itinerant Quaker, was struck by 'the failure of Friends in Ulster Province' in 1774.[173] The first purpose-built meeting house in Dublin was at Meath Street in 1684, but in general Quakers favoured austere, sometimes solitary, meeting houses, of which 120 are known, but of which only sixty survive. Responding to Beaufort's well known 'A new map of Ireland civil and ecclesiastical' in 1792 that highlighted Anglican Ireland, the Quakers produced their own superb map of their fifty-four meeting houses in

167 Roulston, 'Accommodating clergymen'. **168** W. Shee, *The Irish church being a digest of returns* (London, 1852), p. 42. **169** Revd J.B. Leslie published meticulous 'biographical succession lists' for nine dioceses, and the rest are in typescript in the RCB Library. Even the most cursory perusal reveals the recurrence of names. **170** *Irish Church Gazette*, 16 Oct. 1936; Leslie, *Ferns*, p. 121. **171** I. Grubb, *The Quakers in Ireland* (London, 1927), p. 89. **172** Wakefield, *Ire.*, ii, p. 809. This figure implies that there were about 1,000 Quaker families. **173** Diary of Robert Willis, Philadelphia, Historical Society of Pennsylvania, MS 719, p. 327.

1794, with the pragmatic detail of showing market as well as meeting times to facilitate their travelling merchants.[174]

The American Quaker William Savery (1750–1804), visiting Clonmel (Co. Tipperary) in 1798, thought that Irish Quakers were prosperous: 'Friends in Ireland seem to live like princes of the earth more than in any country I have seen – their gardens, horses, carriages, and various conveniences, with the abundance of their tables'.[175] A decade later, John Gough counted sixty in attendance at Garryrone, a meeting house near Clonmel (Co. Tipperary), with twenty to thirty horses and eleven carriages parked on the green surrounding the meeting house.[176] Seven meeting houses were recorded in Co. Wexford in 1794: in the towns of New Ross[177] and Enniscorthy, and rural meetings in townlands with endogamous clusters of closely related families at Forest (Taghmon), Randallsmill (near Castlebridge), Cooladine (near Enniscorthy), Ballintore (near Ferns)[178] and Ballinclay (near Gorey). These were presumably small plain additions to existing domestic dwellings of prominent local Quakers. It was only after 1830 that Quakers began to commission architects.

Another distinctive feature of the Quakers was that they were industriously epistolary, ensuring that they are remarkably well documented. They were also socially progressive and avoided negative entanglements in politics whereas for so many other churches in Ireland their escutcheons could not be seen for the blots. While the Quakers did not entirely withdraw into homogenous communities, some villages and towns were strongly influenced by them and they imparted an entrepreneurial flavour. Examples are Ballitore (Co. Kildare), Portlaw (Co. Waterford), Clara (Co. Offaly), Bessbrook (Co. Armagh), Moate (Co. Westmeath) and Baltyboys (Co. Wicklow).[179] In 1709, Moate was described as 'a pretty little clean-built town, of a different ayre from the generality of the Irish villages in this part of Ireland' with '10 or 12 familys of Quakers'.[180] The landscape around it was 'a well improv'd, well planted country, with trees and orchards, good houses, and, as I hear, English inhabitants'.[181] Bessbrook was laid out after 1845 as a model village around two large squares by the dynamic entrepreneur John Grubb Richardson (1813–91). He refused to allow public houses, pawnbrokers or a police station,

---

174 Map of Friends meetings in Ireland 1794, NLI, 16 B 6. 175 William Savery, *A journal of the life, travels, and religious labors of William Savery, a minister of the Gospel of Christ, of the Society of Friends, late of Philadelphia* (Philadelphia, 1861), p. 401. 176 Gough, *Tour*, p. 39. 177 A 'large new meeting house' was erected at New Ross in 1788 (D. Butler, *The Quaker meeting houses of Ireland* (Dublin, 2004), pp 77–8. 178 The meeting house, single-storeyed with a high-hipped roof, was erected in 1756 by Fossie Thackaberry, 'the preacher', and Joseph Smithson (It was converted to residential use in the 1980s) (D. Rowe & E. Scallan, *Houses of Wexford*, second edition (Ballinakella, 2016), No. 83. 179 J. Hussey, *The Quakers of Baltyboys, County Wicklow, Ireland, 1678–1800* (Dublin, 2017). 180 'Molyneux tour', p. 34. 181 'Molyneux tour', p. 49.

Fig. 35 Map of Friends meetings in Ireland, 1794 (NLI, 16 B 6).

but insisted on a public school open to all denominations. Bessbrook's housing template, with individual privies, yards and allotments, influenced plans for the later and much more celebrated Bournville by George Cadbury (1839–1922) in England. At Portlaw, the mercantile Malcomsons inserted an elaborate street plan after 1859: a set of triangular blocks of uniform housing converging on a market square.

Huguenots

Veterans from the Williamite army inflated Huguenot numbers after 1691: in 1699, there were 'twenty thousand French Protestants who inhabit there now & are daily encreasing'.[182] They settled primarily in Dublin, Lisburn (Co. Antrim) and Portarlington (Co. Laois), under the patronage of Henri de Ruvigny, Lord Galway (1648–1720). Portarlington was described in 1709 as 'a pretty new town well planted by Lord Gallwey with a colony of French'.[183] The Huguenot population in Dublin rose from 2,000 in 1700 to 3,600 by 1720, five per cent of the urban population. In Dublin, the French-speaking Huguenots split into reformed and conformed elements, with separate places of worship. The conformed congregation adopted Anglican liturgy, joined the Church of Ireland, and attended the Lady Chapel of Saint Patrick's Cathedral, and St Mary's Church (northside). The reformed (non-conformist) congregation had meeting houses at Peter Street (southside) and Lucy Lane (northside). Dublin Huguenots, especially the reformed congregation, retained their distinctiveness until the francophone first generation petered out in the mid-eighteenth century.[184] The supposed Huguenot settlement of New Geneva (Co. Waterford) was planned by James Gandon in the 1780s, but the resonant name proved to be the only successful part of this grandiose project.[185] Dublin remained a seedbed for many varieties of Protestant dissent, ranging from White Quakers, Open Brethren, Exclusive Brethren, Plymouth Brethren, Kellyites and Walkerites to Christian Scientists and the Salvation Army.[186]

Moravians

The Moravians were present in Dublin from 1746 but their most celebrated settlement was at Gracehill (Co. Antrim), established as a distinct community in 1765. Like the largest English settlements of Fulneck (1740s, near Leeds) and Fairfield (1785, near Manchester), Gracehill was founded on egalitarian, family-centred and economically self-sufficient principles, the better to protect

182 R. Loeber, D. Dickson & A. Smyth, 'Verdon's account of Dublin city and county in 1699', *Anal. Hib.*, 43 (2012), p. 60.   **183** 'Molyneux tour', p. 51.   **184** R. Hylton, *Ireland's Huguenots and their refuge, 1662–1745* (Brighton, 2005), pp 35, 112, 116.   **185** M. Craig, *The architecture of Ireland from the earliest times to 1880* (London, 1982), pp 311–13. This reproduces the grandiose plan of James Gandon for the new town.   **186** S. Smyrl, *Dictionary of Dublin dissent: Dublin's Protestant dissenting meeting houses, 1660–1920* (Dublin, 2009).

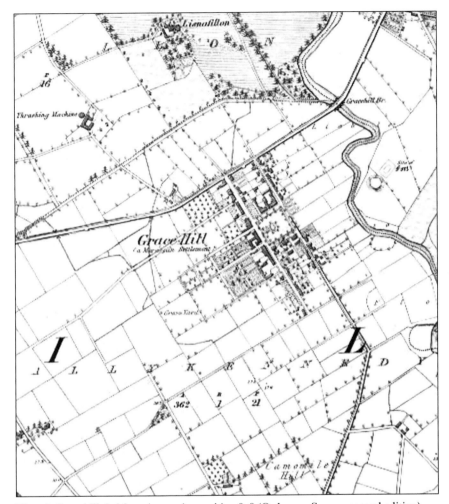

Fig. 36 Gracehill, 'a Moravian settlement' in 1858 (Ordnance Survey, second edition).

their distinctive mission.[187] The template of the highly structured Moravian village was based on the mother settlement at Herrnhut in Germany. Their community was allocated to a series called choirs, strictly based on age, gender and marital status. Each choir (infant, boys, girls, single brothers, single sisters, married, widows, widowers) had specific responsibilities and were assigned dwellings, organised on gender lines. Gracehill was laid out around a square with the church on the centre of the west side. The village was split along the short axis of the church, and this invisible line divided the male and female

187 G. Darley, 'The Moravians: building for a higher purpose', *Architectural Review*, 177 (1998), pp 45–9.

sides, and bisected the graveyard. The residents were primarily tradesmen who
worked for the community and in return were provided with a home and the
essentials of life. A crisp grid of uniform rectangular fields surrounded the
village. Gracehill was intentionally self-contained in terms of the regulation of
life in accordance with its religious beliefs.

Anne Plumptre (1760–1818) described the settlement in 1814:

> The upper end of the green is occupied by the chapel, a boy's school,
> and the house for the single sisters: they are, as the name imports, a
> society of unmarried women. Their number was at this time about sixty,
> and they were of all ages. They live all together, having lodging-rooms
> in common, full of small beds like the wards of an hospital; they eat
> their meals together, sit and work together, and have a seat appropriated
> to them in the chapel. No vow is taken against marriage; but any one
> marrying quits the society immediately, and establishes herself with
> her husband in some of the houses of the village. A variety of works are
> carried on among them; working muslin, making lace, spinning, knitting,
> plainwork of every kind, fancy pin-cushions, housewives' purses, child-
> bed linen and the like. ... The green is inclosed with a paling, and trees
> are planted all round: within is a gravel walk for general recreation and
> relaxation. There are also very good schools both for girls and boys.[188]

In 1824, the educationalist James Glassford praised their schools:

> Two academies and boarding schools for young gentlemen and ladies
> severally [separately]. Two day schools for boys and girls of the lower
> class, all in excellent arrangement, young gentlemen for college, military
> academy, mercantile: young ladies female education, music but no
> dancing. A sisterhood and brotherhood for unmarried persons of the
> order belong to this settlement. Manufacture lace etc ... Farms in good
> state; hedges trimmed, no rags or beggary or idlers.[189]

Methodists

Methodism advanced from an internal religious society within the Church of
England in the 1730s to a major international movement by the 1880s. During
that period, it exerted a significant influence on Ireland and Britain, became
the largest denomination in the United States (with a formative input from

---

188 Plumptre, *Narrative*, p. 160. Thomas Russell (1767–1803) has a long and admiring
earlier description from 1791: *Journals & memoirs of Thomas Russell*, ed. C.J. Woods
(Dublin, 1991), pp 163–70. These moralized landscapes were caricatured in a once famous
novel: 'Too Good Owenite wants to parcel out the world into squares like a chessboard with
a community on each, raising everything for one another' (Thomas Peacock, *Crotchet Castle*
(London, 1831), p. 18.   189 Glassford, *Three tours*, pp 43–5.

Irish immigrants), and sponsored a dynamic global missionary presence. Methodism embraced personal discipline and sobriety, but it was animated by emotion, enthusiasm and even ecstasy.[190] In Ireland, it flourished especially in the decades after the 1798 rebellion, when Methodism responded much more effectively to the advent of secularizing enlightenment influences than the Established Church, by emphasizing inwardness and 'heart religion'. It became more fervent, egalitarian, populist and politically conservative.[191] Like Quakerism, Methodism held a particular appeal for women, who were encouraged to play a leadership role denied to them within Anglicanism.

Methodism flourished most along the ragged border where dominantly Catholic and dominantly Protestant communities abutted on one another. Methodism and the evangelical revival spread along the south Ulster shatter belt, with field and street preaching, and circuit clergy of enormous energy.[192] Methodism made negligible inroads on Catholics but it peeled off other Protestants. Its strength lay in an arc from Sligo across north Roscommon to Cavan, Monaghan, Armagh, Louth and south Down.[193]

Methodism prospered in the parts of south Leinster that had been convulsed in 1798, notably north Wexford and Wicklow. A vignette shows how Methodism gained a hold by instilling seriousness. In 1813, a Methodist chapel was built at Coolafancy (Co. Wicklow), through converting a two-story public house, containing a spacious shop, hall, and parlour to the front and a large kitchen to the rear, 'near the popish chapel, and the ball alley between both'. The Methodists 'pulled down the ball alley, levelled the cock pit, and enclosed a neat yard with a stone wall'.[194] Everything that Methodism abominated – drinking, cock-fighting, sabbath-breaking – was symbolically razed in raising this chapel, all the sweeter for being sited alongside the Catholic chapel.

EVANGELICALISM

Evangelicalism in Britain after the French Revolution was stripped of its radicalism, and politicization of the evangelical impulse moved decisively in a conservative direction.[195] The strengthening evangelicalism of Protestantism was the most significant British cultural response to the French Revolution. The Ulster Evangelical Society was founded in 1798. By promoting

---

190 D. Hempton, *Methodism: empire of the spirit* (New Haven, 2005).   **191** D. Hempton & M. Hill, *Evangelical Protestantism in Ulster society, 1740–1890* (London, 1992). The heartland of Irish Methodism is identified as the 'Linen triangle' and the 'Lough Erne rectangle' (map on p. 31).   **192** D. Cooney, *The Methodists in Ireland: a short history* (Blackrock, 2001).   **193** Whelan, *Bible war*, p. 166.   **194** Memoir of John Buttle, in possession of Magda Loeber, Pittsburgh.   **195** S. Brown, *The national churches of England, Ireland and Scotland, 1801–1846* (Oxford, 2001).

evangelicalism, which dissolved social and denominational barriers, Methodism reinforced a shared Ulster Protestant identity by providing a bridge between Presbyterianism and the Established Church, as was noted in 1824: 'common interest and common danger draw them closer'.[196] Evangelicalism dictated its response to sectarian conflict, by simultaneously narrowing the focus to a choice between reformed religion and Catholic superstition, and widening it to an international eschatological conflict. Ulster Protestants toggled between regarding themselves as a faithful remnant in a hostile land, or as folded into a great, civilizing and Protestant empire. Both ideas were culturally reinforcing, instilling unshakeable confidence, and permitting Protestant populism to trump class interests.[197]

Between 1790 and 1840, an evangelical elite emerged in both Britain and Ireland, with a massive emphasis on moral reform paving the way for Victorian moral earnestness. Their chosen battle ground in Ireland was popular education as a spearhead of moral reformation. Irish evangelicals wished to insert scripture at the core of education and use this covertly to deliver reformation at a local level. The leadership increasingly injected a partisan, triumphalist style, and launched an aggressive assault on Catholicism. This accelerated after 1815, as pride and providence coalesced in a surge of Britishness. By the 1820s, the movement had become ever more militant and confrontational. This created the conditions in which anti-Catholic violence once more disfigured the red-letter calendar days of popular Protestantism on 12 July, 4 November and 5 November. In 1822, the gauntlet was thrown down to the Catholics from the very pinnacle of Irish Protestantism, the pulpit of Archbishop William Magee of Dublin. 'Antithetical' Magee savaged Catholics as 'a church without a religion' and Dissenters as 'a religion without a church'.[198]

Evangelical Protestantism, anti-Popery and imperialism marched tightly together in Ulster, most notably expressed in the Orange Order founded in 1795. In the 1790s, a seam of disturbance ripped open along the Ulster fringes, centred on south Armagh: its influence seeped east and west through the crescent of drumlins and lakes that necklaced and insulated the province. This area incubated both the Defenders and the Orange Order in the 1790s, vernacular political mobilizations with a hard sectarian edge. A generation later, the 'Second Reformation' erupted between 1822 and 1827, centred on Kingscourt (Co. Cavan), and politicized in a conservative direction by powerful landed and political families like Farnham, Roden, Gosford, Mandeville and Lorton, mixing a stiff cocktail of pride, prejudice and providence. The entrenched divide along the Ulster frontier marked the point at which

196 Glassford, *Three tours*, p. 106.   197 D. Hempton, *Religion and political culture in Britain and Ireland: from the Glorious Revolution to the decline of empire* (Cambridge, 1996), p. 110. 198 Whelan, *Bible war*, p. 159.

O'Connellite politics failed to gain public traction, because confrontational opposition met it here in the 1820s. The antiquarian George Petrie (1790–1866) considered that in Sligo 'the gentry and parsons are ferocious bigots' in 1837 [199] while John O'Donovan in the same year commented that there 'the all-absorbing feeling is the conversion of papists'.[200]

The map of Irish Society[201] operations from 1818 to 1827 showed two sharply divided zones of concentration: the same broad south Ulster arc already identified stretching across the drumlin belt from Newport to Newry, and a second one in Munster (with the addition of Kilkenny, which often behaved culturally as if it were a 'Munster' county).[202]

Between 1888 and 1920, Protestant identity cohered around opposition to Home Rule, crystallizing a canopy Protestantism that sheltered and unified the diverse strands within Ulster's confessional complexities. Evangelicalism was crucial to its unity, welding together denominational and class interests around a shared anti-Catholicism. It built bridges between British and Irish Protestantism, between clergy and laity, between the churches and voluntary organizations like the Orange Order, and especially among Anglicans, Methodists and Presbyterians. Evangelicalism was central to the emergence of popular Ulster unionism in the 1880s, with its insistent emphasis on unity. Revd Thomas Ellis exhorted the Orangemen of Portadown (Co. Armagh) in 1885: 'Let us stand together as one man, never divided. In our concord is our glory. In our discipline is our victory. In our union is our strength'.[203]

Evangelical ideology was bifocal, with one eye sternly fixed on the narrow political ground of Ulster and its zero-sum game of Prods versus Taigues ('The loyal sons of Judah amid the faithless men of Israel'),[204] the other elevated towards empire and Protestantism's epic global conflict with Popery. Against the backdrop of post-Famine Catholic migration, evangelicalism was helped by the massive Victorian expansion of empire, pitting the commercial, Christian and civilized British world against the sordid and superstitious Irish Catholic diaspora, notably in America. These tropes, resonant with the mantra of superiority (in religious, racial and civic terms), also attached themselves to a binary racial category of Saxon versus Celt, and British versus Irish. In so doing, it accelerated the invention of a British tradition for Ulster Protestants, rehearsed annually in monumental public displays of memory on 12 July.[205]

---

199 *OS letters, Sligo*, p. 156. **200** J. O'Donovan, Castlekelly (Co. Roscommon) to G. Petrie (Dublin), 13 June 1837, NLI, MS 792 (400). **201** The 'Irish Society for promoting the scriptural education and religious instruction of the Irish-speaking population chiefly through the medium of their own language', founded in 1818, was usually called the Irish Society. **202** P. De Brún, *Scriptural instruction in the vernacular: the Irish Society and its teachers, 1818–1827* (Dublin, 2009) [map on p. 86]. **203** T. Ellis, *God and the nation: a sermon preached to the Orangemen of the district of Portadown* (Armagh, 1885), p. 12. **204** Ellis, *God and the nation*, p. 11. **205** A. Jackson,'Unionist myths', *Past and Present*, 136 (1992), pp 164–85.

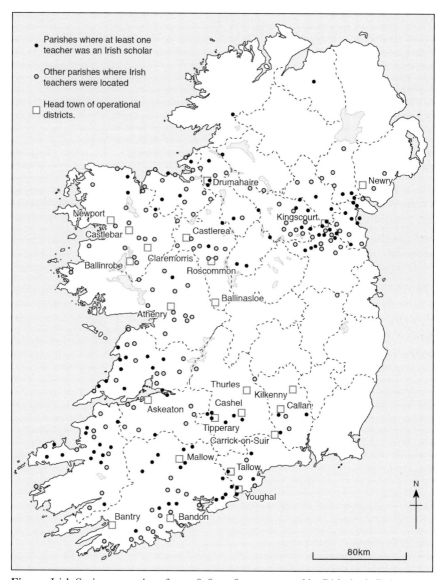

Fig. 37 Irish Society operations from 1818 to 1827, as mapped by Pádraig de Brún.

The proliferation of sects/house groups/pentecostalists/evangelicals/ Baptists remained a potent presence in Protestant-dominated areas of Ulster. This 'bible belt', arguably the most distinctive cultural region in contemporary Ireland, was never a self-contained or cohesive geographical entity: rather, the various sects occurred in separate nodes across Ulster, whose bristling juxtapositions shaped the peculiar religious landscape. The vitality of this Protestant tradition is witnessed in the diffusion of the Elim Pentecostal movement, founded in Monaghan in 1915 by George Jeffreys (1889–1962), a charismatic Welsh preacher, and the more recent spread of the Free Presbyterian church, founded in 1951 by Revd Ian Paisley (1926–2014).[206]

The Elim Pentecostal movement built its first church in Belfast in 1916: it currently enjoys a strong presence down the Lagan valley from Belfast to Armagh, with twelve congregations in the Belfast area. Elsewhere it has churches in Castlebar and Westport (Co. Mayo), Sligo, Carrick-on-Shannon (Co. Leitrim), Roscrea (Co. Tipperary), Bandon (Co. Cork), Monaghan, Kells and Navan (Co. Meath) and four in Dublin (Finglas, Swords, Tallaght, Ballyfermot). The Free Presbyterian church currently has sixty-one congregations in Northern Ireland, with twenty in Co. Antrim, seventeen in Co. Down, nine in Co. Tyrone, five in Co. Derry, two in Co. Fermanagh, two in the Republic of Ireland at Convoy (Co. Donegal) and Coragarry (Drum, Co. Monaghan), fourteen in England, Scotland and Wales, and about 100 globally, once Canada, the United States, Australia and Nepal are added.

Ulster also experienced a proliferation of para-religious buildings like Orange and Masonic Halls, tabernacles and revival halls, expressing a vigorous grassroots religious sensibility. Tin became available as a cheap building material after 1855. The Edinburgh firm Charles Young supplied a prefabricated portable version.[207] These tin buildings were widely used by itinerant preachers. They became a distinctive marker of the Ulster Protestant world.

---

206 Paisley was the butt of the poet W.R. Rodger's withering put down: 'there but for the grace of God goes God'. **207** There is a chapter on Ireland in I. Smith, *Tin tabernacles: corrugated iron mission halls, churches and chapels of Britain* (Pembroke, 2004); B. O'Reilly, 'Ireland's corrugated iron ("tin") churches' in T. Condit & C. Corlett (eds), *Above and beyond: essays in memory of Leo Swan* (Bray, 2005), pp 491–502.

CHAPTER SEVEN

The Catholic Revival

THE HISTORICAL CONTEXT OF IRISH CATHOLICISM in this period is heavily trampled ground.[1] A sensational demographic surge (two million to four million between 1700 and 1800, and a further doubling by the eve of the Famine) in a predominantly Catholic island necessitated building a plethora of new churches without state aid. [2] The nineteenth century proved the heyday of Irish church building, driven by a surge of energies within competing denominations, the population explosion, new architectural imperatives in the ecclesiological realm, and increased resources. The geography of the Catholic Revival is clearly established, with a core in south Leinster and east Munster.[3] This was a fertile agricultural area, with an entrenched, durable and demographically dominant Catholic population, mature towns with maritime trade, a commercially focussed and dynamic big farm group, an outward looking orientation, and successful patterns of clerical recruitment. Here the 'underground gentry'[4] provided the bedrock of Irish Catholicism: these confident families entertained high notions of their own importance, prioritized education, and maintained links with the sympathetic Continent.

When prosperous Catholics could express their willingness to engage in the public life of the state, they did so with alacrity, as, for example, in signing the Catholic Qualification Rolls. Between 1778 and 1800, a total of 6,578 did

---

1 N. Yates, *The religious condition of Ireland, 1770–1850* (Oxford, 2006); E. Larkin, *The pastoral role of the Roman Catholic church in pre-Famine Ireland, 1750–1850* (Dublin, 2006). 2 Catholic church building is discussed in K. Whelan, 'The Catholic church in Co. Tipperary, 1700–1850' in W. Nolan (ed.), *Tipperary: history and society* (Dublin, 1985), pp 215–55 and K. Whelan, 'The Catholic community in eighteenth-century Co. Wexford' in Power & Whelan (eds), *Endurance and emergence*, pp 156–78. On churches in general, there is excellent coverage in the four volumes of the *Buildings of Ireland* architectural guides: A. Rowan, *North West Ulster* (London, 1979), C. Casey & A. Rowan, *North Leinster* (London, 1993), C. Casey, *Dublin* (London, 2005) and K. Mulligan, *South Ulster* (New Haven, CT, 2013). 3 K. Whelan, 'The regional impact of Irish Catholicism 1700–1850' in W. Smyth & K. Whelan (eds), *Common ground: essays on the historical geography of Ireland* (Cork, 1988), pp 253–77. 4 K. Whelan, 'An underground gentry? Catholic middlemen in eighteenth-century Ireland' in J. Donnelly & K. Miller (eds), *Irish popular culture, 1650–1850* (Dublin, 1998), pp 118–72.

so, including 308 females. Strikingly, 68 per cent came from six urban areas: Dublin (2,269, 34.5 per cent), Cork (1,157, 17.5 per cent), Limerick (660, 10 per cent), Galway (176, 3 per cent) and Waterford (114, 2 per cent). There were only seven signatories from Ulster – Down with five and Armagh with two. Roscommon, Sligo and Leitrim had no signatories.[5]

By 1800, there were 1,026 Catholic parishes, amalgamated from 2,445 medieval parishes. This revamped parochial system facilitated new churches being positioned more centrally, almost invariably at crossroads. Forcibly severed from its pre-Reformation roots, the church's evolving flexible chapel and parish building strategy allowed it to follow surging population movements into the remote and poorer regions on the edges of mountains and bogs, the fringes of towns and the backlanes of cities. In 1825, Patrick Grady, the combative parish priest of Killedan (Co. Mayo), accused his bishop of removing 'seats of public worship from silent and central country places to paltry whiskey selling villages'.[6]

John O'Donovan argued in 1837 that the reworked parochial system had eroded the existing religious traditions:

> From the dismemberment of Catholic parishes, many of them have been left without a patron saint at all: when a union of two parishes takes place, the most distinguished of the two patrons is retained, and in many instances the original Milesian [Irish] saint is wholly forgotten, and the parish left without any patron or else placed under the tutelage of the Virgin, St Michael the Archangel or some other distinguished foreign saint. This is the real state of the case, and the surest guide the antiquarian pilgrim has is (when such exists) the holy well of the parish, in the name of which that of the original founder of the parish is most likely to endure.[7]

CATHOLICS AND THE PUBLIC SPHERE

The urgent Catholic commitment to church building in the nineteenth century was driven by an ingrown sense of persecution. This trope entered deep into the Irish Catholic historical consciousness: a broadsheet in Irish on the 1835

---

5 NLI MS 13,060 (2). 6 Grady accused Patrick McNicholas (1818–52), bishop of Achonry, of seizing a new chapel and adjoining dwelling house, erected 'for the most part' at Grady's expense. When one of his congregation opposed the bishop, he 'found his mill next morning consumed to ashes'. The bishop, accompanied by 'an infuriated mob', proclaimed that Grady would be 'dispossessed of his chapel'. After the bishop withdrew, 'the priests and their mob broke in the doors of the chapel', 'burst in the windows' and threw a dead cat on the altar (CSO/RP/1825/950). The disputatious Grady later sought a pension for his services to government: in 1793, against Defenderism; in 1798, against joining the French; in 1807, against the Threshers and in 1825, against the 'Catholic Rent' (CSO/RP/1826/2015). 7 *OS letters, Longford/Westmeath*, p. 18.

Fig. 38 An O'Connellite parade swings onto Sackville Street in 1835 and turns towards Nelson's pillar. The Liberator stands in his triumphal car, holding his Milesian Cap (based on an ancient Irish crown). A costumed bard strums his harp while a modern band plays in front of him. Spectators occupy every vantage point. The captions read 'O'Connell my liberator' (held up by a young boy) and 'A nation brave/who justly do agree/have but to will it/and they must be free'. Richard Lalor Sheil (1791–1851) is seated beside O'Connell (RIA HP 1636).

Cork election lauded 'O'Connell do réabaigh puirt agus do thraochaigh buir/ do chuir eaglais Chríost gan fothain cois claí/suí Aifrinn naofa dha dtréada bhíodh/le heagla an tírnigh ghránna' (O'Connell who breached the barriers and subdued the boors/who shoved Christ's church shelterless into the ditch/ the customary Mass sites abandoned/for fear of the hated landlord).[8] An enthusiastic church builder in mid-nineteenth-century Dublin commented that earlier chapels were 'crouching timidly in the darkest and most loathsome allies and lanes of the city'.[9]

O'Connell instilled a reinvigorated feistiness in Catholics. Priests took on landlords at local level and sought untrammelled leadership of their own communities across every sphere – political, religious, educational, social – in

8 Holohan, 'Two controverted Cork elections', p. 124. 9 W. Meagher, *Notices of the life and character of His Grace Most Rev. Daniel Murray, late Archbishop of Dublin* (Dublin, 1853), p. 90.

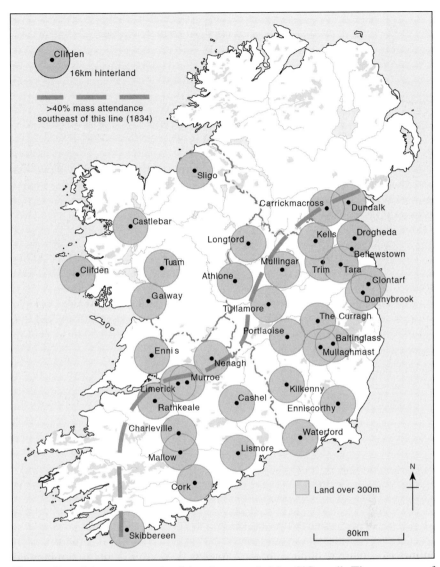

Fig. 39 Repeal 'monster meetings' in 1843 attended by O'Connell. The core area of activism was south of a line linking Dundalk, Limerick and Cork, and it coincided with areas that were also actively Catholic as measured by Mass attendance figures in 1834.

a highly publicized series of bruising confrontations. In a row over Cortown chapel in Bohermeen parish (Co. Meath) in 1823, the parish priest Michael Branagan confronted the landlord Charles Tisdall of Charlesfort.[10] Revd James

10 M. Branagan, *A letter from the Rev. Michael Branagan ... to Charles A. Tisdall, ... containing strictures on the circular letters of that gentleman, addressed to the congregation of*

Callanan of Celbridge (Co. Kildare) similarly challenged Lord Cloncurry in the same year.[11] Edward Synge of Dysart (Corofin, Co. Clare) was excoriated in 1826 by the parish priest John Murphy, who despised his contentious local school. Murphy warned him that only a priest could control the barbarous 'common fellows' who 'hated a Sassenagh', and castigated Synge from the altar for weeks when he refused to close his school.[12] It was later burnt down.[13] In 1828, John Lawler of Rockville (Co. Kildare) complained to his bishop, James Doyle, that his landlord, Sir Gerald Aylmer of Donadea Castle, intended to build a barracks 'for the Peelers' adjacent to the chapel gate at Kilmeague, a proximity designed to 'irritate and annoy' the faithful on holy days, funerals and Sundays. Doyle, never a shrinking violet, warned Dublin Castle of party broils if the barracks were built, because the police have 'rendered themselves very odious to the people'.[14]

The abrasive Martin Doyle, nephew of Bishop James Doyle, became parish priest of Graiguenemanagh (Co. Kilkenny).[15] He berated the local landlord David Burtchaell (1788–1865) of Brandondale in 1829 when the magistrate disinterred the body of John Murphy from the graveyard at Duiske Abbey: 'the putrid remains were carried into the chapel and the head then severed from the body whilst the parts now in a state of putrification were strewed about or overran the floor'. Doyle admonished Burtchaell that 'by the laws of the Catholic Church, a place of divine worship is desecrated by the effusion of human blood, but when such place is used as a charnel house or room for dissecting the dead, the profanation is extreme, and the irreverence done to the presence of the Most High is too great for utterance'.[16]

Cortown chapel (Dublin, 1823): C. Tisdall, *A reply to a letter from the Rev. Michael Branagan ... to Charles A. Tisdall ... containing strictures on the circular letters of that gentleman, addressed to the congregation of Cortown chapel* (Dublin, 1823). **11** J. Callanan, *Letter from the Rev. James Callanan ... to the Right Honourable Lord Cloncurry* (Dublin, 1823). On Cloncurry, see K. Holton, *Valentine Lawless, Lord Cloncurry, 1771–1855* (Dublin, 2018). **12** CSO/RP/OR/1826/215. **13** CSO/RP/OR/1826/286. **14** CSO/RP/1828/1180. On 17 Aug. 1828, Aylmer promptly orchestrated a counter-memorial signed by sixty-eight Kilmeague Catholics stating that they had no reason to fear or object to a constabulary barracks adjoining their chapel as the police enjoyed a harmonious existence in the neighbourhood (CSO/RP/1828/1261). **15** Martin Doyle had erected a Catholic church in Clonegal between 1822 and 1824, costing £1,000, replacing a thatched chapel on the site, and built over and around it. He had likely engaged the expensive architect Thomas Cobden. The new church was 92 x 40 x 28 feet high [3,680 square feet]. It had paired Corinthian pillars and pilasters, with a breakfront pilaster, ceiling plasterwork, a superb altar painting, and galleries with handsome external granite flights of stairs. However locals were unhappy about the cost and his uncle JKL, rebuking him that it was 'a sin to oppress the poor for any purpose, however holy', transferred him to Graiguenemanagh. The villagers sarcastically clapped Doyle out of Clonegal and he allegedly cursed them. By comparison, the Church of Ireland church of 1819 cost £1,200 (architect John Meason) while the tiny Methodist chapel of 1834 cost £250 (OS namebooks, Co. Carlow, 1834).

CATHOLIC CHAPEL BUILDING

The Catholic vernacular typological sequence ran from Mass rock, Mass garden, scalán, bothóg, Mass cabin and Mass house, to chapel before finally embracing the dignity of 'church'. From the Protestant Reformation until 1871, the word 'church' applied officially only to Protestant parish churches. Catholics and Methodists had 'chapels' while Presbyterians and Quakers had meeting houses. Pückler-Muskau observed in 1824 that 'The Catholics are not allowed for instance to call their places of worship churches but only chapels and no bells are allowed'.[17] The linguist P.W. Joyce (1827–1914) noted in 1910 that 'The term chapel has so ingrained itself in my mind that to this hour the word instinctively springs to my lips when I am about to mention a Catholic place of worship; and I always feel some sort of hesitation or reluctance in substituting the word 'church'.[18]

In 1614, the Dublin provincial synod recognized that, however distasteful it might be, the calamitous times dictated that Mass must be permitted in profane places. Mass could be celebrated in 'private houses, in orchards or caves, in the woods or on the mountain tops', so long as 'due reverence was observed'.[19] Outdoor Mass required at a minimum a linen cloth over the altar and protection from wind and rain to the sides and back. Mass was never to be said without at least one lit wax candle.[20] The Mass rock phase was sporadic temporally and geographically but it imprinted itself on the Catholic memory, especially in Ulster.[21] A vivid poem survives in which a Catholic priest from Clogher diocese imagined himself being pursued.

Ní ghoireann cuach ar chraoibh,	The cuckoo doesn't call from its branch
Is ní chluinim faoile i ngleann,	nor the seagull from the valley,
Is ní fheicim feithid nó fuath,	I never glimpse an insect, or a shadow,
Nach saoilim gur slua Gall.	that I do not imagine is a host of the foreigners.
Ní chluinim torann mo chos,	When I hear the sound of my feet,
Is ní tharrngim dos im dhiaidh,	or snag a bush behind me
Nach saoilim gurab í an ruaig,	I think it is the hunt
Bhíos anuas, anoir is aniar.[22]	bearing down on me here, there, everywhere.

From the diocese of Clogher alone, 150 examples of Mass rocks are cited,[23] seventy-five examples are listed from Kilmore[24] while 177 are identified from

---

16 CSO/RP/OR/1829/300. **17** *Letters of a dead man*, p. 553. **18** P.W. Joyce, *English as we speak it in Ireland* (Dublin, 1910), pp 97–100. **19** Moran, *Catholic archbishops of Dublin*, p. 268. **20** A. Forrestal, *Catholic synods in Ireland, 1600–1690* (Dublin, 1998), pp 56–8. **21** H. Bishop, 'Memory and legend: recollections of penal times in Irish folklore', *Folklore*, 129:1 (2018), pp 18–38. **22** D. Ó Doibhlin, 'Penal days' in H. Jefferies & C. Devlin (eds), *History of the diocese of Derry from the earliest times* (Dublin, 2000), p. 174. **23** P. Ó Gallachair, 'Clogher's altars from the penal days: a survey', *Clogher Record*, 2:1 (1957), pp 97–130. **24** D. Gallogly, *Diocese of Kilmore, 1800–1950* (Cavan, 1999), pp 399–401.

Fig. 40 A surviving scalán at Templecarne graveyard (near Pettigo, Co. Donegal). It has a stone table under a segmental-arched hood.

the much larger and more heavily Catholic Cloyne and Ross.[25] O'Donovan described 'the time of the Mountain Masses'.[26] In Coniamstown townland in Bright parish (Co. Down), the Mass rock featured an altar reredos, with two tiny triangular recesses cut into the rock to cradle the cruets.[27] In east Ulster, bothóg was the name for the shed under which the priest said Mass,[28] while the word scalán was used in west Ulster.[29] Scaláns were also designed to shelter the priest as he collected 'offerings' at funerals – an Ulster tradition, sanctioned only in the Archbishopric of Armagh, which remained in vogue there until 1971.[30]

25 H. Bishop, 'Spatial distribution and location of Catholic Mass rock sites in the Diocese of Cork and Ross, Co. Cork, Ireland' in *Geographies of Religions & Belief Systems*, 4:1 (2014), pp 40–78. **26** John O'Donovan visited the townland of South Rosskeen and was shown 'a remarkable fort with subterranean chambers' within which was 'the site of a small chapel which was probably used during the time of the 'Mountain Masses' (*OS letters, Mayo*, p. 185). See also *OS letters, Galway*, p. 181, p. 186. **27** O'Laverty, *Down and Connor*, i, p. 165. **28** O'Laverty, *Down and Connor*, i, p. 199. This is derived from Irish 'both', a cabin, akin to Scotch 'bothy' and English 'booth'. O'Laverty provided systematic coverage of the Mass rock phenomenon. **29** 'A shed such as was used for Mass in penal times' (M. Traynor, *The English dialect of Donegal: a glossary* (Dublin, 1953), p. 241). 'A scallan, a rude shed' (H. Dorian, *The outer edge of Ulster: a memoir of life in nineteenth-century Donegal*, ed. B. Mac Suibhne & D. Dickson (Dublin, 2000), p. 71). **30** F. Sweeney, 'Wake and funeral offerings in the province of Armagh' in Ryan (ed.), *Death and the Irish*, pp 190–3. The community context of wakes and offerings is covered in J. Coll, 'Continuity and change in the parish of Gaoth Dobhair, 1850–1980' in Smyth & Whelan (eds), *Common ground*, pp 287–9.

William Bingley described the situation at Killimard near Donegal town in the 1780s: 'Many thousands of these persons in various parts assemble every Sabbath day at the foot of hills with only a hovel for an altar very much in the form of a cow stall where they hear Mass in the open air and in all kinds of weather'. They were 'bareheaded and on their knees' 'in all weathers' 'in the open air'. The priest 'receives his dues on a Lord's Day in farthings, halfpence and pence dropped into a box set on a stool at the chapel door or the gate of a field if he has no chapel'.[31] Catholics had to improvise: denied bells, they used cow horns to summon the faithful, as in the well-known 'Séipéal na hAdhairce' (the chapel of the horn) in the Nire valley (Co. Waterford). A horn was also used in Glenmore (Co. Kilkenny).

The Welsh antiquarian Edward Lhuyd (1660–1709), travelling from Tipperary via Kilkenny to Dublin in 1688, encountered an early version of a penal chapel:

> I diverted myself for some time in viewing a Popish church. Of this, I must beg leave to give you a rude description, but it falls out well that the homelier it be, the more agreable it is to the subject. In shape it resembled a pedlar's stall, t'was in length 25 foot [7.6m], in breadth 12 [3.6m], in heighth 14 or 15 [4.5m], at the altar end walled up, at ye other end, open to the top. Its walls were of great green clods on the inside whereof grew almost as many plants (spontaneously) as on the hill above mentioned. That part of the roof above the altar covered with straw (not to say thatched) the rest naked, the rafters were birch boughs gently pruned, the altar consisted of two stakes knock'd into the sayd mud wall, fastened to two others stuck fast in the ground upright with ligaments of straw. These four stakes were such as some husbandman would be allowed to stick in a hedge. On the two cross stakes lay the table [altar].[32]

A structure of this size could only have held internally about seventy-five people, if we assume that each standing person occupied (a tight) three square feet, and that the space also accommodated the altar. Early Catholic chapels did not have pews or benches, and the congregation stood or knelt as appropriate, with the weak 'going to the wall'.[33]

In the tightly regulated and scrutinized spaces of cities and towns, difficulties had to be surmounted. Catholics in Waterford successfully petitioned the corporation in 1699 for a site for a chapel in Bailey's Lane. A few years later, they were forced to defend 'their convenient and accustomed exercise of their religion in the city', owing to 'unkindness and severity in their neighbours'. Their defence

---

31 Bingley, *Discontents in Ireland*, pp 16–17. 32 Edward Lhwyd to Richard Jones, Bryn y Hynon, Wrexham, National Library of Wales, Peniarth MS 427, pp 450–1. 33 The first recorded appearance of this proverb is in the Coventry Mystery Plays of *c.*1500: 'The weakest go ever to the wall'.

was that they had previously enjoyed the use of four chapels, but that these had become so dilapidated as to pose a danger. They accordingly determined:

> to provide themselves with in a bye corner or lane as they did and in a place where there was such a dunghill and so much durt and nastyiness ... inclined to make up the present chapple ... for the common convenience of the inhabitants, partly that it was upon the walls of one of the said chapples in King Charles's ye second's time .. it was in a remote corner, soe as not to be exposed to any Protestant family or to the view of the right reverend Lord Bishop or ye Protestant Clergy or to yr lordships in your accustomed walks or stations ... two of the congregation are appointed every Sabbath day at ye door of the chapple to keep [country people] out soe few or none of them doe now come in but do tarry abroade in the little cabbin house chapel made for themselves ... the doore of this chapple is shut up and all service ended by the time they go to church on ye Sabbath ... if forced to go out of gates, there is no home or chapple but such as are too narrow for theyr own parishioners, nor can the old, sick, gouty or decrepit go thither.[34]

Catholics rebuilt in Dublin as well. Obscure alleys opened onto surprisingly large volumes, infiltrated into dense urban blocks, their interior scale hidden in plain sight by their unadorned exteriors.[35] These camouflaged chapels were identifiable only by crosses on Rocque's map of 1756, accessed by narrow lanes and alleys: Hangman's Lane, Dirty Lane, Pill Lane, Skipper's Lane, John's Lane, Limerick Alley, Rosemary Lane. 'Chapel' yards were highly irregular in shape, suggesting incremental expansion to fit whatever space was available around former warehouses and stables. In 1756, no chapel was found east of a line passing through Christ Church and St Patrick's Cathedrals. The social divide in eighteenth-century Dublin was an eastside/westside one, not southside/northside.[36] Successful Catholic merchants preferred to live in the Liberties and Kilmainham, escaping the stifling jurisdiction of the guilds. John Keogh chose Mount Jerome, Luke White (*c.*1750–1824) was at Woodlands (formerly Luttrellstown), Edward Byrne (1740–1804) lived in Mullinahack, Anthony MacDermott on Usher's Quay, Randal MacDonnell (1762–1821) on Usher's Island, Thomas

---

34 'A petition from Waterford Catholics to the Corporation dated circa 1710', *JRSAI*, 6 (1860), p. 128. 35 Compare the situation in Amsterdam. In 1629 Vrijburg, a typical clandestine church, was concealed behind a row of houses fronting on the Keizersgracht, and located at the centre of a block. It was so surrounded by houses on all four sides that it was invisible from any public street. In 1691, the Regents of Amsterdam prohibited Catholics attending Masses from parking their sleds on prominent streets. 36 A superb valuation map of Dublin in 1830 showed that the pattern endured well into the nineteenth century: J. Martin, 'The social geography of mid-nineteenth-century Dublin' in Smyth & Whelan (eds), *Common ground*, p. 178.

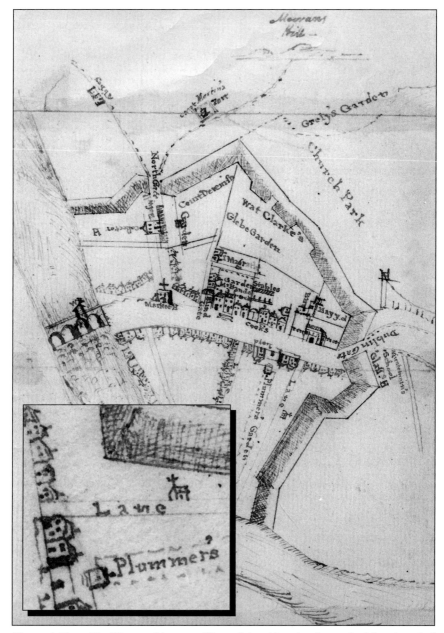

Fig. 41 Athlone (Co. Westmeath) *c*.1750. The peripheral location down a back lane is typical for Catholic chapels in the eighteenth century. The crucifix over the pictogram signalled a Catholic chapel. A Mass house was first recorded in 1719. A T-shaped chapel was shown on a 1784 map and this was replaced by a substantial new church in 1795. This map shows east-bank Athlone, within the 700m-long earthern rampart built in 1652-4 (demolished by 1784), which with the Shannon enclosed a defensible area of 4–5ha (Private collection).

Fig. 42 Detail from a map of Dublin in 1797 drawn by John Brownrigg (1747–1838). The tightly packed Liberties area contained many Catholic chapels (Dublin City Libraries).

Reynolds in the Coombe.[37] Of 137 Dublin city participants in the Back Lane parliament of 1792, the majority were from the south-west of the city, with strong concentrations in Francis Street (9), Ushers Quay (6), Thomas Street (4) and Watling Street (3).[38]

No wonder that it caused a sensation when the rising Catholic star Daniel O'Connell (1776–1847) set himself up ostentatiously on Merrion Square.[39] O'Connell was determined to assert his social status, even to the extent of

37 When **Luke White**, who 'realized the largest fortune ever made by trade in Ireland', died in February 1824, he still faced class condescension: the duke of Bedford sneered to Lady Holland: 'Old Luke White will cut up well and tallow richly on the kidneys. This is butcher's language and I dare say unintelligible to you, but in plain English he must have died immensely rich' (entry on White by D. Fisher & S. Farrell in D. Fisher (ed.), *The history of parliament: the House of Commons, 1820–1832* (Cambridge, 2009). In the same way, Edward Byrne paid a reputed £80,000 a year in taxes but yet was dismissed as a '*quondam* grocer' by John Foster (*An accurate report of the speech of the Right Honourable John Foster, 27 February 1793* (Dublin, 1793), p. 6). **38** C.J. Woods, 'The personnel of the Catholic Convention, 1792–3', *Archiv. Hib.*, 57 (2003), pp 26–76. There were 284 members in all, so Dublin with 137 had the lion's share.   **39** Protestant disdain for O'Connell was still evident in W.B. Yeats's name for his particularly persistent cat – Daniel O'Connell (i.e., the King of the Beggars).

improvidently acquiring a trophy house (Number 58, formerly 30) on Merrion Square in 1809.[40] A Catholic was flaunting himself right at the heart of Ascendancy Dublin – a square ringed by peers, judges, politicians, bishops, surgeons and other pillars of the Protestant establishment. It was a flamboyant if financially reckless move to purchase a house in the bastion of Protestant privilege. His cautious wife Mary was suitably horrified: 'Where on earth will you be able to get a thousand guineas?'[41]

These earlier subdued Catholic chapel spaces were succeeded by more assertive insertions into fine facades, ambiguously suspended between the private and the public spheres, as at Clarendon Street (1793), SS Michael & John on Halston Street (1814), St Francis Xavier on Gardiner Street (1832), St Paul's on Arran Quay (1837), and Saint Andrew on Westland Row (1837). All these were carefully insinuated into Georgian terraces.[42] When the Catholic church rose in status in the nineteenth century, older alley entrances were opened out to the streets through ingenious interventions and clearance of existing buildings, as at St Nicholas of Myra, Whitefriars Street, and Adam and Eve's on Cook Street.[43] Similarly in Belfast, the Mill Street Mass house of 1769 was entered via a narrow passage called in local parlance Squeeze-Gut Entry.[44]

BARN CHAPELS

From the 1740s onwards, as population exploded, 'barn chapels' began to be constructed in the countryside, simple structures designed to hold a large standing and kneeling congregation. Coquebert de Montbret provided an

---

40 This is now the home of the University of Notre Dame in Dublin. The 1830 Dublin valuation (p. 8) has: 'No. 30, O'Connell, £180 valuation, 4 stories, deep yard and stable offices in lock-up yard'. 41 M. O'Connell to D. O'Connell, 18 Sept. 1809 in *O'Connell correspondence*, i, p. 205. 42 McCullough, *Dublin: an urban history*, p. 198. A set of plans of these Catholic churches in their urban contexts is on p. 206. For the two most influential architects of nineteenth-century Catholic churches, see J. Sheehy, *J.J. McCarthy and the Gothic Revival in Ireland* (Belfast, 1977) and B. Grimes, *Majestic shrines and graceful sanctuaries: the church architecture of Patrick Byrne, 1783–1864* (Dublin, 2010). 43 This became the popular name for the set-back Franciscan church here. An alley from the quays led to it, whose entrance was marked by a painted pub sign featuring Adam and Eve. Joyce references it (with a characteristic twist by putting Eve first) in the magnificent first line of *Finnegans wake*: 'riverrun, past Eve and Adam's, from swerve of shore to bend of bay'. On the multiple connotations of 'riverrun', see B. McCrea, 'Dublin, Paris and the world republic of letters' in Joannon & Whelan (eds), *Paris: capital of Irish culture*, pp 227–39. 44 This Mass house, hidden, mean and cramped, served the 800 Catholics of Belfast. The congregation brought bricks or planks to use when kneeling on the clay floor. When its lease was later offered for sale by the parish priest, he described it as suitable for 'a malt kiln, warehouse or factory' (*Belfast Newsletter*, 17 May 1784). P. Rogers, 'Father Hugh O'Donnell, first parish priest of Belfast, 1772–1812' in H.A. Cronne, T.W. Moody & D.B. Quinn (eds), *Essays in British and Irish history in honour of James Eadie Todd* (London, 1949), p. 224.

evocative description of one at Ballyovey (medieval Baile Odhbha, modern Baile Óbha in Partry parish, Co. Mayo) in 1791, including a very early reference to the segregation of male and female attendees:

> La chapelle est sur le bord du chemin. C'est celle de la paroisse de Balliovi. J'y assistai à la messe à onze heures dite par le curé M. Gibbon. Cette chapelle [est] sans banc, basse, couverte de chaume, [a] une seule chandelle, un calice d'étain: cette simplicité bien loin de nuire à la dévotion, me paraît y ajouter. Un sceau d'eau bénite fut distribué parmi les paroissiens. Le curé avait été 7 ans à Nantes. Les hommes étaient d'un côté en habits bleus ou bruns, les femmes de l'autre, décemment vêtues et *chaussées* mais elles ôtent souliers et bas après la messe. Le curé fit suivre la messe d'un sermon en irlandais dans lequel il me dit ensuite qu'il avait parlé de Saint Irelatus [Jarlath], patron du diocèse de Tuam où sa paroisse est située.[45]

An Irish-language song 'Mainistir Bhaile Chláir' (The abbey of Claregalway) recorded a row over the reluctance of local people to pay a levy imposed by the priest to finish building a new chapel:

A's nach mór an chúis náire é do'n phobal 's a liachtaighe fear maith a mBaile-Chláir baisteach anuas a bheith ar an sagart an fhad a bhíonn sé an an t-Aifreann d'á rádh.	And is it not shameful for the congregation when there are so many snug men in Claregalway that the rain pours down on the priest while he is saying Mass.
A's nuair a thosuigheann an pobal ag cruinniughadh bíonn an leacóigín cloiche ag gach fear in a láimh le cur faoi n-a glúnaidh ins an ngreallaigh 's dar mo chúis go mbíonn drab ar na mná,	And as the congregation begins to gather every man has his little flagstone in his hand to slip under his knees on the gravel and for sure the women's clothes are bedrabbled.

The Claregalway congregation was exhorted to pay the levy because then 'Eireochaidh sibh suas as an ngreallaigh/agus sachaidh sibh ar chláracaibh 'pine' (You will rise up off the gravel/and will kneel on pine boards).[46]

45 Bibliothèque Nationale de France, NAF, MS 20098, f. 51v. 'The chapel is by the side of the road, it is the parish church for Balliovi. I attended the 11 o'clock Mass there, celebrated by the parish priest, Fr Gibbon. This chapel [is] low and thatched, [has] no pews and just a single candle and a pewter chalice: far from lessening the sense of devotion, this simplicity seems to me to heighten it. A bucket of holy water was distributed among the parishioners. The parish priest had spent seven years in Nantes. On one side were the men, wearing blue or brown clothes, on the other were the women, decently dressed and <u>wearing shoes</u>, but after Mass they take off both shoes and stockings. After the Mass, the priest preached a sermon in Irish, and told me later that in it he had spoken of St Irelatus [Jarlath], patron saint of the diocese of Tuam, within which his parish lies'. I use a text (abbreviations expanded, spelling and punctuation modernized) kindly supplied by Jane Conroy from her forthcoming edition of de Montbret's travels in Ireland.   46 Mhic Choisdealbha, *Amhráin Mhuighe Séola*, pp 50–2. In 1836, 'one transept was neatly fitted up as a chapel' and Mass was attended by 'men in dark blue frieze and Connemara stockings, the women with the red

Under population pressure, the unicameral structure evolved into T and cruciform shapes. Wooden galleries accessed by external stone steps maximized the interior space. In Slane (Co. Meath) in 1809, the parish priest Michael O'Hanlon observed that 'our old chapels, which formerly contained the congregation, are not, at present, equal to our increased numbers, and new ones are universally building, of from one-third to double the former dimensions'. O'Hanlon reported that 'the present chapels, though more than twice as large as the old ones, are too small for the population'.[47] The population surge between 1800 and 1845 increased the urgency of ministering to the proliferating poor, labourers, cottiers and micro-farmers, and the denizens of the crowded lanes, allies and backstreets of towns and cities. The rapid escalation in population in the first half of the nineteenth century dictated that cramped chapels had to be enlarged, sprouting a profusion of improvised add-on shapes.

The viability of the T-plan for Catholic chapels large and small was advocated by the Dublin architect John Leeson in 1832.[48] For him, its principal virtue was that it made it possible 'to divide the church equally among the poor and the rich, giving the one class no advantage over the other, except that of a separate entrance'.[49] 'Country chapels' were dismissed by Mrs Hall in 1843 as 'huge and ungainly barns', with clay-floored interiors, 'bare whitewashed walls', 'a few deal stools', and altars 'dressed with shabby tinsel ornaments, and hung with miserable coloured prints'.[50] A good impresion of what these pre-Famine chapels looked like can be gained from the relatively unchanged example at Ardmore (Co. Waterford), built there in 1837 by John Mullany (1813–84) of Cahir (Co. Tipperary), complete with its carpenter Gothic confession boxes.[51] The Commission of Public Instruction reported in 1834 that there were 2,109 chapels for 1,029 Catholic parishes, essentially two chapels per parish. The average congregation then was 3,000, served by multiple Masses.

Catholic chapels could provoke opposition. Some examples were discreetly tucked away in rural hollows, as at Clodiagh (Co. Kilkenny) and Poulfur (Co. Wexford), and in backstreet chapel lanes in towns. In 1745, at Macroom (Co. Cork), the elevated site of the new church was taken as a sign of 'popery riding triumphant': 'Its splendid Mass house built on an eminence at the entrance into the town, in imitation of the northern Mass house of the city of Cork, is to signify to

cloaks gracefully hanging over their linsey woollen petticoats' (W.T. Meyler, *St Catherine's bells: an autobiography*, 2 vols (London, 1868), i, pp 75–6). **47** Wakefield, *Ireland statistical and political*, ii, p. 618. In 1781, the population of Slane and Rathkenny parishes was 3,560 Catholic, and 230 Protestant. By 1811, there was 5,948 Catholics and 132 Protestants. **48** Leeson was derided as 'a chapel building clerk' in the satirical *Essay on the rise and progress of architectural taste in Dublin* (Dublin, 1832), p. 10. **49** *FJ*, 9 & 14 Feb. 1832. **50** S.C. & A.M. Hall, *Ireland: its scenery and character*, 2 vols (London, 1843), ii, pp 18–19. **51** Mullany emigrated in 1847, settling first in LaSalla (Illinois) and then in Dubuque (Iowa). He built Catholic churches in Iowa and Illinois.

Table 3: Size of Catholic population per parish in the diocese of Kildare and Leighlin, 1827

Bagenalstown	10,000	Mountrath	10,000	Portarlington	9,000
Rosenallis	8,000	Edenderry	8,000	Borris	8,000
Maryborough	7,500	Rathvilly	7,500	Graignamanagh	7,500
Killeigh	7,500	Monasterevan	7,500	Baltinglass	7,000
Mountmellick	6,500	Stradbally	6,500	Clonegal	6,500
Carlow	6,500	Leighlinbridge	6,500	Philipstown	6,500
Tullow	6,000	Clonmore	6,000	Hacketstown	6,000
Goresbridge	6,000	Ballyadams	6,000	Arles	5,500
Ballinakill	5,000	Abbeyleix	5,000	Kildare	5,000
Killeshin	4,500	Tinryland	4,500	Doonane	4,500
Saint Mullins	4,500	Clonbullogue	4,500	Caragh	4,500
Clane	4,500	Ballina	4,500	Naas	4,000
Myshall	4,000	Ballon	4,000	Carbery	3,500
Kilcock	3,500	Newbridge	3,000	Allen	3,000
Ballyfin	2,500	Kill	2,500	Suncroft	2,500

Total – 244,500   **Parishes – 45**   **Average – 5,430**

the traveller that the papists of that town abound in wealth and want only power'.[52] The pamphleteer then posed the question: 'Why must they have their houses of idolatry on the tops of hills or in the most open publick passages of the town?'[53]

Another hostile commentator in 1763 was concerned by 'new and pompous Mass houses in some of the most conspicuous parts of their great cities, where none had been built before'.[54] Orrery convinced himself in 1735 that conversation in Cork city revolved around how much 'beef and butter sell for the pound'[55] while Lord Shannon in 1795 dismissed it as 'a very popish and gossipy place'.[56] In 1772, a hostile observer lamented the 'great progress Popery had made within these few years in this town' because 'three new chapels have been built at a vast expense, and added to five others here'.[57] In 1775, a visitor counted seven churches, seven chapels and four meeting houses in Cork, and observed 'elegant carriages standing before the door' of the Mass houses.[58] In

52 *Sensible advice to Protestants containing some means of reviving and strengthening the Protestant interest*, second edition (Cork, 1745), p. 14. **53** *Sensible advice to Protestants*, p. 40. **54** J. Lockman, *A history of the cruel sufferings of the Protestants and others by Popish persecutions, in various countries together with a view of the Reformations from the Church of Rome* (Dublin, 1763), p. 123. **55** Countess of Cork and Orrery (ed.), *The Orrery papers*, 2 vols (London, 1903), i, p. 134. **56** Shannon to Boyle, 4 Apr. 1795 in E. Hewitt (ed.), *Lord Shannon's letters to his son* (Belfast, 1982), p. 34. **57** Letter from Cork, 1 Feb. 1772, signed by 'A Protestant', *FJ*, 18 Feb. 1772. **58** [T. Campbell], *A philosophical survey of the south of Ireland* (London, 1777), p. 181.

1774, more than 100 rich Catholics supported the bishop in building chapels in 'this extensive city, a second Dublin, to which Waterford is but a village'.[59] In 1804, Lord Midleton in the same county was still complaining about Cork Catholic uppitiness:

> I object strongly to bringing [chapels] forward to occupy the most conspicuous station in the prospect as I am convinced is the cause with them of engaging into rivalship with the Established Church. That this is the object with them is obvious from the magnificence of the edifices which they are erecting in many parts of Ireland and from their erecting steeples and putting up bells.[60]

In 1813, John Gough complained about Limerick's 'nine Romish chapels, each of which has a good bell, which causes a great rattle through the city every morning'.[61]

COMPETITIVE SPIRES

O'Connell insisted on the necessity for Catholics to be fully incorporated on equal terms within the public sphere of post-Emancipation Ireland. A galling aspect of the penal laws was their relegation of the majority population to a permanent status as non-citizens, excluding them from the public spaces of their own country.[62] In 1778, Michael Skerrett (archbishop of Tuam 1749–85) was wary of the high profile of 'the secular [Catholic] gentlemen of Dublin': 'I was always of opinion that the more insignificant we appeared in the eyes of government the better'.[63] Bishop Patrick Ryan (1760–1819) of Ferns grumped about Irish Protestants: 'They appear more numerous than they really are because they have power and can make a show; we are without it and make none. Look to the chapels on Sunday and look to the churches … They have law on their side and can speak out: we have it against us and must be silent'.[64] James Doyle, the more confrontational bishop of Kildare and Leighlin, commented that 'we are not dumb dogs who know not how to bark'.[65] And bark he did most effectively.

The Catholic Pro-Cathedral was shunted from its preferred Sackville Street site (allocated to the General Post Office) onto a dingy back street (adjacent to the later Monto brothel district), and its elegant footprint was cramped

59 Cited in Fenning, *Dominicans*, p. 412. **60** Lord Midleton (Bath) to Joseph Haynes, Midleton (Co. Cork), 1 Oct. 1804, in Guildford Muniment Room (Surrey), Midleton papers, MS 1248/7–13, ff 20–2. **61** Cited in C.J. Woods, *Travellers' accounts as source material for Irish historians* (Dublin, 2009), p. 99. **62** J. Leerssen, *Hidden Ireland, public sphere* (Galway, 2002). **63** Michael Skerrett to Charles O'Conor, 1 May 1778, RIA, MS B I 1. **64** Wakefield, *Ireland statistical and political*, i, p. 627. **65** Cited in D. Akenson, *The Irish education experiment: the national system of education in the nineteenth century* (London, 1970), p. 203. The Biblical quotation is from Isaiah 56:10.

into a constrained site, 'despite the superior wealth and respectability of the [Catholic] inhabitants'.[66] When it was finally dedicated in 1825, O'Connell's lieutenant Richard Lalor Sheil (1791–1851) was explicit about its role in reclaiming a Catholic public presence in Dublin: 'At last an edifice worthy of the loftiness of our creed stands in the centre of the metropolis. Our religion has at last lifted up its proud and majestic head'.[67] 'That grand and sumptuous pile' elevated the self-esteem of Dublin Catholics.[68] Perhaps luckily, two other grandiose later schemes for cathedrals were abandoned.[69]

The sense of opposition to the state religion expressed itself in the symbolic landscape, featured as a dialogue between opposed churches, and with a constantly intensifying emphasis. Art Mac Cumhaigh (1738–73) staged a debate between a ruined medieval church (An Róimhchill – the Rome church) in Faughart (Co. Louth), speaking in Irish, and an Anglican one (An Teampall Gallda – the foreign church), newly built in Forkhill (Co. Armagh) (often translated to speak in English in macaronic versions).[70] Mac Cumhaigh juxtaposed cill and teampall. Cill was no longer in use as a word meaning church in Irish at that time, so it emitted an archaic flavour, indicating cultural continuity. The spliced neologism Róimhchill (Roman-church) suggested that the Catholic church has deeper roots in the culture. While teampall does not exclusively refer to a Protestant church, it had become the contemporary Irish word for a church by Mac Cumhaigh's time, and its use gestured towards shallow roots for the Anglican church. The term Gallda ('foreign') made it crystal clear that that church should not be considered as indigenous. This type of oppositional thinking surfaced in Newry (Co. Down) in 1828 when an impressive new Catholic church was constructed: a local loyalist, Robert Atkinson, declared in public that it would soon be converted into a Protestant church.[71]

'A discussion between church and chapel [c.1832][72] featured a dialogue between Fr Matthew's proposed 'poor and naked' Capuchin chapel in Cork city and Shandon church, 'sitting in your pomp and grandeur'. The ballad

---

66 Meagher, *Daniel Murray*, p. 95. 67 Cited in M. Purcell, *St Mary's Pro-Cathedral Dublin* (Dublin, 1988), p. 1; M. McCarthy, 'Dublin's Greek Pro-Cathedral' in Kelly & Keogh (eds), *Catholic diocese of Dublin*, pp 237–46. 68 *Elegy on the death of the Most Revd John Thomas Troy* (Dublin, 1823), p. 9. 69 The English town planner Patrick Abercrombie (1879–1957) had proposed a giant cathedral west of O'Connell Street terminating a new boulevard to replace that stretch of Parnell Street in his modernist Dublin city plan of 1920. Archbishop Byrne paid the Pembroke estate £100,000 for Merrion Square in 1930 in anticipation of the Eucharistic Congress and announced his desire to build a gigantic old-fashioned neo-Gothic cathedral there. Archbishop Dermot Ryan (1924–1985), soon after taking office in 1974, generously gifted the park to the citizens of Dublin. 70 B. Ó Buachalla (eag.), *Art Mac Cumhaigh: dánta* (Baile Átha Cliath, 1973), pp 84–7. 71 CSO/RP/OR/1828/735. 72 G.-D. Zimmerman, *Songs of Irish rebellion: Irish political street ballads and rebel songs, 1780–1900* (Dublin, 2002), pp 198–9.

anticipated the future ruin of Shandon, when it will be a 'shelter for owls and ravens'. St Anne's was built in 1722 in mellow Cork limestone. Additional stages were added to its square tower in 1749, literally generating a higher profile (170 feet [52m] high) and creating a notably graceful silhouette above the low-lying city. Presumably this was motivated by a desire to counteract Catholic church building in Cork city.[73] Fr Matthews's ambitious chapel was only completed late in the nineteenth century.

Later examples of poems and ballads include 'The new Catholic church in Gorey' by James O'Reilly [1840],[74] 'Church of Slane' [c.1840], 'A dialogue between St Audeon's church and St Audeon's new chapel High Street '[c.1844], 'New chapel of Killamoate [Co. Wicklow) [c.1846],[75] 'A new song in praise of the Catholic church of Kanturk' [1867] and 'Croaghpatrick mountain and chapel' [1905] by Patrick Walsh.[76] These ballads all exhibited the belief of the entire Catholic population, not just the priests and the middle class, that their revival marked a necessary and long delayed rebalancing of the historical scales in Ireland.

When the O'Connell Monument required funding, careful records were kept of the £12,981 which was contributed. Of that sum, £10,561 can be allocated precisely to specific areas. Dublin understandably dominated with forty-three per cent of the total. The overseas contribution was twenty per cent while the provincial figures were Leinster with sixty-one per cent, Munster with ten per cent, Ulster with five per cent and Connaught with four per cent.

The long lists of contributors to funding campaigns that filled many column inches in nineteenth-century local newspapers are testament to that deep-rooted instinct. The 1855–6 building fund to attract a convent to Ardee (Co. Louth) had over 900 subscribers.[77] A 1908 list of subscribers to the Saint Nicholas church fund in Dundalk contained 2,054 names, close enough to every family in the town when its population in 1911 was 13,128.[78]

We need to avoid the anachronistic assumption that the pennies of the poor were extracted from unwilling or gullible Catholics hoodwinked by cunning and rapacious priests. A hard-nosed New Yorker William Curtis commented in 1909:

> It is astonishing how much money the people of Ireland spend upon their religion, and the twin churches of Wexford are illustrations of the display that is found in every part of the country. It is a common subject of comment and criticism that the bishops should permit such extravagance, but they reply that no man is ever poorer because of what

73 Shandon's four-sided clock frequently gave contradictory times, attracting the nickname 'the four-faced liar'. 74 Esmonde papers, NLI, MS 8519 (11). 75 My thanks to Tim O'Neill for furnishing me with a manuscript copy of this ballad. 76 Colm Ó Lochlainn Collection of ballads, UCD Library [online]. 77 *Newry Express*, 17 Jan. 1855, 3 Feb. 1855, 11 Apr. 1855, 6 Feb. 1856, 28 June 1856. 78 These lists appeared in the *Dundalk Democrat* from May to September 1908.

Table 4: Contributions to O'Connell Monument, 1862–5 (£s)
Source: J. O'Hanlon, *Report of the O'Connell Monument Committee* (Dublin, 1888).

Dublin	4,503	Kilkenny	550	Tipperary	477
Louth	398	Wicklow	234	Kildare	232
Wexford	226	Cork	190	Galway	168
Waterford	165	Cavan	126	Limerick	121
Derry	119	Roscommon	109	Kerry	109
Sligo	108	Westmeath	100	Antrim	93
Longford	92	Laois	67	Meath	56
Down	55	Monaghan	45	Tyrone	39
Carlow	35	Offaly	32	Mayo	31
Leitrim	30	Armagh	29	Clare	23
Donegal	8	Fermanagh	4		
Australia	1,602	England	252	US	70
S. Africa	56	Belguim	23	Argentina	23
France	17	Chile	14	Canada	8
Trinidad	5	Mexico	3	India	3
Malta	1	Spain	1	**Overseas**	**2,105**

he gives for his religion. It may be said, also, that all of the Roman Catholic churches are crowded on Sunday, early and late.[79]

Irish bishops were determined to make Irish churches approximate as imitatively as possible to prevailing continental styles: after Catholic Emancipation, as one acerbic critic phrased it, 'they hurriedly transplanted whole edifices, cheapened to their poverty, either directly from Greece or Rome, or from Puginized or ritualistic England' and 'Ireland took to foreign and ready-made architectural forms like a passive child to a soothing syrup'.[80] The city architect Charles MacCarthy (son of J.J., the most prolific architect for Catholic churches in the second half of the nineteenth century) observed at the 1901 meeting of the Architectural Association of Ireland that contemporary church architecture was 'absolutely without interest' and advised that 'in future, designers should leave out the Carrara marble altar, with its bristling reredos, the vulgar stained glass from Germany, and that impertinent carved oak pulpit from Belgium'.[81] The deracinated Paul Cullen (1803–78), archbishop of Dublin, had lived in Rome from the age of seventeen until middle age, and

---

79 W. Curtis, *An Irish summer* (New York 1909), pp 277–8. 'The "win churches" are two fine Roman Catholic houses of worship, exact duplicates of each other, within two or three blocks, with beautiful spires two hundred and thirty [70m] high. They cost $250,000 each and were paid for by the congregations of this city and neighborhood'. **80** R. Eliott, *Art and Ireland* (Dublin, 1906), p. 96. **81** *Irish Times*, 9 Oct. 1901.

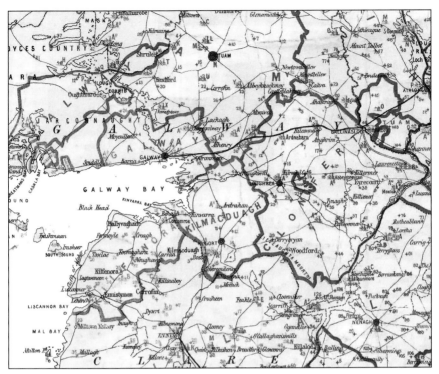

Fig. 43 Detail from the 1859 *Catholic map of Ireland showing the diocesan boundaries, cathedrals, chapels or churches and remarkable ecclesiastical antiquities* (Dublin, M. Allen, 12 Westland Row, 1859). John O'Donovan described this colour map as 'the first attempt made at a pictorial representation of Hibernia "Catholica" (NLI, 16 L 23). The thirty-six page key, of which the only known copy is in the Cardinal Tomás Ó Fiaich Library and Archive in Armagh, identifed the parishes and chapels in each diocese, as well as O'Donovan's listing of the antiquities (M. Herity, 'A Catholic map of Ireland 1859' in *Ossory, Laois and Leinster*, 5 (2013), pp 230–3).

the bulk of Irish bishops were educated on the Continent until the second half of the nineteenth century. That gave them a desire on their return to emulate continental forms: in 1861, Archbishop Patrick Leahy (1806–75) in Thurles stated his desire to have 'the Roman usages – Roman chant, Roman ceremonies, Roman everything'.[82]

After Emancipation, O'Connell led Catholics in a concerted campaign to reclaim the public sphere by putting their presence on ostentatious display. His 'monster meetings' and a series of rallies, parades, processions and funerals around the Dublin streets staked out city spaces as open to Catholics, unhindered by the previous collusion between the state and the gentry to keep them invisible, cowed and marginalized. O'Connell insisted that these

82 C. O'Dwyer, 'Archbishop Patrick Leahy' (MA, Maynooth, 1971), p. 44.

events be literally spectacular: his medium was his message.[83] In that sense too, investment in prominently sited chapels was a political act and regarded as such by all concerned. Nineteenth-century Ireland was alive to the symbolism of the 'competitive spires' phenomenon, Catholics enjoyed the benefit of building later than the Protestants, and they were therefore able to ensure that they built higher, especially through the use of soaring neo-Gothic spires.

In Kenmare (Co. Kerry), the land agent W.S. Trench (1808–72) was accused of interfering in 1867 to prevent the new convent being located in too prominent a position. Trench himself contrasted the new 'neat and unpretending Protestant church' which was 'plain and undecorated' with the large and gorgeous' Catholic church, and posed the question: 'would it have been right to have allowed it in all its size and the convent in all its richness to have overwhelmed our chaste and neat though small Protestant place of worship?'[84] Fr John O'Sullivan had largely financed the Catholic church of 1862: he vied for local control of the town with Trench. It had impressive German wooden angels on hammerhead beams in the ceiling. Its crowning glory was a cockerel on the weather vane, allegedly put there to crow over Trench, who had refused the site initially and was overruled by Lansdowne. The agent then blocked a window in his house so that he was not forced to look at the church. The offending convent was eventually inserted at the rear of the Catholic church rather than in a more prominent location.

CHAPEL VILLAGES

Chapels, developing as the hub of their communities, attracted other functions. Of known locations for posting threatening letters in the first half of the nineteenth century, the chapel was by far the most likely venue.[85] Hedge schools sprang up inside and later alongside the chapels.[86] In 1827, Bishop James Doyle of Kildare and Leighlin advised his priests that 'it is an indispensable requisite that each department of a parish or of a union of parishes be provided with a spacious and convenient school house' and that they should 'use every exertion' 'to build, adjoining or convenient to each chapel a parochial schoolhouse' which should be 'spacious, airy and

---

83 G. Owens, 'Nationalism without words: symbolism and ritual behaviour in the Repeal monster meetings of 1843–5' in Donnelly & Miller (eds), *Irish popular culture*, pp 242–69. 84 Cited in Lyne, *Lansdowne estate*, p. 660. The Protestant church cost £3,000 and ignited a searing social row over pews and precedence (pp 678–9). 85 Gibbons, *Captain Rock, night errant*. 86 M. Tóibín, 'The school beside the chapel' in *The Past*, 8 (1970), pp 18–23. Micheál Tóibín was father of the novelist Colm Tóibín. The very term **'hedge school'** was a semantic deformation. It originated in the common English usage of 'hedge' as 'an attribute expressing contempt' (*OED*), e.g. hedge-doctor, hedge-lawyer, or hedge-alehouse.

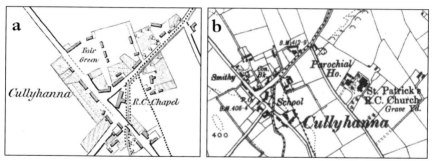

Fig. 44a–b The chapel village of Cullyhanna (Co. Armagh) as shown on the first edition (1834) and third edition (1906) OS maps. In 1834, the T-shaped Catholic chapel was located at the crossroads, facing the fair green, on the main road halfway between Newtownhamilton and Crossmaglen. The new church (shown on the later map) was built in 1893. A school, parochial house, cemetery, constabulary barracks, forge and post office are also shown. In more recent years, Cullyhanna added a GAA clubhouse, now the principal focus for community activities. Its current population is around 300 people.

well lighted'.[87] In 1828, the Catholics of Carndonagh (Co. Donegal) sought government assistance to build a school on the grounds of their new (1826) church.[88] In the same year, the inhabitants of Staplestown (Co. Kildare) solicited help to build a schoolhouse to educate 600 local children, to be attached to their chapel.[89] The English novelist William Thackeray (1811–63) was struck by the proximity of school and chapel in 1842.

> Look at the national school: throughout the country, it is commonly by the chapel side; it is a Catholic school, directed and fostered by the priest; and as no people are more eager for learning, more apt to receive it, or more grateful for kindness than the Irish, he gets all the gratitude of the scholars who flock to the school, and all the fuller influence over them, which naturally and justly comes to him.[90]

These crossroads chapels and schools then acted as a coagulant for a chapel village. Following a change in ecclesiastical law, each priest was required to provide himself with a parochial house after 1850. Catholic parochial houses proliferated in the period from 1860 to 1890, located as close as possible to the chapel.[91]

---

87 J. Doyle, *Pastoral address of the Right Rev. James Doyle, Bishop of Kildare and Leighlin, on the education of the Catholic poor* (Dublin, 1827), p. 30. For the broader context, see T. McGrath (ed.), *The pastoral and education letters of Bishop James Doyle of Kildare and Leighlin, 1786–1834* (Dublin, 2005). **88** CSO/RP/1828/1297. Signed by sixteen parishioners. **89** CSO/RP/1828/1297. Signed by twenty-three parishioners. **90** [W. Thackeray], *Irish sketch book*, 2 vols (London, 1845), i, pp 56–7. **91** A generation earlier, in 1824, Catholic priests' houses on the Tipperary/Limerick border were described as 'generally thatched; some snug little cabins, most of them, some not very good' (G.C. Lewis, *On local disturbances in Ireland; and on the Irish church question* (London, 1836), p. 140).

Table 5: Chapels on which threatening letters were posted, 1806–41

1806	Rathlackin (Sligo)	1823	Clara (Offaly)
1807	Tralee (Kerry)		Springfield (Cork)
	Ballymaguin (Kerry)		Athnaleenta (Cork)
	Odorney (Kerry)	1824	Effin (Limerick)
1812	Gurteen (Sligo)		Easkey (Sligo)
1813	Borris (Derry)	1825	Ballysteen (Limerick)
	Keelogue (Mayo)	1825	Dunlavin (Wicklow)
1815	Ballinsmala (Waterford)	1826	Skreen (Sligo)
1816	Caher (Kerry)	1827	Ring (Waterford)
1820	Kilconnell (Galway)		Innismagrath (Leitrim)
1821	Knockboy (Limerick)		Murghane (Leitrim)
1822	Kilflynn (Kerry)	1829	Kilskeery (Westmeath)
	Lucan (Dublin)	1831	Kill (Offaly)
	Listowel (Kerry)		Trim (Meath)
	Drimsorly (Clare)		Portlaoise (Laois)
	Killorglin (Kerry)		Ballinakill (Laois)
	Aglish (Waterford)		Mayo (Laois)
	Farranhavane (Cork)		Kells (Kilkenny)
	Shanballymore (Cork)		Longwood (Meath)
	Fiddown (Kilkenny)	1841	Magherow (Sligo)
1823	Inchigeela (Cork)		Leighlinbridge (Carlow)
	Coolbahaga (Cork)		

Around this nucleus of chapel, school and parochial house, the extraordinary chapel villages of Ireland emerged.[92] There are thirty examples in Co. Limerick alone, with a clustering in the late settled mountain areas of Sliabh Luachra.[93] The advent of the chapel village bifurcated settlements, where the new centre was constructed away from older medieval or estate villages, as at Castlebellingham/ Kilsaran (Co. Louth), Carnew/Tomacork, Blessington/Valleymount and Enniskerry/Curtlestown (Co. Wicklow), Killedmond/Rathanna and Lorum/ Ballinkillin (Co. Carlow), Timolin/Moone (Co. Kildare), and Killan/Rathnure and Templeshanbo/Ballindaggan (Co. Wexford).

By the middle of the nineteenth century, the resurgent Catholic church had consolidated an efficient national administrative network of parishes. It helped to restore dignity and a renewed sense of cohesion in parish communities. This national network facilitated the diffusion of political, cultural and social

---

92 K. Whelan, 'The Catholic parish, the Catholic chapel and village development in Ireland', *Irish Geography*, 16 (1983), pp 1–15. **93** P. O'Connor, *Exploring Limerick's past: an historical geography of urban development in county and city* (Newcastle West, 1987), p. 116. These chapel villages are Ardpatrick, Anglesborough, Ashford, Ballyagran, Ballyhahill, Ballysteen, Banoge, Broadford, Bulgaden, Caherline, Carrigkerry, Cloncagh, Colmanswell, Donaghmore, Effin, Feohanagh, Feenagh, Garryspillanne, Granagh, Kilcolman, Kilfinny, Meanus, Monagay, Mount Collins, Mungret, Nicker, Raheenagh, Rockhill, Templeglantan and Tournafulla.

Table 6: Dates of Catholic parochial houses, 1857–1920 [sample]

Based on *Dictionary of Irish Architects* website. *Italics* = not built

County	Name	Date	County	Name	Date	County	Name	Date
Monaghan	Killanny	1857	Down	Kilkeel	1886	Kildare	Kill	1909
Louth	Knockbridge	1859	Tipperary	Solohead	1888	Antrim	Ballymena	1910
Down	Finnis	1860	Waterford	Ballybricken	1889	Armagh	Cloghogue	1910
Offaly	Edenderry	1860	Armagh	Cullyhanna	1890	Cork	Eyeries	1910
Laois	Portlaoise	1861	Leitrim	Aughavas	1890	Cork	Grenagh	1910
Louth	Tenure	1864	Waterford	Rathgormack	1890	Donegal	Culdaff	1910
Kildare	Celbridge	1866	Louth	Ravensdale	1892	Meath	Dunshaughlin	1910
Down	Legamaddy	1866	Cork	Caheragh	1896	Down	Dromore	1911
Louth	Tullyallen	1867	Leitrim	Kinlough	1896	Limerick	Askeaton	1911
Cavan	Ballymachugh	1868	Wicklow	Arklow	1898	Mayo	Ballycastle	1911
Down	Ballygalget	1870	Derry	Feeny	1899	Waterford	Tramore	1911
Dublin	Seville Place	1872	Dublin	Balbriggan	1908	Wexford	Rosslare	1911
Longford	Granard	1872	Tyrone	Dunnamanagh	1901	Cavan	Baileborough	1912
Antrim	Loughguile	1873	Antrim	Larne	1903	Clare	Liscannor	1912
Donegal	Lettermacward	1873	Longford	Ardagh	1903	Derry	Craigbane	1912
Meath	Ratoath	1874	Tyrone	Cookstown	1903	Cavan	Corlough	1913
Donegal	*Dunfanaghy*	*1874*	Donegal	Ardara	1904	Kilkenny	Newmarket	1913
Antrim	Rasharkin	1875	Fermanagh	Killesher	1904	Louth	Dromiskin	1913
Louth	Ardee	1875	Roscommon	Roscommon	1904	Tyrone	Fivemiletown	1913
Limerick	Murroe	1876	Sligo	Collooney	1904	Waterford	Kilmeaden	1913
Westmeath	Killucan	1876	Tipperary	Terryglass	1904	Clare	Carron	1914
Donegal	*Dunlewey*	*1876*	Roscommon	Ballinlough	1905	Sligo	Tubbercurry	1914
Donegal	Carrick	1877	Mayo	Mulranny	1906	Tipperary	Rathronan	1914
Meath	Dunboyne	1879	Wexford	New Ross	1906	Derry	Lavey	1915
Antrim	Ballycastle	1880	Donegal	Raphoe	1907	Tipperary	Fethard	1915
Mayo	Attymass	1880	Fermanagh	Garrison	1907	Mayo	Crossmolina	1916
Mayo	Ballaghdereen	1882	Cork	Ballyhea	1908	Limerick	Hospital	1919
Louth	Tallanstown	1882	Derry	Bellaghy	1908	Derry	Garvagh	1920
Meath	Oldcastle	1882	Fermanagh	Beleek	1908	Down	Spinn	1920
Armagh	Lurgan	1884	Limerick	Croom	1908	Leitrim	Glencar	1920
Meath	Ardcath	1885	Limerick	Kilmallock	1908	Tipperary	Moyglass	1920
Tyrone	Eglish	1885	Wexford	Enniscorthy	1908	Cavan	Glangevlin	1920
Down	Ardglass	1886	Cork	Mourneabbey	1909			

organizations, most memorably in the case of the GAA with its distinctive 'parish rule' that specifies that teams must be exclusively recruited from within their Catholic parish.

RATHNURE: A CHAPEL VILLAGE

Rathnure (Co. Wexford), perched on the shoulders of the Blackstairs Mountains, is a chapel village of recent origin. Until 1853, the Rathnure area had formed part of the sprawling Catholic parish of Killegney.[94] The parish was then split, with the new parish of Cloughbawn serving the lowland area

94 W. Grattan Flood, *History of the diocese of Ferns* (Waterford, 1916), pp 52–3.

Fig. 45 The Rathnure and Killan area photographed in 1963 by Kenneth St Joseph (1912–94), with the Blackstairs Mountains rising behind (CUCAP). St Joseph photographed from a Cessna Skymaster and had a brilliant eye for the best angle and height.

around Clonroche, while Rathnure served the upland area to the west. A new stretch of road had been built in the 1830s to bypass a narrow and difficult part of the Newtownbarry (Bunclody) to New Ross road.[95] The older higher stretch via Monamolin and Templeludigan was then abandoned in favour of the easier lower 'new line'.

The parish chapel of Rathnure, built in 1859, was located for reasons of accessibility on the 'new line' at a crossroads, replacing the tiny chapel of ease that had occupied the same location. The site was donated by the Hands (local publicans), who had established a public house/grocery shop here. A second

95 This analysis is based primarily on a detailed account in IFC Schools Manuscript, volume 900, Rathnure (Co. Wexford), Department of Irish Folklore, University College Dublin.

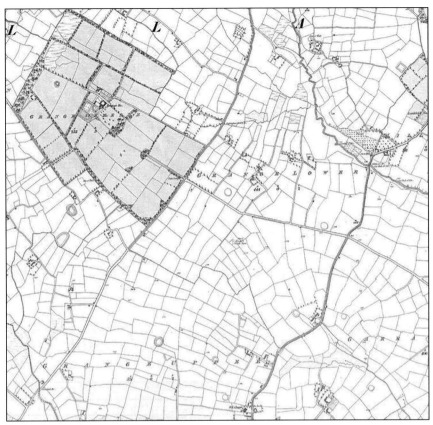

Fig. 46 The same area as shown on the first edition OS map in 1840. The lower and the higher roads clearly structure the settlement pattern. At Rathnure, an isolated Catholic chapel is shown. Monksgrange demesne is a prominent feature.

public house, run by the Brennan family, soon followed.[96] In the 1860s, the Hand family sold out to the Conran family whose descendants still run a leading business in the village.[97] This chapel was on the edge of the Forrestal farm, the most significant Catholic farm in the area.[98] The chapel, and subsequently

96 Despite its centrality in Irish life, remarkably little has been written on the Irish pub. There is simply nothing in the Irish literature to match Joseph Mitchell's essay on the still extant McSorley's at 15 Seventh Avenue, New York: 'The old house at home' in J. Mitchell, *Up in the old hotel* (New York, 1992), pp 3–22. **97** In 1896, Thomas Conran left £200 for an altar designed by James Pearse (father of Patrick) for the Catholic church (G. Binions, *Old Blackstairs families* (Killann [Co. Wexford], 2016), p. 90. **98** Anthony Forrestal (farmer) and Walter (Watt) Forrestall (merchant), both of Rathduffe, signed the Catholic Qualification Rolls in 1780 and 1786. Anthony was killed and his son Patrick was executed in 1798. In the Tithe Applotment Book (1833), Walter, Richard, John and Moses Forrestal held a total of 120 Irish acres in Rathnure. In Griffiths's Valuation in 1853, Anne, Moses and John Forrestal held 187 statute acres in Rathnure Upper.

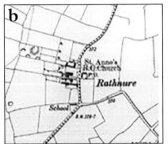

Fig. 47a–c The same area as shown on (a) Valentine Gill's 1811 map of Co. Wexford, where 'Ranure' has no indication of any church or village; (b) 1906 edition of the OS map; (c) 1925 edition of the OS map. Rathnure now has a Catholic church, parochial house, school and post office, and the demesne around Monksgrange has shrunk.

the parish, took its name from the townland in which it was located, as was frequently the case. The active parish priest, Myles Doran (1808–90), quickly added new facilities to the chapel site. First he built a parochial house alongside the chapel. In 1867, he was instrumental in getting the national school for boys shifted from Ballybaun townland (two miles distant) to the chapel yard. In 1882, a national school for girls followed alongside it.

Rathnure continued to evolve, aided by the fact that it stood almost exactly astride the traditional divide between the hinterlands of New Ross and Enniscorthy. It was located at the interface between the small mountain farms of the Blackstairs, and the large lowland farms of the Boro valley and the Castleboro estate below it. By 1933, it consisted of a chapel, national schools, priest's house, a public house/grocery, a forge, a shoemaker's shop, a village hall, a creamery and a string of labourers' cottages. A new school opened in 1953 and a parochial hall in 1955, both in Rathnure. The hall, designed by local engineer Gerald Flood of Castleboro, cost £600, accommodated 1,500 and was lit by its own power plant. The building was 70 x 34 feet [21m x 10m], with a dance floor of 56 x 36 feet [17m x 11m], and a raised stage.[99]

Rathnure developed a plethora of organizations, like Muintir Na Tíre, the Pioneer Total Abstinence Association, the Legion of Mary and the Irish Countrywomen's Association. Growing in community strength, the parish established itself as a social unit, reflected most intensely in the fanatical support for its fine hurling team, backboned by the Rackard and Quigley families, that emerged as the leading force in Wexford club hurling from the 1950s to the 1980s. A set of GAA pitches, a recreational complex with an indoor hurling pitch, a garage and county council housing schemes were more recent additions. In this way, an entire new village had grown up.

The rise of Rathnure has been accompanied by the decay of two neighbouring settlements, Templeudigan and Killann. Templeudigan had been an incipient

99 *Echo*, 24 Sept. 1955.

chapel village in the area in the first half of the nineteenth century. However, once the main road was diverted away from it, it shrank, and today it has a forlorn appearance when compared with its more vigorous neighbour. Killann, the medieval parish centre, had a cluster of ancient ecclesiastical sites: St Anne's holy well, an ancient graveyard, the medieval church. In 1615, this church was still minimally in repair, it was upgraded in 1755–6 and dismantled in 1832, when the materials were sold for sixty pounds (eliciting an acerbic comment from Revd J.B. Leslie: 'what a pity to find ecclesiastics so little regardless of venerable architectural remains').[100] The new church (80 x 60 feet [24m x 18m] of 1832–5 was in the Early English style and cost £1,330. Its location was shifted 200 yards away from the ancient site to the glebeland.

This Protestant church served the needs of the sizeable group of Protestant families who had been established in its vicinity by two local landlords, the Richards of Monksgrange and the Blackers of Woodbrook (in 1831, there were 409 Protestants in the parish). The village also had a Protestant national school built in 1826 and a public house/grocery (later in the possession of the Rackard family). On the first edition six-inch map, Killann, reflecting the vitality of the colony and the support of two active landlords, still far outstripped Rathnure, which was literally not on the map at this stage. However, the demise of landlordism, the retrenchment of the Protestant community and the dynamism of Rathnure arrested Killann's growth. Symbolically, Rathnure and Killann offer vivid landscape testimony of the dialectic of Catholic and Protestant, new and old, hill and plain.[101]

CONVENTS AND SCHOOLS

The geography of Catholic education was sharply differentiated after the rise of teaching orders like the Ursuline and Presentation Sisters, and the Christian Brothers. Highly capable leaders Nano Nagle (1718–84), Edmund Rice (1762–1844) and Mary Aikenhead (1787–1858) founded innovative indigenous religious orders. These emerged first in Munster, spearheaded from Cork (where the Presentation Sisters were founded in 1775) and Waterford (where the Christian Brothers were established in 1802). By 1820, for example, there were nine Christian Brothers monasteries (Waterford, Cork, Limerick, Thurles, Dungarvan, Carrick-on-Suir, Cappoquin, and two in Dublin), with thirty-seven brothers teaching 4,250 children.[102]

---

100 Leslie, *Ferns*, p. 181. **101** The advent of almost universal car ownership and the post-Tiger crash inflicted damage on both villages, which suffered the loss of their post offices. Rackards sold their pub *c.*2002 and it closed permanently *c.*2012. **102** D. Keogh, *Edmund Rice and the first Irish Christian Brothers* (Dublin, 2008).

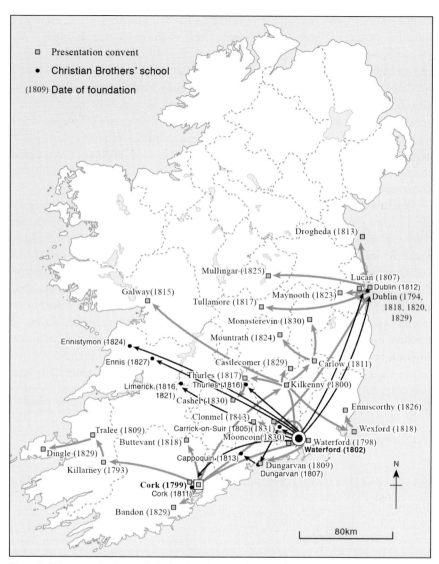

Fig. 48 The spread of the Christian Brothers and the Presentation Sisters (1799–1830). Cork and Waterford rather than Dublin acted as the spearheads for key Catholic institutions – a reminder that Dublin was still predominantly Protestant and England-facing in its 'official' outlook in this period.

Although it began in the last quarter of the eighteenth century,[103] the impressive expansion of convents was primarily a post-Famine phenomenon.

103 R. Raughter, 'Pious occupations: female activism and the Catholic revival in eighteenth-century Ireland' in R. Raughter (ed.), *Religious women and their history: breaking the silence* (Dublin, 2005), pp 25–49.

There were sixteen convents of five orders with 122 nuns in 1800 (Dublin had fifty-six nuns, Cork thirty, Galway eighteen, Drogheda twelve, Killarney four, and Limerick, Kilkenny, Thurles and Wexford all with three).[104] By 1850, this had advanced to ninety-one convents, and by 1900 there were 368 convents of fifty-three different congregations, and 8,031 nuns.[105] The town-based convent schools presided over a reformation of Irish popular culture away from its vernacular pre-Famine expressions towards a more anglicized lower-middle-class sensibility, with respectability, emotional control and conformity as the core values. The nuns helped nudge Catholic Ireland in a more utilitarian anglophone direction, equally distant from a fading Gaelic world on one side and an unsympathetic Protestant colonial one on the other.

In Dublin city alone, there were forty-eight convents with 1,200 nuns by 1871. Among these institutions were the controversial Magdalen asylums, an early expression of the Catholic church beginning to absorb welfare functions from the state.[106] The forbidding nature of nineteenth-century institutional buildings like jails, asylums and workhouses has gloomed Irish towns under damp skies, an austerity accentuated by the greyness of Roman cement, and architecturally undistinguished (nundescript?) convents. The poet Austin Clarke visited the old barracks at Glencree in Co. Wicklow, converted into a punitive borstal by 'the terrible black brethren': 'We could see the wicked boys working in the fields of the Reformatory below, or marching up and down the prison yard with a black Brother as their grim jailer'.[107] At Letterfrack (Co. Galway), another poet Richard Murphy (1927–2018) observed 'poor destitute badly fed shaven-headed cruelly treated boys from eight to sixteen'.[108]

Austin Clarke had fun in the 1930s with the efflorescence of names that all this activity had caused:

> Since the establishment of our republic, many Continental orders have spread again throughout our country. Children of today have for their delight the florality of names such as the Faithful Companions of Jesus, the Handmaidens of the Sacred Heart of Jesus, the Daughters of the Cross, the Sisters of the Cross and Passion, the Blue Sisters, the Poor Servants of the Mother of God, the Sisters of Marie Auxiliatrix, the

---

104 *Castlereagh correspondence*, iv, p. 172.   **105** C. Clear, *Nuns in nineteenth-century Ireland* (Dublin, 1987); M. Luddy, '"Possessed of fine properties": power, authority and funding of convents in Ireland 1780–1900' in M. Van Dijck & J. de Maeyer (eds), *The economics of providence: management, finances and patrimony of religious orders and congregations in Europe, 1773–c.1930* (Leuven, 2012), pp 227–46; J. Castle & G. O'Brien, 'I am building a house: Nano Nagle's Georgian convents', *Irish Architectual and Decorative Studies*, 19 (2016), pp 54–75.   **106** For opposing views, see J. Smith, *Ireland's Magdalen laundries and the nation's architecture of containment* (Notre Dame, 2007) and J. Prunty, *The monasteries, Magdalen asylums and reformatory schools of Our Lady of Charity in Ireland, 1853–1973* (Dublin, 2017).   **107** A. Clarke, *Twice around the Black Church: early memories of Ireland and England* (Dublin, 1990), p. 55.   **108** R. Murphy, *In search of poetry* (Thame, 2017), p. 25.

Little Sisters of the Assumption, Our Lady of the Cenacle, the Little Company of Mary, the Sisters of Bon Secours, the Sisters of Saint Joseph of Chambery, the Sisters of Saint Joseph of Cluny.[109]

Convents became a core element of the Catholic institutional sectors forming in the second half of the nineteenth century.[110] Towns in Ireland developed Catholic institutional sectors in the second half of the nineteenth century, notably in diocesan centres like Thurles (Co. Tipperary), Tuam (Co. Galway), Carlow, Clones (Co. Monaghan), Killarney (Co. Kerry) and Navan (Co. Meath).[111] In the nineteenth century, Catholic diocesan centres displaced their older counterparts, which faded into shabby genteel obsolescence, with many Protestant bishops choosing not to reside in them. Consider the relationship between Enniscorthy and Ferns, Killarney and Ardfert, Carlow and Leighlin, and Loughrea and Clonfert.

Of the newly chosen Catholic diocesan centres, only Cobh (as compared with Mallow, Midleton or Fermoy) might be regarded as poorly situated, and the choice here was favoured because the soaring spire on an elevated site became the last identifiable element that departing emigrants could see as they left Ireland for the last time, 'St Colman's spire shrinking ashore'.[112] As early as 1837, an advertisement for St Patrick's College in Thurles boasted that it 'forms a prominent feature amidst a large group of religious houses, which forcibly remind the stranger of Catholic countries'.[113] Large Irish towns like Wexford, Castlebar (Co. Mayo), Mullingar (Co. Westmeath)[114] and Fermoy (Co. Cork) also exhibited Catholic sectors.[115] Even smaller towns like Ardee (Co. Louth), Adare and Doon (Co. Limerick), Kilrush (Co. Clare), Downpatrick (Co. Down), Oldcastle (Co. Meath), Kilbeggan (Co. Westmeath), Tullow (Co. Carlow) and Dunlavin (Co. Wicklow)[116] could exhibit polarized internal geographies.

109 Clarke, *Twice round the Black Church*, p. 144. 110 D. Murphy, *Sketches of Irish nunneries* (Dublin, 1865); J. Murphy, *Terra incognita or the convents of the United Kingdom*, second edition (London, 1876). 111 K. Whelan, 'A geography of society and culture in Ireland since 1800' (PhD, UCD, 1981), pp 45–59. 112 Derek Mahon's poem 'To Mrs Moore at Inishshannon', voiced by Brigid Moore, the first recorded Irish immigrant at Ellis Island, in a letter home. 113 O'Dwyer, *Cashel and Emly*, p. 308. 114 Satirized in the brilliant parody of the topographic ballad 'Mullingar': 'Ye nine inspire me and with rapture fire me/To sing the buildings both old and new/The majestic courthouse and the spacious workhouse/And the church and steeple which adorn the view./There's a barracks airy for the military/Where the brave repose from the toils of war/Five schools, a nunnery and a thriving tannery/In the gorgeous city of Mullingar'. 115 See the map of Wexford by Billy Colfer in *Atlas of Irish rural landscape*, p. 276. 116 See the map of Dunlavin by Paul Ferguson in *Atlas of Irish rural landscape*, p. 271.

CHAPTER EIGHT

Two Cities, Two Religions: Belfast and Dublin

ULSTER PROTESTANTISM UNDERWENT a dramatic religious renewal in the second half of the nineteenth century, in some ways echoing the Devotional Revolution in Catholicism as both of them responded to dramatic transformations in social structure, inflicted by the Famine, and by the destruction of protoindustrial industry by power-based weaving in the Ulster countryside. Across the Protestant communities of Europe and America experiencing the swift transtion to an urban industrial world, a religious revival based on an evangelical awakening erupted, affecting Scandinavia, Germany, Switzerland, France, Holland, England, Scotland and the United States. One of its very strongest expressions was in Protestant Ulster.

The 1859 revival began in Connor and Ahoghill near Antrim town, spread quickly across the Bann to east Derry, wildfired east into Belfast and north Down, and eventually encompassed most of Ulster, with the exception of its western and southern Catholic fringes.[1] The born-again 'awakening' was especially concentrated among young females of weaving and small farming families, and allowed evangelical Presbyterianism to penetrate many rural communities. Orangeism spread on the coat tails of the revival in the countryside and it was carried into the urban mill communities by displaced migrants.

The mechanization of flax spinning proved a disaster for hand spinners and handloom weavers in Belfast's outer hinterland. Deskilling and deindustrialization decimated south and west Ulster, provoking sustained movement into Belfast. In the 1850s and 1860s, Belfast soaked up 90,000 people from these shattered Famine communities to work in its expanding textile factories, a workforce largely composed of women and children, who cost half the wages of a skilled man. Belfast grew with astonishing rapidity in the nineteenth century, achieving annual growth rates of three per cent. The population shot up from 20,000 in 1800 to 75,000 by 1841 and 349,000 by 1901. In the second half of the nineteenth century, Belfast became the last of

---

1 J. Carson, *God's river in spate: the story of the religious awakening of Ulster in 1859* (Belfast, 1958).

the giant British industrial cities, growing more rapidly than any other city in Britain or Ireland.[2] By 1913, Belfast claimed the largest shipyard, tobacco factory, rope works and linen factory in the world.[3] It had developed a mature evangelical elite, mixing profit, piety and paternalism in a characteristic fashion. Disciplined, hard working and austere, their moneymaking was leavened by public charity and philanthropy: emphatically, urbanization and secularization did not go hand-in-hand in nineteenth-century Belfast, even at the elite level.[4]

Belfast's accelerated growth increased the Catholic component of its population. From eight per cent in 1785, this rose to thirty-two per cent in 1834 before peaking at forty per cent in 1841; Catholic migration then slackened in the post-Famine period, and the Catholic share slipped back to thirty-three per cent in 1860, and twenty-five per cent in 1900.[5] Along the industrialized seams of the Shankill and the Falls, segregation became institutionalized. The first serious sectarian riots, erupting in 1857 and rumbling on until 1886, responded to the shifting sectarian balance of the city: as elsewhere, entrenched urban elites were least able to accommodate new migrant communities, and the Catholic influx from south and west Ulster confirmed Protestant perceptions about their poverty and lack of education. Protestant tolerance diminished in tandem with the escalation of Catholic numbers, and a reviving evangelicalism pitted itself against what it perceived as the aggressive monolith of Irish Catholicism.[6]

Protestant fear of Catholic encroachment created tensions along the interfaces, especially in west Belfast where Catholics concentrated along the spine of the Falls Road and Protestants on the Shankill Road. The 1857 riot featured the Catholic Pound and the Protestant Sandy Row. The Riot Commission Report concluded that 12 July was used 'to remind one party of the triumph of their ancestors over those of the other and to inculcate the feeling of Protestant superiority over their Roman Catholic neighbours'.[7] It was also linked to rising evangelicanism, with an urgent sense of the need for the 'saved' to preach to the 'unsaved': this involved open air preaching to the 'unchurched', involving what the Presbyterian open air preacher Revd Hugh 'Roaring' Hanna (1821–92) called 'the duty of aggression' against the 'audacious and savage outrages of a Romish mob'. Hanna encouraged Protestants to use force if necessary: 'Our most valuable rights have been obtained by conflict'.[8]

2 J. Bardon, 'Belfast at its zenith', *History Ireland*, 1 (1993), pp 48–51; J.C. Beckett & R. Glasscock (eds), *Belfast: the origins and growth of an industrial city* (Belfast, 1967).   3 P. Wicks, *The truth about Home Rule* (London, 1913), p. 54.   4 Hempton, *Religion and political culture*, pp 128–31.   5 S. Baker, 'Orange and green: Belfast, 1832–1912' in H. Dyos & M. Wolff (eds), *The Victorian city* (London, 1973), pp 789–814.   6 D. Hempton & M. Hill, 'Godliness and good citizenship: evangelical Protestantism and social control in Ulster 1790–1850', *Saothar*, 13 (1988), pp 68–80.   7 J. Holmes, 'The role of open-air preaching in the Belfast riots of 1857', *PRIA*, 102, C (2002), pp 47–66.   8 Holmes, 'Open-air preaching'.

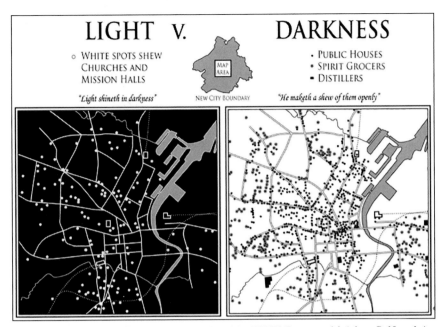

Fig. 49 Belfast in black and white, as depicted by W.J.W. Roome, *A brighter Belfast: being the story of the Shankill Road Mission* (Belfast, 1898).

The Victorian riots copper-fastened the segregationalist impulse. Belfast's breakneck growth widened the sectarian divide. By 1861, thirty per cent of Catholics were illiterate versus ten per cent of Protestants; by 1901, seventy per cent of Protestant homes had gas versus fifty per cent of Catholic ones; one in six of Protestant houses versus one in sixteen of Catholic houses had baths. Catholics were over-represented at one-third in the general labourers category, while they were under-represented in engineering and shipbuilding. In these sectors, an exclusively Protestant workforce had been institutionalized by union apprenticeship schemes and reinforced by intimidation. In 1900, the 9,000-strong work force of the shipyards was universally Protestant in composition.[9]

The novelist James Douglas (1867–1940) created a vivid portrait of 'Bigotsborough' in 1907.

> [Belfast] is a city which suffers from unsatisfied aspirations and baffled aims. Its imagination is starved, and it is oppressed by an intolerably grey monotony. It is the loneliest city in the world. It would be happy if it were on the Clyde, for its blood is Scottish but it lives in exile among an alien race. It has ceased to be Scottish and it is too proud to be Irish. It

9 B. Collins & A. Hepburn, 'Industrial society: the structure of Belfast 1901' in P. Roebuck (ed.), *Plantation to partition* (Belfast, 1981), pp 210–28.

has the hunger of romance in its heart for it has lost its own past, and is groping blindly after its own future. It cannot identify itself with Ireland or with Scotland or with England, and it vehemently endeavours to give itself to each country in turn. It is like a woman who dallies with three lovers, and cannot make up her mind to marry any of them.[10]

The American commentator William Curtis offered a more sympathetic portrait in 1909. He was struck by the crowded church attendances and defined Belfast as 'distinctively a theological town'. He was impressed to 'hear workingmen discussing theology in the streetcars instead of politics, comparing the eloquence of their ministers'. Curtis counted 176 houses of worship: seventy-two Presbyterian (one for every 1,670 inhabitants), thirty-seven Church of Ireland, thirty Methodist, eighteen Catholic, seven Congregationalist, six Baptist, two Moravian, two Plymouth Brethren, one Friends meeting house and one Jewish synagogue). He emphasized how thoroughly religious culture had permeated the lifestyle:

> If you will look through the windows as you pass through the streets, you will see them draped with neat Nottingham curtains and linen shades. There are shelves of books and pictures, neat carpets and center tables with a family Bible and photograph album and religious newspapers and periodicals. There are often books on theology, more so than anything else, commentaries on the Bible and other rational works, for the well-to-do Belfast mechanic is a Presbyterian and always prepared to defend the doctrines of that faith.[11]

NORTHERN IRELAND: PARALLEL SOCIETIES

In Northern Ireland, the impact of partition solidified denominational boundaries along the border, while the macro-distribution of Catholic and Protestants exhibited astonishing stability in broad terms. In 1971, the Catholic population in Northern Ireland was thirty-four per cent, almost unchanged since Partition. The northern state achieved exactly what it was designed to do – copperfasten a perpetual two-to-one Protestant majority. The Troubles that began in 1969 altered the sectarian arithmetic: by 2011, Catholics comprised forty-five per cent of the population. The overall picture is 'of the two main Protestant [Church of Ireland, Presbyterian] denominations in decline almost everywhere and a Catholic population on the increase across wide swathes of Northern Ireland'.[12] In 2011, the population of Northern Ireland was 1.8m

---

10 J. Douglas, *The unpardonable sin* (London, 1907).   11 Curtis, *An Irish summer*, p. 324.
12 N. Cunningham & I. Gregory, 'Religious change in twentieth-century Ireland: a spatial history', *Irish Geography*, 45:3 (2012), p. 227.

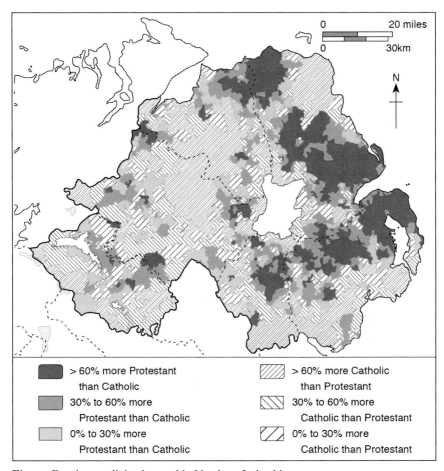

> 60% more Protestant
than Catholic

30% to 60% more
Protestant than Catholic

0% to 30% more
Protestant than Catholic

> 60% more Catholic
than Protestant

30% to 60% more
Catholic than Protestant

0% to 30% more
Catholic than Protestant

Fig. 50 Dominant religion by ward in Northern Ireland in 2011.

(three per cent of the entire UK population – an indication of why Northern Ireland never registered in the initial Brexit debate), of which forty-eight per cent identify as Protestant and forty-five per cent as Catholic.

An outcome of the Good Friday/Belfast Agreement (many things in Northern Ireland have two names, most memorably Stroke City – Londonderry/Derry) was that eighteen watch towers were demolished along the Border.[13] The impact of the Troubles within Belfast cemented existing cleavages, set in stone with peace (actually war) walls, while in Derry the Protestants retreated to the Waterside across the river. One-hundred-and-sixteen peace walls form an interrupted zig-zag along 'interfaces' in Belfast, Derry, Lurgan and Portadown.[14]

13 D. Wylie, *British watchtowers* (London, 2010).

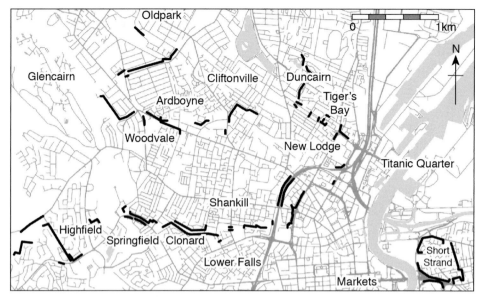

Fig. 51 Peace walls in Belfast in 2018.

Micro-mapping of the religious demography of Belfast between 1971 and 2011 exposed sharpening segregation even within a constantly evolving geography. The Short Strand enclave in Belfast is almost entirely encircled by walls. A wall guards the Fountain estate in Derry/Londonderry where a residual working-class Protestant community was left marooned in a Catholic city once their middle-class co-religionists migrated east to the Waterside across the Foyle. Enrollment figures for 2016/17 showed that ninety-three per cent of children in Northern Ireland are still educated apart from those of the opposing affiliation. In 2000, a mere three per cent of primary schools were integrated and it was still at under six per cent in 2017. Just over five per cent of pupils attended integrated secondary schools in 2000, under nine per cent in 2017. By contrast, rigorous application of legislation has successfully integrated work places (the proportion of Catholics in the police service has shifted from one in ten in 2000 to one in three in 2018), and unemployment rates in the two main religious groupings have converged rapidly.

Northern Ireland still exhibits a frozen form of 'living apart together' within parallel societies.[15] And underneath that deep sectarian permafrost lie the victims of the Troubles: 3,700 dead people, with the map of the casualties exhibiting its own grisly geography.[16] In the words of the Belfast

14 Interactive map online on thedetail.tv.   15 Interactive map by Matthew O'Doherty online on thedetail.tv.   16 I. Gregory et al. (eds), *Troubled geographies: a spatial history of religion and society in Ireland* (Bloomington, 2013).

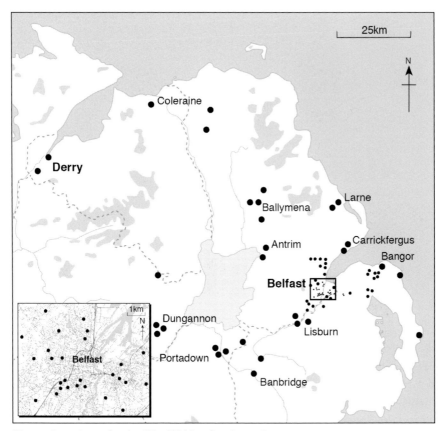

Fig. 52 Locations of major 'Twelfth' bonfires in 2016.

poet Medbh MacGuckian, 'Every inch of the land has been paid for in the blood of a man'.[17] Undefined anomalous spaces at once nondescript but supersaturated inspired photographers Willie Doherty[18] and Paul Seawright. Both foreground sites that are eerily quiet, edgy, banal, marginal, dim, waste ground, interstitial and woebegone. Their photographs foster an instinctual unease in the viewer but their content, the sites of sectarian murders, the lost world of the disappeared, lie beyond pictorial convention. Seawright observes that 'I have always been fascinated by the invisible, the unseen, the subject that doesn't easily present itself to the camera'.[19]

Belfast is the last city in Europe where communities demand functioning walls to manage a divided city. The pallet ziggaurats of the Twelfth bonfires

---

17 As is her wont, McGuckian recyles a phrase from the historian A.T.Q. Stewart (1929–2010).   18 C. Wylie, *Willie Doherty, requisite distance: ghost story and landscape* (Dallas, 2009).   19 P. Seawright, *Sectarian murders*, 1988.

Fig. 53 The materials for the 'Twelfth' bonfires on the Shankill Road (left) and Antrim (right). One banner on the Antrim specimen states: 'We're not racist!!! Just don't like niggers'. Another reads 'Keep Antrim tidy. We're not racist. Just don't like cottonpicking niggers'. An Irish tricolour bears the inscription 'I Ran Away'.

represent a vernacular architectural form of the early twentieth first-century, dreary steeples still puncture the grey Fermanagh skyline. And a lost future haunts this sombre city as expressed by the playwright Stewart Parker (1941– 88) on his native Belfast.

> Why would one place break your heart more than any other? A place the like of that? Brain-damaged and dangerous, continuously violating itself, a place of perpetual breakdown, incompatible voices, screeching obscenely through the smoky dark wet. Burnt out and still burning … we can't love it for what it is, only for what it might have been, if we'd got it right, if we'd made it whole.[20]

DUBLIN AS A CATHOLIC CITY

Between 1800 and 1865, 1,842 Catholic churches were constructed across Ireland, at a cost of £3,098,627.[21] In addition, 217 convents cost £1,058,415,340

---

20 Parker's moving play, *Northern Star*, was first staged in 1984.   21 M. O'Reilly, *Progress of Catholicity in Ireland in the nineteenth century* (Dublin, 1865). The average construction cost per church was £1,682.

colleges cost £308,918, and forty-four hospitals, orphanages and asylums cost £147,135. The total expenditure on Catholic infrastructure reached £4,575,995 in this period. In Dublin city, the number of chapels rose from sixteen in 1628, to nineteen in 1749 to twenty-six in 1825 to twenty-eight (including nine convent chapels) in 1849, and forty-four (city and suburbs) in 1880.[22] From 1800 to 1865, Dublin expended £1,170,100 on religious construction, of which just over half was spent on building churches.

In the late nineteenth century, an aureole of Catholic institutions enveloped the core of Dublin, as the Catholic church assumed ownership of gentry houses and demesnes, and there was a sustained investment in education.[23] Dublin was ringed by a belt of abandoned estates and villas, with no demand for them in a stagnant economy. They suited institutional use once you could endure or impose a high tolerance for cold and draughts. In the post-Famine period, the Catholic church vaulted over Protestant Ascendancy and landlordism, both weakened fatally by disestablishment and the Land Acts, except in south-east Ulster, where landlord control remained strong. Landlord houses were increasingly turned to Catholic uses. An early example was the Jesuits taking over Clongowes Wood from former Catholic owners in 1814, the Loreto Sisters acquired Rathfarnham Hall from the Griersons in 1823, the Society of the Sacred Heart Sisters bought Mount Anville from the entrepreneur William Dargan (1799–1867) in 1865 and the trend accelerated rapidly with the legislative euthanasia of the Irish landlord system in the last quarter of the nineteenth century. Over fifty Big Houses were eventually acquired for a variety of Catholic institutional uses.

Particular energy was possibly devoted to acquiring properties associated in popular memory with mistreating Catholics. In Co. Wexford, the properties of hate figures from 1798 were targetted: Hunter Gowan's Mount Nebo was bought by the Benedictines in 1907, and renamed Mount St Benedict, while the Sisters of Providence took over Lord Ely's Loftus Hall in 1917. The old home of John Foster, the great champion of Protestant Ascendancy, passed into Cistercian ownership in Collon (Co. Louth). The Sisters of the Infant Jesus acquired Drishane Castle (Millstreet, Co. Cork) in 1909 while the Benedictine Sisters acquired Kylemore (Co. Galway) in 1918. Granite salvaged from the burned-out Castleboro was used to build steps leading up to the Catholic church in Taghmon (Co. Wexford). The stones of Mitchelstown Castle (Co. Cork) were sold to the Cistercian monks of Mount Melleray Abbey (Co. Waterford), who used them to build a new abbey. The Patrician Brothers acquired Ballyfin (Co. Laois) from the Cromwellian Cootes in the 1920s, while the De La Salle

22 H. Campbell, 'Religion and the city: the Catholic church in Dublin 1691–1878', *Urban Design Studies*, 3 (1997), pp 1–24.   23 D. Raftery, 'The 'mission' of nuns in female education in Ireland, *c.*1850–1950', *Paedagogica Historica*, 48:2 (2012), pp 299–313.

Table 7 Big Houses turned to Catholic ownership

Belcamp Hall	Dublin	1893	Oblate	Gloster	Offaly	1958	Convent
Belmont	Dublin	1863	Oblate	Gormanston	Meath	1948	Franciscan
Bellinter	Meath	1965	Our Lady of Sion	Killashee	Kildare	[?]	
Besborough	Cork	1922	Sacred Heart Sisters	Kilnacrott	Cavan	1931	Norbertine
Bolton Castle	Kildare	1962	Cistercian	Kylemore	Galway	1918	Benedictine
Burnham	Kerry	1924	Sisters of Mercy	Loftus Hall	Wexford	1917	Sisters of Providence
Cahirmoyle	Limerick	1921	Oblate novitiate			1936	Rosminian Sisters
Carriglea	Waterford	1904	Bon Sauveur Convent	Loughglynn	Roscommon	1909	Franciscan Mission of Mary
Carrignavar	Cork	1950	Sacred Heart Fathers	Moore Abbey	Kildare	1945	Sisters of Charity of Jesus & Mary
Castlebar House	Mayo	1924	Sisters of Mercy				
Castlecor	Longford	1925	Ladies of Mary	Mount Heaton	Offaly	1878	Cistercian [Mount St Joseph, Roscrea]
Castledurrow	Laois	1922	Convent School				
Castle Martyr	Cork	[?]	Carmelite College	Mount Nebo	Wexford	1907	Benedictine
Clogher Palace	Tyrone	1922	Convent	Mount Anville	Dublin	1965	Society of the Sacred Heart
Clongowes Wood	Kildare	1814	Jesuit				
Cloonamahon	Sligo	[?]	Passionist Fathers	Mount Argus	Dublin	1856	Passionists
Dalgan Park	Mayo	1918	Columban	Mount Pleasant	Louth	[?]	Catechesis Centre
Delvin Lodge	Meath	[?]	Convent	Mount Trenchard	Limerick	1953	Sisters of Mercy
Donamon Castle	Roscommon	1939	Divine Word Missionaries	Moyne Abbey	Galway	c.1955	Sacred Heart Fathers
				Myross Wood	Cork	[?]	Sacred Heart Fathers
Dowdstown [Dalgan Park]	Meath	1927	Columban	Newcastle	Longford	1951	African Missionary Nuns
Drishane Castle	Cork	1909	Missionary Sisters of the Infant Jesus	Newmarket Court	Cork		
				Oakley Park	Kildare	c.1955	St John of God Brothers
Dromkeen	Cavan	[?]	Convent				
Drumcar	Louth	[?]	St John of God Bothers	Oriel Temple	Louth	1938	Cistercian
				Orlagh	Dublin	1872	Augustinian
Drumcondra House	Dublin	1842	All Hallows College	Portglenone	Antrim	1948	Cistercian Nuns
Duckspool	Waterford	[?]	Augustinian	Rathfarnham Hall	Dublin	1823	Loreto
Dunboyne Castle	Meath	1950	Good Shepherd Convent	Rathfarnham Cast.	Dublin	1913	Jesuit
				Rockwell	Tipperary	1864	Spiritan
Dundrum	Tipperary	1909	Convent	Roebuck Castle	Dublin	1943	Little Sisters of the Poor
Ennismore	Cork	1952	Religious Order				
Essex Castle (Carrickmacross)	Monaghan	1888	Saint Louis Sisters	Rubane/Echlinville	Down	1950	De La Salle Brothers
				Sion Hill	Dublin	1836	Dominican
Faithlegg	Waterford	1936	De La Salle Brothers	Terenure	Dublin	1860	Carmelite
Gallen Priory	Offaly	1922	Convent	Williamstown	Dublin	1860	Holy Ghost
Glenart Castle	Wicklow	[?]	Religious Order	Castle			(Blackrock College)
Glenstal	Limerick	[?]	Benedictine	Woodlock	Waterford	1901	

Brothers acquired Faithlegg House in the 1930s. In 1926, the parish priest of Glassdrumman (Co. Armagh) bought the ruins of Ravensdale Park (burned in 1922) and recycled its Mourne granite to build his new church.

The foundation of the new state cemented Catholicism in its position of unchallenged ascendancy. Archbishop John Charles McQuaid (1895–1973) orchestrated the building of resolutely retro churches around suburban Dublin. Thirty-four churches were erected in a deliberate ring around Dublin between 1940 and 1965, an ecclesiastical pincers holding the inner suburbs in its grip. Vast examples like Mount Merrion (1956) were islanded in windswept car

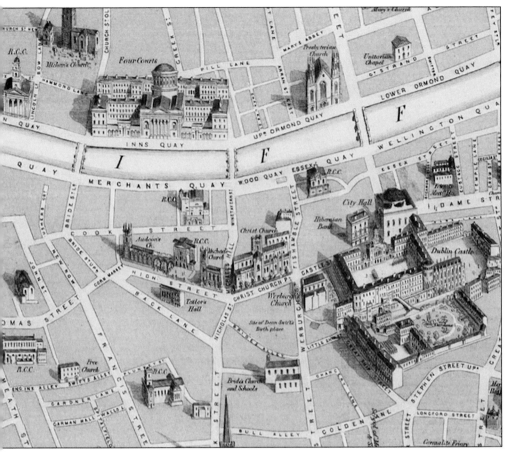

Fig. 54 A detail from 'Dublin in 1861', as mapped by Edward Heffernan, 'civil engineer, 12 Charleville Road Rathmines'. Heffernan enlivened his little-known map with impressively precise isometric drawings of the principal buildings, and thirty-four drawings of buildings and landscapes. On this section, sixteen churches of various denominations are shown.

parks. These reinforced concrete halls were designed to hold congregations of 1,500 people. The Cork-born sculptor Séamus Murphy (1907–75) was amused at the behaviour of Dubliners in the 1930s:

> When they are in a bus, they spend much time raising their hats, or if they are bare-headed, crossing themselves as ostentatiously as possible, not only at every church we pass but at unseen oratories and private chapels in convents, orphanages, colleges, Magdalen Homes, hospitals and industrial schools.[24]

24 S. Murphy, *Stone mad* (Cork, 2005), p. 32. Originally published in 1950, this matchless book celebrates the distinctive culture of the stone masons.

Catholics on buses could readily distinguish Catholic churches from non-Catholic churches in the 1960s and failure to participate in the ritual instantly marked out non-Catholics.[25] The Catholic church preened itself on the spectacular pace of its advance:

> No city of the same, and similarly poor, Catholic population can point to such progress as has taken place in Dublin since the beginning of this century … This external growth of religion is but the manifestation of an improved inner life in the general mass of the population.[26]

This expansion was particularly pronounced on the north side of the city, which became almost monolithically Catholic in the second half of the nineteenth century. In 1861, Cardinal John Henry Newman (1801–90) described the north side as 'the specifically Catholic side of Dublin' and the name 'The Holy Land' became attached to the area around Clonliffe Road with its cluster of institutions.[27] Lower-middle-class Drumcondra ('where they speak the best English')[28] became the quintessential Catholic suburb in Dublin from the 1870s.[29] Dublin city had been seventy-three per cent Catholic in 1834, it reached seventy-seven per cent by 1861, and the city became ever more monolithically Catholic in the second half of the nineteenth century, as Protestants accelerated their migration to the self-governing suburbs of Rathmines, Pembroke and Clontarf, or retreated (like Samuel Beckett's family) to the safety of genteel Greystones (Co. Wicklow).[30] The Protestant church at Greystones, built in 1857, had to be enlarged three times – 1864, 1883, 1898 – to cater for the influx.[31]

CATHOLICISM NEW AND OLD

The cultural retrieval of ancient traces of Irish civilisation began as an immense work of scholarship in the 1830s and 1840s, initially associated with the Ordnance Survey. The wider project included O'Donovan, Petrie, Hardiman, Todd, O'Curry, Reeves, Wilde and Graves, the cumulative impact of whose

---

25 I owe this observation to Christopher J. Woods.   **26** 'Progress of religion in diocese of Dublin' in *Irish Catholic Directory* (Dublin, 1871), p. 158.   **27** K. Whelan, *Dublin through space and time: from Wood Quay to Silicon City* (Dublin, 2015).   **28** As a nettled Stephen Dedalus riposted to the supercilious but dim English Jesuit who queried his use of the archaic English word 'tundish' (Joyce, *Portrait of the Artist*).   **29** M. Daly, 'Catholic Dublin: the public expression in the age of Paul Cullen' in D. Keogh & A. McDonnell (eds), *Cardinal Paul Cullen and his world* (Dublin, 2011), p. 135.   **30** Greystones was also reassuringly distant from vulgar Bray, with its 'real waves and imitation quality'.   **31** In 1883, it had to be enlarged 'for the second time' (*Irish Ecclesiastical Gazette*, 6 Jan. 1883). In 1898, it was enlarged again to seat 150 more people (*Irish Builder*, 1 Jan. 1898). Not to be outdone, a Catholic church was built in 1866 and enlarged in 1886, the dates suggestive of a response to the Church of Ireland's efforts.

work restored time depth and prestige to the Irish countryside. Translations opened the hitherto sealed casket of the Irish literary tradition and made this ancient history accessible to an anglophone population. The results of earlier scholarship gradually migrated into literature.[32] In that sense, these scholars were indispensable precursors of the Irish Literary Revival.[33]

The Irish landscape was re-enchanted by pinning the sagas to specific locations, thus restoring a mythic overlay. William Wilde asserted that the true value of the Ordnance Survey, 'that great national work', was that it 'allowed for topography to be linked to archaeology and literature'.[34] This is the period when Newgrange, Dún Aengus, Tara, Glendalough and Monasterboice were brought to national attention. This is also the period when scholarly interest engaged hagiography, with the capacity to tie earlier literature to precise locations, where there was often a still living tradition of veneration.[35] This new burst of intellectual history helped internal tourism, itself facilitated by faster and more reliable steam ships, and the penetration of the railways into the west. Wilde's and Wakeman's guidebooks fed this renewed interest.[36]

The Irish Revival was invigorated by the rediscovery of the material heritage of Ireland – landmark pieces like the Ardagh Chalice and the Tara Brooch inspired a new range of costume jewellery, now reduced to the level of kitsch but then enormously liberating.[37] The influence on modern work of exposure to the magnificent artefacts of early medieval Ireland can be seen in the popularization of 'Celtic' jewellery from the 1840s onwards by Waterhouse, Acheson and especially Edmond Johnson (*ob.* 1900), the Grafton Street jeweller.

This revivalist emphasis connected with a wider strain in British thinking. Pugin, Ruskin, Newman and Morris were all seeking to reconnect England with the core Greek virtue (idealism) rather than the core Roman one (materialism). The practical, getting and spending imperial values had corrupted the early Roman Republic, and increasingly hovered like the sword of Damocles over England as a warning to the materialist rapacity and acquisitiveness of the British Empire. This in turn inspired the Hiberno-Romanesque movement in Irish architecture as a turning away from the Gothic Revival. Hiberno-Romanesque showcased the high cultural achievements of pre-conquest Ireland, and was therefore eminently suitable as a signature style of post-

32 Wilde, *Beauties of the Boyne*, p. 6.   **33** V. Mercier, *Modern Irish literature: sources and founders* (Oxford, 1994), pp 10–11.   **34** Wilde, *Beauties of the Boyne*, p. 29.   **35** J. Shearman, *Loca Patriciana: an identification of localities chiefly in Leinster visited by St Patrick* (Dublin, 1879); E. Hogan, *Onamasticon Goedilicum: locorum et tribuum Hiberniae et Scotiae: an index with identifications to the names of places and tribes* (Dublin, 1910).   **36** W.F. Wakeman, *A handbook of Irish antiquities, pagan and Christian: especially such as are of easy access from the metropolis* (Dublin, 1848). This guidebook raced through many later editions.   **37** J. Sheehy, *The rediscovery of Ireland's past: the Celtic Revival, 1830–1930* (London, 1980); N. Netzer, 'Art/full ground: unearthing national identity and an early medieval Golden Age' in V. Kreilkamp (ed.), *Eire/land* (Boston, 2003), pp 49–56.

Fig. 55 The priests's graveyard at Maynooth College presents a petrified forest of Celtic Crosses.

colonialism. Hiberno-Romanesque churches of this period offered another example of what antique dealers call a 'distressed' (deliberately archaic) style. Among the finest examples are the Catholic cathedral in Loughrea (1897–1902, Co. Galway), the Honan Chapel (1915–16, Cork) and the whimsical parish church in Spiddal (1903–7, Co. Galway) by William Scott (1871–1921), with its curious donkey-eared pinnacles.[38]

In the second half of the nineteenth century, a new style appeared on Irish gravestones, influenced by the Irish Revival, and inspired by an intellectual and artistic emphasis on Irish high crosses. The display of the superb plaster casts[39] of historic Irish high crosses proved a crowd-pleaser at major international exhibitions (London, 1851 and 1854, Dublin 1853, Paris 1867, Philadelphia 1876, Chicago 1893). In 1857, the artist Henry O'Neill (1798–1880) produced his superbly illustrated *Sculptured crosses of ancient Ireland*.[40] By the 1860s, monumental sculptors were able to reproduce generic slimmed-down versions for use as gravestones. The High Cross was increasingly adopted as a visual icon of Irish identity.

38 P. Larmour, '"The drunken man of genius": William A. Scott (1871–1921)', *Irish Architectural Review*, 3 (2001), pp 28–41. The phrase is Yeats's: Scott was in charge of the restoration of Thoor Ballylee.   39 Some of these are now on display in the Medieval Mile Museum in Kilkenny.   40 H. O'Neill, *Illustrations of some of the most interesting sculptured crosses of ancient Ireland drawn to scale and lithographed by Henry O'Neill* (London, 1857); P. Harbison, *Henry O'Neill of the 'Celtic Cross': Irish antiquarian artist and patriot* (Bray, 2014).

Irish graveyards soon petrified this aspiration, as stone forests of Celtic-cross-style gravestones sprouted in the graveyards. They were regarded as political statements, as indicated by the 1903 removal of a Celtic Cross memorial from the Protestant graveyard in Bandon (Co. Cork) on the grounds that it was 'Romish, idolatrous and ritualistic'.[41] This extraordinary change was commented on by Oscar Wilde (1854–1900): 'everywhere in our cemeteries there are now to be seen stately and graceful Irish crosses' and these 'have quite displaced the urns and sarcophagi formerly so common'. These gravestones were by far the most prolific settlement expression of the Irish Revival, which otherwise lacked a vernacular landscape expression.[42]

THE IRISH CATHOLIC EMPIRE

In the nineteenth century, the Irish Catholic church exported anglophone Catholicism as an epiphyte[43] on the British Empire.[44] It also exported its architectural model.[45] In Irish-influenced St Johns in Newfoundland, the Irish template for a Catholic institutional sector was followed exactly. At least 20,000 Irish nuns served outside Ireland between 1800 and 1960.[46] The Ursulines were in New York by 1812, the Sisters of Mercy in Great Britain by 1830, the Presentation Sisters in Newfoundland by 1833, and the Loreto in Kolkota by 1841. The College of All Hallows, opened in 1842 to educate missionaries, had produced 1,500 by 1900.[47] By the 1880s, the Christian Brothers operated in China and in Kolkota. The Society of African Missions was founded in 1877.

The new Irish identity was exported to the Irish diaspora, bestowing a worldwide projection and a dominant role to Irish Catholicism in the English-

41 *Irish Times*, 20 Jan. 1904.   **42** D. Kiberd & P.J. Mathews (eds), *Handbook of the Irish Revival: an anthology of Irish cultural and political writings, 1891–1922* (Dublin, 2015). Section Seven, 'The natural world', pp 180–99.   **43** An **epiphyte** is an organism that is supported nonparasitically on the surface of another plant.   **44** J.J. O Kelly, *Ireland's spiritual empire: St Patrick as a world figure* (Dublin, 1952); F. Bateman, 'Ireland's spiritual empire: territory and landscape in Irish Catholic missionary discourse' in H. Carey (ed.), *Empires of religion* (London, 2008), pp 267–87; S. Roddy, *Population, providence and empire: the churches and emigration from nineteenth-century Ireland* (Manchester, 2014), pp 181–223; C. Barr & H. Carey (eds), *Religion and greater Ireland: Christianity and Irish global networks, 1750–1969* (Montreal, 2015).   **45** Among many possible examples, see M. Casey, 'Cornerstone of memory: John Hughes and St Patrick's Cathedral', *American Journal of Irish Studies*, 12 (2015), pp 10–56; M. Thurlby, 'St Patrick's Roman Catholic church, school and convent in St John's: J.J. McCarthy and Irish Gothic Revival in Newfoundland', *Journal of Society for the Study of Architecture in Canada*, 28:3 (2003), pp 13–20. John Mannion's 'Point Lance: an Irish settlement in Newfoundland' is a scintillating example of how to dissect the settlement impact of the Irish overseas (*Atlas of Irish rural landscape*, pp 387–409).   **46** D. Raftery, ' "Je suis d'aucune nation": the recruitment and identity of Irish women religious in the international mission field, c.1840–1940', *Paedagogica Historica*, 49:4 (2013), pp 513–30.   **47** K. Condon, *The Missionary College of All Hallows, 1842–91* (Dublin, 1986).

Fig. 56 An Indian hurling team in 1921, organised by an Irish missionary. The English managed to spead their stick-and-ball games of cricket and hockey into India with remarkable success. Hurling never took off. Note the much thinner shinty-like sticks with their sharp blades at this time, when the game placed a huge emphasis on ground strokes.

speaking world. At the First Vatican Council of 1867–70, thirty per cent of the 730 bishops were either Irish or of Irish descent. The novelist Canon Sheehan (1852–1913) noted in 1881: 'Wherever the mightier race has gone, the weaker race has followed and established a spiritual empire coterminous with that political empire'.[48]

These global ambitions within Irish Catholicism intensified markedly after the founding of the Irish Free State in 1922. The Irish Catholic church serviced the Irish diaspora in the United States, United Kingdom and Australia and supported missionary activities in Asia, Africa and South America. Any consideration of 'Irish Catholicism' from the Famine to Vatican II should include the version that was exported across the anglophone world of the British Empire and beyond. Ireland became the epicentre of a global religious enterprise nourished by an exceptional level of vocations. The Maynooth Mission to China (established in 1911, with its College built in 1918) extended to the Philippines in 1929, to Korea in 1933, and to Burma in 1936. The Missionary Sisters of Our Lady of the Rosary were founded in 1924 to minister in Nigeria, followed in 1937 by the Medical Missionaries of Mary (also focussed on Nigeria).

By 1964, over 6,000 Irish missionaries served outside Ireland. This glut of recruits encouraged missionary-oriented continental congregations seeking

48 P. Sheehan, 'The effect of emigration on the Irish church' in *Irish Ecclesiastical Record*, third series, iii (1882), p. 611.

anglophones to locate Irish outposts in the small farm world of the west and the drumlin belt in the first half of the twentieth century.[49] Their distribution is glaringly at odds with the previous geography of Irish convents, which was solidly rooted in Munster and south Leinster. The Franciscan Mission of Mary established itself in Loughglynn in 1903 and the Divine Word Missionaries at Donamon Castle in 1939, both in Co. Roscommon. The shortage of English teachers forced the francophone Missionary Sisters of the Infant Jesus to turn to Ireland to recruit and train missionary teachers. In 1909, Mother Beatrice Foley, who had returned from Singapore, established Drishane Convent (Co. Cork) to train anglophone teachers for the Asian mission. Within five years, the convent was despatching teaching sisters to Asia and South America. In 1932, St Patrick's Missionary Society located themselves in the small farm hill country of Kiltegan (Co. Wicklow).

The missionary college of All Hallowes targeted young men of modest or limited means, and its leading county for recruits from 1842 to 1891 was Cavan (191), followed by Cork (180), Kerry (168), Limerick (162), Tipperary (143), Longford (120) and Clare (88).[50] An equivalent institution for nuns was St Brigid's Missionary College in Callan (Co. Kilkenny), run by the Sisters of Mercy but not exclusive to them.[51] It opened in 1884 and closed in the 1950s, having educated 2,000 missionary nuns. Its leading counties for recruits were Cork (105), Kilkenny (99), Tipperary (85), Clare (59) and Limerick (56).

CATHOLICISM AND COLONIALISM

For its most psychologically acute critic James Joyce (1882–1939), Ireland had been eviscerated by a dual colonialism, 'the English tyranny and the Roman tyranny', that complicity of British imperialism and Roman Catholicism which made Ireland 'the scullery maid of Christendom'[52] and the home of 'the gratefully oppressed'.[53] Irish culture had been so thoroughly destroyed that it could never be resuscitated even by a determined policy of cultural revival: 'Just as ancient Egypt is dead, so is ancient Ireland'.[54] To believe otherwise was to plunge one's self into a crepuscular world, dim witted and dimly lit by 'the broken lights of ancient myth'.[55] The only reality that the Irish past bequeathed

49 A map showing the distribution in 1959 is in K. Whelan, 'A geography of society and culture in Ireland since 1800' (unpublished PhD thesis, UCD, 1981), p. 113.   **50** Condon, *All Hallowes*, pp 289–364.   **51** C. Barr & R. Luminiella, ' "The leader of the virgin choirs of Erin": St Brigid's Missionary College, 1883–1914' in T. MacMahon, M. De Nie & P. Townend (eds), *Ireland in an imperial world: citizenship, opportunism and subversion* (London, 2017), pp 155–78.   **52** J. Joyce, *A portrait of the artist as a young man*, ed. S. Deane (London, 1992), p. 222.   **53** 'After the race' in J. Joyce, *Dubliners*, ed. T. Brown (London, 1992), p. 35.   **54** J. Joyce, *Occasional, critical and political writing*, ed. K. Barry (Oxford, 2000), p. 125.   **55** Joyce, *Portrait*, p. 184.

was a treadmill of brute repetition, the endless circling of Johnny Morkan's horse around King William's statue in the short story 'The Dead' (written in 1906). Modern Ireland was haunted by the afterlife of that deeper world from which it was permanently estranged. And here lay Joyce's most profound insight: the Irish in this condition were not deprived of modernity: they literally embodied it as a form of paralysis.[56] Irish Catholicism had therefore developed its identity through two sets of filters – British and Roman – that cut it doubly off from its indigeneous roots.

That malign hybrid of British colonialism and Roman Catholicism injected timidity into the culture, turning Ireland, in the cutting phrase of Seán Ó Faoláin (1900–91), into 'a nation of apple-lickers' (if tempted by Satan, an Irish Adam would at most have given the apple a cautious lick). The result was summed up by the artist Tony O'Malley (1913–2003): 'the parish priest pretending to be sober, and the bank clerks pretending to be drunk'. O'Malley believed that the malaise was greatest in the small towns: 'God made the country, man made the town but the Devil made the small town'.

The post-Famine Irish Catholic church cast a withering eye on vernacular culture and enforced middle-class values. In Connemara in 1906, an extensive Catholic grazier Thomas Francis Joyce, who held fourteen farms, sought to obtain further land from the Congested Districts Board. His application was opposed by Fr John Flately on the grounds of social justice. Joyce immediately informed his archbishop that it was 'too bad for priests to be interfering with a man who had only the income of two farms and the ambition of his whole life was to make a priest of his one son and nuns of his two daughters'. The turbulent Flately was rapidly exiled to Clare Island (Co. Mayo).[57] In 1913, a woman in Templenoe parish (Co. Kerry) objected to the usurpation of her pew in the chapel: the priest replied that she lacked respectability: 'Do you have asparagus? A privy house? Cucumber? Cups and saucers on your table?[58] The recognized attributes of a strong farmer in Co. Limerick was 'a priest in the parish, a piano in the parlour,[59] a pump in the yard and bulled his own cows'.[60]

56 S. Deane, 'Dead ends: Joyce's finest moments' in D. Attridge & M. Howes (eds), *Semicolonial Joyce* (Cambridge, 2000), pp 21–36.   57 Evidence of Rev. John Flately in *Royal commission on congestion in Ireland, volume ix* (Dublin, 1908), p. 14. There is a long and sympathetic account of Flately in Fenton, *It all began*, pp 185–222.   58 Cited in C. Delay, 'Confidantes or competitors: women, priests and conflict in post-Famine Ireland', *Éire-Ireland*, 40:1–2 (2005), p. 114.   59 H. Keeley, 'Flung open: walking into the parlour in Victorian Irish fiction' in R. Richman Kenneally & L. McDiarmid (eds), *The vibrant house: Irish writing and domestic space* (Dublin, 2018), pp 107–24.   60 Kevin Danaher RIP, personal communication. Tim O'Neill remembers another Limerick version from Newcastle West: 'A pump in the yard, a son a Jesuit, and bulled his own cows'.

CHAPTER NINE

Catholicism in the New State

F ROM THE 1930S, THE CHIEF IDEOLOGICAL INFLUENCE on the new state
was exerted by Éamon de Valera (1882–1975).[1] In one sense, de Valera
belonged to the Irish Revival and its rediscovery of the west of Ireland, a project
with deep roots in European Romanticism. In the preface to their *Children's and
household tales* (1812–57), the Grimm brothers employed the analogy of a great
storm that had laid waste to a wide cultivated field, leaving only a small patch of
it intact. This small patch – cúinne an ghiorria in Irish parlance[2] – became the
remnant of the once vast crop of folk wisdom. The storm is modernity, which
has almost completely effaced that tradition, destroying its vitality and thereby
ravaging the basis of the authentic unity of German culture. The Grimms
conceived of their enterprise as an effort to restore that lost unity by recovering
whatever could be salvaged of the original tradition.

The romantic mindset was above all restorative,[3] celebrating surviving
specimens of ancient tradition as 'the last of their kind', final remnants of a
vanishing inheritance on the brink of extinction – 'ní bhéadh ár leithéidí arís
ann'. The German linguist Heinrich Wagner (1895–1946) observed about
the Irish language:

> We are not dealing with a language spoken over a wide area but rather with
> the ruins of a language. We compare our work with the archaeologist's
> task of reconstructing an old building from a heap of stones, lying here
> and there in the place where the original building stood.[4]

---

1 De Valera is an easy – too easy – target for satire: Gogarty described him as 'a cross
between a corpse and a cormorant'. 2 **Cúinne an ghiorria** means 'the hare's corner'. In
traditional Irish farming practice, the farmer when harvesting a corn field left one corner
uncut to shelter and nurture the hare. Metaphorically, it signalled the desirability of leaving
a space for tradition and nature to flourish, and to suggest the significance of opening
ourselves to the unknown. Cúinne an ghiorria represents survival but also transformation
(the hare is a shape-shifter in Irish mythology) and possibility. The problem with this
conception is that it suggests that an unsullied realm of tradition still survives; by its nature,
any living culture is in constant flux. In a colonized context like Ireland, we need to pay
equally careful attention to the stubble and the aftergrass. 3 R. Pogue Harrisson, *Forests:
the shadow of civilization* (Chicago, 1992), p. 173. 4 H. Wagner, *Linguistic atlas and survey
of Irish dialects* (Dublin, 1958).

Surveying the Galway landscape dense with place names and memories of narratives and songs, William Butler Yeats in 1903 had convinced himself that in the west of Ireland the seemingly inexorable victory of the modern might not be total. He imagined the different kind of poetry that might be possible if the poet (in his archaic role as bard) immersed himself in the 'great river' of the people. Yeats equated 'The Galway Plains' with Homeric Greece:

> There is still in truth upon these great level plains a people, a community bound together by imaginative possessions, by stories and poems which have grown out of its own life, and by a past of great passions which can still waken the heart to imaginative action ... England or any other country which takes its tune from the great cities and gets its taste from schools and not from old custom may have a mob, but it cannot have a people.[5]... One could still if one had the genius, and had been born to Irish, write for these people plays and poems like those of Greece. Does not the greatest poetry always require a people to listen to it?[6]

De Valera took on that Revivalist project with its emphatic emphasis on the west of Ireland and the Gaeltachts. But he had competing pressures to contain. De Valera had to steer among the competing claims of capitalism (deemed to be fatally wounded by the Wall Street crash of 1929), communism and fascism.[7] Unlike other Catholic countries (Italy, Spain, Portugal), de Valera ensured that Ireland did not succumb to the fatal Catholic fascination with fascism. He developed a late version of Jeffersonian republicanism, a curious hybrid of the classical republican emphasis on frugality and the Catholic emphasis on corporatism, restraint and personal discipline. In practical terms, de Valera promoted a strong version of the rural family as the bedrock of Christian civilization and the bulwark of social order. The landscape impact included the efforts of the Land Commission and the support of small farming. A long-term result has been that the Republic of Ireland has successfully maintained a rural culture that has been dramatically hollowed out elsewhere in Europe.

However, there were costs to this approach, notably the promotion of family over individual rights (with serious adverse consequences for women), the reservation of a special status for the Catholic church (violating republican principles), and a stifling emphasis on the rights of property. The novelist John MacGahern (1934–2006), that most acute analyst of this Irish world, described the society that he experienced: 'That the climate was insular, repressive and

5 W.B. Yeats, 'The Galway plains' in *William Butler Yeats: selected criticism*, ed. A.N. Jeffares (London, 1978), p. 129. 6 Yeats, 'The Galway plains', p. 130. 7 For the 1932 Eucharistic Congress, in a fit of post-colonial sartorial angst, de Valera agonized over whether to wear formal morning wear of the British kind, before deciding to appear dressed in a sober republican lounge suit to greet the Papal Legate Lorenzo Lauri. Lauri simply swept past him on landing, assuming that De Valera was a plain clothes policeman.

sectarian is hardly in doubt, but there is also little doubt that many drew solace from its authoritarian certainties'.[8] MacGahern stressed the power wielded by the uniformed classes: above all clerics, but equally 'civil servants, teachers, doctors, nurses, policemen, tillage inspectors': these people, not just the Catholic church, created 'the narrow, emerging world of the people who belonged to the lower echelons of the new infant State'. [9] MacGahern concluded that lives were lived within small compasses: 'People did not live in Ireland then. They lived in small, intense communities, and the communities could vary greatly in spirit and character, even over a distance of a few miles'.[10] He emphasized the 'little republics' of the family farms. The Land League activist Matthew Harris (1826–90) had warned in the 1880s: 'When the farmers would be emancipated and get their lands, such men would look on the boundary of their farms as the boundary of their country, because farmers as a rule are very selfish men'.[11] MacGahern was equally clear that 'much of what went on was given no more than routine lip service'. 'Most people went about their sensible pagan lives as they had done for centuries, seeing this conformity as just another veneer they had to pretend to wear like all the others they had worn since the time of the Druids'.[12]

DEATH IN CONTEMPORARY IRELAND

In recent decades, death has declined in the Western world in its presence and its vividness. People now seek to avoid the sight of dying, or even being in the presence of a dead person. Death, once a public process, has been banished from the world of the living. As death approaches, people are removed from their homes, to languish in hospitals or hospices.

With the rise of the cemetery in the secularizing nineteenth century, the dead were separated from the living, as they had not been when they were interred in or near places of worship. The promiscuous older graveyards united the dead by faith, birth and dwelling place, and these all-encompassing graveyards remain culturally relevant in Ireland, where they have not lost ground to sprawling urban parkland cemeteries, with their dead carefully stratified by social status and wealth. Whole areas of Irish Catholic practice have evaporated with extraordinary rapidity in recent decades but what has barely weakened at all is the Irish funeral.[13] Only in

---

8 J. MacGahern, 'Whatever you say, say nothing', *Irish Times*, 30 Dec. 1999. 9 MacGahern, *Memoir*, p. 2. 10 MacGahern, *Memoir*, p. 210. 11 Cited in P. Bew, *Land and the national question in Ireland, 1858–82* (Dublin, 1978), p. 229. 12 J. MacGahern, *Memoir* (London, 2005), p. 211. 13 On anthropological perspectives, see H. Hartman, *Der totenkult in Irland: ein beitrag zur religion der Indogermanen* (Heidelberg, 1952); N. Witoszek & P. Sheeran, *Talking to the dead: a study of Irish funerary traditions* (Amsterdam, 1998); L. Taylor, 'Bás in Éirinn: cultural constructions of death in Ireland', *Anthropological Quarterly*, 62:4 (1989), pp 175–87; Ryan (ed.), *Death: a miscellany*.

Ireland would a heated public row erupt (in 2016) over the insistence of the Healy Raes in turning up uninvited at Kerry funerals, while a Wexford politician said that 'I'd walk out on the altar with the priest if I could' at funerals. Many half-believe that Mayo's efforts to win an All-Ireland are doomed because of the failure of their last winning team in 1951 to respect a passing funeral. Irish newspapers still feature the serried ranks of the recently departed, and this tradition has migrated seamlessly to local radio notifications of deaths and funerals each morning and the high-trafficked website RIP.ie. A defining feature of Irish funerals is that you don't have to be invited to attend. In a sense, all funerals are local: 'what other kind is there?' as the poet Micheal Coady asked.[14]

Cremation (which has given us a new word 'cremains') and domesticated ash urns remain a marginal activity in the still-vibrant Irish culture of death, although cremation is a cheaper option than burial.[15] In 2016, cremation rates were above seventy-five per cent in England and had edged up over fifty per cent in the US but in Catholic cultures, burial was still dominant, with Ireland leading the way at eighty-two per cent followed by seventy-seven per cent in Italy. In Ireland in 2013, the average cost of a funeral was €5,000 (versus £3,700 in the UK), but this could double at the higher (lower?) end. In general, undertaking globally is switching from providing products (coffins) to become more like event management, as the actual disposal of the body itself is increasingly private, and a celebration of the life replaces the funeral.[16]

Full engagement with Irish life requires becoming a connoisseur of funerals. The funeral became a centrally embedded ritual in the fabric of Irish life, stitching together the private and the public spheres. Irish literature also showcased the funeral: Caoineadh Airt Uí Laoghaire, Joyce's 'Ivy Day in the Committee Room', the Paddy Dignam funeral in *Ulysses*, *Finnegans wake* (indebted to the rollicking song of the same name), Máirtín Ó Cadhain's pathologically loquacious dead in *Cré na Cille* (1949),[17] Samuel Beckett ('I have no bone to pick with graveyards'), Seamus Heaney's *North* (1975), with its meditation on modern victims of the Northern Ireland Troubles, and John MacGahern's masterpiece *Amongst women* (1990). Even in the ghoulish horrors of the Troubles, graves were respected on all sides of the conflict.

Dignified treatment of the forgotten or disregarded dead remains a pressure point of pain in contemporary Irish society, as in the debate on appropriate emotional infrastructure, ranging from famine memorials, to First World

---

14 M. Coady, *Given light* (Oldcastle, 2017), p. 58. 15 T. Saad, 'The moral inadequacy of cremation', *The New Bioethics*, 23:3 (2017), pp 249–60. 16 'Funerals of the future', *Economist*, 14 Apr. 2018, pp 52–4. In 2017, the funeral industry was worth sixteen billion pounds in the US, 2.6 bn in Great Britain (employing 20,000), 2.5 bn in France and 1.56 bn in Germany (employing 27,000). 17 The novel, with its vigorous, variegated and colloquial Connemara Irish, had a notoriously fraught translation history. *Graveyard clay*, translated by Liam Mac An Iomaire and Tim Robinson, appeared in 2016.

War victims, to the forlorn fate of the disappeared during the Troubles, or the barbaric treatment of infants in Tuam and elsewhere.[18] History is what hurts, what is not over and done with, what is not dead and buried and resting in peace. A posthumous accounting for the disregarded dead requires proper naming, proper burial and proper acknowledgment of lives cast away like rubbish. Neglected dignity has to be restored by attending to the specificity of each life and each person. The triple circuit of name, body and mourning needs to be completed. The impersonal archives can be mined to restore a healing intimacy and an acknowledgement of personal value.

A continuing vernacular expression of interest in marking death can be seen in the proliferation of roadside memorials to crash victims, where (as in the earlier tradition of leachtaí) specifying the exact death place is extraordinarily foregrounded, and which attract their own deeply personal mourning suites – teddies, photographs, cards, flowers ...[19] This can be regarded as an updating of the older tradition of funerary cairns.[20] Spectral white bicycles in Dublin are elevated above the sites where cyclists were killed, serving both as a protest and a memorial.

Burials still have the power to stir deep emotions. On 1 July 2010, 63-year-old bachelor Cecil Tomkins shot and killed his bachelor brother 66-year-old Walter Tomkins at the family farm that they shared at Cronelea (Shillelagh, Co. Wicklow) because he had not followed his mother's burial wishes. Their mother, Bella Tomkins, had been buried locally a few days earlier in Aghowle with her husband. Her original wish was to be interred with her family in Kilcormick (Co. Wexford), but she later reserved a plot in Gorey and left a letter expressing her desire to be buried there, and enclosing the money to cover the costs.[21]

CATHOLICISM TODAY

There were two truly remarkable features to the nineteenth-century surge of Catholicism in Ireland. The first was that it occurred in tandem with the catastrophic population collapse after the Famine (the population halved from 1845 to 1900) and the second was that it largely lacked state support. Ostracism by the British state ensured that Catholics were forced to derive their financial resources from within their own community, forging a democratic consensus between clerics and congregations. Once the Irish Free State came into

---

18 E. Mark-Fitzgerald, *Commemorating the Irish Famine: memory and the monument* (Liverpool, 2013); D. Farrell, *Innocent landscapes* (Manchester, 2001). 19 H. Everett, *Roadside crosses in contemporary memorial culture* (Denton, TX, 2002). 20 Mac Néill, 'Wayside death cairns'; U. MacConville & R. McQuillan, 'Continuing the tradition: roadside memorials in Ireland', *Archaeology Ireland*, 19:1 (2005), pp 26–30. For photographs, see P. Connell, *Irish roadside memorials* (Dublin, 2012). 21 *Irish Independent*, 24 Apr. 2012.

existence, there was the presumption, and then the reality, of a close-to-the-point-of-coercive relationship between church and state, driven by a historic sense that an independent Irish state must support Catholicism in a way that the adversarial British one never did.

A vignette from 1921, when a Catholic lord lieutenant (Viscount Fitzalan) was appointed, is revealing about official British attitudes. The Dublin Castle chapel had to be refitted: 'It was decided to secure a suitable picture of the Madonna, Joseph and the infant Jesus to hang above the altar. When the Viceroy and His Lady arrived to inspect the chapel, they found a picture of Charles the Second, Lady Castlemaine and their baby'.[22] The state's origin was dramatic and bloody, and it then subsided into the lassitude of a peripheral, pious and poor European state. Many functions of a welfare state were handed off hastily without scrutiny to the Catholic church, whose personnel, property, infrastructure and visibility swelled to bloated proportions. By 1972, there were 297 religious congregations and 1,569 priests in the Dublin archdiocese alone.[23]

However that seeming power masked a spiritual dessication, a dry rot most clearly evident in the rash of poorly designed mediocre churches that appeared in Ireland after the second Vatican Council (1962–5). In 1964, the first post-Vatican II church, Our Lady Queen of Peace by Andrew Devane, was located appropriately enough at Dublin Airport. Two years later, Ronald Tallon (1927–2014) brought Mies Van Der Rohe (1886–1969) – a rectangular box on a plinth – to a bemused Knockanure in rural Kerry. The sense of dislocation was added to by the destructive impact of cars, with parking needs trumping any efforts at careful insertion. The architectural integrity of the attractive estate town at Bunclody (Co. Wexford) was destroyed by ripping out the streetline in the 1960s to facilitate a car park and inserting a remarkably ugly concrete church. Many chapels, which eloquently spoke the vernacular language of the Irish architectural tradition, were heedlessly and deliberately destroyed, replaced by inferior modernist successors, which have never been loved as their homely predecessors were. Hundreds of new and remodelled churches were built after Vatican II, but only a handful of commissions, notably those by Liam McCormick, produced worthwhile architecture. Atrocities were perpetrated by parish priests ignorant of the legacy bequeathed to them, in collusion with builders and architects who took the money and ran with lowest-common-denominator buildings. The spiritual and aesthetic malaise evident in these sterile buildings prefigured institutional collapse. Among the sorrowful mysteries of gutted Catholic chapels are Clonegal (Co. Carlow) and Loughmore (Co. Tipperary).

22 T. Jones, *Whitehall diary*, 3 vols (London, 1969–71), iii, pp 98–9.   23 Kelly & Keogh (eds), *Catholic diocese of Dublin*, p. 380.

Fig. 57 This cartoon appeared in the London-published *Evening Standard* on 6 Dec. 1930. Its caption reads: 'Attempted Revolution in Dublin: capture of desperate person found to be in possession of complete set of Marie Stopes'. Stopes (1884–1973) was a pioneer advocate of birth control via contraception (but not abortion). The Irish Free State confiscated contraceptives mailed from England, the butt of this cartoon. It shows the 'Prisidint' [there was none at this time], who looks like W.T. Cosgrave, squashed between two bloated bishops, and the censor [James Montgomery (1884–1973)] mounted on an old-fashioned horse. The depiction of the Irish people teeters on the edge of the old *Punch* simian style figures. The cartoon was by New Zealand-born Sir David Low (1891–1963), the most radical and fearless British political cartoonist since Gillray. Low arrived in England in 1919, and developed a distaste for English snobbery: 'I came from the outside world without respect for institutions and persons that have no right to respect'. His forceful and epigrammatic draughtsmanship was groundbreaking. Low invented the walrus-faced and complacently stupid Colonel Blimp in 1934 as a symbol – and later dictionary definition – of 'an extreme die-hard type of outlook' (T. Benson, *Low unpublished* (London, forthcoming)).

Liam McCormick (1916–96) was the sole architect who rose to the challenge of creating uplifting spiritual spaces in his twenty-seven churches.[24] McCormick was inspired by the sweeping vista from Crockaulin, the mountain above Greencastle (Co. Donegal) where he lived: 'This arc of land holds nearly all my personal history. It has provided me with all of my inspiration. It has

---

24 C. Pollard, *Liam McCormick: seven Donegal churches* (Kinsale, 2011). These are Milford (1961), Murlog (1964), Desertegney (1964), Burt (1967), Creeslough (1971), Glenties (1974) and Donoughmore Presbyterian (1977). Burt was voted the best Irish building of the twentieth century in a 1999 popular poll.

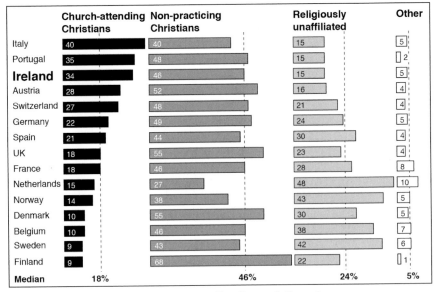

	Church-attending Christians	Non-practicing Christians	Religiously unaffiliated	Other
Italy	40	40	15	5
Portugal	35	48	15	2
Ireland	34	46	15	5
Austria	28	52	16	4
Switzerland	27	48	21	4
Germany	22	49	24	5
Spain	21	44	30	4
UK	18	55	23	4
France	18	46	28	8
Netherlands	15	27	48	10
Norway	14	38	43	5
Denmark	10	55	30	5
Belgium	10	46	38	7
Sweden	9	43	42	6
Finland	9	68	22	1
Median	18%	46%	24%	5%

Fig. 58 Religious practice in Europe, 2015 (Pew Research Center).

moulded my personality and my outlook as it has moulded so much of my design and of my work'.[25] He achieved this effect while remaining architecturally ambitious and in sympathetic dialogue with landscape context, primarily in the Atlantic north-west.

The Republic of Ireland is currently converging on the post-religious European norm (a catch-up phase, mimicking what has happened in the economic arena), thereby becoming part of the hollowed-out religious experience of Europe, in contrast to the United States and the Islamic world, which are marked by a strong presence of religion in the public sphere. The crucial historic context to understand is not the 'collapse' of Irish Catholicism (more accurately regarded as a reversion of the Irish experience towards a European norm) but how the real anomaly, its staggering predominance, surfaced in the first place.

Catholicism in Ireland is subsiding from an exceptional intensity towards the more general Catholic level. The anomaly in Irish Catholicism concerned timing rather than intensity. A reciprocal link between church and state dominated early modern Europe. This bundling of religion, nation and state was 'delayed' in Ireland until well into the twentieth century, tightening after independence in 1921, at a time when these bonds were loosening across Europe. The recent collapse of Devotional Revolution Catholicism carried

25 Cited in D. Martyn, 'A resonant architecture: Liam McCormick and the sonorities of place', *Landscape Studies*, 43:2 (2018), pp 260–74.

Ireland into the global Catholic mainstream. Ireland between the Famine and Vatican II was an aberration in transnational Catholic terms: the challenges that the Catholic church confronts in Ireland are now closer to those it confronts in other continents than was the case even a generation ago. A once 'hot' Irish Catholicism has 'cooled' to become more like Catholicism elsewhere.[26]

Globally a similar decline has affected mainstream liberal Protestants (episcopalians, Presbyterians), where there has been a shift to conservative and evangelical churches that make strong personal demands on behaviour and belonging as a way of conferring meaning on life. The age of embedded religion, where specific religion traditions went with the territory, has passed. Religious behavior was stitched into neighbourhoods, schools, parish churches and a web of other institutions, generating a parallel culture in which religious identity was absorbed, shaped and transmitted through shared habits. The age of individualization has untied the bonds of belief, behaviour and belonging that underpinned religious observance: a woven fabric has unravelled into a flaccid tangle of hanging threads.

That shift has encouraged moral relativism: a self-protective non-judgmental shield behind which everyone should be free to judge for themselves what is right and wrong, and that judgment should be based on how it makes the individual feel, a therapeutic effect that helps us to feel good about ourselves. The digital world has laid waste communal life and eroded structured time: we all live in Oakland now, where, in the celebrated aphorism of Dorothy Parker (1893–1967): 'there is no there there'. An increasing cohort in the Western world self-identify as 'spiritual but not religious'. In the United States in 2015, thirty-seven per cent of those unaffiliated to any religious group so regarded themselves. Close to one-fifth of people in the United Kingdom choose the same category.[27] Many Irish people have drifted disenchanted from their birth church. Buddhism, a religion of practice rather than dogma, is among the fastest-growing faiths in Ireland, increasing by twelve per cent in the 2016 census. An Irish Buddhist Union was formed in Dublin in 2018.

Unlike its European counterparts, nineteenth-century Irish Catholicism was never required to pay a political reckoning for its stances within a state regime that was hostile to it. It escaped the fate of its European counterparts who lost support for at best not resisting and at worst supporting Fascist regimes in the mid-twentieth century. However, the Irish church eventually paid a severe accumulated price for uncontested power when a rapidly transforming Irish economy, society and state detached itself from the church/state consensus in the 1990s. An institutionally rigid Catholicism had calcified in Ireland,

---

26 The best comparative article is J. Cleary, 'The Catholic Twilight?' in E. Maher & E. O'Brien (eds), *Tracing the cultural legacy of Irish Catholicism: from Galway to Cloyne and beyond* (Manchester, 2017), pp 209–25. **27** Pew survey, 2015.

severed from its Gaelic roots in the name of Romanization. It installed a smug and domineering leadership style that sidelined the laity, marginalized, condescended to and mistreated women, promoted a prim pernickety piety rather than spirituality, scorned intellectual debate, and inflicted routine cruelty in the name of unchallenged power and prestige within an all-too-docile flock. Unable to resist the knocker's ball that hit it in the 1990s, this brittle construction crumbled as it deserved to crumble. Letterfrack, Tuam, Goldenbridge, Cloyne, Ferns and too many others generated their own litany of shame. A hurt child is always and only a hurt child and the abyss gaped open the second that this was forgotten. The tragedy of the evil was compounded by the fact that it was inflicted most on the weak, the vulnerable, the fragile, the timid, the female, the poor, and the marginalized. A class element was always in play: the Catholic middle class escaped, but they also shut their eyes, their mouths and their hearts.

As usual, there were regional dimensions. The collapse was swiftest and most severe in Dublin in recent years, as the Catholic church has downsized. In the great divestment of the geek-chic Tiger years, many of its large properties were sold off and have increasingly reverted to becoming country clubs, golf courses, apartment blocks and especially hotels, as at Ballyfin (Co. Laois), Faithlegg (Co. Waterford), and St Helens (Booterstown, Co. Dublin).[28] In the North, with its fraught bundling of politics, identity and religion, the impact has been noticeably more muted. In a society polarized by identity politics, conversion becomes emotionally fraught, an intimate act of cultural betrayal. Unlike the American experience, where religious 'consumers' shop around for alternative models, the normal default in Ireland is to become non-practicising rather than converting. In the boom years, more gyms were built than churches. Abandoned churches and homes with their melancholy iconography are irresistible catnip for photographers.[29] The institutional Catholic church faced disestablishment and downsizing in the twenty-first century, a shrinking exercise in planned obsolescence for religious orders, cardiganed congregations, shuttered churches, imported clergy and new uses for old buildings.[30] The cavernous Catholic church in Finglas West, built in 1967 to hold a congregation of 3,500, closed on 8

---

28 A former Loreto hostel on 77 Stephen's Green (originally built for the earl of Glandore in 1765) with planning approval for a luxury 81-bedroom hotel, was offered for sale in 2018, inviting offers in excess of €16 million. It was sold by the Loreto nuns in 2017 for €7.55 million. The former chapel will be converted into a distinctive restaurant and bar. The Loreto Sisters bought it in 1911 as a hostel for country girls attending the National University at nearby Earlsfort Terrace, which had begun admitting women students in 1908. Loreto Hall remained in use until the 1990s (*Irish Times*, 31 Jan. 2018).   **29** D. Creedon, *Ghosts of the faithful departed* (Cork, 2011); T. Blake, *Abandoned churches of Ireland* (Cork, 2015).   **30** [Ulster Historic Churches Trust], *New life for churches in Ireland: good practice in conservation and reuse* (Belfast, 2013).

October 2018. It is to be demolished to be replaced by a church one-tenth of its size to house 350 people, with the freed space being allocated generously to social and sheltered housing.[31]

During the Celtic Tiger, while the Dublin skyline was crane-crowded, no new Catholic churches were added, despite the explosion of construction in Dublin and its sprawling commuter belt. Of modern churches, the intimate chapels at Glenstall (1987, Co. Limerick) by Jeremy Williams and in the Irish College (2004, Rome) by Marko Ivan Rupnik can be regarded as exceptions to the run-of-the-mill construction of modern Catholic churches. Celbridge (Co. Kildare), in the Dublin commuter belt, with a population of 3,000 in the early 1970s and with 20,000 in 2018, still has only one Catholic church. From the 1830s onwards, thirty-nine places of worship have closed in Dublin: of these, nineteen were Church of Ireland, five were Presbyterian, five were Methodist, two Jewish, only one was Catholic, and seven other churches also closed.[32] The weakening of Mass attendance as a cementing communal force has damaged social cohesion and social capital.[33]

Yet the Republic of Ireland is far from being a secular society. Some churches have been allocated to New Irish Catholic communities, as in the Polish-speaking St Audeon's in Dublin. In 2016, the number of civil marriages exceeded the number of Catholic ceremonies only in Dublin, Cork and Waterford, indicating that the bulk of Irish marriages still take place in churches. The First Communion and the funeral remain securely rooted in Irish culture. The divorce rate in Ireland was 0.6 divorces per 1,000 population in 2015, the lowest rate in the EU. Ireland had the second-highest fertility rate in the EU in 2015 at 1.92; the EU average was considerably lower at 1.58. It is indubitably true that the majority of European Christians (not just Catholics) are now non-practicing but globally the number of Catholics increased by over seven percent between 2010 and 2015, primarily in the global south. Europe now contains just over one-fifth of global Catholics so the Irish decline forms part of a much wider picture.[34]

The secularization model implied that religious practice in the advanced capitalist world has entered an inexorable downward spiral, in which religion suffers an irreversible loss of social significance and exists increasingly as a privatized minority practice. Religion still displays remarkable resilience when subaltern groups convert religious difference into collective social or political

31 *Irish Times*, 9 Oct. 2018. 32 A. Horner, 'Reinventing the city: the changing fortunes of places of worship in inner city Dublin' in Clarke, Prunty & Hennessy (eds), *Surveying Ireland's past*, pp 665–89. 33 K. Andersen, 'Irish secularization and religious identities: evidence of an emerging new Catholic habitus', *Social Compass*, 57:1 (2010), pp 15–39; M. Breen & C. Reynolds, 'The rise of secularism and the decline of religiosity in Ireland: the pattern of religious change in Europe', *International Journal of Religion & Spirituality in Society*, 1 (2011), pp 195–212. 34 These statistics are based on two reports by the Pew Research Centre: *The changing global religious landscape* (2017) and *Being Christian in Western Europe* (2018). Pewresearch.org.

effort, and practical identity politics. The 'rise' of religious fundamentalism and of political Islam evidences this. When once-dominant religions decline, substantial sections convert to alternative or new religions. In Latin America, Protestant evangelical churches erode the space once dominated by Catholicism, and across Europe inward migrations have created substantial Islamic and Hindu religious communities. Ireland has also been more deeply politically integrated into the European Union, and now straddles three wider social spheres: the European, the Anglo and the American. Religious change in those three contexts is divergent and volatile, and after the Trump and Brexit votes, only the most hubristic of commentators would predict how future changes in these wider zones will impact on Ireland. Commentators do well to remind themselves frequently that they are Monday-morning quarter backs, hurlers on the ditch not the pitch.

NEW AGE, NEW CHURCHES

The Republic of Ireland is shedding a monopoly version of religion and transitioning towards a detraditionalized spirituality, often grouped under the term 'New Age'. The precipitous retreat of a chastened Catholicism has opened a space for alternative and more individualistic religious expressions.[35] New Age spirituality globally represents 'a tectonic shift in the sacred landscape' in creating forms of believing without belonging.[36] Detached from the institutional supervision and affiliation of formal churches, it remains geographically unstructured and imposes minimal credal requirements. Stressing a cosmological oneness between the individual and creation, it asserts that the human self is fundamentally good, and that evil exists as an expression of traumatic life experiences or negative global circumstances that damage the fundamentally healthy self.

New Age practices seek to restore individuals to wellbeing, as a means of releasing their optimal potential. Rather than being the collateral benefits of religious practice, health, self-confidence, prosperity and supportive relationships are the desired end goals. Meditation, relaxation exercises, holistic healing, oneness with nature and self-discovery techniques all offer paths to self-realization. New Age spirituality can be regarded as closely connected to the individualistic character of late modernity, and its syncretic ideas are compatible with late capitalist subjectivism, consumerism and multiculturalism, as well as the needs and neuroses that New Age addresses.

---

35 G. Daniel, *Transforming post-Catholic Ireland: religious practice in late modernity* (Oxford, 2016).   36 P. Heelas & L. Woodhead, *The spiritual revolution: why religion is giving way to spirituality* (Oxford, 2005), p. 16.

Table 8: Churches in Dublin city, 2013			
Catholic churches	50	Hindu temples	3
Protestant churches	26	Sikh gurdwaras	3
Islamic mosques	10	Jewish synagogues	2
Orthodox churches	7	Bahá'í temples	1
Buddhist centres	6	**Total**	**108**

New Age turns towards experiential spirituality, as, for example, pilgrimages. While conventional Christianity struggles to retain adherents, the great European sites like the Camino de Santiago, Assisi, Lourdes, Glastonbury, Taizé, Częstochowa, Fatima and Croagh Patrick have grown in popularity.[37]

Exuberant evangelical and Pentecostal African churches are flourishing in Ireland. The migrant-led churches that emerged in the wake of immigration are predominantly Pentecostal: two-thirds of 243 churches self-identified as Pentecostal in 2009.[38] Start-up and improvised churches are often hidden in plain view, in warehouses, factories, industrial units and abandoned cinemas. These spaces were attractive to fledgling congregations because they were cheap to rent, provided easy parking for a scattered congregation and had large flexible interiors. They also did not attract NIMBY middle-class neighbours quick to take legal umbrage. Their drab exteriors conceal kaleidoscopic internal colour with drapes, fabrics and lights. By contrast, the well-heeled Church of Scientology established their national office on Merrion Square in 2016 and opened a Centre in Firhouse, with a pristine (if never used) GAA pitch attached.

These changes carry Ireland into a new global reality: post-secularism as a core aspect of multi- (or better pluri-) culturalism.[39] (Multi-culturalism implies a blended identity, whereas pluri-culturalism acknowledges the persistence of difference). The resurgence of religion globally in the twenty-first century marked the advent of a post-secular age.[40] In a post-secular world, religious and secular perspectives are accorded equal status. Rather than stratification and separation, a dialogue between religious people and secularist people encourages a tolerant co-existence. That stance requires a movement beyond regarding the secularization of Ireland as uni-directional and irreversible, a necessary liberation for Irish citizens from the oppressive weight of religion, a

37 P. Margry, 'European religious fragmentation and the rise of civil religion' in U. Kockel, M. Nic Craith & J. Frykman (eds), *A companion to the anthropology of Europe* (Chichester, 2012), pp 275–94. **38** L. Thompson, 'Pentecostal migrants and the churches in Ireland', *Search*, 33:3 (2010) pp 185–93. **39** C. Taylor, *A secular age* (Cambridge, MA, 2007); M. Ratti, *The postsecular imagination: postcolonialism, religion and literature* (London, 2013); U. Parmaksiz, 'Making sense of the postsecular', *European Journal of Social Theory* (2016), pp 98–116. **40** I. Johnson, *The souls of China: the return of religion after Mao* (London, 2017).

release from the handcuffs of history. The older assumption that modernization would inevitably lead to secularization is increasingly discredited. Modern states need to adjust to accommodate this co-existence of faith and reason.

World cities increasingly bristle with multiple religions. In London, for example, forty per cent of the population were not born in the UK, fifty-five per cent are not white: there are 1.3 million Muslims, 750,000 Christian church attenders, 450,000 Hindus, many Jews, Buddhists, and other faith-oriented people, living alongside but often invisible to secularists.[41] In a pluri-cultural Ireland, a secular state necessarily excludes the faith-based values of the majority of the New Irish, and therefore limits both inclusive citizenship and cosmopolitanism.

41 B. Judah, *This is London: life and death in the world city* (London, 2016).

CHAPTER TEN

Conclusion: Landscape and Imagination

T HE HISTORIC IRISH LANDSCAPE cannot be properly understood without due
appreciation of how saturated it was in a spiritual sensibility. We should
regard this legacy as an intellectual and imaginative resource, one that is
constantly fed by scholarship. In Patrick Kavanagh's words, 'On the stem of
memory, imagination blossoms'. From his own extensive repertoire, Seamus
Heaney's personal favourite poem ['Lightenings' VIII)] was inspired by reading
the scholar's Proinsias Mac Cána's evocation of the memorable Clonmacnoise
air ship story.[1] Mac Cána was paraphrasing from earlier scholarship a fragment
known as 'A ship seen in the air'.[2]

> One day the community of Clonmacnoise were assembled in conclave
> on the floor of the church. As they were conversing, they saw a ship
> sailing above them in the air, moving as if it were upon the sea. When
> the crew of the ship saw the conclave and the settlement below them,
> they cast out the anchor; and so the anchor came down onto the floor of
> the church, so that the clerics seized it. A man from the ship came down
> after the anchor, swimming as if through water; but when he reached the
> anchor they seized him. 'For God's sake let me go!' said he, 'for you are
> drowning me'. Then he went from them, swimming through the air and
> taking the anchor with him.

Heaney has explained his attraction to this poem:

> I was devoted to this poem because the crewman who appears is situated
> where every poet should be situated: between the ground of everyday
> experience and the airier realm of an imagined world. And the essential

1 P. Mac Cána, 'Mythology in early Irish literature' in R. O'Driscoll (ed.), *The Celtic
consciousness* (Portlaoise, 1981), pp 143–54. The Annals of Ulster laconically recorded ships
with crews in the air above Clonmacnoise in 749 (AU, i, p 213). 2 J. Carey, 'Aerial ships and
underwater monasteries: the evolution of a monastic marvel', *Harvard Celtic Colloquium*,
12 (1992), pp 16–28; K. Meyer (ed.), 'Stories from the Edinburgh MS XXVI (Kilbride
Collection No. 22)' in O. Bergin, R. Osborn, R. Best, K. Meyer & J. O'Keeffe (eds), *Anecdota
from Irish manuscripts* (Halle & Dublin, 1910), pp 8–9.

thing – whether you're the poet or the crewman – is to be able to move
resourcefully between these two realms, not to get yourself bogged down
in the quotidian, yet not to lose your head in the fantastic.

> The annals say: when the monks of Clonmacnoise
> Were all at prayers inside the oratory
> A ship appeared above them in the air.
> The anchor dragged along behind so deep
> It hooked itself into the altar rails
> And then, as the big hull rocked to a standstill,
> A crewman shinned and grappled down the rope
> And struggled to release it. But in vain.
> 'This man can't bear our life here and will drown',
> The abbot said, 'unless we help him'. So
> They did, the freed ship sailed, and the man climbed back
> Out of the marvellous as he had known it.[3]

FROM 'THE PEACOCK'S TALE' TO THE 'TAJ MICHEÁL'

In retrospect, the completion of Galway cathedral in 1965 marked a climactic
point architecturally and ecclesiastically for the Catholic church in Ireland.
Michael Brown (1895–1980), the pharaonic bishop of Galway from 1937 until
1976, rejected the site previously chosen for the new cathedral as lacking
sufficient room for cars. In 1941, he acquired a new site around the old jail.
Construction began in 1958, using ashlar limestone rather than concrete, and
designed to seat 1,500 people in a cavernous building (91m x 48m wide, in total
4,366 square metres). President Kennedy, who had visited Galway in 1963,
featured in a kitschy mosaic high up in the mortuary chapel, flanked by one
dedicated to Patrick Pearse. The cathedral, widely considered to be grey and
gloomy, is bereft of landscaping and is marooned in its car park.[4] Galwegians
christened their expensive new cathedral (it eventually cost just under one
million pounds) the 'Taj Micheál' in an ironic nod to their domineering bishop.[5]

Contrast this cathedral with the earliest identified Irish church: the mid-
fifth to early sixth-century church at Caherlehillan (Co. Kerry), built of

---

3 S. Heaney, *Seeing things* (London, 1991), p. 62. Copyright estate of Seamus Heaney.
4 M. Browne, *Cathedral of Our Lady Assumed into Heaven and Saint Nicholas Galway*
(Galway, 1967). 5 Browne was popularly known as 'Cross Michael' (from his many
newspaper letters signed '+ Michael' and from his headstrong personality), and he refused
to listen to even sympathetic or well-informed criticism of 'his' cathedral. There were also
torrents of adversarial comment: I once heard a Galway professor describe the cathedral as
'a heap of compressed fog'.

posts, wattle and sods. Its external measurement is 3.8m x 2m (7.6 square metres).[6] Five-hundred-and-seventy-four Caherlehillans would fit into Galway cathedral.

6 J. Sheehan, 'A peacock's tale: excavations at Caherlehillan, Iveragh, Ireland' in N. Edwards (ed.), *The archaeology of the early medieval Celtic churches* (Leeds, 2009), pp 191–206.

APPENDIX

Fifty National Maps of Religion

1 Early medieval churches by Matthew Stout [*Atlas of Irish rural landscape*, p. 51].
2 Early churches pre-AD 600 by Matthew Stout [*Early medieval Ireland*, p. 25].
3 Recorded Ferta sites by Elizabeth O'Brien ['Burial among the ancestors to burial among the saints', p. 265].
4 Early Irish hand bells by Cormac Bourke [Corlett & Potterton (eds), *Church in medieval Ireland*, p. 268].
5 High crosses by Peter Harbison [Harbison, *High crosses of Ireland*].
6 Round towers by Brian Lalor [Lalor, *Irish round tower*].
7 Pre-Romanesque and early Romanesque stone church types, 900–1130 by Tomás Ó Carragáin [Ó Carragáin, *Churches in early medieval Ireland*, opposite p. 1].
8 Date ranges for pre-Romanesque mortared churches by Tomás Ó Carragáin [Ó Carragáin, *Churches in early medieval Ireland*, p. 119].
9 Civil parishes in Ireland, 1850 by W.J. Smyth [Smyth, *Mapmaking, landscapes and memory*, p. 366].
10 Cantreds and trícha céts of Ireland 1200 [a proxy for rural deaneries] by Paul MacCotter [MacCotter, *Medieval Ireland*, pp 258–61].
11 Irish medieval figure sculpture by John Bradley [Rynne (ed.), *Figures from the past*, p. 263].
12 Grange townlands by Geraldine Stout [*Atlas of rural Ireland*, p. 55].
13 Spread of religious orders to 1169 by Matthew Stout [Stout, *Early medieval Ireland*, p. 246].
14 Medieval nunneries by Tracy Collins [Lyttleton & Stout (eds), *Church and settlement in Ireland*, p. 147].
15 Spread of religious orders, 1169–1320 by F.X. Martin [NHI, ix, pp 30–1].
16 Spread of religious orders, 1320–1420 by F.X. Martin [NHI, ix, p. 32].
17 Ecclesiastical valuations for Great Britain and Ireland, early fourteenth century, by Bruce Campbell [Cunliffe (ed.), *Penguin atlas of British and Irish history*, p. 101].
18 Spread of religious orders, 1420–1530 by F.X. Martin [NHI, ix, p. 32].
19 Madonna and Child representations pre-1600 by John Bradley [Rynne (ed.), *Figures from the past*, p. 261].
20 Dissolution of the religious houses, 1534–1610 by Brendan Bradshaw [NHI, ix, p. 33].
21 Age of the Reformation in Great Britain and Ireland by John Morrill [Cunliffe (ed.), *Penguin atlas of British and Irish history*, p. 115].
22 Irish Colleges abroad, 1590–1800 by John Silke [NHI, ix, p. 48].
23 Wayside and churchyard crosses, 1600–1700 by Heather King [King, 'Irish wayside and churchyard crosses, 1600–1700'].
24 Sheela-na-gigs [Freitag, *Sheela-na-gigs*, p. 6].
25 Holy wells by Ronan Foley [Foley, *Healing waters*, p. 22].

26 Coarbs and erenaghs by Katharine Simms [Simms, 'Frontiers in the Irish church']. [This volume, p. 33].
27 Spread of dissenting congregations in Ireland by Alan Gailey [Gailey, 'The Scots element in North Irish popular culture']. [This volume, p. 128].
28 Continental-trained priests in Ireland in 1704 by Kevin Whelan [Smyth & Whelan (eds), *Common ground*, p. 256].
29 Conditions for Mass attendance in Ireland, 1731 by W.J. Smyth [Smyth, *Mapmaking, landscapes and memory*, p. 372].
30 Protestant population by barony, 1732 by W.J. Smyth [Smyth, *Mapmaking, landscapes and memory*, p. 409].
31 Masonic lodges, 1798 by Kevin Whelan [Whelan, *Fellowship of freedom*, p. 38].
32 Birthplace of Christian Brothers, 1800–21 by Dáire Keogh [Keogh, *Edmund Rice*, p. 98].
33 Spread of Christian Brothers, 1802–30 by Dáire Keogh [Keogh, *Edmund Rice*, p. 148].
34 Catholic rent by county, 1824–5 by Fergus O'Ferrall [O'Ferrall, *Catholic Emancipation*, p. 67].
35 O'Connellite local organization, 1825–30 by Fergus O'Ferrall [O'Ferrall, *Catholic Emancipation*, p. 67].
36 O'Connell Annuity, 1832–4 by Kevin Whelan [Smyth & Whelan (eds), *Common ground*, p. 265].
37 Irish Society Operations [Bible teachers], 1818–27 by Pádraig de Brún [De Brún, *Scriptural instruction in the vernacular*, p. 86]. [This volume, p. 172].
38 D. Miller, 'Mass attendance in Ireland in 1834' [Brown & Miller (eds), *Piety and power*, pp 158–79].
39 Ratio of Catholic priests to people by diocese, 1800 and 1840, by Emmet Larkin [Larkin, *Pastoral role of Roman Catholic church*, pp 15–16].
40 O'Connell's monster meetings, 1843 by Kevin Whelan [Whelan, *Fellowship of freedom*, p. 122]. [This volume, p. 177].
41 Catholic parishes and chapel villages by Kevin Whelan [*Atlas of rural Ireland*, p. 275].
42 Medieval parish boundaries lost in creation of modern Catholic parish network by W.J. Smyth [Smyth, *Mapmaking, landscapes and memory*, p. 369]; Continuities and losses in the distribution of modern Catholic parish boundaries as compared with the medieval parish network by W.J. Smyth [Barry (ed.), *Settlement in Ireland*, p. 175].
43 Convents in Ireland, 1850 by Catríona Clear [Clear, *Nuns in nineteenth-century Ireland*, p. 38].
44 Percentage by county of nuns recruited for four congregations, 1845–1926 by Barbara Walsh [*History Ireland*, 11:4 (2003), p. 25].
45 Orange Halls in 1910 by Estyn Evans ['The personality of Ulster', p. 16].
46 Presbyterian and Methodist churches, 1910 by Kevin Whelan [*Atlas of Irish rural landscape*, p. 240].
47 Catholics and Protestants in Ulster, 1911 by K.M. Davies [NHI, ix, p. 81].
48 Condemnation by Catholic priests of IRA violence, 1919–21 by Brian Heffernan [Crowley et al. (eds), *Atlas of Irish Revolution*, p. 499].
49 Religion by all denominations, 1971 [Haughton (ed.), *Atlas of Ireland*, p. 86].
50 Nine maps of folk traditions by Caoimhín Ó Danachair [Haughton (ed.), *Atlas of Ireland*, p. 90].

Bibliography

H. von Achen, 'Fighting the disenchantment of the world: the instrument of medieval revivalism in nineteenth-century art and architecture' in H. Laugerud & S. Ryan (eds), *Devotional cultures of European Christianity, 1790–1860* (Dublin, 2012), pp 131–54.

A. Shafto Adair, *The winter of 1846–7 in Antrim with remarks on outdoor relief and colonization* (London, 1847).

K. Andersen, 'Irish secularization and religious identities: evidence of an emerging new Catholic habitus', *Social Compass*, 57:1 (2010), pp 15–39.

C. Armstrong, 'Processional cross, pricket candlestick and bell, found together at Sheephouse, near Oldbridge, Co. Meath', *JRSAI*, 95 (1915), pp 2–31.

[R. Bairéad], *Riocard Bairéad amhráin*, eag. N. Williams (Baile Átha Cliath, 1978).

J. Bardon, 'Belfast at its zenith', *History Ireland*, 1 (1993), pp 48–51.

C. Barr & H. Carey (eds), *Religion and greater Ireland: Christianity and Irish global networks, 1750–1969* (Montreal, 2015).

— & R. Luminiella, 'The leader of the virgin choirs of Erin': St Brigid's Missionary College 1883–1914' in T. MacMahon, M. De Nie & P. Townend (eds), *Ireland in an imperial world: citizenship, opportunism and subversion* (London, 2017), pp 155–78.

P. Barry, 'The journals of Samuel Molyneux in Ireland, 1708–1709', *Anal. Hib.*, 46 (2015), pp 1–84.

T. Barry, 'The Pope Nicholas IV taxation of the early fourteenth century and Irish medieval rural settlement archaeology: a case study', *L'urbanisme: mélanges d'archéologie médiévale* (2006), pp 8–15.

— (ed.), *A history of settlement in Ireland* (London, 2000).

R. Bartlett, *Why can the dead do such great things?: saints and worshippers from the martyrs to the Reformation* (Princeton, 2013).

F. Bateman, 'Ireland's spiritual empire: territory and landscape in Irish Catholic missionary discourse' in H. Carey (ed.), *Empires of religion* (London, 2008), pp 267–87.

D.A. Beaufort, *A new map of Ireland civil and ecclesiastical* (London, 1792).

G. De Beaumont, *Ireland: social, political, and religious*, ed. T. Garvin & A. Hess (Boston, [1839–42] 2006).

J.C. Beckett & R. Glasscock (eds), *Belfast: the origins and growth of an industrial city* (Belfast, 1967).

R. Bell, *A description of the condition and manners of the peasantry of Ireland* (London, 1804).

A. Ben-Amos, *Funerals, politics and memory in modern France, 1789–1996* (Oxford, 2000).

[G. Beranger], *Memoir of Gabriel Beranger and his labours in the cause of Irish art and antiquities from 1760 to 1780*, ed. W. Wilde (Dublin, 1880).

H. Bhabha, *The location of culture* (London, 1993).

E. Bhreathnach, 'The mendicant orders and vernacular Irish learning in the late medieval period', *IHS*, 37:147 (2011), pp 357–75.

—, J. MacMahon & J. McCafferty (eds), *The Irish Franciscans, 1534–1990* (Dublin, 2009).

W. Bingley, *An examination into the origin and continuance of the discontents in Ireland* (London, 1799).

G. Binions, *Old Blackstairs families* (Killann [Co. Wexford], 2016).

H. Bishop, 'Spatial distribution and location of Catholic Mass rock sites in the diocese of Cork and Ross, Co. Cork, Ireland', *Geographies of Religions & Belief Systems*, 4:1 (2014), pp 40–78.

—, 'Memory and legend: recollections of penal times in Irish folklore', *Folklore*, 129:1 (2018), pp 18–38.

S. Booker, *Cultural exchange and identity in late medieval Ireland: the English and Irish of the four obedient shires* (Cambridge, 2018).

E. Boran, 'Persecution and deliverance in sixteenth-century Kilkenny: the *Vocacyon of Johan Bale* 1553', *Old Kilkenny Review*, 69 (2017), pp 71–92.

A. Partridge [Bourke], *Caoineadh na dtrí Muire: teáma na paise i bhfilíocht bhéil na Gaeilge* (Baile Átha Cliath, 1983).

A. Bourke, 'The Irish traditional lament and the grieving process', *Women Studies International Forum*, 11 (1988), pp 287–91.

—, 'Caoineadh na marbh', *Oghma*, 4 (1992), pp 3–11.

—, 'The virtual reality of Irish fairy legend', *Éire-Ireland*, 31:1–2 (1996), pp 7–25.

—, *The burning of Bridget Cleary: a true story* (London, 1999).

—, et al. (eds), *The Field Day anthology of Irish writing, volume IV: Irish women's writing and traditions* (Cork, 2002).

—, *Voices underfoot: memory, forgetting and verbal art* (Hamden, CT, 2016).

E. Bourke, *'Poor green Erin': German travel writers' narratives on Ireland* (Frankfurt, 2011).

J. Bradley, 'The Ballyhale Madonna and its iconography' in E. Rynne (ed.), *Figures from the past: studies on figurative art in Christian Ireland in honour of Helen M. Roe* (Dublin, 1979), pp 258–77.

N. Brady, 'Mills in medieval Ireland: looking beyond design' in S. Walton (ed.), *Wind and water in the Middle Ages: fluid technologies from antiquity to the Renaissance* (Tempe, AR, 2006), pp 39–68.

W. Brady (ed.), *State Papers concerning the Irish church in the time of Queen Elizabeth* (London, 1868).

G. Branigan, *Ancient and holy wells of Dublin* (Dublin, 2012).

N. Brannon, 'A lost seventeenth-century house recovered: Dungiven, Co. Londonderry' in A. Hamlin & C. Lynn (eds), *Pieces of the past: archaeological excavations, 1970–1986* (Belfast, 1988), pp 81–4.

L. Breatnach, 'Canon law and secular law in early Ireland: the significance of *Bretha nemed*', *Peritia*, 3 (1984), pp 439–59.

M. Breen & C. Reynolds, 'The rise of secularism and the decline of religiosity in Ireland: the pattern of religious change in Europe', *International Journal of Religion and Spirituality in Society*, 1 (2011), pp 195–212.

W. Brenneman & M. Brenneman, *Crossing the circle at the holy wells of Ireland* (Charlottesville, 1994).

[W. Brereton], *Travels in Holland, the United Provinces, England, Scotland and Ireland, 1634–1635*, ed. E. Hawkins (Manchester, 1844).

C. Brett, *Roger Mulholland: architect of Belfast* (Belfast, 1976).

M. Bric, 'The tithe system in eighteenth-century Ireland', *PRIA*, 86, C (1986), pp 271–88.

M. Bridge, 'Locating the origins of wood resources: a review of dendroprovenancing', *Journal of Archaeological Science*, 39:8 (2012), pp 28–34.

M. Briody, *The Irish Folklore Commission, 1935–1970: history, ideology, methodology* (Helsinki, 2007).

E. Broderick, *Patterns and patrons: the holy wells of Waterford* (Waterford, 2015).

S. Brown, 'The New Reformation movement in the Church of Ireland, 1801–1829' in S. Brown & D. Miller (eds), *Piety and power in Ireland, 1760–1960: essays in honour of Emmet Larkin* (Belfast, 2000), pp 180–208.

—, *The national churches of England, Ireland and Scotland, 1801–1846* (Oxford, 2001).

A. Browne, *A compendious view of the ecclesiastical law of Ireland, second edition with great additions* (Dublin, 1803).

P. Browne, *Through the eye of a needle: wealth, the fall of Rome and the making of Christianity in the West, 350–550 AD* (Princeton, 2012).

F.D. Brullaughan, *Opusculum de missione et missionariis tractans* (Metz, 1747).

P. De Brún, *Scriptural instruction in the vernacular: the Irish Society and its teachers, 1818–1827* (Dublin, 2009).

E. Brynn, *The Church of Ireland in the age of Catholic Emancipation* (New York, 1982).

T. Burke, *Hibernia Dominicana: sive historia Provinciæ Hiberniæ Ordinis Prædicatorum, ex antiquis manuscriptis, probatis auctoribus, literis originalibus* (Cologne [Kilkenny], 1762).

J. Burtchaell, 'The south Kilkenny farm villages' in Smyth & Whelan (eds), *Common ground*, pp 110–23.

D. Butler, *The Quaker meeting houses of Ireland* (Dublin, 2004).

I. Butler, A journey to Lough Derg [1745] [CELT].

P. Butler & M. Davies, *Wicklow through the artist's eye: an exploration of County Wicklow's historic gardens, c.1660–c.1960* (Bray, 2014).

M. Byrne, *Waterford 1470: Dean John Collyn and the chantry chapel of St Saviour* (Drogheda, 2013).

N. Mandeville Caciola, *Afterlives: the return of the dead in the Middle Ages* (Ithaca, NY, 2016).

[Giraldus Cambrensis], *The history and topography of Ireland*, ed. & trans. J. O'Meara (London, 1982).

B. Campbell, 'Benchmarking medieval economic development: England, Wales, Scotland, and Ireland c.1290', *Economic History Review*, 61:4 (2008), pp 896–945.

H. Campbell, 'Religion and the city: the Catholic church in Dublin, 1691–1878', *Urban Design Studies*, 3 (1997), pp 1–24.

J. Graham-Campbell (ed.), *The archaeology of medieval Europe, i, eighth to twelfth centuries AD* (Aarhus, 2009).

[T. Campbell], *A philosophical survey of the south of Ireland* (London, 1777).

J. Carey, 'Aerial ships and underwater monasteries: the evolution of a monastic marvel', *Harvard Celtic Colloquium*, 12 (1992), pp 16–28.

W. Carrigan, *The history and antiquities of the diocese of Ossory*, 4 vols (Dublin, 1905).

C. Carroll, *Exiles in a global city: the Irish and early modern Rome, 1609–1783* (Leiden, 2018).

J. Carroll, 'The excavation of the old Presbyterian meeting house at Ramelton, Co. Donegal', *Archaeology Ireland*, 3:2 (1989), pp 61–3.

M. Carroll, *Irish pilgrimage: holy wells and popular Catholic devotion* (Baltimore, 1999).

J. Carson, *God's river in spate: the story of the religious awakening of Ulster in 1859* (Belfast, 1958).

P.J. Carty, 'The historical geography of County Roscommon' (MA, University College Dublin, 1970).

M. Carver & J. Klapste (eds), *The archaeology of medieval Europe, ii, twelfth to sixteenth centuries* (Aarhus, 2011).

C. Casey, *Dublin* (London, 2005).

C. Casey & A. Rowan, *North Leinster* (London, 1993).

M. Casey, 'Cornerstone of memory: John Hughes and St Patrick's Cathedral', *American Journal of Irish Studies*, 12 (2015), pp 10–56.

R. Cashman, *Storytelling on the Northern Irish border: characters and community* (Bloomington, 2011).

J. Castle & G. O'Brien, 'I am building a house: Nano Nagles's Georgian convents', *Irish Architectual and Decorative Studies*, 19 (2016), pp 54–75.

[Castlereagh], *Memoirs and correspondence of Viscount Castlereagh*, 4 vols, ed. C. Vane (London, 1849).

J. Channing, 'Ballykilmore, Co. Westmeath: continuity of an early medieval graveyard' in Corlett & Potterton (eds), *Church in early medieval Ireland*, pp 23–38.

A. Cherryson, Z. Crossland & S. Tarlow, *A fine and private space: the archaeology of death and burial in post-medieval Britain and Ireland* (Leicester, 2012).

E. Mhic Choisdealbha, *Amhráin Mhuighe Séola: traditional songs from Galway and Mayo* (Dublin, 1918).

W. Christian, *The stranger, the tears, the photograph, the touch: divine presence in Spain and Europe since 1500*, second edition (Budapest, 2017).

A. Clarke, *Twice around the Black Church: early memories of Ireland and England* (Dublin, 1990).

H. Clarke, 'Quo vadis? Mapping the Irish "monastic town"' in S. Duffy (ed.), *Princes, prelates and poets in medieval Ireland: essays in honour of Katharine Simms* (Dublin, 2013), pp 261–78.

—, R. Johnston & S. Dooley, *Dublin and the Viking world* (Dublin, 2018), pp 103–12.

—, J. Prunty & M. Hennessy (eds), *Surveying Ireland's past: multidisciplinary essays in honour of Anngret Simms* (Dublin, 2004).

C. Clear, *Nuns in nineteenth-century Ireland* (Dublin, 1987).

J. Cleary, 'The Catholic twilight?' in E. Maher & E. O'Brien (eds), *Tracing the cultural legacy of Irish Catholicism: from Galway to Cloyne and beyond* (Manchester, 2017), pp 209–25.

B. Clesham, 'A voyage to the kingdom of the Joyces in 1756', *Journal of the South Mayo Family Research Society*, 7 (1994), pp 2–5.

B. Colfer, *The Hook peninsula, Co. Wexford* (Cork, 2004).

J. Coll, 'Continuity and change in the parish of Gaoth Dobhair, 1850–1980' in Smyth & Whelan (eds), *Common ground*, pp 278–95.

B. Collins & A. Hepburn, 'Industrial society: the structure of Belfast 1901' in P. Roebuck (ed.), *Plantation to partition* (Belfast, 1981), pp 210–28.

T. Collins, 'Timolin: a case study of a nunnery estate in later medieval Ireland', *Anuario de Estudios Medievales*, 44:1 (2014), pp 51–80.

—, 'An archaeological perspective on female monasticism in the Middle Ages in Ireland' in J. Burton & K. Stöber (eds), *Women in the medieval monastic world* (Turnhout, 2015), pp 229–51.

—, 'Isolated in the wilderness?: an archaeological exploration of nunneries in the medieval landscape of Ireland' in Lyttleton & Stout (eds), *Church and settlement*, pp 142–56.

Comhairle Mhic Clamha ó Áchadh na Muileann: the advice of Mac Clave from Aughnamullen, S. Ó Dufaigh & B. Rainey ed. & trans. (Lille, 1981).

K. Condon, *The Missionary College of All Hallows, 1842–1891* (Dublin, 1986).

C. Connell, *Glasnevin cemetery Dublin, 1832–1900* (Dublin, 2004).

P. Connell, *Irish roadside memorials* (Dublin, 2012).

J. Connery, *The reformer* (London, 1836).

S. Connolly & A. Moroney, *Stone and tree sheltering water: an exploration of sacred and secular wells in Co. Louth* (Drogheda, 1998).

T. Coomans, *Life inside the cloister: understanding monastic architecture: tradition, reformation, adaptive reuse* (Leuven, 2018).

D. Cooney, *The Methodists in Ireland: a short history* (Blackrock, 2001).

[A. Cooper], *An eighteenth-century antiquary: the sketches, notes and diaries of Austin Cooper (1759–1830)* ed. L. Price (Dublin, 1942).

A. Corbin, *Village bells: sound and meaning in the nineteenth-century French countryside* (New York, 1998).

M. ac Cordhuibh, 'Ros Dumhach Erris [Kilcummin (Co. Mayo)]: leachtaí cloch', *Bealoideas*, 16 (1946), pp 64–71.

P.J. Corish (ed.), *A history of Irish Catholicism*, 6 vols (Dublin, 1968).

—, 'An Irish Counter-Reformation bishop: John Roche', *Irish Theological Quarterly*, 25 (1958), pp 14–32, 101–23; 26 (1959), pp 105–16, 313–30.

C. Corlett, 'Cursing stones in Ireland', *JGAHS*, 64 (2012), pp 1–20.

—, *Here lyeth: the eighteenth-century headstones of Co. Wicklow* (Wicklow, 2015).

C. Corlett & M. Potterton (eds), *Settlement in early medieval Ireland in the light of recent archaeological excavations* (Bray, 2011).

—, *The church in early medieval Ireland in the light of recent archaeological excavations* (Bray, 2014).

D. Corry, 'Ancient church sites and graveyards in County Fermanagh', *JRSAI*, 9 (1919), pp 35–46.

E. Costello, 'Medieval memories and the reformation of religious identity: Catholic and Anglican interactions with parish church sites in County Limerick, Ireland', *Post-Medieval Archaeology*, 51:2 (2017), pp 332–53.

V. Costello, *Irish demesne landscapes, 1660–1740* (Dublin, 2015).

M. Craig, *The architecture of Ireland from the earliest times to 1880* (London, 1982).

T. Crofton Croker, *Researches in the south of Ireland* (London, 1824).

—, *The keen of the south of Ireland* (London, 1844).

A. Crookshank & Knight of Glin, *Ireland's painters, 1600–1940* (New Haven, 2002).

F. De Cuellar, 'Carta de uno que fué en la Armada de Yngaleterra y cuenta la jornada' in P. Gallagher & D.W. Cruickshank (eds), *God's obvious design: papers from the Spanish Armada symposium, Sligo* (London, 1990), pp 201–21.

L.M. Cullen, *The emergence of modern Ireland, 1600–1900* (London, 1981).

E. Culleton, *On our own ground: Co. Wexford parish by parish, volume 1* (Wexford, 2013).

[Cummian], *Cummian's letter* De controversia Paschali *together with a related computistical text* De rationae computanti, ed. & trans. M. Walsh & D. Ó Cróinín (Toronto, 1988).

B. Cunliffe et al. (eds), *The Penguin atlas of British and Irish history* (London, 2002).

B. Cunningham, *The Annals of the Four Masters: Irish history, kingship and society in the early seventeenth century* (Dublin, 2010).

N. Cunningham & I. Gregory, 'Religious change in twentieth-century Ireland: a spatial history', *Irish Geography*, 45:3 (2012), pp 209–33.

J.S. Curl, *Classical churches in Ulster* (Belfast, 1980).

—, *Death and architecture* (Stroud, 2002).

J. Curtin, *Tales of the fairies and of the ghost world collected from oral tradition in south-west Munster* (Boston, 1895).

W. Curtis, *An Irish summer* (New York 1909).

A. Dallas, *A mission tour-book in Ireland: showing how to visit the missions in Dublin, Connemara, etc.* (London, 1860).

G. Daniel, *Transforming post-Catholic Ireland: religious practice in late modernity* (Oxford, 2016).

G. Darley, 'The Moravians: building for a higher purpose', *Architectural Review*, 177 (1998), pp 45–9.

J. Davies, *A discovery of the true causes why Ireland was never entirely subdued* (London [1612], 1786).

S. Deane, 'Dead ends: Joyce's finest moments' in D. Attridge & M. Howes (eds), *Semicolonial Joyce* (Cambridge, 2000), pp 21–36.

C. Delay, 'Confidantes or competitors: women, priests and conflict in post-Famine Ireland', *Éire-Ireland*, 40:1–2 (2005), pp 107–25.

E. Dennehy, 'Children's burial grounds', *Archaeology Ireland*, 15:1 (2001), pp 20–3.

—, 'Dorchada gan phian: the history of ceallúnach in Co. Kerry', *Kerry Archaeological and Historical Society Journal*, 2 (2003), pp 5–21.

Description of Ireland and the state thereof as it is at this present in anno 1598, ed. E. Hogan (Dublin, 1878).

Diary of Viscount Percival afterwards First Earl of Egmont, volume 1, 1730–1733 (London, 1920).

D. Dickson, 'Jacobitism in eighteenth-century Ireland: a Munster perspective', *Éire-Ireland*, 39:3–4 (2004), pp 38–99.

—, *Old world colony: Cork and south Munster 1630–1830* (Cork, 2005).

—, 'Seven sisters?: the seaport cities of mid-eighteenth century Ireland' in T. Truxes (ed.), *Ireland, France and the Atlantic in a time of war* (Abington, 2017), pp 93–107.

P.S. Dineen & T. O'Donoghue (eds), *Dánta Aodhagáin Uí Rathaille / The poems of Egan O Rahilly*, second edition revised & enlarged by B. Ó Buachalla (London, 2004).

'Discourse on the mere Irish of Ireland', 1608 [CELT].

G. Doherty, *The Irish Ordnance Survey: history, culture and memory* (Dublin, 2006).

A. Dolan, 'The large medieval churches of the dioceses of Leighlin, Ferns and Ossory: a study of adaptation and change', *Irish Architectural and Decorative Studies*, 2 (1999), pp 26–65.

C. Donnelly, P. Logue & J. O'Neill, 'Timber castles and towers in sixteenth-century Ireland: some evidence from Ulster', *Archaeology Ireland*, 21: 2 (2007), pp 22–5.

C. Donnelly & E. Murphy, 'The origins of cillíní in Ireland' in E. Murphy (ed.), *Deviant burial in the archaeological record* (Oxford, 2008), pp 191–222.

C. Downham, *Medieval Ireland* (Cambridge, 2017).

The Dublin Cemeteries Act, 1846 and bye-laws for the management and maintenance of the cemeteries at Golden Bridge, and Prospect, Glasnevin in the city and county of Dublin (Dublin, 1901).

E. Duffy, *The stripping of the altars: traditional religion in England, 1400–1580* (New Haven, 1992).

—, *Reformation divided: Catholics, Protestants and the conversion of England* (London, 2017).

P. Duffy, *Landscapes of south Ulster: a parish atlas of the diocese of Clogher* (Belfast, 1993).

— & W. Nolan (eds), *At the anvil: essays in honour of William J. Smyth* (Dublin, 2012).

P.J. Dunning, 'The Arrouasian Order in medieval Ireland', *IHS*, 4 (1944–5), pp 297–315.

P. Dwyer, *The diocese of Killaloe from the Reformation to the close of the eighteenth century* (Dublin, 1878).

D. Edwards, 'Lordship and custom in Gaelic Leinster: select documents from Upper Ossory, 1559–1612', *Ossory, Laois & Leinster*, 4 (2010), pp 1–47.

R.D. Edwards, *Church and state in Tudor Ireland: a history of penal laws against Irish Catholics, 1534–1603* (London, 1935).

T. Charles-Edwards, *Early Christian Ireland* (Cambridge, 2000).

— & F. Kelly (eds), *Bechbretha: an old Irish law-tract on bee-keeping* (Dublin, 1983).

M. Egeler, *Islands in the West: classical myth and the medieval Norse and Irish geographical imagination* (Turnhout, 2017).

[Egerton], *The Egerton papers: a collection of public and private documents, chiefly illustrative of the times of Elizabeth and James I, from the original manuscripts*, ed. J. Collier (London, 1840).

C. Eire, *Reformations: the early modern world, 1450–1650* (New Haven, 2016).

R. Eliott, *Art and Ireland* (Dublin, 1906).

T. Ellis, *God and the nation: a sermon preached to the Orangemen of the district of Portadown* (Armagh, 1885).

M. Empey, ' "We are not yet safe, for they threaten us with more violence": a study of the Cook Street riot 1629' in W. Sheehan & M. Cronin (eds), *Riotous assemblies: rebels, riots and revolts in Ireland* (Cork, 2011), pp 64–79.

E. Estyn Evans, 'The personality of Ulster', *Transactions of the Institute of British Geographers*, 51 (1970), pp 1–20.

T. Fanning, 'Excavation of an early Christian cemetery and settlement at Reask, Co. Kerry', *PRIA*, 81, C (1981), pp 67–172.

G. Farrell, *The 'mere' Irish and the colonisation of Ulster, 1570–1641* (London, 2017).

C. Fatovic, 'The anti-Catholic roots of liberal and Republican conceptions of freedom in English political thought', *Journal of the History of Ideas*, 66:1 (2005), pp 37–58.

H. Fenning, *The undoing of the friars of Ireland: a study of the novitiate question in the eighteenth century* (Louvain, 1972).

—, *Irish Dominican province, 1698–1797* (Dublin, 1990).

—, *The Black Abbey: the Kilkenny Dominicans, 1225–1996* (Kilkenny, 1996).

S. Fenton, *It all happened: reminiscences of Séamus Fenton* (Dublin, 1948).

S. Ferguson, *Brief biographical sketches of some Irish Covenanting ministers* (Londonderry, 1897).

J. Ferrar, *The prosperity of Ireland displayed in the state of 54 Charity Schools in Dublin* (Dublin, 1796).

P. Ferritéar, 'Bean chaointe a cosaint féin', *Éigse*, 3 (1939), p. 222.

T. Finan, 'The medieval bishops of Roscommon and the lost church of Kilteasheen' in Duffy (ed.), *Princes, prelates, poets*, pp 352–61.

N. Finlay, 'Outside of life: traditions of infant burial in Ireland from cillíní to cist', *World Archaeology*, 31:3 (2000), pp 407–22.

E. Mark-Fitzgerald, *Commemorating the Irish Famine: memory and the monument* (Liverpool, 2013).

E. FitzPatrick & C. O'Brien, *The medieval churches of Co. Offaly* (Dublin, 1998).

W.J. Fitzpatrick, *History of the Dublin Catholic cemeteries* (Dublin, 1900).

D. Flanagan, 'Ecclesiastical nomenclature in Irish texts and placenames: a comparison', *Proceedings of the tenth International Congress of Onomastic Science* (1969), pp 355–88.

M.-T. Flanagan, *The transformation of the Irish church in the twelfth century* (Woodbridge, 2013).

R. Foley, *Healing waters: therapeutic landscapes in historic and contemporary Ireland* (Farnham, 2010).

W. Follett, 'Religious texts in the Mac Aodhagáin Library of Lower Ormond', *Peritia*, 24–5 (2013–14), pp 213–29.

A. Ford, 'Martyrdom, history and memory in early modern Ireland' in I. McBride (ed.), *History and memory in modern Ireland* (Cambridge, 2001), pp 43–66.

A. Forrestal, *Catholic synods in Ireland, 1600–1690* (Dublin, 1998).

C. Fox, 'Swift's Scotophobia', *Bullán*, 6 (2002), pp 43–65.

B. Freitag, *Sheela-na-gigs: unravelling an enigma* (London, 2004).

J.F. Fuller, *Omniana: the autobiography of an Irish octagenarian*, second edition (London, 1920).

A. Gailey, 'The Scots element in North Irish popular culture', *Ethnologica Europeae*, 11:1 (1975), pp 2–22.

J. Gamble, *Sketches of history, politics and manners taken in Dublin and the north of Ireland in the autumn of 1810* (London, 1811).

—, *Views of society and manners in the north of Ireland* (London, 1819).

M. Geaney, 'Timber bridges in medieval Ireland', *Journal of Irish Archaeology*, 25 (2016), pp 89–104.

G. Gelléri, 'An unknown "creator" of picturesque Ireland: the Irish sketches and notes of Luttrell Wynne', *Irish Architectural and Decorative Studies*, 18 (2016), pp 44–65.

N. Nic Ghabhann, *Medieval ecclesiastical buildings in Ireland, 1789–1915* (Dublin, 2015).

S. Ní Ghabhláin, 'Church and community in medieval Ireland: the diocese of Kilfenora', *JRSAI*, 125 (1995), pp 61–84.

—, 'The origin of medieval parishes in Gaelic Ireland: the evidence from Kilfenora', *JRSAI*, 126 (1996), pp 37–61.

S. Gibbons, *Captain Rock, night errant: the threatening letters of pre-Famine Ireland, 1801–1845* (Dublin, 2004).

D. Gimster & R. Gilchrist (eds), *The archaeology of Reformation, 1480–1580* (London, 2003).

J. Glassford, *Notes of three tours in Ireland in 1824 and 1826* (Bristol, 1832).

H. Glassie, 'Tradition', *Journal of American Folklore*, 108:430 (1995), pp 395–412.

—, *Passing the time in Ballymenone*, second edition (Bloomington, 1995).

J. Gough, *A tour in Ireland in 1813 and 1814* (Dublin, 1817).

[La Boullaye le Gouz], *Les voyages et observations du sieur de La Boullaye Le Gouz* (Paris, 1653).

M. Grant, *Sketches of life and manners with delineation of scenery in England, Scotland and Ireland* (London, 1804).

M. Greengrass, *Christendom destroyed: Europe, 1517–1648* (London, 2014).

I. Gregory et al. (eds), *Troubled geographies: a spatial history of religion and society in Ireland* (Bloomington, 2013).

D. Griffiths, *Vikings of the Irish Sea: conflict and assimilation, AD 790–1050* (London, 2010).

B. Grimes, *Majestic shrines and graceful sanctuaries: the church architecture of Patrick Byrne, 1783–1864* (Dublin, 2010).

W. Grimshaw, *Incidents recalled or sketches from memory of the cotton manufacture in Ireland, the Irish Volunteers, the rebellion of 1798 & the Irish parliament* (Philadelphia, 1848).

E. Grogan, 'Eighteenth-century headstones and the stone mason tradition in Co. Wicklow: the work of Dennis Cullen of Monaseed', *Wicklow Archaeology and History*, 1 (1998), pp 41–63.

I. Grubb, *The Quakers in Ireland* (London, 1927).

J. Guldi, 'Landscape and place' in S. Gunn & L. Faire (eds), *Research methods for history* (Edinburgh, 2012), pp 66–80.

C. Haigh, *English Reformations: religion, politics and society under the Tudors* (Oxford, 1993).

D. Hall, *Women and the church in medieval Ireland, c.1140–1540* (Dublin, 2003).

S.C. & A.M. Hall, *Ireland: its scenery and character*, 2 vols (London, 1843).

J. Hamill, *The Herdman family and Sion Mills* (Belfast, 2017).

T. Hamling & C. Richardson, *A day at home in early modern England: material culture and domestic life, 1500–1700* (New Haven, 2017).

G. Hand, 'The dating of the early fourteenth-century ecclesiastical valuations of Ireland', *Irish Theological Quarterly*, 24:3 (1957), pp 271–4.

P. Happe & J. King (eds), *The vocacyon of Johan Bale* (New York [1593], 1990).

P. Harbison, *The high crosses of Ireland: an iconographical and photographic survey*, 3 vols (Bonn, 1991).

—, *Pilgrimage in Ireland: the monuments and the people* (London, 1991).

—, *William Burton Conyngham and his Irish circle of antiquarian artists* (New Haven, 2012).

—, *Henry O'Neill of the 'Celtic Cross': Irish antiquarian artist and patriot* (Bray, 2014).

M. Haren, 'Social structures of the Irish church: a new source in papal penitentiary dispensations for illegitimacy' in L. Schmugge (ed.), *Illegitimitat im spatmittelalter* (Munich, 1994), pp 207–26.

R. Pogue Harrison, *The dominion of the dead* (Chicago, 2003).

H. Hartman, *Der totenkult in Irland: ein beitrag zur religion der Indogermanen* (Heidelberg, 1952).

[J. Hartry], *Triumphalia chronologica monasterii Sanctae Crucis in Hibernia de Cisterciensium Hibernorum viris illustribus*, ed. D. Murphy (Dublin, 1891).

G. Haskins, *Ireland* (Boston, 1856).

J. Haughton (ed.), *Atlas of Ireland* (Dublin, 1979).

A. Hayden, 'Early medieval shrines in north-west Iveragh: new perspectives from Church Island, near Valentia, Co. Kerry', *PRIA*, 113, C (2013), pp 67–138.

J. Healy, *History of the diocese of Meath*, 2 vols (Dublin, 1908).

P. Heelas & L. Woodhead, *The spiritual revolution: why religion is giving way to spirituality* (Oxford, 2005).

D. Hempton, *Religion and political culture in Britain and Ireland: from the Glorious Revolution to the decline of empire* (Cambridge, 1996).

—, *Methodism: empire of the spirit* (New Haven, 2005).

—, *The church in the long eighteenth century* (London, 2011).

— & M. Hill, 'Godliness and good citizenship: evangelical Protestantism and social control in Ulster, 1790–1850', *Saothar*, 13 (1988), pp 68–80.

— & M. Hill, *Evangelical Protestantism in Ulster society, 1740–1890* (London, 1992).

Henry's Upper Lough Erne in 1739, ed. C. King (Dublin, 1892).

E. Hogan, *Onamasticon Goedilicum: locorum et tribuum Hiberniae et Scotiae: an index with identifications to the names of places and tribes* (Dublin, 1910).

J. Holmes, 'The role of open-air preaching in the Belfast riots of 1857', *PRIA*, 102, C (2002), pp 47–66.

P. Holohan, 'Two controverted Cork parliamentary elections and a broadsheet poem in the Irish language', *JCHAS*, 113 (2008), pp 114–30.

K. Holton, *Valentine Lawless, Lord Cloncurry, 1771–1855* (Dublin, 2018).

H.F. Hore (ed.), 'An account of the barony of Forth, in the county of Wexford, written at the close of the seventeenth century', *Kilkenny and South-East of Ireland Archaeological Society Journal*, new series, 4:1 (1862), pp 53–84.

P.H. Hore, *History of the town and county of Wexford*, 6 vols (London, 1900–11).

A.A. Horner, 'Through the fractured lens of the Civil Survey: an appraisal of buildings across the mid-seventeenth century Dublin region' in Duffy & Nolan (eds), *At the anvil*, pp 215–40.

—, 'Reinventing the city: the changing fortunes of places of worship in inner city Dublin' in Clarke, Prunty & Hennessy (eds), *Surveying Ireland's past*, pp 665–89.

— & R. Loeber, 'Landscape in transition: descriptions of forfeited properties in Counties Meath, Louth and Cavan in 1700', *Anal. Hib.*, 42 (2011), pp 59–180.

—, 'Retrieving the landscapes of eighteenth-century Co. Kildare: the 1755–60 maps of John Rocque', *Archaeology Ireland*, 31:2 (2017), pp 19–23.

J.E. Howard, *The island of saints or Ireland in 1855* (London, 1855).

T. Jones Hughes, 'Landholding and settlement in the Cooley peninsula of Co. Louth', *Irish Geography*, 4:3 (1961), pp 149–74.

—, 'Town and baile in Irish placenames' in N. Stephens & R. Glasscock (eds), *Irish geographical studies* (Belfast, 1970), pp 244–58.

J. Hunt, 'Rory O'Tunney and the Ossory tomb sculptures', *JRSAI*, 80:1 (1950), pp 22–8.

R.J. Hunter, *Ulster transformed: essays on plantation and print culture, c.1590–1641* (Belfast, 2012).

L. Hurley, 'Death in the garden: Patrick Byrne's mortuary chapel at Goldenbridge Cemetery, Dublin', *Irish Architectural and Decorative Studies*, 19 (2017), pp 76–89.

J. Hussey, *The Quakers of Baltyboys, County Wicklow, Ireland, 1678–1800* (Dublin, 2017).

T. Hussey, *A pastoral letter to the Catholic clergy of the united dioceses* [sic] *of Waterford and Lismore* (Dublin, 1797).

R. Hylton, *Ireland's Huguenots and their refuge, 1662–1745* (Brighton, 2005).

V. Igoe, *Dublin burial grounds and graveyards* (Dublin, 2001).

N. Jackman, C. Moore & C. Rynne (eds), *The mill at Kilbegly* [Co. Roscommon] (Dublin, 2013).

A. Jackson, 'Unionist myths' in *Past and Present*, 136 (1992), pp 164–85.

R. Wyse Jackson, 'Lewis Prytherch's manuscript', *NMAJ*, 4 (1945), pp 143–51.

E. Jamroziak, *The Cistercian Order in medieval Europe, 1090–1500* (Abingdon, 2013).

H. Jefferies, 'Bishop George Montgomery's survey of the parishes of Derry diocese: a complete text from *c.*1609', *Seanchas Ard Mhacha*, 17:1 (1996–7), pp 44–76.

—, 'Erenaghs in pre-Plantation Ulster: an early seventeenth-century account', *Archiv. Hib.*, 53 (1999), pp 16–19.

—, 'Derry diocese on the eve of the plantations' in G. O'Brien (ed.), *Derry: history and society* (Dublin, 1999), pp 175–204.

—, 'Erenaghs and termonlands: another early seventeenth-century account', *Seanchas Ard Mhacha*, 19:1 (2002), pp 55–8.

—, 'Elizabeth's Reformation in the Irish Pale', *Journal of Ecclesiastical History*, 66:3 (2015), pp 524–42.

B. Jennings, 'Donatus Moneyus, de Provincia Hiberniae S. Francisci', *Anal. Hib.*, 6 (1934), pp 12–138.

— (ed.), *Wadding papers, 1614–38* (Dublin, 1953).

M. Johnson, *An archaeology of capitalism* (Oxford, 1996).

M. Johnson, ' "Vengeance is mine": saintly retribution in medieval Ireland' in S. Throop & P. Hyams (eds), *Vengeance in the Middle Ages: emotion, religion and feud* (Abingdon, 2016), pp 5–50.

[Jonas], *Jonas of Bobbio; life of Columbanus, life of John of Réomé, and life of Vedast*, ed. & trans. A. O'Hara & I. Wood (Liverpool, 2017).

B. Kaplan, 'Fictions of privacy: house chapels and the spatial accommodation of religious dissent in early modern Europe', *American Historical Review*, 107 (2002), pp 1031–64.

—, *Religious conflict and the practice of toleration in early modern Europe* (Cambridge, MA, 2007).

H. Keeley, 'Flung open: walking into the parlour in Victorian Irish fiction' in R. Richman Kenneally & L. McDiarmid (eds), *The vibrant house: Irish writing and domestic space* (Dublin, 2018), pp 107–24.

M. Kelly ' "Unheard-of mortality": the Black Death in Ireland', *History Ireland*, 9:4 (2001), pp 12–17.

D. Keogh, *Edmund Rice and the first Irish Christian Brothers* (Dublin, 2008).

W.D. Killen, *Ecclesiastical history of Ireland*, 2 vols (London, 1875).

H. King, 'Late medieval crosses in Co. Meath, *c.*1470–1635' *PRIA*, 84, C (1984), pp 79–115.

—, 'Irish wayside and churchyard crosses, 1600–1700', *Post-Medieval Archaeology*, 19:1 (1985), pp 13–33.

—, 'Late medieval Irish crosses and their European background' in C. Hourihane (ed.), *From Ireland coming: Irish art from the early Christian to the late gothic period and its European context* (Princeton, 2001), pp 333–50.

W. King & C. King, *A great archbishop of Dublin: William King, DD, 1650–1729* (London, 1906).

H.T. Knox, *Notes on the early history of the dioceses of Tuam, Killala and Achonry* (Dublin, 1904).

M. Krasnodebska-D'Aughton, 'Prayer, penance and the passion of Christ: the iconographic program of the Franciscan friary at Ennis, Ireland' in *Studies in Iconography*, 37 (2016), pp 75–108.

A.J. Lafaye, 'The Dominicans in Ireland: a comparative study of the east Munster and Leinster settlements', *Journal of Medieval Monastic Studies*, 4 (2015), pp 79–108.

S. Lalonde & A. Tourunen, 'Investigating social change through the animal and human remains from Carrowkeel, east Galway', *Archaeology Ireland*, 21:4 (2007), pp 36–8.

B. Lalor, *The Irish round tower: origins and architecture explored* (Dublin, 1999).

J. Langtry & B. Fay, 'Mount Jerome cemetery of Dublin' in S. Carmen Giménez (ed.), *Arte y arquitectura funeraria/Arte e architettura funeraria/Funeral art and architecture XIX–XX* (Madrid, 2000), pp 106–91.

T. Laqueur, *The work of the dead: a cultural history of mortal remains* (Princeton, 2015).

E. Larkin, *The pastoral role of the Roman Catholic church in pre-Famine Ireland, 1750–1850* (Dublin, 2006).

P.J. Larkin, ' "Popish riot" in south Co. Derry 1725', *Seanchas Ard Mhacha*, 8:1 (1975–6), pp 97–110.

K. Lavezzo, *Angels on the edge of the world: geography, literature and English community, 1000–1534* (Ithaca, 2006).

M.L. Legg (ed.), *The census of Elphin 1749* (Dublin, 2004).

I. Leister, *Peasant openfield farming and its territorial organisation in County Tipperary* (Marburg, 1976).

E. Lenihan, 'Bronze medieval crucifix: a recent important find', *The Other Clare* (1989), pp 18–20.

C. Lennon, 'The chantries in the Irish Reformation: the case of St Anne's Guild Dublin, 1550–1630' in R. Comerford, M. Cullen, J. Hill & C. Lennon (eds), *Religion, conflict and co-existence in Ireland* (Dublin, 1989), pp 6–25.

—, 'Political thought of Irish Counter-Reformation churchmen: the testimony of the *Analecta* of Bishop David Rothe' in H. Morgan (ed.), *Political ideology in Ireland, 1541–1641* (Dublin, 1999), pp 181–202.

—, 'Mass in the manor house: the Counter-Reformation in Dublin, 1560–1630' in J. Kelly & D. Keogh (eds), *History of the Catholic diocese of Dublin* (Dublin, 2000), pp 112–26.

K. Lilly (ed.), *Mapping medieval geographies: geographical encounters in the Latin West and beyond, 300–1600* (Cambridge, 2013).

P. Lionard, 'Early Irish grave-slabs', *PRIA*, 61, C (1961), pp 95–170.

J. Lockman, *A history of the cruel sufferings of the Protestants and others by Popish persecutions, in various countries together with a view of the Reformations from the Church of Rome* (Dublin, 1763).

M. Loeber & R. Loeber, 'Louisa Beaufort's diary of her travels in south-west Munster and Leinster in 1842 and 1843', *Anal. Hib.*, 46 (2015), pp 121–205.

R. Loeber, 'Sculptured memorials to the dead in early seventeenth-century Ireland: a survey from Monumenta Eblanae and other sources', *PRIA*, 81, C (1981), pp 267–93.

—, *The geography and practice of English colonisation in Ireland* (Athlone, 1991).

— & M. Stouthamer-Loeber, 'The lost architecture of the Wexford plantation' in K. Whelan (ed.), *Wexford: history and society* (Dublin, 1987), pp 173–200.

—, & K. Whelan, 'An early eighteenth-century house: Clonegal Rectory, Co. Carlow', *Wexford Historical Society Journal*, 13 (1990–91), pp 135–41.

—, D. Dickson & A. Smyth, 'Journal of a tour to Dublin city and the counties of Dublin and Meath in 1699', *Anal. Hib.* 43, (2012), pp 47–67.

J. Logan, 'Tadhg O'Roddy and two surveys of Co. Leitrim', *Breifne*, 4:14 (1971), pp 76–81.

A.K. Longfield, *The eighteenth-century memorials by Dennis Cullen of Monaseed* ([Dublin], 1958).

J. Loveday, *Diary of a tour in 1732 through parts of England, Wales, Ireland and Scotland* (Edinburgh, 1840).

A.T. Lucas, *Penal crucifixes* (Dublin, 1958).

[P. Luckombe], *A tour through Ireland in 1779* (Dublin, 1780).

M. Luddy, '"Possessed of fine properties": power, authority and funding of convents in Ireland, 1780–1900' in M. Van Dijck & J. de Maeyer (eds), *The economics of providence: management, finances and patrimony of religious orders and congregations in Europe, 1773–c.1930* (Leuven, 2012), pp 227–46.

A. Lynch, *Tintern Abbey, Co. Wexford: Cistercians and Colcloughs: excavations, 1982–2007* (Dublin, 2010).

G. Lyne, *The Lansdowne estates in Kerry under W.S. Trench, 1849–1872* (Dublin, 2001).

—, 'The Mac Finín Duibh O'Sullivans of Tuosist and Berehaven', *Kerry Archaeological and Historical Society Journal*, 9 (1976), pp 32–67.

— & M. Mitchell (eds), 'A scientific tour through Munster: the travels of Joseph Woods, architect and botanist, in 1809', *NMAJ*, 27 (1985), pp 15–61.

P. Lysaght, *The banshee: the Irish supernatural death messenger* (Dublin, 1996).

—, 'Caoineadh os cionn coirp: the lament for the dead in Ireland', *Folklore*, 108 (1997), pp 65–82.

—, 'Old age, dying and mourning' in E. Biagini & M. Daly (eds), *The Cambridge social history of Ireland* (Cambridge, 2017), pp 282–6.

J. Lyttleton, 'Molana Abbey and its New World master', *Archaeology Ireland*, 24:4 (2010), pp 32–5.

— & M. Stout (eds), *Church and settlement in Ireland* (Dublin, 2018).

W. MacAfee, 'The colonisation of the Maghera region of south Derry during the seventeenth and eighteenth centuries', *Ulster Folklife*, 23 (1977), pp 70–91.

C. Mac Aonghusa, 'Thomond in a European context: the Uí Bhriain dynasty, 1450–1581' (MA thesis, University College Cork, 2005).

J. McCafferty, 'A mundo valde alieni: Irish Franciscan responses to the Dissolution of the Monasteries, 1540–1640', *Reformation & Renaissance Review*, 19:1 (2017), pp 50–63.

P. Mac Cána, *Celtic mythology* (Feltham, 1983).

—, 'Mythology in early Irish literature' in R. O'Driscoll (ed.), *The Celtic consciousness* (Portlaoise, 1981), pp 143–54.

E. Mac Cárthaigh, 'Gofraidh Óg Mac an Bhaird ceccinit: 2 Do dúiseadh gaisgeadh Ghaoidheal', *Ériú*, 66 (2016), pp 77–110.

M. McCarthy, 'Dublin's Greek Pro-Cathedral' in Kelly & Keogh (eds), *Catholic Diocese of Dublin*, pp 237–46.

R.B. McCarthy, 'The Church of Ireland in south Tipperary in the twentieth century', *Tipperary Historical Journal* (2007), pp 145–52.

U. MacConville & R. McQuillan, 'Continuing the tradition: roadside memorials in Ireland', *Archaeology Ireland*, 19:1 (2005), pp 26–30.

F. McCormick, 'Iona: the archaeology of the early monastery' in C. Bourke (ed.), *Studies in the cult of Saint Columba* (Dublin, 1997), pp 45–68.

—, 'Reformation, privatisation and the rise of the headstone' in A. Horning, R. Ó Baoill, C. Donnelly & P. Logue (eds), *The post-medieval archaeology of Ireland, 1150–1850* (Bray, 2007), pp 355–70.

—, *Struell wells* (Downpatrick, 2011).

—, 'Agriculture, settlement and society in early medieval Ireland', *Quaternary International*, 346 (2014), pp 119–30.

—, 'Mass houses and meeting houses: Catholic and Presbyterian church design in eighteenth-century Ireland' in Lyttleton & Stout (eds), *Church and settlement in Ireland*, pp 208–28.

P. MacCotter, *Medieval Ireland: territorial, political and economic divisions* (Dublin, 2008).

—, 'Túath, manor and parish: kingdom of Fir Maige, cantred of Fermoy', *Peritia*, 22 (2012), pp 211–48.

C. Mac Craith, *Dánta na mBráthar Mionúr* 1 (Baile Átha Cliath, 1967).

M. Mac Craith, 'Litríocht an 17ú h-aois: tonnbhriseadh an tseanghnáthaimh nó tonnchuthú an nuaghnáthaimh?', *Leachtaí Cholm Cille*, 26 (1996), pp 50–82.

—, 'Do chum glóire Dé agus an mhaitheasa phuiblidhe so/For the glory of God and this public good': the Reformation and the Irish language', *Studies*, 106:424 (2017–8), pp 476–83.

D. MacCulloch, *The Reformation: Europe's house divided, 1490–1700* (London, 2003).

—, *All things made new: writings on the Reformation* (London, 2016).

N. McCullough, *Dublin: an urban history: the plan of the city* (Dublin, 2007).

—, *Palimpsest: change in the Irish building tradition*, second edition (Dublin, 2014).

S. Mac Giollarnáth, 'Seanchas fola: folklore from east Galway', *JGAHS*, 64 (2012), pp 106–27.

B. McGrath, 'A fragment of the Minute Book of the Corporation of New Ross 1635', *JRSAI*, 144–5 (2014–15), pp 100–12.

T. McGrath (ed.), *The pastoral and education letters of Bishop James Doyle of Kildare and Leighlin, 1786–1834* (Dublin, 2005).

N. MacGregor, *Living with the Gods: on beliefs and peoples* (London, 2018).

L. McInerney, *Clerical and learned lineages of medieval county Clare* (Dublin, 2014).

—, 'A "most vainglorious man": the writings of Antonius Bruodin', *Archiv. Hib.*, 70 (2017), pp 202–83.

C. MacKenzie, E. Murphy & C. Donnelly (eds), *The science of a lost medieval Gaelic graveyard: Ballyhanna* (Dublin, 2015).

C. MacKenzie & E. Murphy, *Life and death in medieval Gaelic Ireland: the skeletons from Ballyhanna, Co. Donegal* (Dublin, 2018).

C. Mac Mhurchaidh (ed.), *Lón anama: a collection of religious poems in Irish with translations in English* (Dublin, 2005).

M. Mac Néill, 'Wayside death cairns in Ireland', *Béaloideas*, 15 (1946), pp 49–63.

E. McParland, *Public architecture in Ireland, 1680–1760* (New Haven, 2001).

B. MacShane, 'Negotiating religious change and conflict: female religious communities in early modern Ireland *c.*1530–*c.*1641', *British Catholic History*, 33:3 (2017), pp 357–82.

M. Maddox, 'Re-conceptualising the Irish monastic town', *JRSAI*, 146 (2016), pp 21–32.

E. Magennis, 'A Presbyterian insurrection?: reconsidering the Hearts of Oak disturbances of July 1763', *IHS*, 31:122 (1998), pp 165–87.

M. Maguire, 'Churches and symbolic power in the Irish landscape', *Landscapes*, 5:2 (2004), pp 91–113.

A.P.W. Malcomson, *Archbishop Charles Agar: churchmanship and politics in Ireland, 1760–1810* (Dublin, 2002).

—, *Primate Robinson, 1709–94* (Belfast, 2003).

C. Manning, 'References to church buildings in the Annals' in A. Smyth (ed.), *Seanchas: studies in early medieval Irish archaeology, history and literature* (Dublin, 2000), pp 37–52.

—, 'The adaptation of early masonry churches in Ireland for use in later medieval times' in M. Meek (ed.), *The modern traveller to our past: festschrift in honour of Ann Hamlin* (Southport, 2006), pp 243–8.

—, 'A note on dairthech' in E. Purcell, P. McCotter, J. Nyhan & J. Sheehan (eds), *Clerics, kings and Vikings: essays on medieval Ireland in honour of Donnchadh Ó Corráin* (Dublin, 2015), pp 323–5.

J. Mannion, 'Point Lance: an Irish settlement in Newfoundland' in *Atlas of Irish rural landscape*, pp 387–409.

P. Margry, 'European religious fragmentation and the rise of civil religion' in U. Kockel, M. Nic Craith & J. Frykman (eds), *A companion to the anthropology of Europe* (Chichester, 2012), pp 275–94.

J. White Marshall & G. Rourke, *High Island: an Irish monastery in the Atlantic* (Dublin, 2001).

P. Marshall (ed.), *The Oxford illustrated history of the Reformation* (Oxford, 2014).

—, *Heretics and believers: a history of the English Reformation* (New Haven, 2017).

J. Martin, 'The social geography of mid nineteenth-century Dublin' in Smyth & Whelan (eds), *Common ground*, pp 173–88.

H. Martineau, *Letters from Ireland* (London, 1852).

D. Martyn, 'A resonant architecture: Liam McCormick and the sonorities of place', *Landscape Studies*, 43:2 (2018), pp 260–74.

W. Shaw Mason, *A statistical account or parochial survey of Ireland*, 3 vols (Dublin, 1814–19).

W. Monck Mason, *The life of William Bedell D.D. lord bishop of Kilmore* (Dublin, 1843).

T. Massingham, *Florilegum insulae sanctorum seu, vitae et acta sanctorum Hiberniae* (Paris, 1624).

W. Meagher, *Notices of the life and character of His Grace Most Rev. Daniel Murray, late Archbishop of Dublin* (Dublin, 1853).

S. Meigs, *The Reformations in Ireland: tradition and confessionalism, 1400–1690* (Dublin, 1997).

P. Melvin, *Estates and landed society in Galway* (Dublin, 2013).

K. Meyer (ed.), 'Stories from the Edinburgh MS XXVI (Kilbride Collection No. 22)' in O. Bergin, R. Osborn, R. Best, K. Meyer & J. O'Keeffe (eds), *Anecdota from Irish manuscripts* (Halle & Dublin, 1910), pp 8–9.

M. Ní Mharcaigh, 'The medieval parish churches of south-west Co. Dublin', *PRIA*, 96, C (1997), pp 245–96.

D. Miller, 'Landscape and religious practice: a study of Mass attendance in pre-Famine Ireland', *Éire-Ireland*, 40:1 & 2 (2005), pp 90–106.

J. Mitchell, 'The ordination in Ireland of Jansenist clergy from Utrecht, 1715–16: the role of Fr Paul Kenny O.D.C.', *JGAHS*, 42 (1990), pp 1–29; 43 (1991), pp 46–81.

[C. De Montbret], 'A new view of eighteenth-century life in Kerry, ed. S. Ní Chinnéide', *Kerry Archaeological and Historical Society Journal*, 6 (1973), pp 83–100.

R. Moore, *The formation of a persecuting society: authority and deviance in Western Europe, 950–1250* (London, 2007).

P.F. Moran, *History of the Catholic archbishops of Dublin since the Reformation* (Dublin, 1864).

— (ed.), *Spicilegium Ossoriense, being a collection of original letters and papers illustrative of the history of the Irish church from the Reformation to the year 1800*, 3 vols (Dublin, 1874–84).

—, *The Catholics of Ireland under the penal laws in the eighteenth century* (London, 1900).

V. Morley, *The popular mind in eighteenth-century Ireland* (Cork, 2017).

H.V. Morton, *In search of Ireland* (London, 1930).

K. Morton, 'A spectacular revelation: medieval wall painting at Ardamullivan', *Irish Arts Review*, 18 (2002), pp 104–13.

[F. Moryson], 'The Irish sections of Fynes Moryson's unpublished itinerary', ed. G. Kew (Dublin, 1998).

R. Moss, 'Continuity and change: the material setting of public worship in the sixteenth-century' in T. Herron & M. Potterton (eds), *Dublin and the Pale in the Renaissance, 1494–1660* (Dublin, 2011), pp 182–206.

D. Murphy, *Sketches of Irish nunneries* (Dublin, 1865).

E. Murphy et al., 'The "lost" medieval Gaelic church and graveyard at Ballyhanna, Co. Donegal' in Corlett & Potterton (eds), *Church in early medieval Ireland*, pp 125–42.

E. Murphy & M. Le Roy (eds), *Children, death and burial: archaeological discourses* (Oxford, 2017).

J. Murphy, *Terra incognita or the convents of the United Kingdom*, second edition (London, 1876).

[H. von Pückler-Muskau], *Letters of a dead man: Prince Hermann Fürst von Pückler-Muskau*, ed. & trans. L. Parshall (New York, 2016).

H. Mytum, 'A long and complex plot: patterns of family burials in Irish graveyards from the eighteenth century', *Church Archaeology*, 5–6 (2004), pp 31–41.

—, 'Popular attitudes to memory, the body and social identity: the rise of external commemoration in Britain, Ireland and New England', *Post-Medieval Archaeology*, 40:1 (2006), pp 96–110.

N. Netzer, 'Art/full ground: unearthing national identity and an early medieval Golden Age' in V. Kreilkamp (ed.), *Eire/land* (Boston, 2003), pp 49–56.

A. Nicholson, *Ireland's welcome to the stranger or an excursion through Ireland in 1844 & 1845 for the purpose of personally investigating the condition of the poor* (Dublin, [1847] 2002).

J. Nolan, 'Excavation of a children's burial ground at Tonybaun, Ballina, Co. Mayo' in J. O'Sullivan & M. Stanley (eds), *Settlement, industry and ritual* (Bray, 2006), pp 89–101.

M. Nolan, 'Irish pilgrimage: the different tradition', *Annals of the Association of American Geographers*, 73:3 (1983), pp 421–38.

W. Nolan, *Fassadinin: land, settlement and society in southeast Ireland* c.1600–1850 (Dublin, 1979).

L. Nugent, 'Gatherings of faith: pilgrimage in medieval Ireland' in F. Beglane (ed.), *Gatherings: past and present* (Dublin, 2017), pp 20–30.

T. Ó hAnnracháin, *Catholic Europe, 1592–1648: centre and peripheries* (Oxford, 2015).

—, 'The bishop's role in two non-Catholic states: the cases of Ireland and Turkish Hungary considered', *Church History & Religious Culture*, 95:2–3 (2015), pp 245–55.

J. Obert, *Postcolonial overtures: the politics of sound in contemporary Northern Irish poetry* (Syracuse, 2015).

E. O'Brien, 'Pagan and Christian burial in Ireland during the first millennium AD: continuity and change' in N. Edwards & A. Lane (eds), *The early church in Wales and the West: recent work in early Christian archaeology, history and placenames* (Oxford, 1992), pp 130–7.

—, 'Burial practices in Ireland: first to seventh centuries AD' in J. Downes & A. Ritchie (eds), *Sea change: Orkney and Northern Europe in the later Iron Age, AD 300–800* (Angus, 2003), pp 63–72.

—, 'Burial among the ancestors to burial among the saints: an assessment of some burials in Ireland from the fifth to the eight centuries AD' in N. Edwards, M. Ní Mhaonaigh & R. Flechner (eds), *Transforming landscapes of belief in the early medieval insular world and beyond* (Turnhout, 2017), pp 259–86.

W. O'Brien, *Irish ideas* (London, 1893).

B. Ó Buachalla (eag.), *Art Mac Cumhaigh: dánta* (Baile Átha Cliath, 1973).

—, *An caoine agus an chaointeoireacht* (Baile Átha Cliath, 1995).

—, *Aisling ghéar: na Stíobhartaigh agus an t-aos léinn 1603–1788* (Baile Átha Cliath, 1996).

T. Ó Carragáin, 'The architectural setting of the cult of relics in early medieval Ireland', *JRSAI*, 133 (2003), pp 130–76.

—, 'Habitual masonry styles and the local organisation of church building in early medieval Ireland', *PRIA*, 105, C (2005), pp 99–149.

—, 'Skeuomorphs and spolia: the presence of the past in Irish pre-Romanesque architecture' in R. Moss (ed.), *Making and meaning in insular art* (Dublin, 2007), pp 95–109.

—, 'From family cemeteries to community cemeteries in Viking Age Ireland?' in C. Corlett & M. Potterton (eds), *Death and burial in early medieval Ireland in the light of recent excavations* (Bray, 2010), pp 217–26.

—, *Churches in early medieval Ireland: architecture, ritual and memory* (London, 2010).

—, 'Is there an archaeology of lay people at early Irish monasteries?', *Bulletin du centre d'études médiévales d'Auxerre* (2015), pp 1–29.

—, 'Churches and social power in early medieval Ireland: a case study of Fir Maige' in J. Sánches Pardo & M. Shapland (eds), *Churches and social power in early medieval Europe* (Turnhout, 2015), pp 99–156.

—, 'Christianising the landscape of Mag Réta: home territory of the kings of Laígis' in Lyttleton & Stout (eds), *Church and settlement in Ireland*, pp 60–85.

S. Ó Catháin & P. O'Flanagan, *The living landscape: Kilgalligan, Erris, Co. Mayo* (Dublin, 1975).

S. Ó Cillín, *Travellers in Co. Clare, 1459–1843* (Galway, 1977).

C. Ó Clabaigh, *The friars in Ireland, 1124–1540* (Dublin, 2012).

S. Ó Coiléan, 'The Irish lament: an oral genre', *Studia Hib.*, 24 (1984–8), pp 97–117.

B. Ó Conchúir (eag.), *Amhráin Eoghan Rua Ó Súilleabháin* (Baile Átha Cliath, 2009).

A. O'Connor, *Child murderess and dead child traditions* (Helsinki, 1991).

—, 'To hell or to purgatory? Irish folk religion and post-Tridentine Counter-Reformation Catholic teachings', *Béaloideas*, 80 (2012), pp 115–41.

—, 'Perspectives on death from Irish folklore' in S. Ryan (ed.), *Death and the Irish: a miscellany* (Dublin, 2016), pp 179–82.

M. O'Connor, *The history of the Irish Catholics from the settlement in 1691, with a view of the state of Ireland from the Invasion by Henry II to the Revolution: part I* (Dublin, 1813).

P. O'Connor, *Exploring Limerick's past: an historical geography of urban development in county and city* (Newcastle West, 1987).

D. Ó Corráin, 'Viking Ireland: afterthoughts' in H. Clarke, M. Ní Mhaonaigh & R. Ó Floinn (eds), *Ireland and Scandinavia in the early Viking Age* (Dublin, 1998), pp 485–98.

—, 'Ireland c.800: aspects of society' in D. Ó Cróinín (ed.), *A new history of Ireland, i: prehistoric and early Ireland* (Oxford, 2005).

—, 'From sanctity to depravity: church and society in medieval Ireland' in N. Ó Ciosáin (ed.), *Explaining change in cultural history* (Dublin, 2005), pp 140–62.

—, 'Island of saints and scholars: myth or reality?' in O. Rafferty (ed.), *Irish Catholic identities* (Manchester, 2012), pp 32–61.

—, *The Irish church, its reform and the English invasion* (Dublin, 2017).

C. Ó Crualaoich, 'The identification of Leac Mhic Eochaidh in north Wexford 1592', *The Past*, 32 (2016), pp 52–72.

—, 'Townland and defunct placenames in Sligo: evidence for surnames' (forthcoming).

— & A. Mac Giolla Chomhghaill, *Logainmneacha na hÉireann IV; Townland names in County Wexford* (Dublin, 2016), pp 83–107.

G. Ó Crualaoich, *The book of the cailleach: stories of the wise-woman healer* (Cork, 2003).

C. Ó Danachair, 'The bothán scóir' in E. Rynne (ed.), *North Munster studies* (Limerick, 1967), pp 489–98.

D. Ó Doibhlin, 'Penal days' in H. Jefferies & C. Devlin (eds), *History of the diocese of Derry from the earliest times* (Dublin, 2000), pp 167–86.

P. O'Donoghue, 'Opposition to tithes payment in 1830–1831', *Studia Hib.*, 6 (1966), pp 69–98.

J. O'Donovan, 'Elegy on the death of Rev. Edmond Kavanagh by the Rev. James O'Lalor', *Journal of the Kilkenny and South-East of Ireland Archaeological Society*, n.s., 5 (1858–9), pp 118–42.

J. O'Donovan Rossa, *Rossa's recollections* (New York, 1898).

S. Ó Duilearga, *Leabhair Sheain Í Chonaill* (Baile Átha Cliath, 1948).

C. O'Dwyer, 'Archbishop Patrick Leahy', (MA thesis, Maynooth, 1971).

—, *Archdiocese of Cashel and Emly* (Strasbourg, 2008).

S. Ó hEochaidh, *Síscéalta ó Thír Chonaill/Fairy legends from Donegal*, trans. M. Mac Néill (Dublin, 1977).

C. Ó Fearghail, 'The evolution of Catholic parishes in Dublin city from the sixteenth to the nineteenth centuries' in F.H. Aalen & K. Whelan (eds), *Dublin, city and county from prehistory to present* (Dublin, 1992), pp 63–71.

F. Ó Fearghail, 'Bishop Wheeler's visitation of Ossory 1622', *Ossory, Laois and Leinster*, 6 (2016), pp 129–200.

F. O'Ferrall, *Catholic Emancipation: Daniel O'Connell and the birth of Irish democracy, 1820–1830* (Dublin, 1985).

T. Ó Fiach, 'The fall and return of John Mac Moyer (and his connection with the trial of Blessed Oliver Plunkett)', *Seanchas Ardmhacha*, 3:1 (1958), pp 50–86.

—, 'Irish poetry and the clergy', *Leachtaí Cholm Cille*, 4 (Má Nuad, 1975), pp 30–56.

P. Ó Gallachair, 'Clogher's altars from the penal days: a survey', *Clogher Record*, 2:1 (1957), pp 97–130.

D. Ó Giolláin, *Locating Irish folklore: tradition, modernity, identity* (Cork, 2000).

—, 'Revisiting the holy well', *Éire-Ireland*, 40:1–2 (2005), pp 11–41.

C. Ó Gráda, *An drochshaol: béaloideas agus amhráin* (Baile Átha Cliath, 1995).

[J. O'Hanlon], *Irish folklore: traditions and superstitions of the country* (Glasgow, 1870).

—, *Report of the O'Connell Monument Committee* (Dublin, 1888).

A. O'Hara, 'Carmen de hibernia insula: the earliest poem about Ireland' in S. Ryan (ed.), *Treasures of Irish Christianity, volume 3. To the ends of the earth* (Dublin, 2015), pp 20–4.

J.J. O'Kelly, *Ireland's spiritual empire: St Patrick as a world figure* (Dublin, 1952).

M.J. O'Kelly, 'Church Island near Valencia, Co. Kerry', *PRIA*, 59, C (1958), pp 57–136.

J. Olafsson, *The life of the Icelander Jón Ólafsson* [1661] [CELT].

J. O'Laverty, *An historical account of the Diocese of Down and Connor, ancient and modern*, 5 vols (Dublin, 1878–95).

S. Ó Loingsigh (ed.), 'An excursion to Co. Cavan 1809', *Breifne*, 8 (1965), pp 495–504.

T. O'Loughlin, *Adomnán and the holy places* (London, 2007).

B. Ó Madagáin (eag.), *Gnéithe den chaointeoireacht* (Baile Átha Cliath, 1978).

T.S. Ó Máille, *Seanfhocla Chonnacht* (Baile Átha Cliath, 2010).

T. O'Malley, 'Inscape: life and landscape in Callan and south Kilkenny' in W. Nolan & K. Whelan (eds), *Kilkenny: history and society* (Dublin, 1900), pp 617–32.

C. Ó Maonaigh (eag.), *Seanmónta Chúige Ulaidh* (Baile Átha Cliath, 1965).

S. Ó Mórdha, 'An anti-tithe speech in Irish', *Éigse*, 9 (1958–61), pp 233–6.

N. Ó Muraile (eag.), *Amhráin agus dánta Raiftearaí le Dúghlas de Híde* (An Spideál, 2018).

H. O'Neill, *Illustrations of some of the most interesting sculptured crosses of ancient Ireland drawn to scale and lithographed by Henry O'Neill* (London, 1857).

M. O'Neill, 'The medieval parish churches of Co. Meath', *JRSAI*, 132 (2002), pp 1–56.

—, 'The medieval parish churches of Co. Kildare' in W. Nolan & T. McGrath (eds), *Kildare: history and society* (Dublin, 2006), pp 153–93.

— (ed.), *Episcopal visitations of the diocese of Meath, 1622–1799* (Dublin, 2017).

T. O'Neill, *Merchants and mariners in medieval Ireland* (Dublin, 1987).

—, *The Irish hand: scribes and their manuscripts from the earliest times*, second edition (Cork, 2014).

D. Ó hÓgáin, *Myth, legend, & romance: an encyclopaedia of the Irish folk tradition* (London, 1990).

R. Uí Ógáin & T. Sherlock, *The otherworld: music and song from Irish tradition* (Dublin, 2012).

B. O'Reilly, 'Ireland's corrugated iron ("tin") churches' in T. Condit & C. Corlett (eds), *Above and beyond: essays in memory of Leo Swan* (Bray, 2005), pp 491–502.

J. O'Reilly, 'Islands and idols at the ends of the earth: exegesis and conversion in Bede's *Historia Ecclesiastica*' in S. Lebecq, M. Perrin & O. Szerwiniak (eds), *Bède le vénérable* (Villeneuve d'Ascq, 2005), pp 119–45.

P. Ó Riain, *A dictionary of Irish saints* (Dublin, 2011).

T. O'Rorke, *The history of Sligo town and county, volume I* (Dublin, 1889).

[Orrery], *An answer to a scandalous letter lately printed and subscribed by Peter Welsh* (Dublin, 1692).

Countess of Cork and Orrery (ed.), *The Orrery papers*, 2 vols (London, 1903).

S. Osborne, *Gleanings in the west of Ireland* (London, 1850).

C. Ó Scea, 'Erenachs, erenachships and church landholding in Gaelic Fermanagh, 1270–1609', *PRIA*, 112, C (2012), pp 271–300.

M. Ó Siochrú, 'Rebuilding the past: the transformation of early modern Irish history', *The Seventeenth Century* (2018), forthcoming.

S. Ó Súilleabháin, 'Adhlacadh leanbhaí', *JRSAI*, 69:3 (1938), pp 143–51.

—, *Irish wake amusements* (Cork, 1967).

—, *Miraculous plenty: Irish religious folktales and legends*, trans. W. Caulfield (Dublin, 2012).

A. O'Sullivan & D. Boland, *The Clonmacnoise bridge: an early medieval river crossing in County Offaly* (Bray, 2000).

A. O'Sullivan, F. McCormick, T. Kerr & L. Harney, *Early medieval Ireland, AD 400–1100: the evidence from archaeological excavations* (Dublin, 2013).

A. O'Sullivan & F. MacCormick, 'Early medieval Ireland: investigating social, economic and settlement change, AD 400–1100' in M. Shanley, R. Swan & A. O'Sullivan (eds), *Stories of Ireland's past* (Bray, 2017), pp 10–32.

J. O'Sullivan & T. Ó Carragáin, *Inishmurray: monks and pilgrims in an Atlantic landscape: archaeological survey and excavations* (Cork, 2008).

É. Ó Tuathail, *Sgéalta Mhuintir Luinigh/Munterloney folktales: Irish traditions from Co. Tyrone*, trans. S. Watson (Dublin, 2015).

C. Otway, *A tour in Connaught, comprising sketches of Clonmacnoise, Joyce Country and Achill* (Dublin, 1839).

K. Overbey, *Sacral geographies: saints, shrines and territory in medieval Ireland* (Turnhout, 2012).

G. Owens, 'Nationalism without words: symbolism and ritual behaviour in the Repeal monster meetings of 1843–5' in Donnelly & Miller (eds), *Irish popular culture*, pp 242–69.

A. Rackard & L. O'Callaghan, *Fishstonewater: holy wells of Ireland* (Cork, 2001).

U. Parmaksiz, 'Making sense of the postsecular', *European Journal of Social Theory* (2016), pp 98–116.

J. Payne, *Twelve designs of country-houses, of two, three and four rooms on a floor, proper for glebes and small estates* (Dublin, 1757).

R. Payne, *A briefe description of Ireland made in this year 1589* (London, 1589) [CELT].

F. Peacock, 'Church bells: when and why they were rung' in W. Andrews (ed.), *Curious church customs* (Hull, 1895), pp 33–48.

M. Pepperdene, 'Baptism in the early British and Irish churches', *Irish Theological Quarterly*, 22 (1955), pp 110–23.

M. Phelan, 'The O'Kerin school of monumental sculpture in Ossory and its environs in the sixteenth and seventeenth centuries', *JRSAI*, 126 (1996), pp 167–81.

H. Pike, *Medieval fonts of Ireland* (Greystones, 1989).

C. Plummer (ed.), *Beatha naem nÉrenn*, 2 vols (Oxford, 1922).

A. Plumptre, *Narrative of a residence in Ireland during the summer of 1814 and that of 1815* (London, 1817).

The letters of Saint Oliver Plunkett, 1625–1681, ed. J. Hanly (Dublin, 1979).

C. Poirtéir, *Famine echoes* (Dublin, 1995).

C. Pollard, *Liam McCormick: seven Donegal churches* (Kinsale, 2011).

P. Power, 'The bounds and extents of Irish parishes' in S. Pender (ed.), *Féilscríbhinn Torna: essays and studies* (Cork, 1947), pp 218–24.

D. Iogna-Prat, 'Churches in the landscape' in T. Noble & J. Smith (eds), *The Cambridge history of Christianity: early medieval Christianities, c.600–c.1100* (Cambridge, 2008), pp 363–79.

J.P. Prendergast, *Ireland from the Restoration to the revolution, 1660–1690* (London, 1887).

J. Prunty, *Dublin slums, 1800–1925: a study in urban geography* (Dublin, 1998).

—, *The monasteries, Magdalen asylums and reformatory schools of Our Lady of Charity in Ireland, 1853–1973* (Dublin, 2017).

E.C. Rae, 'Irish sepulchral monuments of the later Middle Ages: Part II: the O'Tunney atelier', *JRSAI*, 101 (1971), pp 1–39.

D. Raftery, 'The "mission" of nuns in female education in Ireland c.1850–1950', *Paedagogica Historica*, 48:2 (2012), pp 299–313.

—, ' "Je suis d'aucune nation": the recruitment and identity of Irish women religious in the international mission field, c.1840–1940', *Paedagogica Historica*, 49:4 (2013), pp 513–30.

J. Rainford, 'Feakle's Biddy Early: a victim of moral panic?', *History Ireland*, 20:1 (2012), pp 28–31.

M. Ratti, *The postsecular imagination: postcolonialism, religion and literature* (London, 2013).

R. Raughter, 'Pious occupations: female activism and the Catholic revival in eighteenth-century Ireland' in R. Raughter (ed.), *Religious women and their history: breaking the silence* (Dublin, 2005), pp 25–49.

R. Refaussé, 'Visitation notebook of Charles Lindsay, 1804–1808', *Journal of the Kildare Archaeological Society*, 17 (1987–91), pp 121–47.

S. Rheinisch, 'Uncovering an Anglo-Norman manor and deserted medieval village', *Archaeology Ireland*, 27:3 (2013), pp 32–5.

B. Rich, *A new description of Ireland* (London, 1610).

A. Ridge, *Death customs in rural Ireland: traditional funerary rites in the Irish midlands* (Galway, 2009).

J.M. Rigg (ed.), *Calendar of State Papers relating to English affairs preserved principally at Rome in the Vatican Archives and Library, 1558–1578*, 2 vols (London, 1916–26).

K. Ritara, *Pilgrimage to heaven: eschatology and monastic spirituality in early medieval Ireland* (Turnhout, 2016).

K. Robertson, 'Medieval things: materiality, historicism and the pre-modern object', *Literature Compass*, 5 (2008), pp 1–21.

P. Robinson, *The plantation of Ulster: British settlement in an Irish landscape, 1600–1670* (Dublin, 1984).

T. Robinson, *Mementos of mortality: cenotaphs and funerary cairns of Árainn* (Roundstone, 1991).

S. Roddy, *Population, providence and empire: the churches and emigration from nineteenth-century Ireland* (Manchester, 2014).

P. Rogers, *The Irish Volunteers and Catholic Emancipation: a neglected phase of Ireland's history* (London, 1934).

M.V. Ronan, *The Reformation in Dublin, 1536–1558* (Dublin, 1926).

— (ed.), 'Archbishop Bulkeley's visitation of Dublin 1630', *Archiv. Hib.*, 8 (1941), pp 56–98.

W. Roulston, 'The provision, building and architecture of Anglican churches in the north of Ireland, 1600–1740' (PhD, QUB, 2003).

—, 'The role of the parish in building and maintaining Anglican churches in the North of Ireland, 1660–1740' in E. FitzPatrick & R. Gillespie (eds), *The parish in early medieval and early modern Ireland* (Dublin, 2006), pp 325–44.

—, 'Accommodating clergymen: Church of Ireland ministers and their houses in the north of Ireland, 1600–1870' in T. Barnard & W. Neely (eds), *The clergy of the Church of Ireland, 1000–2000* (Dublin, 2006), pp 106–27.

A. Rowan, 'Irish Victorian churches: denominational distinctions' in B. Kennedy & R. Gillespie (eds), *Ireland: art into history* (Dublin, 1994), pp 207–30.

M. Ryan, *Biddy Early: the wise woman of Clare* (Cork, [1978] 1991).

E. Rynne, 'The round tower, evil eye, and holy well at Balla, Co. Mayo' in C. Manning (ed.), *Dublin and beyond the Pale: studies in honour of Paddy Healy* (Bray, 1998), pp 177–84.

A. Ryrie, *Being Protestant in Reformation England* (Oxford, 2013).

T. Saad, 'The moral inadequacy of cremation', *The New Bioethics*, 23:3 (2017), pp 249–60.

W. Savery, *A journal of the life, travels, and religious labors of William Savery, a minister of the Gospel of Christ, of the Society of Friends, late of Philadelphia* (Philadelphia, 1861).

G. Scally, *High Island (Ard Oileán), Co. Galway: excavation of an early medieval monastery* (Dublin, 2014).

J. Scott, *Weapons of the weak: everyday forms of resistance* (New Haven, 1985).

Seasonable advice to Protestants containing some means of reviving and strengthening the Protestant interest, second edition (Cork, 1745).

St John D. Seymour, 'The eschatology of the early Irish church', *Zeitschrift für celtische philologie*, 14 (1923), pp 179–211.

R. Sharpe, 'Some problems concerning the organization of the church in early medieval Ireland', *Peritia*, 3 (1984), pp 23–70.

—, 'Churches and communities in early medieval Ireland: towards a pastoral model' in J. Blair & R. Sharpe (eds), *Pastoral care before the parish* (Leicester, 1992), pp 81–109.

—, *Roderick O'Flaherty's letters to William Molyneux, Edward Lhwyd and Samuel Molyneux, 1696–1709* (Dublin, 2013).

—, 'Medieval manuscripts found at Bonamargy friary and other hidden manuscripts', *Studia Hib.*, 41 (2015), pp 49–85.

H. Shearman, *Privatising a church: the disestablishing and disendowment of the Church of Ireland* (Lurgan, 1995).

J. Shearman, *Loca Patriciana: an identification of localities chiefly in Leinster visited by St Patrick* (Dublin, 1879).

W. Shee, *The Irish church being a digest of returns* (London, 1852).

J. Sheehan, 'A peacock's tale: excavations at Caherlehillan, Iveragh, Ireland' in N. Edwards (ed.), *The archaeology of the early medieval Celtic churches* (Leeds, 2009), pp 191–206.

J. Sheehy, *J.J. McCarthy and the Gothic Revival in Ireland* (Belfast, 1977).

—, *The rediscovery of Ireland's past: the Celtic Revival, 1830–1930* (London, 1980).

K. Simms, 'Frontiers in the Irish church: regional and cultural in colony and frontier' in T. Barry, R. Frame & K. Simms (eds), *Medieval Ireland: essays presented to J.F. Lydon* (London, 1995), pp 177–200.

L. Simpson, 'The priory of All Hallows and the Old College: archaeological investigations in Front Square, Trinity College Dublin' in S. Duffy (ed.), *Medieval Dublin XIII* (Dublin, 2013), pp 246–316.

B. Smith (ed.), *The Cambridge history of Ireland, volume I, 1000–1550* (Cambridge, 2017).

I. Smith, *Tin tabernacles: corrugated iron mission halls, churches and chapels of Britain* (Pembroke, 2004).

J. Smith, *Ireland's Magdalen laundries and the nation's architecture of containment* (Notre Dame, 2007).

K. Smith, 'An investigation of the material culture of Donegal Franciscan friaries in the late sixteenth and seventeenth centuries', *Donegal Annual*, 63 (2011), pp 96–104.

S. Smyrl, *Dictionary of Dublin dissent: Dublin's Protestant dissenting meeting houses, 1660–1920* (Dublin, 2009).

W.J. Smyth, 'Excavating, mapping and interrogating ancestral terrains: towards a cultural geography of first names and second names in Ireland' in Clarke, Prunty & Hennessy (eds), *Surveying Ireland's past*, pp 243–80.

—, *Mapmaking, landscapes and memory: a geography of colonial and early modern Ireland c.1530–1750* (Cork, 2006).

J. Soderberg, 'Feeding communities: monasteries and urban development in early medieval Ireland' in S. McNally (ed.), *Shaping communities: the archaeology and architecture of monasticism* (Oxford, 2001), pp 67–77.

—, 'Anthropological *civitas* and the possibility of monastic towns', *JRSAI*, 144–5 (2014–5), pp 45–59.

Some thoughts on the tillage of Ireland (Dublin, 1741).

R. Stalley, *The Cistercian monasteries of Ireland: an account of the history, art and architecture of the White Monks in Ireland from 1142–1540* (New Haven, 1987).

—, Gothic survival in sixteenth-century Connacht' in M. Meek (ed.), *The modern traveller to our past: festschrift in honour of Ann Hamlin* (Dublin, 2006), pp 302–14.

—, 'Masons and their materials in medieval Ireland' in V. Olson (ed.), *Use of limestone in medieval buildings* (Farnham, 2011), pp 209–26.

C. Stancliffe, 'Religion and society in Ireland' in P. Fouracre (ed.), *The new Cambridge medieval history*, c.*500*–c.*700* (Cambridge, 2005), pp 397–425.

L. Lux-Sterritt & C. Mangion, 'Gender, Catholicism and women's spirituality over the longue durée' in L. Lux-Sterritt & C. Mangion (eds), *Gender, Catholicism and spirituality: women and the Roman Catholic church in Britain and Europe, 1200– 1900* (Basingstoke, 2011), pp 1–18.

G. Stout, 'The Abbey of the Port of St Maria, Dunbrody, Co. Wexford: an architectural study' in I. Doyle & B. Browne (eds), *Medieval Wexford: essays in memory of Billy Colfer* (Dublin, 2016), pp 97–123.

—, & M. Stout, *Excavation of an early medieval secular cemetery at Knowth Site M, Co. Meath* (Dublin, 2008).

—, & M. Stout, *The Bective Abbey project, Co. Meath: excavations, 2009–2012* (Dublin, 2016).

—, R. Loeber & K. O'Brien, 'Mellifont Abbey, Co. Louth: a study of its post-dissolution architecture 1540–1727', *PRIA*, 116, C (2016), pp 191–226.

M. Stout, 'The distribution of early medieval ecclesiastical sites in Ireland' in Duffy & Nolan (eds), *At the anvil*, pp 53–80.

—, *Early medieval Ireland 431–1169* (Bray, 2017).

L. Stutz, 'Building bridges between burial archaeology and the archaeology of death: where is the archaeological study of the dead going?', *Current Swedish Archaeology*, 24 (2016), pp 13–35.

F. Sweeney, 'Wake and funeral offerings in the province of Armagh' in Ryan (ed.), *Death and the Irish*, pp 190–3.

C. Tait, *Death, burial and commemoration in Ireland, 1550–1650* (Basingstoke, 2002).

—, 'Riots, rescues and "grene bowes": Catholics and protest in Ireland, 1570–1640' in T. Ó hAnnracháin & R. Armstrong (eds), *Insular Christianity: alternative models of the church in Britain and Ireland, 1570–1700* (Manchester, 2013), pp 66–87.

C. Taylor, *A secular age* (Cambridge, MA, 2007).

L. Taylor, 'Bás in Éirinn: cultural constructions of death in Ireland', *Anthropological Quarterly*, 62:4 (1989), pp 175–87.

—, *Occasions of faith: an anthropology of Irish Catholics* (Dublin, 1995).

C. Teeling, *Observations on the history and consequences of the Battle of the Diamond* (Belfast, 1838).

N. Terpstra, *Religious refugees in the early modern world: an alternative history of the Reformation* (Cambridge, 2015).

L. Thompson, 'Pentecostal migrants and the churches in Ireland', *Search*, 33:3 (2010), pp 185–93.

G. Thomson, *Lettering on gravemarkers in Britain and Ireland* (Bray, 2011).

P. Thorsheim, 'The corpse in the garden: burial, health and the environment in nineteenth-century London', *Environmental History*, 16 (2011), pp 38–68.

M. Timoney, *Had me made: a study of grave memorials of Co. Sligo from 1650 to the present* (Sligo, 2005).

[J. De La Tocnaye], *A Frenchman's walk through Ireland, 1796–7*, ed. J. Stevenson (Belfast, 1917).

[A. de Tocqueville], *Alexis de Tocqueville's journey to Ireland, 1835*, ed. E. Larkin (Dublin, 1990).

J.H. Todd (ed.), 'Autograph letter of Thady O'Roddy', *Miscellany of the Irish Archaeological Society*, 1 (1846), pp 112–25.

M. Tóibín, 'The school beside the chapel' in *The Past*, 8 (1970), pp 18–23.

M. Traynor, *The English dialect of Donegal: a glossary* (Dublin, 1953).

J.B. Trotter, *Walks through Ireland in the years 1812, 1814 and 1817: described in a series of letters to an English gentleman* (London, 1819).

[Ulster Historic Churches Trust], *New life for churches in Ireland: good practice in conservation and reuse* (Belfast, 2013).

R. Usher, *Protestant Dublin, 1660–1760: architecture and iconography* (Basingstoke, 2012).

Valor beneficiorum ecclesiasticorum in Hibernia: or the first-fruits of all the ecclesiastical benefices in the kingdom of Ireland, as taxed in the King's books (Dublin, 1741).

J. Venedy, *Ireland*, 2 vols (Leipzig, 1844).

C. Voght, 'Schilderung von Irland, bruchstücke aus dem tagebuche eines reisenden im herbst 1794' in *Der genius der zeit*, 8 (1796), pp 566–653 [CELT].

H. Wagner, *Linguistic atlas and survey of Irish dialects* (Dublin, 1958).

E. Wakefield, *An account of Ireland statistical and political*, 2 vols (London, 1812).

W.F. Wakeman, *A handbook of Irish antiquities, pagan and Christian: especially such as are of easy access from the metropolis* (Dublin, 1848).

J.C. Walker, *An historical essay on the dress of the ancient and modern Irish* (Dublin, 1778).

B. Walsh, 'Lifting the veil on entrepreneurial Irish women: running convents in nineteenth-century England and Wales', *History Ireland*, 11:4 (2003), pp 23–8.

P. Walsh, *Gleanings from Irish manuscripts* (Dublin, 1933).

A. Walsham, *Catholic Reformation in Protestant Britain* (London, 2014).

T.J. Westropp, *A folklore survey of County Clare*, website of Clare County Library.

I. Whelan, *The Bible war in Ireland: the 'Second Reformation' and the polarisation of Protestant-Catholic relations, 1800–1840* (Dublin, 2007).

K. Whelan, 'The regional impact of Irish Catholicism, 1700–1850' in W. Smyth & K. Whelan (eds), *Common ground: essays on the historical geography of Ireland* (Cork, 1988), pp 253–77.

—, *Fellowship of freedom: The United Irishmen and 1798* (Cork, 1998).

—, 'Clachans: landscape and life in Ireland before and after the Famine' in Duffy & Nolan (eds), *At the anvil*, pp 453–75.

—, 'Reading the ruins: the presence of absence in the Irish landscape' in Clarke, Prunty & Hennessy (eds), *Surveying Ireland's past*, pp 263–94.

—, *Dublin through space and time: from Wood Quay to Silicon City* (Dublin, 2015).

—, 'Paris: capital of Irish culture' in P. Joannon & K. Whelan (eds), *Paris, capital of Irish culture: France, Ireland and the Republic, 1798–1916* (Dublin, 2017), pp 33–76.

J. White, 'The Cusack papers: new evidence on the Knock apparition', *History Ireland*, 4:4 (1999), pp 39–43.

N.B. White, *Extents of Irish monastic possessions, 1540–1541* (Dublin, 1943).

N. Whitfield, 'A suggested function for the holy well?' in A. Minnis & J. Roberts (eds), *Text, image, interpretation: studies in Anglo-Saxon literature and its insular context in honour of Éamonn Ó Carragáin* (Turnhout, 2007), pp 495–563.

N. Whyte, *Inhabiting the landscape: place, custom and memory, 1500–1800* (Oxford, 2009).

C. Wickham, *Medieval Europe* (New Haven, 2016).

P. Wicks, *The truth about Home Rule* (London, 1913).

[Willes], *The letters of Lord Chief Baron Edward Willes to the earl of Warwick, 1757–1762*, ed. J. Kelly (Aberystwyth, 1990).

N. Witoszek & P. Sheeran, *Talking to the dead: a study of Irish funerary traditions* (Amsterdam, 1998).

A. Wood, *The memory of the people: custom and popular senses of the past in early modern England* (Cambridge, 2013).

W. Wood-Martin, *The history of Sligo county and town, from the close of the Revolution of 1688 to the present time* (Dublin, 1895).

C.J. Woods (ed.), 'Johan Friedrich Hering's description of Connacht 1806–7', *IHS*, 25:99 (1987), pp 311–21.

—, 'The personnel of the Catholic Convention, 1792–3', *Archiv. Hib.*, 57 (2003), pp 26–76.

—, *Travellers' accounts as source material for Irish historians* (Dublin, 2009).

D. Wooley (ed.), *The correspondence of Jonathan Swift, DD*, 4 vols (Frankfurt, 1999–2005).

J. Wooley (ed.), *Jonathan Swift and Thomas Sheridan*, The Intelligencer (Oxford, 1992), pp 228–9.

A. Wycherley, *The cult of relics in early medieval Ireland* (Turnhout, 2015).

C. Wylie, *Willie Doherty, requisite distance: ghost story and landscape* (Dallas, 2009).

N. Yates, *The religious condition of Ireland, 1770–1850* (Oxford, 2006).

A. Young, *A tour in Ireland with general observations on the present state of that Kingdom made in the years 1776, 1777 and 1778*, 2 vols (Dublin, 1780).

E. Zadoro-Rio, 'The making of churchyards and parish territories in the early medieval landscape of France and England in the 7th–12th centuries: a reconsideration', *Medieval Archaeology*, 47 (2003), pp 1–19.

—, 'Territoires paroissiaux et construction de l'espace vernaculaire', *Medievales*, 49 (2005), pp 105–20.

W. Zelinsky, 'The uniqueness of the American religious landscape', *Geographical Review*, 91:3 (2001), pp 565–85.

G.-D. Zimmerman, *The Irish storyteller* (Dublin, 2001).

Index of People and Places

Irish placenames are listed under their respective counties. Dioceses are listed alphabetically.
Illustrations are indicated by page numbers in bold.